National Security in the Obama Administration

"The Bush Doctrine is more condemned than understood, let alone defended. Stanley Renshon not only defends the Doctrine but makes it clear that most of the critics have failed to come to grips with the real and pressing problems that will confront the Obama administration. With strong arguments and a penetrating view of the world, this is a stimulating and important book."

Robert Jervis, Columbia University

"*National Security in the Obama Administration* is a serious, fascinating, and timely account of the Bush Doctrine, its legacy, and its implications for the Obama administration's unfolding foreign policy."

Robert Kagan, Carnegie Endowment for International Peace

"Stanley Renshon's book transcends the bitterly polarized and all too often unedifying foreign policy debates that characterized much of the presidency of George W. Bush. In this important new work, he not only provides a welcome reassessment of the Bush Doctrine, but explains how external threats and pressing foreign policy challenges shape the choices of the Obama administration. While major alterations of style and method are evident in Obama's foreign policy, changes in substance and doctrine appear to be far less pronounced. Renshon's important new book illuminates the reasons why."

Robert J. Lieber, Georgetown University

Many observers claim the Bush Doctrine is dead. At least that's what critics hope. But while new U.S. national security challenges emerge, many post-9/11 threats still persist and the policies of George W. Bush offer one set of strategic answers for how President Obama can confront those dangers. Neither a polemic nor a whitewash, this book provides a careful analysis of the Bush Doctrine—its development, application, and rationale—and assesses its legacy: How will Obama respond to the many foreign policy challenges that await him?

Through an examination of psychology as much as policy, Renshon, in the first comparative analysis of the Bush Doctrine and the developing Obama Doctrine, analyzes the range of national security issues Obama will face and the political divisions that permeate U.S. national security debates. It is essential reading for anyone looking to understand how presidents assess security risks generally and how Obama specifically is likely to adapt the Bush Doctrine to his own worldview.

Stanley A. Renshon is a Professor of Political Science at the City University of New York Graduate Center. He is the author of over ninety articles and fourteen books and is a certified psychoanalyst.

National Security in the Obama Administration

Reassessing the Bush Doctrine

Stanley A. Renshon

WITHDRAWN

Routledge
Taylor & Francis Group
NEW YORK AND LONDON

First published 2010
by Routledge
270 Madison Ave, New York, NY 10016

Simultaneously published in the UK
by Routledge
2 Park Square, Milton Park, Abingdon, Oxon OX14 4RN

Routledge is an imprint of the Taylor & Francis Group, an informa business

© 2010 Stanley A. Renshon

Typeset in Galliard by Taylor & Francis Books
Printed and bound in the United States of America on acid-free paper by
Edwards Brothers, Inc.

Library of Congress Cataloging in Publication Data
Renshon, Stanley Allen.
    National security in the Obama administration : reassessing the Bush
doctrine / Stanley A. Renshon.
    p. cm.
    Includes bibliographical references.
    1. National security–United States. 2. United States–Military policy. 3.
United States–Foreign relations–2009- I. Title.
    UA23.R443 2009
    355′.033073–dc22

                                                           2009011811

ISBN 10: 0-415-80406-X (hbk)
ISBN 10: 0-415-80405-1 (pbk)
ISBN 10: 0-203-87451-X (ebk)

ISBN 13: 978-0-415-80406-6 (hbk)
ISBN 13: 978-0-415-80405-9 (pbk)
ISBN 13: 978-0-203-87451-6 (ebk)

For Alexander L. George [1920–2006]
Mentor, Political Psychology Colleague and,
above all, Friend

Contents

Preface

The focus of this book lies at the intersection of post-9/11 national security dilemmas that face the United States and its allies, the development and application of the strategic doctrines and policies that respond to those circumstances, and the presidential leadership and judgment that are brought to bear, for better or worse, on these issues.

This book is an analysis of two presidencies and the doctrine that both connects and separates them. The Bush Doctrine grew out of the 9/11 attacks and represented President Bush's response to what he and his advisors saw as the key issues and lessons to emerge from those attacks. Those attacks reframed the Bush Administration's view of the most serious problems it faced and what to do about them. The potential for the linkage between catastrophic terrorism and the leakage of knowledge or weapons of mass destruction material, either inadvertent or deliberate, raised the national security stakes enormously for the United States. Or at least so the Bush Administration thought, and acted accordingly.

For a brief moment after 9/11 the country and many in the world were united in their rhetorical support of this country and many allies, even those who had not been America's friend, offered various kinds of help, whether out of fear or solidarity, to bring the perpetrators to justice. But Mr. Bush had more serious concerns than revenge. A sophisticated, ruthless, and deadly enemy had pulled off a stunning and severely damaging attack on American soil against major national icons. Either the White House or Congress barely escaped the devastation because of the heroic acts of Americans who gave their lives so that one hijacked plane could not complete its mission. The next time America might not escape catastrophic and irreversible harm.

The Bush Administration put into place a large set of policies designed to prevent another, more deadly attack. These policies were controversial both domestically and abroad. And it is partially on the basis of those disagreements that Barack Obama ran for and was elected to the presidency. A first question that arises then is: what will he do with the national security architecture that he has inherited from the Bush Administration? This has understandably been a focus of attention as the new president takes office and begins to address his responsibilities and exercise his judgment on the many national security matters he will face.

However, those instances—and no president can fully escape from them regardless of the preferred focus of his attention—raise an equally important question for the new Obama Administration: how will he respond to the many other foreign policy challenges that await him?

The answers to that second critical question are also to be found in a series of overlapping layers, each level of which becomes progressively closer to the president's basic operational worldview and set of strategic assumptions.

At the first level are those questions of concrete policy. Here the new president will face many national security questions for which the Bush Doctrine cannot and was not developed to give answers. What does one do about a resurgent Russia? What should the president do about the loose alliance of dictatorships that is gathering momentum linking South America, parts of Eastern Europe, East Asia, and South East Asia? What policies are best suited to handle "revisionist" powers? Should the United States intervene in actual or potentially genocidal wars like Darfur, and if so, in what circumstances?

Underlying these and similarly concrete issues is a second level of inference and analysis that raises some very basic questions for the president. What is the proper role of American power and leadership in the post-9/11 world? How does one relate to our competitors and enemies? How much can he expect from our allies and what do they have a right to expect from us? And of course, the most basic national security question of all: under what circumstances should the United States consider and then use military force?

The Bush Doctrine provides answers to some of these questions, but President Obama will have to see his way clear to his own views. Beneath the Bush Doctrine and whatever doctrine Obama may decide to develop and implement lie a series of strategic assumptions, resting on the foundation of the president's worldview and those of his advisors. That is the third and most basic operational level at which the president and his advisors' thinking operate. What is the nature of the international system and the various actors within it? How can common ground be reached or disaster avoided? What policy tools are likely to work, in what circumstances and with whom?

As should be clear, these are as much questions of psychology as they are of pure policy. What the president and his advisors think, why they think as they do, and what policies they develop as a result are all closely connected with each other, even if they are not ordinarily thought of in that way. This analysis then is a study in the psychology that underlies the national security thinking of the Obama Administration, as well as some of the central issues that their thinking will have to address.

Which parts of the Bush Doctrine, if any, should the Obama Administration retain? No answer can be given to that question without a fair appraisal of that Doctrine. And the Doctrine cannot be appraised or understood apart from the changes that 9/11 brought about in the Bush Administration's national security thinking. Whether those circumstances have sufficiently changed, and if so how, is central to considering how much, if any, of the Bush Doctrine remains relevant. Some have argued it never was; others that it no longer is.

The analysis begins with the position that those conclusions are best reached after a fair consideration of the doctrine, its strengths, weakness, and rationales. Providing that analysis is a major purpose of this work.

This book proceeds along the following lines. Chapter 1 sets out the range of national security issues facing the new administration and the ambivalent relationship between the Bush Doctrine and policies and President Obama's strategic worldview. We further consider the nature of risk in the post-9/11 world and how assessments of it influence the development of any new doctrine or policies. We end with a series of basic national security questions that the Obama Administration will have to address, as did the Bush Administration after the 9/11 attacks. The question raised is: what parts of the Bush Doctrine, if any, are necessary to successfully answer those questions?

Chapter 2 sets out the intellectual and worldview foundations of the Bush Doctrine and details how and why it developed. Chapter 2 analyzes the five major elements of the Bush Doctrine, its misunderstood strategic logic and its underappreciated association with a decidedly realist worldview. Its realist origins are one major, but not the only, example of the mischaracterization and myth surrounding the Doctrine. All of these myths impede our ability to clearly assess the Doctrine. The Doctrine's real contributions and limitations to American national security are analyzed in Chapters 3 and 4 and are the basis for considering how the Obama Administration might modify or make use of them.

Debates about the future of American national security policy require us to take into account the nature of risk and the consequences of uncertainty in the post-9/11 world and the best means for managing them. This is the focus of Chapter 5. We can think of risk as entailing the probability of loss or gain multiplied by their expectancy. In reality, there is a range of possible losses and gains associated with each of the security dilemmas that the United States faces, few metrics available for assessing likely outcomes, spillover effects as decisions made for one issue affect others, and few useful likelihood figures that can be given for any outcome, except perhaps at the extremes. The prime element of national security decisions is uncertainty. How leaders frame and understand the national security problems they face, what they know and don't know about the circumstances they are called on to decide, and what they can know or infer about their adversaries' intentions all carry enormous weight. Often however, such assessments are based on inferences whose basis is frequently unexamined. This is a recipe for trouble.

However threats to national security are framed, special attention will need to be paid to the nature of the post-9/11 world, the psychological assumptions we make about the actors in it, and the usefulness and limitations of the various strategies that are available. National security strategies that rest on ideas like deterrence, reassurance, legitimacy, coercion, prevention, and democratic peace are no stronger than the conceptual foundations on which they are built. The assumptions that underlie our major conceptual views of national security policy, the tools of strategic psychology, need to be rethought in our post-9/11 circumstances. That is the focus of Chapter 6.

At the core of the debate about the Bush Doctrine and the new post-9/11 strategic world lies the critical issue of force—if and when to use it. There is no doubt that the new Obama Administration will have to face this dilemma sooner or later. Force has always been a complex dilemma for a democracy like the United States that plays many important but paradoxical roles in the international community. Given that catastrophic attack is a real possibility and legitimacy a crucial ingredient of American international leadership, it is important to develop a clearer understanding of the circumstances in which force may be necessary. Toward that end, Chapter 7 develops the concept of dangerousness and begins to address its psychological and political elements.

If the Bush Doctrine is really dead, and President Obama declines to make use of it, we must answer the question: what should take its place? Pundits are unsure and the number of "grand strategy" replacement contenders has multiplied accordingly. Conventional wisdom has yet to crown a successor. Chapter 8 addresses these various alternative proposals and strategies. Comparing the Bush Doctrine with its possible replacements allows us to better understand the advantage and limitations of both, as well as an opportunity to deepen our understanding of the complex issues involved in the post-9/11 national security environment.

The assessment of risk is not only a matter of intelligence information but of judgments given substantial uncertainty. This fact coupled with the controversial nature of policies associated with the Bush Doctrine have given rise to efforts to develop a new smoking gun standard for the possible use of force. The gap between being able to obtain this level of certainty, the need to make necessary national security decisions, and their controversial nature exposes leaders to a built-in credibility dilemma, the nature of which is explored in Chapter 9.

In the end, whatever national security strategies are chosen, political leaders must be able to carry them out and the public must understand and support them. The debates surrounding the Bush Doctrine have made it very clear that the strategic choices that face the United States place a large psychological and political burden on the presidency and on the American public. This burden is exacerbated by the substantial divide emerging between our two major political parties on these matters. Chapter 10 takes up the profound political divide that permeates our national security debates, how they played out in the 2008 presidential election and analyzes their implications for the Obama Administration.

Although Americans now have a new president, they will still be living in a post-9/11 national security world. That requires an understanding of what it will take to survive our enemies, checkmate aggressive dictatorships, and develop firm and realistic relationships with our allies and the rest of the world. In a word this will require leadership. Chapter 11 offers some observations on these issues in relationship to the new Obama Administration.

Acknowledgments

The origins of the book lie in a long-standing interest in the psychology of international conflict and its intersection with presidential leadership and decision-making. Recalling the first allows me to express the too long delayed appreciation for those who helped shape and facilitate those interests.

In the spring of 1968 I began a Master's Program in the School of International Service at American University. My plan was to become a diplomat. One of my first courses was a seminar in unconventional warfare taught by James E. Cross, a senior official with the Institute for Defense Analysis. There I discovered my interest in political psychology and turned my career ambitions from diplomacy to scholarship.

As a political science doctoral student at the University of Pennsylvania, I was able to go outside of my disciplinary home base to follow my interests and that was how I found my way to a seminar in the Psychology Department entitled "The Psychology of International Conflict." That course was taught by a young assistant professor, Allan I. Teger, with a large National Science Foundation grant to study the psychology of conflict escalation. That was the start of a lifelong friendship and the consolidation of an equally long interest in that substantive area.

Over time, an interest in presidential psychology and judgment led naturally in some circumstances, to a substantive focus on their foreign policies. George W. Bush was clearly one such president, because of 9/11 and Barack Obama became one too because of the critical questions of how he would approach America's post-9/11 circumstances.

An earlier psychologically framed biography of Mr. Bush and his presidency naturally led to a consideration of the impact of the 9/11 attacks on him personally, his presidency, and his strategic response. At that intersection, the Bush Doctrine was born and it became immediately clear that both the attacks and Mr. Bush's response were critically important for the country and for thinking about American national security.

His successor, Barack Obama, faces many of the same national security issues. Yet, his actual policy preferences at this point remain a matter of some debate and mystery, and this includes how he will address the Bush Doctrine.

It is the intersection among the United States' post-9/11 national security dilemmas, strategic doctrine in response to them and presidential leadership and judgment that frames the analysis that follows. I draw on international relations theory, American politics and foreign policy, the psychology of international conflict, theories of risk assessment and judgment, and the psychology of strategic assumptions that underlie "grand theories."

This is a large substantive territory and I have had a great deal of help trying to cover it. Over the course of work on this book, I have greatly benefited from the gracious donations of their time from scholars at professional conferences, in preparing an edited volume on the Bush Doctrine, in personal correspondence, and those who have read drafts and shared their views on a range of issues that this book addresses. My sincere thanks to those scholars: Gerhard Alexander, Douglas Foyle, Richard Friedman, Alexander George, Jack Levy, Jerrold Post, Jonathan Renshon, Janice Stein, Peter Suedfeld, and Marvin Zonis.

In the spring of 2006 I taught a graduate seminar on "American Foreign Policy & National Security after 9/11," and in the Fall of 2008 I taught a seminar entitled "Presidential Decision Making in Foreign Policy." Both were exceptionally stimulating classes for me, and I hope for the students in them, and I benefited a great deal from lively and thoughtful discussions. My thanks for their fine seminar work there to Kora Andrieu, Michael Brenes, Darren DuClos, Rob Domanski, David Frinquelli, Bobbi Gentry, Billie Jo Hernandez, Eli R. Khazzam, Deborah Kim, Alan Koenig, Kevin Mulvihill, Nicholas Petaludis, Matt Polazzo, Danielle Zach Kalbacher, and Michael Waugh.

One of the students from that class, Nicholas K. Petaludis, subsequently became my research assistant and has done a terrific job in every aspect of his many responsibilities. It is a source of great comfort to know that you are working with someone who is both smart and responsible.

This work was facilitated by two grants (# 68018–00 37 and # 69706–00 38) from the City University of New York Research Foundation. I would like to thank the anonymous external reviewers for their helpful comments. Along similar lines, the press sent out both a detailed book proposal and the final manuscript for external review. The three reviewers provided very helpful comments and these are much appreciated.

A special word of thanks is due to Robert Jervis who served as one of the external reviewers (waiving anonymity) and who provided extensive commentary. This book has greatly benefited from considering his perspectives. On some matters, we have agreed to differ; on others we have found common ground. In any event, his close reading of the almost final draft is much appreciated both personally and professionally.

At Routledge Press I would like to thank Siân Findlay for overseeing a fast-track production process and doing it so well. Thanks to Heidi Cormode for her excellent copyediting skills, and to Felicity Watts for proofreading.

A special note of appreciation is due to Michael Kerns, acquisitions editor for the press. His support of this project and my work is deeply appreciated.

In working on this book, as in my life more generally, I have been extraordinarily fortunate to have the love and support of my wife of 30 years, Judith Beldner, and the pleasure of my wonderful children David and Jonathan. My love for them is beyond measure.

Last, but in no way least, allow me a few words about the man to whom this book is dedicated, Alexander L. George. He was an unusual man—a distinguished scholar of international relations, but also a conceptual and methodological pioneer. My thinking about the intersection of foreign policy decision-making, presidential leadership and judgment, and the hard issues of force and diplomacy has been immeasurably enriched by a thirty-year professional and personal friendship.

I discussed many of the issues in this book with Alex. He was not a supporter of the Bush Administration (and did not live to see President Obama take office), but even so he remained a supporter of examining the difficult national security issues that this country now faces in a direct and fair-minded way. I can only hope that this work lives up to that high professional standard of which he was an example.

1 The Obama Presidency and the World he Inherits

President Barack Obama takes office facing a large array of complex national security issues.[1] He will have to address a resurgent Russia intent on demonstrating its great power status and carving out a sphere of influence in areas of the former Soviet Union. It is ready to bully and invade its neighbors to do so, but is still willing to be helpful to the United States in some matters like supplying the North Atlantic Treaty Organization (NATO) troops in Afghanistan. He will have to address a potential East Asian colossus in China that is testing out its newly developing power and influence in Africa, Asia and on the world stage more generally. This has included its increasing military assertiveness in some areas including a testing of limits and wills by "harassing" a United States Navy vessel in what the Pentagon claims are international waters.[2] This must be done at the same time that the United States and China are sorting out a deeply entwined but not always harmonious economic relationship, And he will have to address a host of world difficulties ranging from the continuing crisis in Darfur, to the growing threats of nuclear proliferation, failed states like Somalia, severely troubled states like Pakistan,[3] increasingly troubled states like Mexico, the emergence of a nuclear armed Iran and even a modern-day resurgence of piracy.[4]

He will have to deal with older allies such as Great Britain, Germany and France whose basic support can generally be counted on, but whose specific policy support cannot be taken for granted. He will also have to deal with countries such as Pakistan and Saudi Arabia whose friendship is complicated and equivocal. For Barack Obama, as it was for George W. Bush, the post-9/11 world will be a complex and difficult one.

The new president will also have to deal with the widely held perception that the United States' power and influence have declined. America's economic troubles including a recession, an emphasis on spending at the expense of saving, and a failure of regulation and oversight seem to some more evidence of the erosion of American leadership, power, and influence.

The State of American World Leadership

President Obama will also have to deal with the view that the Bush Administration's policies and rhetoric damaged American leadership and legitimacy. It is a view that the president and his closest advisors appear to hold very strongly. In his invited campaign article for the establishment journal *Foreign Affairs* entitled "Renewing American Leadership," Obama wrote: "To renew American leadership in the world, I intend to rebuild the alliances, partnerships, and institutions necessary to confront common threats and enhance common security. Needed reform of these alliances and institutions will not come by bullying other countries to ratify changes we hatch in isolation. It will come when we convince other governments and peoples that they, too, have a stake in effective partnerships."[5] The not so oblique reference to Mr. Bush's supposed "you're either with us or against us" psychology and to his supposed unilateralism are hard to miss. President Obama's emphasis, both as a candidate and president, on consultation and outreach to all those willing to "unclench their fists," seems to give rhetorical weight to what he promises will be a new American leadership style.

Mr. Obama and his chief foreign policy advisors say they are determined to erase the damage to American leadership and reputation. In that effort they will doubtless be helped by the global enthusiasm that has greeted his presidency. Worldwide, the election of this new president has unleashed a euphoric surge of high expectations.

One editorial noted that, "At least three-quarters of people surveyed by the Financial Times in Britain, France, Germany, Italy and Spain (including 93 percent in France) believe that the new president will have 'a positive impact on international relations'."[6] Some anticipate a new American stance toward the world because the president, as candidate, repeatedly promised one. Some take this to mean that the new administration will abandon what they consider the various crusades of Mr. Bush, among them his focus on expanding democracy's reach, the war against terror, and his skeptical stance toward international organizations and agreements.

Yet, that same editorial noted that, "in Europe and elsewhere, there is a disconnect between Mr. Obama's popularity and receptiveness to his likely policies." One illustration of this fact is found in the repeated American requests to some of its NATO allies to increase their troop commitments to the war in Afghanistan and change their rules of engagement to allow more robust offensive actions. A two-day meeting of NATO defense ministers produced no further commitments for President Obama than previous entreaties had produced for President Bush.[7]

Countries, whether allies or opponents, that have had to deal with the consistent determination of the Bush Administration to avoid another, worse, 9/11 are now hopeful that the new president will be more receptive to their views and wishes. Indeed given what they see as America's diminished circumstances they are not shy about expressing their expectations. France's president Nicholas Sarkozy, who took office in 2007 with clear public pro-American sentiments, still insisted that he needed to, "let us make things clear: in the 21st century, there is no longer one nation that can tell what must be done or what one must think."[8] Foreign Minister Sergei V. Lavrov, bluntly asserted that "America has to recognize the reality of a 'post-American' world."[9]

He is joined in this view by Fareed Zakaria, *Newsweek's* foreign policy pundit.[10] Zakaria's point is not only that there are many ways to have power and influence and that the United States no longer has a monopoly on them, but that there are a number of countries that have gained on the United States and even suppressed it in some of those spheres. Other academics are blunter. Robert Pape writes: "Simply put, the United States is now a declining power. This new reality has tremendous implications for the future of American grand strategy."[11] One of them, as we shall see, is the new emphasis on "realism."

President Obama's Response: The More Things Change ... ?

President Obama responded to, perhaps confirming, these expectations in his first days in office. In his first interview with a foreign news organization (Al Arabiya) Obama said that he recognizes that, "all too often the United States starts by dictating – in the past on some of these issues – and we don't always know all the factors that are involved,"[12] a sentiment reminiscent of what he said in his *Foreign Affairs* article. At almost the same time, he also signed executive orders setting out a time frame for the closing of the prisoner facility at Guantánamo Bay Naval Base,[13] requiring all interrogations to be conducted according to the procedures laid out in the U.S. Army Field Manual,[14] and to review detainee policy.[15] These three presidential initiatives led one *Washington Post* correspondent to declare on page one, "Bush's War on Terror Comes to a Sudden End."[16]

Perhaps. But each of those directives contained caveats whose importance is yet to be determined.[17] On interrogations, his directive created a task force to study whether harsher methods might be needed in some cases. His directives also keep in place the controversial policy of "extraordinary renditions," the secret abductions and transfers of prisoners to countries that cooperate with the United States, so long as it is done on a "short-term" basis.[18] President Obama's Justice Department appears to be continuing the Bush Administration's practice of urging domestic courts to throw out civilian cases involving rendition and torture allegations on the grounds of "state secrets."[19] It also applied for an emergency stay motion at the 9th Circuit, asking it to freeze a district judge's order in a lawsuit challenging the legality of President Bush's warrantless surveillance program.[20] Elena Kagan, President Obama's choice to represent his administration before the Supreme Court, told a key Republican Senator during hearings that she believed the government could hold suspected terrorists without trial as war prisoners.[21] And in arguments before the Supreme Court on the issue of whether the president has the power to order the indefinite military detention of a legal resident, the Obama Administration took the position that, "Any future detention – were that hypothetical possibility ever to occur – would require new consideration under then-existing circumstances and procedure."[22] In other words, circumstances might arise where that might be necessary and if so, the Obama Administration would feel legally justified in doing so. Consistent with this position, the administration has gone to court to overturn a decision granting habeas corpus rights to prisoners kept at Bagram Air Base outside of Kabul, Afghanistan.[23] Along similar lines the administration announced that it was dropping the term "enemy combatant" that the Bush Administration had used as part of its rationale for detaining captured terrorists, but also argued that it had wide authority to detain such persons without filing criminal charges—thus keeping the Bush policy but dropping a term.[24] It has also reinstituted the system of military tribunals that the Bush Administration had spent years developing and defending.[25]

The new administration has also continued the Bush Administration policy of using remotely piloted aircraft to attack militants within Pakistan's borders,[26] and has expanded the target list.[27] And finally, the administration has committed 17,000 new American troops to the War in Afghanistan,[28] although the top U.S. Commander, General David McKiernan, had asked for 55,000 troops,[29] and the president has cautioned that the final number of troops will be decided after a review of American and NATO strategy.[30] Given all these apparent parallels, it is not surprising that a *New York Times* article reviewing these developments was titled, "Obama's War on Terror May Resemble Bush's in Some Areas."[31]

It is clear that the Obama Administration does not believe that the war on terror is over or relatively unimportant. It is also clear that the Obama Administration is not dismantling the national security architecture developed by the Bush Administration. What is not clear is how the new administration will respond to the key strategic challenges that it faces, what its strategic worldview and premises are, and how risk acceptant the administration will be when confronted with assessing any differences between its operational premises and the hard circumstances that it will face. Sighs of relief[32] or self-reassurance against worries[33] that the new administration is not so different from its predecessor are premature.

Bush and Obama: A Hybrid National Security Doctrine?

Herein lies a paradox in the relationship between the Bush Doctrine and the Obama Administration. A president's national security doctrine is both a set of policies and a set of premises on which they are built. The Bush Doctrine is no exception. One central question about the Obama Administration's approach to American national security is whether it is adapting the premises of the Bush Doctrine or just some of its policies. It is possible that the Obama Administration considers the tough-minded premises and policies of the Bush Doctrine as a foundation on which to try out a more conciliatory worldview and set of strategies. During the campaign one supporter said that "Obama is offering the most sweeping liberal foreign-policy critique we've heard from a serious presidential contender in decades."[34]

On the other hand, the fact that the new administration has not immediately discarded, as critics had feared and some supporters had hoped, some key national security policies of the Bush Administration, suggests that they are viewed by the Obama Administration as having some standing as a legitimate and effective response to our national security dilemmas. One reason this comes as a surprise to some is that the array of policies that define the Bush Doctrine are not widely known or understood.[35] Most commentary has focused on its most controversial elements, such as "extraordinary rendition," the development of the concept of "enemy combatant," and the use of "enhanced interrogation techniques." It is also this set of specific policies that have garnered the most attention as the new Obama Administration's national security policies take shape.

However, the national security policies of the Bush Doctrine are not limited to detainee detentions and interrogations. They cover a broad array of national security areas. The Bush Doctrine strategy is *not* a "call for a policy of uni-lateral action and preventive war."[36] These are *possible* options, not doctrinal requirements. The reporter whose story resulted in the end of the war on terror story committed the common mistake of equating a few highly contentious Bush Doctrine policies with the Doctrine itself.

A narrow focus on the most controversial policies does not help us to appreciate the reasoning behind them and in some ways the premises of the Doctrine are as important as the policies that developed from them. These premises grew out of the administration's understanding of the essential issues and features that define the post-9/11 security environment. And the admin-istration's view of the best way to address these issues ultimately rests on the president's worldview and strategic premises and those of his key advisors. The same is and will be true of the Obama Administration.

So, there are really two levels at which the Obama Administration's response to the Bush Doctrine and America's national security issues can be assessed. The first is at the level of specific policies. The second is at the level of specific premises. Ordinarily, we can expect on some level a fit between a presidential doctrine's premises and policies. Yet, it is unclear whether the premises of the Obama Administration's security policies, in their larger philosophical and worldview sense, are ultimately compatible with the premises that underlie the Bush Doctrine and the specific policies growing out of it that President Obama has appeared to adopt.

It is far too early to speak authoritatively of an Obama Doctrine as some have tried to do,[37] but some elements of it can be seen. In the second Democratic Party presidential debate the following Q & A took place:[38]

QUESTION: American diplomatic history books recount the Monroe Doctrine, the Truman Doctrine and will likely discuss the Bush Doctrine. When future historians write of your administration's foreign policy pursuits, what will be noted as your doctrine and the vision you cast for U.S. diplo-matic relations?

OBAMA: Well, I think one of the things about the Obama Doctrine is it's not going to be as doctrinaire as the Bush Doctrine, because the world is complicated … But I think the basic concept, and I've heard it from some of the other folks, is that increasingly we have to view our security in terms of a common security and a common prosperity with other peoples and other countries. And that means that if there are children in the Middle East who cannot read, that is a potential long-term danger to us. If China is polluting, then eventually that is going to reach our shores.

This is a rather expansive national security worldview. It potentially involves the United States in unprecedented levels of involvement in the domestic development of many nations, and in a host of problems that might conceivably effect us. And it seems to run counter the "realism of limits" that the administration seemed to promise in response to its view that overreaching was a key failing of the Bush Administration. John F. Kennedy observed, "there cannot be an American solution to every world problem."[39] President Obama seems to feel that a wide range of military, ecological and social problems effect us and thus are, to some degree, American problems. There may not be an American solution to world problems, but he does seem to contemplate that to them all, America owes a response.

On the use of force, Mr. Obama as a candidate was even more explicit: "No president should ever hesitate to use force—unilaterally, if necessary—to protect ourselves and our vital interests when we are attacked or imminently threatened."[40] This sounds almost Bush-like, but beyond the strong sentiment lie some basic unanswered questions. What does the president consider our vital interests? Granted a 9/11-type attack on American soil would bring reprisals, but what does the president think of as an imminent threat? Most thinking on imminence reflects a pre-9/11, nation state perspective. When armies mass and missiles sites are made operational the possibilities of harm increase, but not necessarily to certainty. With what level of risk does the president feel comfortable himself, and on behalf of the American people? The two are not synonymous.

And what of unconventional threats, and of allies? We can be more certain that Iran will not launch nuclear missiles against the United States barring some severe threat to its existence, but do we have the same level of confidence regarding Israel? Does that matter? Does that calculation then give Iran a free hand to expand its hegemony under nuclear cover through subversion? Strong general affirmations of the willingness to use force can melt or flare depending on the president's understanding of the stakes, the risks, and his actual willingness to "pull the trigger." Most modern presidents have learned the language of forcefulness; the actual commitment is always harder.

These preliminary considerations of a possible Obama Doctrine are important because every president adopts a stance that reflects his strategic worldview and develops policies that he thinks reflect it. President Obama will be certainly no exception. He has after all, already displayed his intention to accumulate and centralize the levers of presidential power in the White House.[41] One report notes, "President Barack Obama is taking far-reaching steps to centralize decision-making inside the White House, surrounding himself with influential counselors, overseas envoys and policy 'czars' that shift power from traditional Cabinet posts."[42]Another White House reporter has written, "it is clear that the center of Barack Obama's administration will be Barack Obama himself."[43] This is entirely consistent with Obama's publicly stated view that reporters and the public should, "Understand where the vision for change comes from, first and foremost. It comes from me. That's my job, is to provide a vision in terms of where we are going, and to make sure, then, that my team is implementing."[44]

Obama then is a president who views himself as the chief source of his administration's vision and he is also continuing a tradition of all modern presidencies by accumulating power in the White House. Yet, he has inherited a set of national security policies built on a set of strategic premises from George W. Bush that he does not appear to fully share. His adaptation of several Bush policies while rhetorically insuring his distance from them suggests that it is a grudging acceptance, one that runs against his grain. One irony of an Obama presidency is that the candidate, who ran against Mr. Bush and his Doctrine, seems to be adopting some of its important policies, which of course includes some of its major premises. It may be possible for Obama to combine his core views with the Bush Doctrine then in some form of creative hybrid, but liberal worldview premises are an awkward fit with those of his predecessor.

The potentially awkward marriage between Bush Doctrine policies and Obama Doctrine premises, to the extent that they differ, will gradually find the latter displacing the former. This is simply a by-product of the passage of time, the accumulation of new circumstances, and the formulations of new policies designed to meet them that reflect the administration's basic national security premises. It is quite possible that President Obama will start out with some Bush Doctrine policies, but eventually end with national security policies that reflect his own distinctive premises.

Realism and Engagement

One source of uncertainty about the ultimate reconciliation of Bush Administration premises and Obama Administration policies lies in the new president's ambiguous rhetorical emphasis on his vision of America in the world. In his inaugural address,[45] Obama said: "We will not apologize for our way of life nor will we waver in its defense" and "For those who seek to advance their aims by inducing terror and slaughtering innocents, we say to you now that, 'Our spirit is stronger and cannot be broken. You cannot outlast us, and we will defeat you.'" These sentiments cheered conservatives and realists.

However, he also emphasized: our "ideals still light the world, and we will not give them up for expedience's sake," and "we reject as false the choice between our safety and our ideals." As to the threats that America faces, he said that our founding fathers "understood that our power alone cannot protect us, nor does it entitle us to do as we please. Instead, they knew that our power grows through its prudent use." Moreover, "our security emanates

from the justness of our cause; the force of our example; the tempering qualities of humility and restraint." To those "who cling to power through corruption and deceit and the silencing of dissent," "we will extend a hand if you
are willing to unclench your fist." Obama envisioned an America, "that exercises
its power with a sense of justice, humility and restraint, and an America that,
while believing its values still light the world, pledges to promote them
through cooperation and understanding as much as military might."[46] Those
sentiments doubtlessly cheered foreign policy liberals.

President Obama often expresses the view that adherence to our ideals will give
the United States the high moral ground in the war against extremists.[47] This
may be correct, but those ideals will need to be tested against the risks that policies
derived from them might pose. There is some evidence that the new administration is seeking to hedge its idealism with a dose of realism. In keeping the
policy of "extraordinary rendition," for example, the Obama Administration
has appeared to come to the conclusion that the policy is needed, even though it
has been a flash point for foreign criticism of American national security practices.

Other administration calculations of risk are less clear. During his presidential campaign Obama said, "And I actually believe that we need missile
defense, because of Iran and North Korea and the potential for them to obtain
or to launch nuclear weapons."[48] Yet, the administration offered Russia a deal,
in which it would reconsider the need for a missile defense system partially
based in Eastern Europe in return for Russian help in stopping the Iranian
nuclear program. Obama's thinking, conveyed in the letter was that, "the
removal of the Iranian threat would eliminate the need to defend against it."[49]
The administration letter was sent in the hope that it would help bring about a
"comprehensive new strategic relationship [that] will encourage Russia to be
more helpful in achieving U.S. goals in Afghanistan and Iran."[50]

This relational "reset" and "fresh start" is in the service of a more general
policy stance of engagement. It is clear even at the very start of the Obama
Administration that it is seeking deals and grand bargains with America's
adversaries and not always friendly competitors. In the case of Russia, that
stance runs the risk of downplaying its reawakened great power ambitions and
allowing those greater latitude in the service of building on supposedly
common interests which are in reality asymmetric. Although the Obama
Administration clearly believes that Russia has no reason to encourage the
development of a nuclear-armed Iran, it is very unclear that the threats to
American and Russian interests in the matter are comparable.

Some expressed concern over the impact of such a deal on Poland and the
Czech Government whose leaders risked substantial political capital in signing
these defense agreements with the United States, and reliability of the United
States as a protective ally. These are serious and legitimate concerns. However,
there is another more basic set of psychological factors at work here. And they
concern Russian regime motivations.

Secretary of Defense Gates has written, "it must be remembered that what is
driving Russia is a desire to exorcize past humiliation and dominate its 'near

abroad'—not an ideologically driven campaign to dominate the globe."[51] Let us assume his argument is correct; what policies follow? Since Russia is trying to exorcize past humiliations should we allow them to invade or bully their neighbors? Would it be good advice to let a belligerent drunk get his/her way so that they might feel better about themselves in the morning? How much coercive assertion should be allowed if some line is drawn? And is the experience of pushing others around and getting your way a motivational pattern that gets reinforced when it is felt to have been successful?

There is also the somewhat practical question of how the new administration calculates the likelihood of getting Russia to act forcefully by pressuring its Iranian ally and business partner, and how effective that would be even if they were to do it wholeheartedly. And there remains the issue of verification for any agreement arrived at with Iran either through some "grand bargain" or as a result of a grudging and forced Iranian retreat in the face of concentrated allied pressure.

Among the most important elements of any administration's national security policy is how much risk they are willing to accept, and what steps they are prepared to take in order to hedge it. The highest levels of the Obama Administration, including the president himself,[52] have now concluded that, "there is no question that Tehran is seeking the bomb."[53] The only questions remaining are when that ambition will reach fruition and what to do about it. The United Nations (U.N.) estimated that Iran has already "built up a stockpile of enough enriched uranium for one nuclear bomb."[54] Admiral Mike Mullen, Chairman of the Joint Chiefs of Staff, agreed with that assessment in an interview.[55] Secretary of Defense Gates however, publicly disagreed, saying, "They're not close to a stockpile, they're not close to a weapon at this point and so there is some time."[56] How much he didn't say.

The Obama Administration hopes that it can convince Iran to put aside its pursuit of the bomb and is determined to test those waters by developing a dialogue.[57] For example, it contemplates a "big tent" meeting on Afghanistan at which Iran would be invited.[58] Further talks regarding Iran's nuclear ambitions that would include "major powers," Russia, China and the E.U., are doubtless being considered.

Debate to date has focused on whether it is wise to legitimize Iran's defiance of U.N.-imposed sanctions, its status as a state supporter of terrorism and its own documented involvement in covert military action against those it views as enemies, including the United States,[59] by entering into talks. Clearly, there are dangers in engaging in dialogue with competitors and enemies, but there are also opportunities. The more important question for the Obama Administration is what it hopes to gain by these talks, what it is prepared offer, how it will insure that any bargain reached is honored, and what it will do about the regional and international threat that Iran poses, if talks fail.

Talks are obviously a form of engagement and are based on the premise, which in the case of declared enemies is really the hope, that ultimately common ground can be reached and incentives can modify state interests.

Whether it is talks with Iran or a decision to drop sanctions and engage the Burmese military junta,[60] or to downplay human rights concerns in order to reach common economic ground with China,[61] the Obama Administration seems to be placing a bet on the utility of "soft power" and engagement, which it considers a form of realism.

One long understood consequence of realism is that it tends to downplay the connection between morality and politics. A less appreciated consequence is that it can easily lead to an ad hoc series of decisions. Each of these may have their merits, but collectively they may well wind up leading in diverse directions. In this case the whole would be less than the sum of its parts.

So whereas the Bush Doctrine has been criticized for excessive moralism, an emphasis on accommodation and deal making may leave any Obama Doctrine without a compass or steady strategic direction. One observer has noted, "There is no Obama Doctrine because Obama is not a doctrinaire kind of leader who operates according to fixed policies. Instead, Obama believes in a set of principles (democracy, security, liberty) for the world and tries to come up with practical measures for incrementally increasing US security and global freedom."[62] He is already being applauded in some quarters for precisely this,[63] but a strategic vision is useful to any president given the ways in which events and pressures that demand quick and substantial response can easily arise.

In real presidential life, as critical national security decisions are being made, the best definition of realism is one that looks at leaders, states and circumstances directly and sees them as they are and are likely to be, not as we hope they are or wish they will become. The new administration offers assurances that this is precisely how they see the world. Secretary of State Hillary Clinton says that when it comes to Iran "Our eyes are wide open."[64] This suggests that any outreach is based on a clear understanding of the nature of that regime and its intentions. Yet, those core elements are precisely the ones that are the subject of debate.

As in the Russian reset initiative, basic questions of regime motivation are relevant here as well. Is the Iranian regime seeking nuclear weapons for security? Do they want them for prestige? Will they be used as part of their aspirations for regional hegemony? All of these questions have profound implications. If the Iranians seek weapons because they are insecure in a tough world, American reassurance may, or may not help. If they want those weapons as matter of prestige, will a new non-nuclear status in the world community suffice? And if they are part of an aspiration to achieve a felt entitlement to regional primacy and status as a "great power" will economic inducements be enough?

We do not know the answer yet to the administration's thinking on these questions, and no reporter has yet thought to ask them. What is clear is that the answers to these questions are critical to the conduct of the "tough" diplomacy that the administration has promised.[65] And it is also clear that the answers to these questions are the unavoidable foundation of assessing whether those eyes, which are wide open, are still peering through rose-colored glasses.

While engagement and accommodation are often considered to reflect the virtues of pragmatism and flexibility, they also run the risk of undercutting moral legitimacy, reinforcing an unstable and inadvisable status quo, while allowing a state to assume that it has successfully engaged an issue when in fact it has only delayed a day of reckoning. That realist sensibility was prominently on display with the administration's appointee to chair the National Intelligence Council responsible for developing that agency's national security estimates and also briefing the president. He is on record as having criticized the Chinese for not cracking down sooner and more forcefully on pro-democracy demonstrators in Tiananmen Square in 1989 which resulted, according to Chinese officials, in the deaths of two to three hundred demonstrators.[66] He also was on record as favoring the view that a small Jewish lobby had disproportionate influence on American foreign policy in the Middle East. In both these views, and in other matters, his realism crossed the line from being clear-eyed to unblinking and he was forced to withdraw his nomination.[67]

In the policy debates between realists and their critics it is often pointed out, correctly, that it is a matter of emphasis. No administration could afford to conduct its foreign policies as if American ideals and values, democracy among them, have no place in national security considerations. It is, as conventional wisdom is quick to point out, a matter of degree.

Yet, it is also true that departures of emphasis carry with them their own policy commitments and momentum. Every administration will say it is using all the elements at its disposal, and the Obama Administration is particularly insistent that it will do so in formulating and implementing their national security policies. However, there should be no illusion that policy choices, especially basic changes in stance resting on broad changes in national security perspective and the weight accorded different elements, do not have consequences.

A Realism of Limits and Engagement: "Smart Power"

Many see Obama's emphasis on "engagement" as a "return to realism."[68] However, that term has traditionally been associated with the hard-headed pursuit of key national interests, by threats or use of military power where necessary. Of course, that term has come to have many meanings, but to critics of recent American national security policy, one of them entails matching means to ends and ambitions to capacities. The doyen of foreign policy realism puts it this way: "The enlightened realist would say we always hope to do somewhat more than we think we are able to do, but never try to do more than we clearly know we can."[69] This sounds prudent as well as Zen like until you consider that what we *think* we are able to do is not synonymous with what we actually can do, and what we *can do* is often a matter of debate. Invoking "realism" is no substitute for finding a fitting solution to a problem that recognizes its essence or essential character and tries to develop a real solution.

Among the many criticisms of the Bush Administration is that it did not recognize the limits of American power and as a result, squandered its influence. Exhibit A for critics is the Bush Administration's overreach in efforts to transform the Middle East by regime change in Iraq. They argue that America's diminished world stature has been brought about by its overly ambitious plans to bring democracy to Iraq, reckless disregard of its allies, a failure to work with and through international institutions, and an impulsive readiness to use military force rather than rely on persuasion, pressure, and persistence. Overreaching in the view of critics was the administration's original sin.

However, that critique misses the essential point of what went wrong in Iraq, which was not the president's plan to plant and nurture the seeds of democracy. The war presented the Bush Administration with many choices, a number of which proved to be critical, and none of which were without substantial risks. The three major debates centered on troops numbers, the depth of the debathification program and the failure to quickly reconstitute the Iraqi Army. None of these three major issues had clear, no-downside solutions. More troops meant better security, but a larger American footprint to stimulate anti-American nationalist feelings. Allowing those who had power to continue exercising it ran counter to plans for a new democratic beginning (the question was at what level to draw the line and who would make those decisions). Other criticisms included a lack of post-Saddam planning and the assumption of rosy scenarios.[70]

There is no doubt our military was unprepared with either effective counter-insurgency doctrine, sufficient numbers of troops, or effective military commanders to deal with the insurgency that took root and caused such brutal carnage over several years. More recently, with a new apparently more effective strategy and a new set of field commanders in place, the situation has improved. If, in the years to come, Iraq emerges a relatively stable, pro-Western, more democratic than dictatorial country the costs of that war will have been somewhat redeemed.

Yet, the new hope is that by being prudent and modest, as Obama suggested in his inaugural address that his administration would be, the United States can achieve more influence. That influence can be multiplied when the United States listens to its allies and takes into account the views of the "international community," a diverse group that ranges from the most brutal dictatorships through the most liberal democracies, led by those who range from the progressive to the repressive and, increasing non-governmental advocacy organizations dedicated to make the world listen and act on their singular causes.

In the view of those who see the United States as one among many powers, and power itself having many sources not all of them military, realism is not only a preferred policy for America's new circumstances, it is a necessary one. In line with this, some foreign policy scholars and practitioners advocate a new somewhat self-congratulatory term "smart power" as the preferred approach to American foreign policy.[71] This is defined as integrating both hard and soft power into American foreign policy design, a combination presumably under-utilized by the Bush Administration's supposed emphasis on military force.

"Smart power" is an especially congenial concept for a president who prides himself on his powers of analysis and is likely to become the new face of realism in the Obama presidency.

"Smart power" emphasizes using "soft power" tools like public diplomacy and a strategy of investing in "global goods," "providing things that people and governments in all quarters of the world want but cannot obtain in the absence of American leadership."[72] This is desirable as a matter of prudent policy, but it is not a policy that will fit all circumstances, and may be especially ill advised in some of the toughest. Many people want to get rid of their governments, say in Egypt. Would it be an exercise in smart power to help them?

And sometimes what is called "smart power" seems really to be a continuation of what is already being done, with a new name. A case in point is President Obama's description of his Afghanistan policy: "At the heart of a new Afghanistan policy is going to be a *smarter Pakistan policy*. As long as you've got safe havens in these border regions that the Pakistani government can't control or reach, in effective ways, we're going to continue to see vulnerability on the Afghan side of the border. And so it's very important for us to reach out to the Pakistani government, and work with them more effectively."[73] This appears to be the very same policy as the Bush Administration followed with then President Musharraf. Indeed, as one "senior official" in the new administration conceded in discussing national security policy in the area, "There are not too many brand-new ideas."[74]

However, it would seem essential that Pakistan retains its very own specific strategic focus given the dangers that exist there.[75] Pakistan's government signed an accord with the Taliban which allowed them to impose Sharia Law in the populous Swat Valley. As a result, "Thousands of Islamist militants are pouring into Pakistan's Swat Valley and setting up training camps here, quickly making it one of the main bases for Taliban fighters and raising their threat to the government in the wake of a controversial peace deal."[76] With this new success, the Taliban now controls territory only 60 miles away from the capital city of Islamabad. Moreover, the new democratically elected Pakistan leader, Asif Ali Zardar, "is emerging as a divisive figure at a time when Pakistan faces a rising Islamist insurgency and a stuttering economy."[77]

While a dual focus on the Afghanistan–Pakistan link ("Af-Pak," as the administration terms it) may represent a smarter framing of that specific problem, it may wind up in retrospect, to miss the larger issue. Were the Taliban and its allies to gain effective control of Pakistan and its nuclear arsenal, it would represent a catastrophic setback and an existential danger. The Obama Administration doubtlessly knows this; and hopefully it knows that its new "smarter," "Af-Pak" strategy concept is no substitute for addressing what has emerged as a dire set of strategic circumstances. "The administration appears to have belatedly come to this more realistic position."[78]

The issue of the viability of smart power in the service of realism confronts one of its most difficult problems in the question of what to do about a nuclear-armed Iran. Mr. Bush attempted for most of his time in office to find a key that would result in getting agreement from Iran to stop its pursuit of dual-use nuclear technology and the purification of uranium used in the making of bombs. In those efforts he relied on America's European allies to broker a deal using inducements offered in the context of mild economic sanctions. Those efforts had failed to reach a successful conclusion by the time Mr. Bush had left office.

The Obama Administration is thus left with the question: What is the "smart power" approach to avoiding that outcome? When President Obama said in his speech on the drawdown of troops in Iraq that his administration was "developing a strategy to use all elements of American power to keep Iran from developing a nuclear weapon," what exactly, did he mean?[79] Talks? Incentives? Isolation? Economic sanctions? The threat of military action? That phrase, "all the instruments of American power," might presumably involve some or all of these.

Smart Power and International Norms

Smart power advocates say "an increasing number of American leaders have turned away from a norms-based approach to global engagement. They have come to view international law as a suggestion rather than binding, alliances as outdated and dispensable and international institutions as decrepit or hostile."[80] No specific recent administrations are named, but the point and culprit, are clear nonetheless. Naturally, "smart power" proponents propose an adherence to international law as they see and understand it, a commitment to alliances with the attendant implication that the United States will seek and operate on a foundation of harmonious agreement with our allies, while renewing our commitment to global institutions, chief among them the United Nations. These positions look a great deal like the "liberal strategies for peace" that Oli Holsti described so well in his classic 1997 study of national security differences between Democrats and Republicans,[81] a division that is still pervasive.

Still, these observations of America's new place in the world and whether a realism borne of either relative decline or inherent limits coupled with smart power would restore America's prestige and influence begs the question of whether they are accurate. Is the United States really now "first among equals"?[82] If so, that would seem to imply that the Obama presidency will unfold in an international context in which the United States is just one of a number of "great powers" jockeying for position in a new world dominated by the search for balance of power advantage.[83] If that is the case, hopes for a "return to realism" will have found fertile international soil.

Realism is a strategic worldview eminently fitted to a world of defined interests and limited ambitions. It imposes discipline on limited options. It is also a worldview tailored to dealing with the world as it is, which includes doing what must be done, but often reaching agreements necessary to forestall harsher choices. So when Hillary Clinton said of her willingness to raise human rights issues with the Chinese, "We have to continue to press them. But our pressing on those issues can't interfere with dialogue on other crucial topics" she captured and embodied a realist perspective.

In that stance there are both advantages and risks. The most obvious risk is that the Chinese or others will take our "realism" as a signal that they needn't make any accommodations, domestically or internationally, on these matters. A more serious general risk of realism as a policy of limits arises in the case of the new Obama Administration-recommended emphasis on limited counter-insurgency goals in Afghanistan,[84] rather than on democratic governance and nation building. The Bush Administration came to the reluctant view that economic and political development was necessary for long-term security in Iraq. What makes Afghanistan different?

Finally, there is a tension in the Obama presidency between the difficult choices that realists are prepared to make and core idealism that seems to be the foundation of the president's worldview. Asked about views of American military intervention during humanitarian crises during the second presidential debate he said:[85]

> Well, we may not always have national security issues at stake, but we have moral issues at stake … So when genocide is happening, when ethnic cleansing is happening somewhere around the world and we stand idly by, that diminishes us … And so I do believe that we have to consider it as part of our interests, our national interests, in intervening where possible. But understand that there's a lot of cruelty around the world. *We're not going to be able to be everywhere all the time.* That's why it's so important for us to be able to work in concert with our allies.

His inaugural address, announcing a "new" approach mixing ideals and noble sentiments, contained many standard American foreign themes, but the test of these sentiments and themes lies on the president's shoulders. Para-doxically, one test of courage in national security policy is sometimes the ability to go against core convictions, when they are inconsistent with the president's larger obligation to "preserve and protect." Herein lies President Obama's core national security dilemma: he appears to hold the basic core convictions of liberal foreign policy premises but is faced with a world, and some particular players in it, that do not share it.

9/11 Risks: Fading, Exaggerated, or Still Real?

The lack of any major post-9/11 attack on the United States has heated up a debate about whether the danger of catastrophic terrorism has subsided, was never as much of a threat as it was presented to be, or still remains a threat that President Obama is required to take seriously. The national intelligence services seem to take the last of those three positions.

The final report of the 9/11 Commission stated unequivocally, "*Our report shows that al Qaeda has tried to acquire or make weapons of mass destruction for at least ten years. There is no doubt that the United States would be a prime target.*"[86] A year later, the third report of the 9/11 Public Discourse Project, a successor to the 9/11 Commission, bluntly stated "Preventing terrorists from gaining access to weapons of mass destruction *must be elevated above all other problems of national security because it represents the gravest threat to the American people.*"[87] And finally, in his 2007 testimony before Congress, John Negroponte, Director of National Intelligence said that the top two problems facing the United States were terrorist threats to the homeland, our national security interests and our allies, and as well "the efforts of dangerous nation states and terrorists to develop and/or acquire dangerous weapons."[88] This threat is not receding.[89] Indeed the 2007 National Intelligence Estimate on the terrorist threat to the U.S. homeland said that al Qaeda's intentions to attack the United States again were "undiminished," and assessed that al Qaeda would "continue to try to acquire and *employ* chemical, biological, radiological or nuclear weapons in attacks and *would not hesitate to use them ... *"[90]

While Dennis Blair, President Obama's Director of National Intelligence added economic instability as the most immediate threat facing the United States, he also said in his testimony before Congress, "We assess that countries that are still pursuing WMD programs will continue to try to do so ... Nuclear, chemical, and/or biological weapons or the production technologies and materials to produce them may also be acquired by states that do not now have such programs; and/or *by terrorists or insurgent organization; and by criminal organizations, acting along or through middlemen.*"[91]

The National Intelligence Council examination of national security trends concludes that, "Opportunities for mass-casualty terrorist attacks using chemical, biological, or less likely nuclear weapons will increase as technology diffuses and nuclear power (and possibly weapons) programs expand."[92] The 2007 National Intelligence Estimate entitled "The Terrorist Threat to the U.S. Homeland" judged that, "The U.S. Homeland will face a persistent and evolving terrorist threat over the next three years ... [coming primarily] from Islamic terrorist groups and cells, especially al-Qa'ida driven by their undiminished intent to attack the homeland and a continued effort by terrorist groups to adapt and improve their capabilities." What kinds of threats are involved? The report states unequivocally, "We assess that al-Qa'ida will continue to try to acquire *and employ* chemical, biological, radiological, or nuclear material in attacks and *would not hesitate to use them* if it develops what it deems is sufficient capability."[93]

President Obama seems to agree. In his first presidential debate with John McCain he said, "the biggest threat to the United States is a terrorist getting their hands on nuclear weapons," and further "the biggest threat that we face right now is not a nuclear missile coming over the skies. It's in a suitcase."[94] So if multiple and independent assessments by American intelligence agencies are credible, there is no evidence that the post-9/11 world and the basic security dilemmas that it brought for the United States and its allies have changed in any fundamental way. President Obama, like President Bush before him still faces a world where, for the first time, potentially catastrophic attacks on the United States are not only a real possibility, but are actively being pursued by smart, determined groups with the intent and the will to deliver a mortal or crippling blow to the United States or its primary allies, preferably with weapons of mass destruction.

Yet, some argue that this risk is "overblown" and inflated. Muller for example, argues that political leaders have inflated these national-security threats as has "the terrorism industry."[95] How do we know that threats of catastrophic terrorism are "inflated"? The term itself suggests a gap between perception and evidence.[96] And both of these terms reflect a complex aggregation of information, evidence, understanding, inference and, finally, judgment. It is difficult to assess the exact probabilities of unique events which themselves depend on unknown and at this stage unknowable probabilities that our efforts to avoid such an outcome are not more than matched by developing capabilities to accomplish it. In those circumstances, given the consequences, what president would not wish to err on the side of prudence?

Assessing Threat

Still, how then do we know when a threat is inflated? For some, it is a simple matter. We simply look for cases defined by "an effort by elites to create a concern for a threat that goes beyond the scope and urgency *that disinterested analysts would justify.*"[97] Who these "disinterested analysts" are, what and how accurate their understanding of the facts is, and how they assemble them to reach the conclusion that a threat is "inflated" are rarely self-evident except in the most extreme cases, and then often only in retrospect.

The problem is that in the most important cases, reliable unambiguous evidence is hard to get. Whether it's Iranian progress in developing nuclear weapons[98] or whether North Korea has a secret uranium enrichment program,[99] underestimating risks is as dangerous and damaging to national security interests as overestimating them. And as Richard Posner has argued, the United States has a long history of underestimating risks, among them the chances of a civil war, the Japanese attack on Pearl Harbor, Soviet spying in the United States during the Cold War, Soviet missiles placed in Cuba, the Iranian revolution, and 9/11, to name a few of many.[100] Moreover, in matters of core national security threats prudence and command responsibility might require giving more weight to dangerous risks than to hopeful solutions.

It is true that national leaders sometimes exaggerate threats for purposes of public mobilization in support of their foreign policy aims. This is the critique that several scholars make regarding the Bush Administration's decision to invade Iraq and his administration's "War on Terror."[101] The chief facts put forward in support of this view entail the failure to find suspected weapons of mass destruction (WMD) programs and weapons, the linking of Saddam Hussein to other terrorists including members of al Qaeda which some said suggested that Hussein was somehow involved in the 9/11 attack, and the use of vivid imagery like the administration's stated intention not to wait until there was a mushroom cloud to act.[102]

Of course the whole idea of "selling" a war, as one of these articles is subtitled, carries with it a slightly unsavory connotation, perhaps because of its association with Madison Avenue whose prime rationale is to instill in buyers the desire to have things they don't really need. But of course, all presidents must make their case to the public, especially when it involves matters of war and peace. In any event, each of the critics' points can be addressed with counterpoints. For example, the view that Saddam Hussein had a WMD program was based on 1991 post-invasion evidence that he had a robust program that came as a surprise to allied intelligence agencies. It was also the conclusion of all of our allies' intelligence services in assessments made before the 2001 invasion. Saddam Hussein did support terrorists and had provided haven and medical treatment of al Qaeda members and associates. When asked directly whether Saddam Hussein has played an operation role in 9/11, Bush said no. The vivid imagery was a reflection of administration fears that Saddam would hand off either technology or WMD information to groups anxious to get and use it. The worry may have been stronger than the likelihood, but on what "objective" basis could that determination be made? Moreover, even assuming that the worry was stronger than the likelihood, what were the risks of action or inaction? That is a calculation that the Bush Administration directly faced after 9/11, and the Obama Administration will face with Iran and perhaps other countries.

Critics of the administration's decision to invade Iraq, and of the use of force more generally, weaken their case by failing to consider the array of facts, understandings and circumstances that the administration faced, as they understood them. The fact that no stockpiles of WMD weapons were found cannot logically be used to bolster the "threat inflation" case since that fact was discovered only after the invasion. Moreover, the Duelfer Report to the CIA concluded that international sanctions were eroding and that Saddam "wanted to recreate Iraq's WMD capability."[103] No threat inflation critic of the Bush Administration has considered this report or its findings.

Threat Assessment and Leadership Rationality

"Threat inflation" critics believe that even dangerous leaders can be deterred. They base this view primarily on the premise that such leaders are "rational" and thus risk adverse when it comes to their own power or life. We can see these assumptions at work in the debate over containing Saddam Hussein, but we are also seeing them again with regard to the developing debate about the "rationality" of Iranian leaders.

The Bush Administration concluded that Saddam was dangerous because he was well documented to be a murderous and feared dictator (whose behavior supported that reputation), had regional hegemonic ambitions, had an inflated view of himself as the successor to Iraq's historical great leaders, and had a tendency to make dangerous misjudgments. Placing those elements in a composite analysis requires us to go beyond narrow questions of "rationality." The latter turned to the somewhat narrow argument as to whether Saddam was "rational." This minimalist term only requires that leaders believe that it is possible for particular policies to advance their own ambitions. This definition of rationality, however, presumes that leaders can reasonably assess the possible consequences of their actions and be deterred from taking action if prudence requires. That term is not useful for leaders whose psychology and position lead them to overestimate the chances of their success and who have not sufficiently considered the risks of failure.

A good illustration of why depending on the minimal definition of rationality as initiating any plan that *might* succeed is in John Mearsheimer and Stephen Walt's well-known analysis of whether Saddam Hussein could have been contained.[104] Their analysis is that his decisions to invade Iran and later Kuwait show his rationality. What is their logic?

They argue that in both cases Saddam was reacting rationally to threats. They write of his decision to invade Iran, "Facing a grave threat to his regime but aware that Iran's military readiness had been temporarily disrupted by the revolution, Saddam launched a limited war against his bitter foe on September 22, 1980." The authors conclude "that the war was an opportunistic response to a significant threat."[105] In others words, Iran's military capacity had been disrupted by the revolution, undercutting the argument that it was a dire and immediate threat, but that Saddam nonetheless, or perhaps because of this period of Iranian weakness, launched an "opportunistic" war. Opportunistic is another way of saying taking advantage of a window of opportunity, which suggests that the impulse to strike won out over prudence.

What of Saddam's invasion of Kuwait? Mearsheimer and Walt argue this too was "defensive." It was designed to deal with Iraq's "vulnerability" that arose because his economy had been badly damaged by "its earlier war with Iran (1980–88)."[106] The authors write that Saddam felt, "he was *entitled* to additional aid [from Kuwait] for one simple reason: Iraq had ruined its own economy in a war that helped protect Kuwait and other Gulf States from Iranian expansionism."[107]

So to rephrase, the authors argue that Saddam was rational because he felt vulnerable. And because of that insecurity, he launched a window of opportunity war against Iran whose military position had been weakened by their revolution. Then, because of that war of attrition that lasted for eight years and severely damaged Iraq's economy, Saddam again felt insecure and further that he was *entitled* to recover his costs of a misadventure from others. Therefore, he invaded Kuwait when it refused to pay him.

One can argue, as the authors have, that these decisions should give us confidence in Saddam's rationality. The authors even view Saddam's decision to stay in Kuwait after being unequivocally warned to leave or else as a sign that he was rational because, among other reasons, "he had reason to believe that hanging tough would work." Why? American public and Congressional opinion was "ambivalent," the Iraqi army was thought to be formidable, and if the fighting dragged on the coalition might collapse, and "public opinion might turn against the war." The authors admit those forecasts look "foolish," but argue that they were "conventional wisdom" at the time. They certainly were and we now know that nowhere were they more strongly believed than among Saddam and his inner circle. However, that doesn't make them more than wishful thinking.

It seems more consistent with the facts to say that the author's character-izations of Saddam's "rationality" reveal strong aggressive and impulsive ele-ments in his psychology heightened by a sense of entitlement and a tendency to misread the consequences of his actions. This last point is a crucial matter, because often the real crux of the decision to use force against an adversary doesn't really depend on them being "rational" in the very limited sense of that word described above, but on being able to reach prudent and reasonable judgments. This Saddam Hussein repeatedly had trouble doing.

We have some direct evidence of this from The Iraqi Perspective Project. This was a two-year study that included a series of intensive interviews with high-level members of the Saddam Hussein regime conducted after the war.[108] Those interviews provide evidence of a distorted worldview and faulty infor-mation assessment that could well have been a chapter in Robert Jervis' classic analysis of misperception in international politics.[109] Among his psychological traits that hampered prudent and accurate assessments were "a supreme, even mystical confidence in his own abilities" (p. 12), "a growing conviction of his own infallibility coupled with the desire to become the new Saladin and lead the Arab world against the 'New Crusader' state of Israel" (p. 15). Among the faulty assumptions that the Project documented were: (1) not taking his opponents, the Americans and their allies seriously (p. viii); (2) a basic mis-understanding of military doctrine (p. ix); (3) a belief that he could "intimidate or buy off foreign opponents his potential foes in Iraq" (p. 14); (4) that America was a timid, spent power (p. 16); (5) a failure to appreciate how the 9/11 attacks changed American strategic calculations (p. 16); (6) the belief that France and Russia would be able and willing to stymie any American invasion plans (p. 26); (7) a belief that Iraqi soldiers were "intrinsically superior fighters to Americans" (p. 29); and (8) "that if an invasion did occur Amer-icans would again be satisfied with something less than regime change" (p. 31). These mistaken views and assumptions were exacerbated by a climate of deadly fear of saying anything Saddam Hussein did not wish to hear. How rational can a leader be in these circumstances?

Consider the case of a country that once was and aspires again to be a great regional and even world power. Imagine that country's leaders are the second generation of a religious revolution that swept the former pro-Western leaders from power. Imagine further that these leaders are not only dedicated to maintaining their political power and religious hegemony, but are actively involved in military activities against their neighbors, harbor the wish to anni-hilate one of them, and see the United States as the embodiment of the movement to stop them from gaining their rightful place in the region and the world. Finally, imagine further that this regime concentrates power in a small group of extremely like-minded leaders suspicious of American intentions and determined to remove or mitigate that influence from their regional sphere. Acquiring WMD weapons would be one powerful way to realize a number of these ambitions.

The "rationality" issue with Iran is not so much that they will decide to directly attack the United States with nuclear weapons. The more likely threat is likely to come in the form of threats, veiled and otherwise, that the regime hopes will lead others to hesitate or comply with their wishes and could well lead others to feel increasingly hemmed in and compelled to strike out. There is also the danger with regimes whose revolutionary fervor has yet to cool, that they will be tempted to undertake adventures, especially through proxies.

This was the history of the other revolutionary power, the Soviet Union, that we faced during the Cold War. The Chinese go-signal to North Korea was one such proxy adventure; the Soviet Union's attempt to introduce missiles into Cuba another. Revolutionary leaders, whether their worldview is shaped by ideology or religion, who feel themselves beset by strong enemies, and acquiring the offensive weapons that they feel will protect them, have many inducements to calculate their "rational choices" in a way that violates our conventional notions of what they ought to do.

The Real Post-9/11 World: Questions for the Obama Administration

As President Bush did before him, President Obama will have to try and provide successful answers to the most serious national security questions that have arisen after 9/11:

- How can the United States avoid being the victim of another major terrorist attack, this time with weapons of mass destruction (WMDs)?
- What roles do the doctrines of prevention, preemption, containment, and deterrence play in the range of threats with which the United States and its allies must now contend?
- How can the United States resolve the dilemma of needing the cooperation of allies to address common threats, while having to deal with allies' different priorities and understandings of these very threats that may require the United States to act alone?
- How can the United States resolve the dilemma of needing international institutions to further develop a liberal democratic world order and its own legitimacy with the fact that the "international community" is sometimes not democratic, liberal, nor supportive of basic American national security concerns?
- How can the United States address the challenge of a fervent and aggressive religious ideology, some of whose elements are potentially attractive to billions of followers worldwide?

The answers to these profound national security questions will reflect the circumstances that President Obama sees as he looks out on the world, the advice that he receives, but most of all, they will reflect his own strategic worldview and judgments. Mr. Obama is a relative novice in foreign policy and national security. His background as a community organizer, State Senator, and one-term United States Senator understandably did not provide him with a long foreign policy resumé or a history of delving deeply into the full range of America's national security problems. It is likely that in these circumstances he will find himself depending on and proceeding from his own worldview. Other than advice, it is the only foundation available to him, to help sort through the options. As he gains confidence in doing so, his worldview will increasingly be the compass of his decisions, and those decisions will eventually result in a clearly defined national security stance, perhaps even a doctrine.

Whither the Bush Doctrine?

In the meantime, the new president will not face these problems in a vacuum. As noted, President Obama inherits national security policies Mr. Bush put into place after 9/11. How he will make use of, modify or discard his predecessor's policies and on what strategic basis is a major issue now facing the new president.

Obama also takes office with an American public politically exhausted by the harsh debates of two Bush terms, longing for partisan reconciliation but still deeply divided, worried about the economy and yet still understandably worried about the threats that they face. The modern presidents who followed Truman were more fortunate. They were bequeathed a policy, containment, that enjoyed broad support and legitimacy. Each president then modified those basic policies in response to circumstances or preferred emphasis, but the essential foundations remained intact. Not so the Obama presidency.

The Obama presidency inherits a contentious set of policies, the Bush Doctrine, whose soundness and legitimacy are widely questioned. The Doctrine is often presented as favoring a policy of preventive wars, using military force to change regimes the United States finds objectionable, disregarding the advice of allies and making clear to those that oppose us that we will not tolerate them, and spreading democracy—by policy if possible, by force if necessary. These, the most frequent characterizations of the Bush Doctrine, are caricatures.

The real Doctrine is a highly complex set of policies that attempt to develop comprehensive national security architecture to deal with the profound and difficult questions for American national security in the post-9/11 environment. The new Obama Administration is under pressure to put Mr. Bush and all his policies behind it. Yet, surely, as long as the United States still faces unique post-9/11 threats of catastrophic terrorism aimed against it and its allies, it would be foolish to cavalierly discard the Bush Doctrine without seriously considering the issues that it faced and the adequacy of the policies put into place to address them.

Still the questions of what parts if any, of the Doctrine should be retained, what parts should be modified, and what parts should be discarded can only be assessed after fairly and clearly setting out and analyzing the Bush Doctrine, in reality. Before we jettison the Bush Doctrine it would be prudent to understand what it really is. Before, we conclude that it is useless, it would be prudent to answer the question: what strategic national security premises and grand strategies should replace it? And finally, before we discard the Bush Doctrine it would be crucial to examine whether its strategic premises don't more accurately match the national security circumstances that the United States continues to face.

Part I

The Bush Doctrine Reconsidered

2 The Evolution of a Post-9/11 National Security Perspective

The Evolution of a Post-9/11 National Security Perspective

On a crisp early September morning in 2001, four groups of Muslim terrorists boarded the planes they would use as instruments of destruction, aimed symbolically and literally at the heart of America's economic, political, and military institutions. Two planes targeted and demolished the World Trade Towers, icons of American entrepreneurial spirit. A third plane struck the South Wing of the Pentagon, headquarters and worldwide symbol of America's military primacy. The fourth plane whose target was either the White House or Congress, hearts of American democracy, crashed in Pennsylvania after passengers recaptured control of the plane from the terrorists. That plane's intended target was the highest level of our political leadership, a strike which, had it been successful, would have been politically and psychologically catastrophic.

The immediate result of the attack could be counted in the thousands killed, the tens of thousands more deprived of their husbands, wives, fathers, mothers, sisters, and brothers. It could also be tallied in the billions of dollars lost in actual physical destruction and the many billions more lost in economic consequences. It was also a devastating psychological blow.

Those attacks demonstrated that the United States was vulnerable. Oceans were not enough to protect it. Nor seemingly, was the most prodigious military in the world's history. Americans awoke on September 11 to discover that they were personally vulnerable at home and at work, as well as abroad. They soon learned that the United States is a primary target of individuals and groups that would like to deliver a mortal or crippling blow to it. September 11 demonstrated that these enemies have the intent, the capacity, and the will. Their clear intent is to acquire WMDs and use them, hence the most fitting term "catastrophic terrorism."[1] As Francis Fukuyama pointed out, "The possibility that a small and weak non-state organization could inflict catastrophic damage is something genuinely new in international relations, and it poses an unprecedented security challenge."[2]

Thus was born the highly contentious "Bush Doctrine."

A Misunderstood, and Vilified Policy

To call the Bush Doctrine controversial would be an understatement. Vilified is a much more fitting word. It is hardly surprising that critics on the left would find much to disparage in the Doctrine. They recoil from its muscularity, assertiveness, willingness to act forcefully and if necessarily militarily on behalf of American national interest as the administration conceived it after 9/11, unwillingness to accede to allies' wishes or international community protest, as well as a willingness to lean, hard if necessary, on those reluctant to support us.

More surprising, perhaps, is the decline of conservative support for the Doctrine. Conservatives have criticized the Bush Doctrine on two primary grounds: what they saw as its lack of assertiveness and its failures in anticipating and managing the post-Saddam occupation. The first group's plea is: Unleash the Bush Doctrine! They wanted to know why the Bush Administration did not militarily confront the other charter members of the "axis of evil," and has let Syria and Iran get away with encouraging terrorist infiltration into Iraq.[3] The second group was appalled by Iraq's unceasing carnage, religious and tribal factionalism and a "unity government" dependent on and making use of murderous militias.[4]

Common Ground?

So, some conservatives and liberals have found surprising common ground, although for wildly divergent reasons. Liberals prefer the comfort of traditional allies, international institutions, and treaty agreements. They generally think the Iraq War was unnecessary and the brutal post-Saddam developments a reflection of the administration's arrogance, ideological blindness, and incompetence. They refused to consider that the choices made regarding the conduct of the war—the number of solders committed, the debathification process, and the favoring of democracy over an American-imposed government—presented dilemmas that were extensively analyzed and debated and for which there were no difficulty-free answers.

Most conservatives saw cause for removing Saddam, but are upset with the brutal and complex strategic morass that Iraq became before the relative success of the surge. They are displeased with the results of the war and the uncertain future of Americans' attempts to change the political and economic foundation of a dangerous region. Unlike most liberals, they believe in the application of American power, and therefore its failure to accomplish its purpose leaves their primary national security assumptions in disarray and in psychological limbo.

For some conservatives, there is a search for some explanation that will preserve their assumptions. If the Bush Administration can be shown to have waged the war incompetently then their assumptions about the legitimacy and efficacy of asserting American power will remain intact. Yet, it is also curiously naïve for conservatives, something they are not often accused of being, to forget that even well thought through plans can run into difficulty, if only because there are many enemies who are working night and day to insure that it happens.

Liberals on the other hand, while loathing the administration, its politics and its war took a different approach. They approached the difficult and complex national security issues that this country faced after 9/11 as if every choice with the singular and limited example of regime change in Afghanistan was wrong and every mistake avoidable. Their repeated complaints about "disastrous mistakes" in Iraq, administration "hubris," and Mr. Bush's "imperial presidency" are less about the wish for the Bush Doctrine's success than a chance to further undercut the premises of an approach that they are conceptually, strategically, and ideologically opposed to.

An Orphaned Policy?

On the surface then, the Bush Doctrine seems at the start of the Obama Administration to be in the odd political position appearing to have no constituency beyond Mr. Bush. Yet, President Obama will face many of the exact same questions that confronted the Bush Administration after 9/11. It would therefore seem prudent to explore the real nature of the Bush Doctrine.

The Bush Doctrine is best understood as a set of strategic premises or a framework for analysis to be applied, with modifications, to specific circumstances. The clearest evidence of this point is the different treatment accorded the three members of the "axis of evil"—Iraq, Iran, and North Korea.

Critics point to the different treatment these states received as evidence of the Doctrine's inconsistency. Yet, each of these countries was and two still are dangerous dictatorships while at the same time not sharing other characteristics (aspirations for regional hegemony, domestic constraints) that would make treating them exactly alike foolish policy. In reality, the war in Iraq was an application of only *one* element of the Bush Doctrine, what I call *assertive realism*. That tenet holds that action is prudent when one faces dangerous states with murderous leaders at their head, who are capable of or have developed weapons of mass destruction (WMD) technology and also have a history of support for terrorist groups. That basic strategic principle has been lost in the carnage and complexity of the Iraq War, but the difficulties of the Iraq War do not necessarily negate the premise.

The confusion that equates Iraq with the Doctrine is part of a larger set of misunderstandings about what the Bush Doctrine actually entails. In some cases, as when liberals decry the Doctrine's imperious unilateralism or when conservatives and realists argue against the supposed primacy of preventive war,[5] the confusion could be easily remedied by looking at the actual facts.

The 9/11 Origins of the Bush Doctrine

The Bush Doctrine grew most directly out of the 9/11 attacks and the strategic questions that they raised. The Bush Administration had to respond to the strategic implications of the 9/11 attack immediately. They had to establish responsibility for the attack, and had to assess what the attack meant.[6] Was it a single strike? Was it part of a concerted campaign? If it was the latter, what was its purpose? As horrendous and traumatic as the attack was, its implications were far more alarming. Pearl Harbor had suggested that oceans didn't guarantee security, 9/11 proved it.

Had the terrorists been sponsored in any way by another country or countries? If so, that fact held enormous implications, for the attack was clearly a more traditional act of war. Yet, if no country had substantially aided the attackers this was not necessarily good news either. It meant that the attack was not the work of a sophisticated nation state, but a relatively small group with the striking sophistication of one. And, chillingly, it had brazenly attacked the world's only superpower on its home ground.

The Bush Administration's core insight in the period immediately after the attack was to put together two essential facts. First, there were groups who were capable of launching major terror strikes against the United States and its allies, and intended to do so with nuclear, chemical or biological weapons if possible. This fact added weight to another, that there were dangerous leaders in power who were motivated by grandiose regional aspirations, murderous proclivities and whose drive for power was permeated by sadism, revenge and the wish for domination.[7]

It was hard to envision a strategy of containment or deterrence working well with such leadership psychologies. Worse, because of isolation and few internal or external checks on their psychologies, these kinds of leaders are also given to poor judgment. Ordinarily a purely rational calculation would lead decision-makers away from being associated in any way with terrorists who wanted to launch a major attack against the United States. However, the Bush Administration made the judgment that there were some leaders for whom the assumption of pure rationality was a poor national security risk.

Once it became clear that al Qaeda was behind the attacks, it also became clear that the group had worldwide reach and resources. This in turn required the administration to frame their response in geographically expansive and strategically comprehensive ways. Since 9/11, the geographical trail has led to the Middle East, East Asia, the Far East, Africa, Canada, Western Europe, South America, and of course the United States.

The substantive trail led to a major rethinking of issues of alliances, cyber security, homeland security, intelligence, terrorism, public diplomacy, and new initiatives to counter WMD and their proliferation. Along the way, the administration had to reconsider the fundamental grand strategies that had been the strategic mainstay of the United States since the Cold War—deterrence, containment, and compellence. The administration also reached back and revived the concepts of preemption and prevention and reframed the concept of imminence to help make those two actionable. The speed and range of the Bush Doctrine's substantive development coupled with the geographical range of its actionable implications are a very substantial, but little acknowledged, aspect of the administration's response.

Realism and the Worldview Origins of the Bush Doctrine

The Bush Doctrine did not spring forth fully developed like Athena from Zeus' head from a small group of neoconservatives.[8] Nor are its origins to be found in the premises of liberal internationalism.[9] It is true that the latter shares with neoconservative foreign policy thinkers a view that favors involvement and even intervention abroad. However, the "old liberal internationalist" tradition arose when America was indisputably needed, its allies dependent, and its adversaries had a home address and no wish to die for the heavenly glory of their cause.

The intellectual origins of the Bush Doctrine can be traced to a conservative-leaning group nicknamed the "Vulcans." They included such prominent figures as William Kristol, Francis Fukuyama, Paul Wolfowitz, Donald Rumsfeld and Dick Cheney. They were concerned with the drift of U.S. foreign policy during the Clinton Administration.[10] Their statement of principles included increasing defense spending and strengthening relationships with democratic allies. The next year, in 1998 this same group sent an open letter to President Clinton warning that, "the policy of 'containment' of Saddam Hussein has been steadily eroding over the past several months." They argued, "If Saddam does acquire the capability to deliver weapons of mass destruction, as he is almost certain to do if we continue along the present course, the safety of American troops in the region, of our friends and allies like Israel and the moderate Arab states, and a significant portion of the world's supply of oil will all be put at hazard." And they ended by urging President Clinton to act decisively by "implementing a strategy for removing Saddam's regime from power."[11] President Clinton seemed to agree. He said, "One way or the other, we are determined to deny Iraq the capacity to develop weapons of mass destruction and the missiles to deliver them. That is our bottom line" (February 4, 1998). On October 31, 1998, Mr. Clinton signed the Iraqi Liberation Act of 1998 that, "Declares that it should be the policy of the United States to seek to remove the Saddam Hussein regime from power in Iraq and to replace it with a democratic government."

The Vulcans, it is easy to see, favored a "forward-leaning" national security policy. Their policy stance is permeated with active verbs. They want to *promote* freedom and democracy, *challenge* hostile regimes, *extend* our preferred international order, and of course *remove* Saddam Hussein from power.[12] These suggestions sound remarkably predictive of elements that were later to become the strategic underpinnings of the Bush Doctrine. The only thing missing from this mix was Mr. Bush himself and those he surrounded himself with once in office. Rumsfeld, Rice, Cheney, and Powell were Cold War realists, not neoconservatives. Before 9/11, Bush himself was a nationalist and a realist not a Vulcan. He was certainly not a neoconservative. After 9/11, he remained a nationalist,[13] but adopted many of the positions associated with neoconservatives.

An early view of Mr. Bush's foreign policy inclinations can be found in his 1999 speech at the Reagan Ranch that he gave while running for president.[14] The themes that he addressed in that speech reflect his worldview and are helpful in understanding the impact 9/11 had in cementing them.[15] In his speech he spoke about the fact that evil remains despite of the fall of the Soviet Union and alludes to the fact that there are enemies who "hate" American values. He also adapted an independent muscular stance on matters of defense and retribution.

They are the words of an American nationalist. However, these phrases also clearly reflect a worldview that any international relations "realist" would find compatible. Mr. Bush sees the world as dangerous; realists would say it is anarchic.[16] That is to say, the international system is populated by wholly self-interested states, who frequently, if not always resort to military and strategic self-help to advance their interests in the absence of any rule-enforcing authority. In this speech, Mr. Bush clearly favors a forward-looking offensive stance toward national security. This is entirely consistent with realist-in-chief John Mearsheimer's major premise that, "the best defense is a good offense."[17] Even so-called "defensive realists" insist that states must be prepared for the worst even if they hope for the best."[18] Mr. Bush from the beginning let national security concerns take precedence over international agreements, guarding against "the false promise of institutions,"[19] another very realist principle.

Mr. Bush's worldview and his understanding of the nature of the international system were consistent both pre- and post-9/11. The 9/11 attacks reaffirmed and strengthened those views; they did not bring them into existence. The key elements of the Bush Doctrine grew very comfortably out of the president's basic realist foreign policy premises.

The Evolution of the Bush Doctrine

No useful strategic doctrine escapes modification, and for good reason. The Clinton Administration's national security strategy *A National Strategy of Enlargement and Engagement* went through three versions.[20] The Truman Doctrine began with George F. Kennen's 1946 "long telegram" outlining the sources of Soviet conduct, picked up steam with American aid to Greece and Turkey in 1948, was consolidated in the 1950 NSS-68 document,[21] and then developed further.

The impetus behind the changes was clear. Containing the Soviet Union in Western Europe pre- and post-Soviet nuclear power were two different matters. Containing the Soviet Union was one thing, containing an alliance of Communist powers yet another. In fact as circumstances change, strategic doctrines must as well if they are to remain useful. So, the fact that the Bush Doctrine evolved should not be surprising. And it is the failing of Bush Doctrine critics that they fail to recognize this fact. Whether the new Obama Administration will take a serious look at the Doctrine and retain what is useful, even if it is associated with Mr. Bush, is an open question.

It is easy to see the changes in the Doctrine by looking at some of the texts, speeches, and official declarations since 9/11 that have helped to define and articulate it. The most comprehensive statement of the Bush Doctrine is found in NSS 2002.[22] In it, Mr. Bush frames the struggle against shadowy networks of terrorists as a direct descendant of the twentieth-century struggles between liberty and totalitarianism, but with one critical difference. The gravest danger of the new struggle is the "intersection of radicalism and technology." These enemies are determinedly seeking WMD, and America and its allies "*will* act" against such dire threats "before they are fully formed." As a result, "we must be prepared to stop rogue states and their terrorists' clients before they are able to threaten or use weapons of mass destruction." Doing this is a matter of simple "common sense and self-defense." To defeat this threat, "we must make use of every weapon in our arsenal—military power, better homeland defense, law enforcement, intelligence and vigorous efforts to cut off terrorist financing."[23] In this war of "uncertain duration," "no nation can build a safer better world alone." As in the past, "Alliances and multilateral institutions can multiply the strength of freedom-loving nations." However, facing novel and dangerous challenges, "Coalitions of the willing can augment these permanent institutions." And, "America will encourage the advancement of democracy *because they are the best foundations for domestic stability and international order.*"

What stands out about the 2002 NSS is how thoroughly conventional it is in many respects. One prominent scholar characterized it as "unexceptional."[24] With the exception of the clearly proactive stance toward threats of nuclear terrorism, it is remarkably within the general historical traditions of American foreign policy. And as we will discuss shortly, it evolved.

Doctrines evolve for many reasons. Most obviously and importantly, principles are declarations of preference and intent whose implementation must be responsive to circumstances. Those who believe they have uncovered something profound in the fact that Mr. Bush treated members of the "axis of evil" differently would be legitimately aghast if he had treated them the same.

The worldview foundations of the Bush Doctrine, as we have seen, were in place well before 9/11 and, as we have also seen, 9/11 brought new circumstances and new understandings on the part of senior administration officials and, as a result, new policies. The administration could not tolerate the risk involved in the transfer of WMD components or technical information from or to dangerous countries. This policy was certainly a by-product of Mr. Bush's pre-9/11 nationalist realist views. Since the world is a dangerous place, it is best to be prudent and when necessary tough when it comes to core security issues. 9/11 added to that foreign policy stance the understanding that the combination of WMD and ruthless tyrants and groups were a recipe for destruction.

Doctrines frame and reflect strategic understandings but policies must be developed to carry out those understandings. The issue therefore is whether the core understanding that is the foundation of the policy is clear-eyed and accurate. How well that understanding is implemented is another, separate matter. It is perfectly possible for the Bush Doctrine to be correct in its major foundation premises, and for decision-makers not to have carried out the policies that flow from them as well as they could have, or even well at all. No doctrine, however conceptually sound, guarantees successful implementation.

Even when the worldviews of a grand strategy are essentially accurate, major new events can have a dramatic effect on the doctrine and lead to modifications. One example is the change in foreign policy from President Bush's pre-9/11 worldview to the actual formulation of the Bush Doctrine after 9/11. Another example is the Bush Doctrine's stress on democratization. That was not mentioned during Mr. Bush's 2000 presidential campaign and was not in evidence in the months before 9/11. Its first mention by the president was during his West Point speech in June 2002, nine months after 9/11.[25] Mr. Bush brought it up again in the administration's official 2002 National Security Strategy document, and in his September 2002 speech at the United Nations. It was a major focus in an October 2002 speech by Condoleezza Rice at the Manhattan Institute.[26] After the invasion of Iraq and the failure to find WMD, it became a staple of the president's and his senior advisors' rhetorical emphasis.[27] It is now officially an indelible part of the Bush Doctrine, despite its relatively late arrival as a primary emphasis.[28]

Doctrines and their associated implementation policies may and should change in response to the lessons learned while applying and refining the doctrine. For example, consider the force structure of the American armed forces. In the past, it was oriented toward fighting *two* conventional wars. The new Quadrennial Defense Review (QDR) has clearly been revised in accord with the lessons of post-9/11 conflicts and the threat of catastrophic terrorism.[29] In the 2001 version, the Pentagon envisioned being able to "swiftly defeat" two adversaries in overlapping military campaigns, while perhaps overthrowing a hostile government in one. In the new strategy, one of those two campaigns can be a large-scale, prolonged "irregular" conflict, such as the counter-insurgency in Iraq. The strategy also envisions conducting combat operations, if necessary, in countries that we are *not* at war with and operating as necessary on a worldwide, rather than a limited regional basis.[30]

Refining the Bush Doctrine

Refining strategic doctrines in practice also can lead to reconceptualization. Consider the concept of deterrence. That doctrine was developed and refined as American national security policy during a Cold War that featured two nuclear-armed and ideologically opposed superpowers. Of course, deterrence and its variants (coercive diplomacy, compellence) were applied outside the arena of direct American–Soviet confrontation, but the strategic reality of mutual assured destruction was never far from consideration during that period.

The basic idea of deterrence involves an actual or implied threat to take action if an adversary does not refrain or desist from certain actions.[31] However, as Sir Lawrence Freedman has noted, the concept has had its ups and downs.[32] The question raised by the 9/11 attacks is whether deterrence still has a role to play in American national security strategy, and if so, what is it?

The new Bush Administration defense review thought that it did and anticipated using "tailored deterrence."[33] This would entail developing doctrine and capabilities that aid deterrence in at least three different domains: advanced military competitors (read China), regional WMD states (for example, Syria, Iran, North Korea), and non-state terrorist threats. The *Quadrennial Review* is a strategic concept document, not a fully refined operational theory. It therefore provides little in specifics beyond some general statements of the capacities needed to address these three separate domains. Nonetheless, conceptualizing three different deterrence domains raises the important theoretical questions of what is similar and what is different about the three areas, and how these understandings affect the development and application of deterrence in each.

The Bush Doctrine Revised

The second, revised iteration of the administration's National Security Strategy was issued March 16, 2006.[34] That document reaffirms the major elements of the 2002 version, but it also refines them. The 2002 version extolled democracy, presenting it as key to domestic stability and international order. It devoted considerable attention to the administration's views and policies on the subject.[35]

The 2006 version, coming after the election victory of Hamas (officially designated as a terrorist organization) in the Palestinian territories, forced the administration to draw an important distinction between being democratically voted into office and continuing an avowed policy of "armed conflict including terrorism." The focus in this new iteration is on "effective democracy"; in the case of Hamas, any government that does not honor these principles (renouncing violence and terror), "cannot be considered fully democratic, however it may have taken office."[36]

The revised National Security Strategy also incorporates a lesson bitterly learned in Iraq. Post-conflict stabilization matters a great deal. It has become clear from a variety of assessments, that post-war planning for the aftermath of the Iraq War was deeply flawed.[37] The failures to adequately anticipate and prepare for the post-Saddam security environment seem particularly critical. Iraq has proven a bloody and very difficult lesson in the failure to anticipate the consequences of the brutal mix of suppressed inter-ethnic and religious conflict, the psychological consequences of decades of brutal dictatorship, severely damaged economies and infrastructure, the development and consolidation of governmental institutions of repression and domestic terror, and the powerful effects of anti-occupation nationalism.

How much these failures to anticipate were a by-product of Mr. Bush's well-known aversion to "nation building" and how much was the by-product of a failure to anticipate that wholesale social, economic, political and psychological *reconstruction* were needed is unclear. However, the 2002 National Security Strategy document did not mention the term "post-conflict stabilization and reconstruction." The 2006 revision does and specifically calls for the development of an Office of Coordinator of Reconstruction and Stabilization located in the Department of State—an explicit transfer of these responsibilities from the Department of Defense that was given responsibility for post-Saddam security and redevelopment.

The 2002 NSS mentioned public diplomacy only twice, in passing.[38] The 2006 version takes seriously the fact that the United States is both at war and also engaged in a "battle of ideas"[39] that requires efforts to limit "sub-cultures of conspiracy and misinformation."[40] The policies for addressing these issues are not only "public diplomacy," but also "transformational diplomacy" that include "actively engaging foreign audiences" and "enlisting the support of the private sector."[41] The catchiness of the concept phrasing is much less important than the fact that it reflects recognition of a key strategic element in future American national security policy.

Finally, the 2006 NSS strategy rearranged the foreign policy universe of allies, rivals, and enemies. Al Qaeda remains a principal enemy.[42] North Korea is a power that destabilizes its region.[43] Russia appears to have moved from friend to intermittent strategic partner, but on the issue of democracy, a disappointment.[44] India has moved from a standoffish, possible ally to a more fully functional strategic partner.[45] China has gone from a strategic competitor to a global player with an important role to play, if it acts as a "responsible stakeholder that fulfills its obligations and works with the United States and others to advance the international system that has enabled its success."[46]

The NSS 2006 restates the doctrine of preventive attacks on terrorist groups[47] and elsewhere refers to "anticipatory action to defend ourselves."[48] These policies renew preemption and preventive force without so naming them. It also singled out one country for particular strategic scrutiny: "We face no greater challenge from a single country than from Iran."[49] The 2006 NSS also makes another subtle, but important language shift. Gone are the political theology references in which the president stated that it was the responsibility of America to "rid the world of evil."[50] In its place is a focus on tyrants and tyranny,[51] two terms that bring to mind America's earliest indictment against King George III. The focus on tyranny and tyrants replaces the language of primal religious categories with much more politically familiar and acceptable terms. Thus, in such subtle phrasing, reconceptualization, and refinement does a doctrine evolve.

It is possible to anticipate a similar set of developments taking place as the Obama Administration applies its strategic premises to the problems it faces. For example, the Obama Administration clearly is emphasizing engagement and in so doing might make conceptual and policy strides as it adds its experience to the array of tools available to the United States. In its outreach to Syria, Iran, and even North Korea and perhaps Cuba, it can refine our understanding of some basic principles. Can incremental steps lead to grand bargains? What level of risk is appropriate to agreements meant to explore common ground? What is the tradeoff between engagement and getting real policy change that is critical? To what extent can engagement be a response to and help to ameliorate the basic psychological issues that drive our adversaries, without running the risk of encouraging these very trends?

The fact is that the Bush Doctrine leaves open the question of whether there can be a blending between the national security premises and policies of the Bush and Obama Administrations. Yet, before we can assess this question it is first necessary to gain a realistic perspective on just what, in reality, the Bush Doctrine entails, and how it addresses the central national security questions of our time. Those are the subjects to which we now turn.

3 The Real Bush Doctrine

The Bush Doctrine like any grand strategy is an attempt to set out a response to a fundamentally new and consequential set of national security challenges. And what could be more distinctive than the fact that the United States was now a, if not *the*, chief target of terrorists with the intention, capacity, and determination to inflict catastrophic damage? It is a basic strategic fact the Obama Administration would do well to keep in mind.

Moreover, like any grand strategy addressing a new set of strategic circumstances the Bush Doctrine had to accomplish three things. It had to accurately diagnose the problem. Second, it had to develop new conceptual and strategic tools to address novel strategic circumstances. It did this by developing what Tony Smith calls "a presidential proclamation of purpose likely to rank in historical significance with any of its predecessors save the farewell address."[1] Lastly, the doctrine had to assess just how these strategic tools, both old and new, should be applied to the *range* of circumstances that the new critical national security issues raise. It would have been foolish of the Bush Administration to rely on just one strategic tool, like preventive war, and it didn't.

General grand strategies begin with general questions. Presidential doctrines try to answer them.[2] Thus, Barry Posen and Andrew Ross for example, ask four questions of grand strategy: "What are U.S. interests and objectives? What are the threats to whose interests? What are the appropriate strategic responses to those threats? What principles should guide the development of U.S. policy and strategy?"[3] This is a reasonable and useful set of questions for *general* grand strategies, like "selective engagement," or "offshore balancing." However, at least with regard to the novel circumstances of post-9/11 security issues, these questions put the cart before the horse. Before we consider which general grand strategies, if any, are best suited to post-9/11 circumstances, it is first necessary to be clear about the nature of the new security issues and the critical questions that they raise.

In response to the shattering 9/11 attacks, the Bush Administration was faced with questions of how it could avoid another, perhaps more devastating attack, what new strategies had to be developed and old strategies refined, how the United States could balance new national security needs with the sometimes different perspectives of its allies, how it could retain international legitimacy while adapting an assertive strategic stance, and how it might combat the appeal of a fervent and necessarily aggressive religious ideology, some of whose elements are potentially attractive to millions of followers worldwide.

Difficult Judgments

Answering these questions require difficult judgments that balance profound theoretical, strategic, and political uncertainties. They often require consideration of staggering causal complexities under enormous time pressures while trying to integrate disparate and contested information from a variety of institutional sources of uneven performance. Regretfully, those with command responsibilities cannot depend on the academic theories put forward by those who either advise or criticize them. Professional knowledge, as opposed to myriad theories, is simply not up to that task presently.

Obviously, when it comes to the many issues that the Bush Doctrine raises, and what parts of it, if any, the Obama Administration should adopt, there should be vigorous public and professional debate, even impassioned and heated debate. Reasonable people can and should disagree. The questions are too important to be left unexamined or, alternatively, drained of understanding by snappy sound bites. But the key to useful debate, even if passionate and heated, is fair play. That requires taking the Doctrine as a serious-minded, good faith attempt, however flawed, to provide answers to the terrible security dilemmas that this country faces.

The Bush Doctrine, in Reality

The real Bush Doctrine, as is the case with other presidential doctrines, is found in official policy documents, presidential speeches and importantly presidential actions.[4] What stands out about the Bush Doctrine is its comprehensiveness. Its formal enunciation is contained in two National Security Strategy statements, one in 2002 and a revised version in 2006. It was further explicated in a Quadrennial Defense Review Report,[5] a national strategy to combat terrorism which was first issued in 2003[6] and then revised in 2006.[7] In addition, it also includes a National Strategy for Homeland Security,[8] a National Strategy to Combat Weapons of Mass Destruction,[9] a National Intelligence Strategy,[10] a National Strategy for Public Diplomacy,[11] a National Strategy to Secure Cyberspace, and the first major revision of the U.S. Army Field Manual for Counterinsurgency in 20 years.[12] The Bush Doctrine has also been explicated, explained, developed, and revised by the president and his advisors repeatedly since 2001 in press conferences, formal addresses, and interviews.[13] None of this is to say that each, or any of these strategy documents represent the last word on the subject. However, they do represent a very comprehensive explication of the Bush Administration's thinking and the linkages between those strategic assessments and the policies they developed as a result.

Many of these documents represent the first time that the government has made a concentrated effort in an area like homeland security, combating weapons of mass destruction, or the protection of cyberspace. Those initiatives, however imperfect, should be welcomed as focused responses, developed under conditions of great threat and little time to erect barriers against further attacks. There can be little doubt that developing and putting that architecture in place enhanced American national security.

This is *not* to argue that the administration's strategic assessments were necessarily correct. Nor is it to argue that even if they were, the policies they followed were necessarily adequate to the implementation task at hand. In Iraq they clearly weren't for several brutal years. What is being argued is that the Bush Administration gave clear expression to its strategic assumptions and the evidence that it used to reached them. They may have been incorrect, but if the Obama Administration reaches different strategic conclusions based on new evidence or a new reading of the old evidence, it owes the American public an explanation of both its thinking and the evidence for it.

One can gain some comparative sense of the great range and specificity of the Bush Doctrine by comparing it to its closest competitor on these matters—the Truman Doctrine. The latter, announced in a speech to Congress on March 12, 1947 laid out a policy of aiding Greece and Turkey in addressing subversive threats orchestrated by the Soviet Union. Other Western European countries at risk also received American aid. That policy was an outgrowth of containment theory developed by George F. Kennan in 1946–47 and formally incorporated in NSC-68 issued April 14, 1950.

Both the Bush and Truman Doctrines underwent change as they developed and were applied to new circumstances. This was a reflection of the underlying reality of any strategic doctrine: however sound, it has to be appropriate for the specific situations in which it is to be applied. Both doctrines received substantial criticism, although for different reasons—the Bush Doctrine for being too assertive, the Truman Doctrine for being too reactive. And both were carried through and applied by strong-minded and strong-willed leaders who felt they were doing what was right for the country, despite low public approval ratings.

The premises of the Bush Doctrine reflect five related strategic elements. These are: American primacy, assertive realism, stand-apart alliances, a new internationalism, and democratic transformation.

American Primacy

Critics credit President Bush with the view that America should be, and should remain, the world's preeminent global power. However, that view has become the predominant presidential view in the aftermath of World War II and the Cold War. Even President Clinton, whose grand strategy started out with the language of cooperative security and selective engagement actually "evolved to a point where it has many of the trappings of primacy."[14]

As noted, there are doubts among some pundits, foreign leaders, and some academics about the power and status of the United States. They see this country as either in absolute or relative decline. We might term this the misperception of decline since these views fail to acknowledge that whatever American power and status remains after accounts of its relative decline vis-à-vis others or in regard to the elements that go into such state rankings, the United States is the single most powerful country in the world.[15]

Yet, as Samuel Huntington pointed out well before critics pointed to the loss of stature brought about by an assertive Bush Doctrine, all this power doesn't necessarily translate to effective influence.[16] Nor does national power and status automatically result in achieving desired goals. Critics point to our difficulties in Iraq as an obvious example and they have a point, but not necessarily, as noted in Chapter 1 for the reasons they suggest. War is a blunt and uncertain instrument whose risks are exacerbated by hard trade-offs with uncertain and often unknowable odds, myriad ways in which unfolding realities can disrupt even the best-made plans, and consequences which can often not be foreseen much less controlled. All of these elements make military power a complicated and risky tool of national strategy and one to be used only very sparingly. The point of primacy is not as critics of the Bush Doctrine contend to use it as a handy tool of strategic policy, but to make its use unnecessary in all but the gravest circumstances.

That is just one of the ways that the meaning of the term primacy has often been misunderstood. Basically, "the objective for primacy … [is to] preserve U.S. supremacy by politically, economically, and militarily outdistancing any global challenger."[17] However, for some, the term carries with it very different connotations with regard to the *purposes* and *use* of that power. Some equate primacy with American domination, the imposition of a modern-day *pax Romana*. Seen in that light, primacy would be defined as a strategy "by which the United States literally rules the world … and uses its military power to impose order among all the states and make them conform internally to its values."[18] So, when Charles Kupchan writes, "Unipolarity rests on the existence of a polity that not only enjoys preponderance, but is also prepared to expand its dominant resources to keep everyone in line … "[19] he equates primacy with dominance in the *use* of power. This equivalence also fuels criticism that America wishes to establish an "empire"[20] which also seems to be an implicit assumption of others who ask: what's so bad about an American empire?[21]

American political culture and national identity will encourage and, if necessary, support American primacy; it will not support empire. And it will certainly not support the imposition of a *pax Americana* worldwide by military force. The idea that America would impose its values, by invading say China, Iran or Russia to make it more democratic is simply absurd. The Iraq example confounds a purpose with a by-product. To anticipate an argument that I will take up at greater length in Chapter 7, Mr. Bush invaded Iraq because he came to the conclusion that Saddam Hussein was extremely dangerous to American national security and could not be contained or deterred. Developing Iraqi democracy was a by-product of that central judgment, not its motivating reason.

Presidential candidate George W. Bush in his 2000 debate with presidential rival Al Gore and in his 1999 major foreign policy speech at the Reagan Ranch did use the word "humility" in speaking of American foreign policy and power.[22] That humility lay in "not dominating others with our power."[23] Yet, he also envisioned a world, "in which no great power, or coalition of great powers dominates or endangers our friends."[24] Of course the latter can only happen if numerous states suddenly renounce their interest in power and prestige. No president, whether a "realist" or not, is likely to base their plans for American national security on that possibility. What then is left is to insure that the United States is stronger than any threatening powers or groups of powers, and that is what primacy has come to mean in the arena of national security, both during the Cold War and post-9/11. That is why Condoleezza Rice specifically confirmed Mr. Bush's American primacy assumption in a 2002 speech at the Manhattan Institute. In it, she bluntly stated, "We will seek to dissuade any potential adversary from pursuing a military build-up in the hope of surpassing, or equaling, the power of the United States."[25]

America's preeminence and unique position as the most powerful country in the world raises a number of critical issues. Chief among them: for what purposes will, and ought, the United States use its preeminent position? And of course, is primacy worth it?[26] The Bush Doctrine is rhetorically quite clear on these matters. In NSS 2002 it states that, "The United States possesses unprecedented—and unequalled—strength and influence in the world. Sustained by faith in the principles of liberty, and the value of a free society, this position comes with unparalleled responsibilities, obligations, and opportunity. The great strength of this nation must be used to promote a balance of power that favors freedom."[27] It is tempting to dismiss this statement as rhetorical cover for a policy of American hegemony. There is, after all, the admission that American power is unprecedented and unequaled. Yet, it is also fair to note that the idea that America has a special role to play on the international stage is one long familiar in American diplomatic history.[28] And notice, the imperative injunction "must be used." If ever there was a rationale or formula for American international leadership, that is clearly it. However, it is not only the Bush Doctrine's wish for primacy that results in American leadership worldwide. World demands for American support and commitment are a large part of the reason that our interests are worldwide. America's world leadership thus begins with a paradox.

Worldwide America is, as Richard Neustadt famously said of the modern presidency, both a leader and a clerk.[29] The United States has many constituencies and they expect us to do their bidding. Worse, like other conflicted dependency relationships, these countries want many, often inconsistent things, from the United States. They want us to be the reluctant, but available, world sheriff. They want us to be the Good Samaritan in times of natural disaster. They want us to maintain and use our power where necessary to pre-serve local and regional stability, but also wish to insure that it is restrained by the wishes of the "international community." They want the United States to help guarantee their autonomy and freedom to act, even if those actions run counter to American interests. And they want to be "listened to" which often seems to translate into the wish to have the United States adopt their preferred policies. These are the understandable wishes of our allies. The less conflicted strategic motives of our enemies and competitors are quite a different and more dangerous matter.

Whether indispensable, preeminent, or primary, American power certainly spurs contradictory impulses in the world. The election of Barack Obama not withstanding, American primacy reassures some, scares others, and angers more than a few. For a country of people who want to be liked and belong, this is a difficult and paradoxical position. The dilemmas of world leadership for the United States flow from its three, not always reconcilable, roles in the world today.[30] It is the chief architect and guarantor of the liberal international order that has developed since World War II. It is the major power, while not always the leader, in a series of bilateral and regional alliances that both underlie the liberal international order but also have their own regional and local security rationales. And it is a country, like many others yet in some ways more so because of its worldwide leadership roles, that has its own national security concerns.

Critics mistake these three roles for "empire." However, it is a strange empire indeed, when the citizens of this "hegemonic power" would generally prefer to go about their business and not that of other countries. It is stranger still when many countries demand the attention of the United States and complain when they don't get enough of it. Given that the world prefers American involvement in many areas as long as it is on their terms, America's international role is bound to be controversial and conflicted. America's allies expect it to live up to what they think of as its international responsibilities. Yet they forget that the United States, while being the major world power now, has its own national security interests that are not only commensurate with its worldwide responsibilities, but a direct result of them.

Some of America's worldwide roles do or could more fully reinforce the strategic aims of the Bush Doctrine. Being a Good Samaritan in times of national disasters is one way of doing the right thing and earning at least some international credit. But such a stance has its limits. The United States cannot be the "first responder" for every ethnic conflict, nor can it right every unfolding wrong. As previously noted John F. Kennedy wisely observed that "there cannot be an American solution to every world problem."[31]

And what is President Obama's stance on this matter? At this point, he sends conflicting signals. He has said,

> In this uncertain world, the time has come for a new beginning, a new dawn of American leadership to overcome the challenges of the 21st

century and to seize the opportunities embedded in those challenges. We will strengthen our capacity to defeat our enemies and support our friends. We will renew old alliances and forge new and enduring partnerships. We will show the world once more that America is relentless in the defense of our people, steady in advancing our interests and committed to the ideals that shine as a beacon to the world—democracy and ... because American values are America's greatest export to the world.[32]

That sounds reminiscent of sentiments that almost every recent president including George W. Bush would find a comfortable fit.

Elsewhere Obama has written of "America's great promise and historic purpose in the world."[33] And further, "I dismiss the cynics who say that this new century cannot be another when, in the words of President Franklin Roosevelt, we lead the world in battling immediate evils and promoting the ultimate good."[34] That sounds like the continuation of a historical perspective that can easily be traced to Woodrow Wilson.

In that same speech he said, "America cannot meet the threats of this century alone, but the world cannot meet them without America."[35] It seems that President Obama thinks American leadership and power are, to borrow a phrase, "indispensible." And what of the military component of national power?

On that element of primacy, Obama has said that to protect American security, "We must call on the full arsenal of American power and ingenuity." Thereafter follows a list of power elements that he argues have been downplayed or ignored including the "strengthening of alliances," getting "our fiscal house in order," and freeing "ourselves from our own oil addiction," but then there is this revealing statement: "None of these expressions of power can supplant the need for a strong military. Instead, they compliment our military."[36]

It would seem that the premise of the importance of superior American power, hard as well as soft, the critical nature of American international leadership, and the intention to exercise it are an integral part of Obama's national security worldview.

Assertive Realism

There is probably no more necessary, overused, and misunderstood word in American foreign policy than "realism." It is a mantle that almost every group of foreign policy scholars aspires to don. This is not really surprising since its opposite, naïve idealism, is hardly the kind of platform on which to stake your political career or professional analysis.

Still, the many groups vying for the status they think that term confers leads to a certain amount of confusion. So when the Baker Commission presented its much-anticipated report on Iraq strategy in early 2007, the *Washington Post*'s headline ran, "The Realists' Repudiation of Policies for a

War, Region."[37] The article went on to say that, "The Iraq Study Group report released today might well be called 'The Realist Manifesto.'" Why? Because, "many of its recommendations stem from the 'realist' school of foreign policy … " The chief recommendations are considered realist because they advocate direct talks with Syria and Iran to help solve the Iraq problem, and a "new emphasis on solving the Israel-Arab War, including pressing Israel to reach a peace deal with Syria," which were part of a "New Diplomatic Offensive."

That definition of realism as involving, if not requiring, talks and diplomacy with one's adversaries as well as allies, is a key element of the Obama national security worldview. There are many examples: "To constrain rogue nations, we must use effective diplomacy and muscular alliances."[38] Or, "the world must prevent Iran from acquiring nuclear weapons and work to eliminate North Korea's nuclear weapons program … In pursuit of this goal, we must never take the military option off the table. *But our first line of offense here must be sustained, direct and aggressive diplomacy.*"[39] Or, finally, "we must harness American power to reinvigorate American diplomacy. Tough-minded diplomacy, backed by the whole range of instruments of American power – political, economic, and military – could bring success even when dealing with long-standing adversaries such as Iran and Syria."[40]

Initiating talks with adversaries can be a reflection of "realism," if you believe as Obama has said that "the notion that somehow not talking to countries is punishment to them – which has been the guiding diplomatic principle of this administration – is ridiculous."[41] Obama here slides over the obvious disadvantages of such talks including legitimizing your opponents, conveying an eagerness that can appear to undercut resolve and thus results, and also conveying a mistaken impression while engaging in the talks as Kennedy apparently did in his first meeting with Krushchev. And there are the additional issues of the expectations of others that talks bring and the added pressure to reach agreement, which if successful, can lead to taking more risks. Of course, having talks with adversaries can be "realistic" if expectations are kept in check, the desire to reach agreement does not interfere with reaching the goals that it was the purpose of the talks to achieve, and there are mechanisms to insure that parties actually adhere to what they have promised.

President Obama's emphasis on talks is couched in strong rhetorical phrasing, especially its adjectives. There will be "direct and aggressive diplomacy." There will be "tough-minded diplomacy." It will be "tough direct diplomacy." It will be "effective" and rely on "muscular alliances." It sounds almost as if Obama has reversed Carl Von Clausewitz's famous dictum and views diplomacy as a continuation of war by other means.

There are understandably reasons to couch diplomacy this way, especially when the initiative to talk to "anyone anywhere,"[42]coupled with a lack of national security experience invites the criticism of naïveté. However, this raises an important question regarding assertiveness about Obama's view of talk as a new element of his realism: how willing is Obama to use the stick? Or, to put it another way, how assertive is his realism?

Bush's view of assertive realism contained a preference when it came to critical national security problems for an offensive stance, rather than a defensive crouch. The administration's judgment was that when it came to catastrophic terrorism, the best defense was a strong offense. Offense, it should be emphasized, is not synonymous with military action. Indeed, military force may have nothing to do with active, assertive policies meant to forestall damage to American national interests. The Bush Doctrine's National Strategy to Secure Cyberspace and its Strategy for Homeland Security and National Intelligence are cases in point. They are assertive because they seek to develop and shape new security architecture in these areas, assertively filling in the gaps with appropriate programs where dangerous gaps previously existed.

In the past, the advance of military technology fueled an "ideology of the offensive" in aggressive nation states.[43] Importantly, this is not the case for the Bush Doctrine. It is not assertive because of a "use it or lose it" window of opportunity psychology generated by technological advances. Rather, it is assertive because it is an active response to groups that have already successfully attacked the United States and would like to repeat their success. The strategic premise of the administration's posture is found in Donald Rumsfeld's observation that, "it is not possible to defend ourselves against every conceivable attack, in every conceivable location at every minute of the day or night, [therefore] the best, and in some cases, the only defense is a good offense."[44]

Bob Jervis writes, "Offensive realism perhaps provides the best explanation for what the US is doing because it sees states as always wanting more power in order to try to gain more security for an uncertain future."[45] However, he misses an important point. Yes, the Bush Doctrine translates into support for higher military budgets, more attention to domestic security, forceful rhetoric, and in several notable cases, the use of military force. Yes, the Bush Doctrine recognizes that preventive action may sometimes be necessary. However, the Doctrine's assertive stance is not primarily to gain power for some future, as yet undefined threat, but one that is quite present, real, and active.

Obama's view on these issues is somewhat of a question mark. He did say during the campaign that as president he would keep "all options on the table." However, he did also say during the first democratic political debate in response to a question that, "I think it would be a profound mistake for us to initiate a war with Iran. But have no doubt, Iran possessing nuclear weapons will be a major threat to us—and to the region."[46] Noting this quote is not meant to imply that initiating a war with Iran would be sound policy; it is only to indicate that "keeping all options on the table" is presidential speak for having a military option. Its purpose is to avoid having to use military force by putting it in the service of deterrence.

As already noted, Obama has also said, "we should never hesitate to use military force ... to protect the American people or our vital interests whenever we are attacked or imminently threatened ... "[47] The first circumstance seems crystal clear, the second opaque.

In opposing the Iraq War Obama said, "I don't oppose all wars. What I am opposed to is a dumb war."[48] He then mentioned the American Civil War and World War II as wars that met his criteria. Obama has called the acquisition of nuclear weapons by Iran a "game changer" and said "I will do everything required to prevent it."[49] Yet, he also said that military action would be a "grave mistake." Again, the point here is not that military action is necessary or desirable. It is the question: what will happen in "game changing" circumstances when a preference for strong alliances and strong talk may not be enough?

Finally, in answer to a question about his response to the Russian invasion of Georgia, he answered, "Their actions were unacceptable. They were unwarranted. And at this point it is absolutely critical for the next president to make clear that we have to follow through on our six-party–six point cease fire."[50] Six weeks into his presidency Obama supported the re-established ministerial engagement with Moscow through the NATO-Russia Council that was frozen following Moscow's move in August to send troops into Georgia in a dispute over the territory of South Ossetia. He also offered a deal not to implement a missile defense system that placed those facilities in Poland and the Czech Republic, to which Russia had objected.[51] A rational "revisionist hegemon" might conclude that the invasion had many desirable outcomes. It had gotten the attention of the new Obama Administration. It forced them to choose between possible future cooperation and a continuing policy of isolation. It had demonstrated to others that Russia was again a major player in the international system and was to be courted and feared. And had by its behavior learned that the Obama Administration's realism could pay Russia dividends.

Stand-apart Alliances

The third element of the Bush Doctrine is a focus on strategic, stand-apart alliances most notably encapsulated in the phrase "coalition of the willing."[52] That term raises in a direct way the differences among American international relationships of convenience, necessity, and true friendship. Here is yet another area where the basic tenets of realism and the Bush Doctrine are close enough to be identical twins. Realists may disagree about many things, but there is one matter on which they concur: international cooperation is extremely difficult because states are always tempted to go their own way and there is little to stop them from doing it.[53]

Institutionalists respond that even if international actors are egotistic and live in an anarchic world where self-help is prevalent and no authorities can enforce the rules, cooperation can and does occur. That is true. However, many of their examples are economic and it is perfectly reasonable to suppose that the domains of national security and international economics and trade operate according to different decision rules.

Here, as elsewhere, the complexity of international relations theory has not yet caught up with the complexity of the post-9/11 international landscape for the United States. The post-9/11 alliance landscape has rearranged the traditional groupings of ally, rival, and enemy, as the examples of France, Germany, India, Pakistan, Saudi Arabia, Yemen, among others, make clear. Critics of the Bush Doctrine give iconic status to a few, but not all, of the European countries the United States rescued from Nazi occupation, rebuilt after World War II, and had as our allies during the Cold War. They exclude consideration of our developing friendships with the new more recently liberated countries like Poland and Czechoslovakia, and major Bush Administration initiatives to India and strengthening our partnership with Japan.

American tensions with our "traditional" allies France and Germany have been gathering steam for some time.[54] The reasons transcend the Bush Administration's direct response disagreements over the war in Iraq.[55] The European grand national security strategy is focused on developing European-wide, political, economic, social and legal institutions, all under the protection of American power, if needed. Paradoxically, they are also quite keen, in Kagan's words, to "tame and civilize American hegemony."[56] Before 9/11, as a practical matter, no American president could go very far in responding favorably to attempts at hemming in its strategic options. After 9/11, it was impossible to do so.

Americans have ambivalent feelings about alliances and have been historically skittish about putting too many of their national security eggs in other countries' baskets. The Bush Administration understood from the start the lesson that every administration eventually learns even if it doesn't say it publicly; allies have different levels of sympathy with and commitment to American national security (and other) policies, few allies are supporters on every matter, and every ally has interests that may or may not coincide with ours on particular matters.

It is certainly true that the Bush Administration's assertive stance toward retaining its options carried over to foreign policy more generally, as can be easily seen in its views on the Kyoto Protocol, the International Criminal Court, and the ABM Treaty. To the Bush Administration such a stance simply reflected the realities of the international system and its assessment of what it needs to do to protect the United States. Others see it as unnecessarily unilateral. While the administration might have done more to "package" its self-protective stance in a soft wrapper, and the Obama Administration will doubtlessly attempt to do that, the fact of distinct interests and perspectives cannot be easily disguised. Alliances are, at base, associations of mutual interests, buttressed to a degree by compatible values and ideals.

The importance of particular alliances and relationships also reflects a common geo-political center of gravity for security interests. The Cold War made Europe and our allies there a center of American geo-political focus. With the demise of the Soviet Union, the end of the Cold War, and the global reach of catastrophic terrorism it was inevitable that America's focus would shift. Asia—the Near, Central, and Far East—along with South East and South Asia and, of course, the wider Middle East now loom much larger in the calculation of American national security interests.

This has thrust the United States into new alliance territory. Who would have imagined that the United States Vice President Cheney would fly to Yemen to try and find common national security ground,[57] or that the Obama Administration would have to work hard to keep our military base in Kyrgyzstan?[58] Old allies have less leverage and less interest in these new areas. As has so often been the case in American history, America has been drawn into these new areas, not because it is seeking empire, but because it needs partners. New cornerstone alliances, like those with India are developing as the United States looks for strategic help in what used to be called the "periphery." That very term however, may need to be retired, at least for American national security interests. Given the globalization of information, people and threats few places are absolutely irrelevant (peripheral).

Realists, as noted, emphasize that cooperation is rare because states can always defect. However, a more complicated reality has emerged for American alliances. As was the case during the Cold War, the search for common security has resulted in some very peculiar strategic alliances. We are in alliance with *parts* of the government in Pakistan and Saudi Arabia, while other parts of those governments continue to pursue interests that are unhelpful and may even be damaging to American and Western interests.

The United States tolerates this because we have to. These two countries (and there are others) are central to American and wider Western interests. The difficult reality is that the United States cannot afford to lose Saudi Arabia and especially Pakistan as an ally in the fight against Muslim extremists. Both are strategically located, "know" many of the players in the region, operate in linguistic and cultural contexts central to that fight and which they understand, and one of them has nuclear weapons. Congressional or executive threats to the contrary, the United States needs Pakistan as an ally and thus there are limits to what it can ask, demand, or threaten.

A radical Muslim government in either place would be a strategic problem of the first magnitude. These would be governments paralleling Iran, which are ruled by a religious oligarchy, intent on imposing and maintaining a fundamentalist religious framework on both their domestic arrangements and foreign policies. Their fundamentalist views would be inconsistent with the assumptions of Western freedom and secularism and their foreign policies would very likely be very antagonistic to American national security interests. Pakistan already has nuclear weapons, so were a radical group to gain power it would represent a dire turn of events for the United States. Should the same happen in Saudi Arabia, the control of their oil resources by a radical government would be almost as dire.

One further complication has emerged in considering post-9/11 alliances, and that is the critical role that state leaders play in alliance relationships. The Bush Administration has been through several key leadership transitions during its time in office and each of these has had an important impact. Changes in government and leadership in Spain, Germany, Italy, Canada, and France have moved these countries in either a more (Germany, Canada, France) or less

(Spain, Italy) supportive stance toward elements of the Bush Doctrine. Mr. Bush's rhetorical stance that "you're either with or against us" has had to address a far more complex reality than critics allow.

The United States has had and continues to have very strong and supportive allies in Europe, Asia, and Africa. Yet, it also continues to have determined enemies. It continues to have needed equivocal allies, as well as fair-weather bandwagoning "friends," and a few long-standing and deep policy partnerships (England, Australia, and Israel come readily to mind). Moreover, even when governments were "against" the United States and the public hostile to Bush policies, a substantial amount of government-to-government cooperation went on at a number of levels on common security concerns.

While President Obama has repeatedly emphasized the importance of our alliances and the need for consistent consultation, the fact is that common interests will sustain common policies and divergent interests will lead to policy differences. Some policy differences like how to handle the transmission of passenger flight information on international flights can and were resolved, by the Bush Administration and the EU after arduous negotiations.[59] Some of them like whether Saddam Hussein had to be removed from power can only be resolved if allies have the same risk assessment and propensity. Perhaps it will turn out that under the Obama Administration the United States, France and Germany will all come to the common view that a nuclear-armed Iran can be contained and over time, its ambitions modified. In that case, some would be reassured that we are on the same policy as our allies. Yet, becoming closer with our allies will be small comfort, if such a policy is undertaken and proves wrong.

A New Internationalism and Selective Multilateralism

How, exactly, should American national security policy engage international institutions? This is a question that fundamentally concerns the Bush Doctrine. The Bush Doctrine views these institutions as not currently structured or operating in a way that allows them to effectively fulfill their important roles. Certainly, the United States cannot fully depend on them when concerns of vital national security arise.

Given domestic and world public opinion, it is necessary for the United States to take the United Nations (U.N.) and other organizations into account. Yet, it is also clear that this iconic organization has many problems that make it an unreliable ally for American national security interests. Though that isn't the U.N.'s purpose, no president can afford to place the security of the United States in its hands. Members of the Security Council share no common outlook or goals. American national security concerns are not theirs and some of its members, like Russia, are very interested in reasserting *their* national power and interests. Others, like France insist on their prerogatives as a "great power." China as a growing regional and international power is at the very beginning of finding its international role. It is not clear if it will be a supporter of the global international system, or a challenger to it.

The General Assembly is more problematic. Demagogues, democrats and terrorists share membership. The concern with broad principles of international justice and procedure is often inconsistent with a particular member's behavior at home and abroad. Regional, cultural and religious groupings spell further trouble for American interests. Many members want to reign in or thwart the American "hegemon." As the recent attempt to develop a common perspective on sanctions for Iran's nuclear program demonstrates, the United States would be foolish to count in any strategic way on the U.N.

Yet, in spite of these drawbacks, the U.N. has iconic status as the voice of the "international community." This puts the United States in a difficult and paradoxical position. It must support the U.N., even as it must of strategic necessity often bypass it. This dilemma is an easy target for American critics, but not a particularly enlightening one.

What, if anything, can be done to minimize the damage to America's international reputation given this paradoxical relationship? Could the U.N. and other international institutions be developed into a helpful vehicle for managing the risks the United States and other allied countries face? The Bush Administration has directly challenged the U.N. to live up to its responsibilities several times, most notably in enforcing its previously passed resolutions regarding Iraq and its attempts to develop common ground on sanctions against Iran's nuclear programs. These efforts have not proved noticeably successful. Even critics of the Bush Doctrine admit that, "in many instances, and especially in hardcore security questions, the United Nations falls far short."[60]

Some might consider this "falling short" assessment quite understated. Neoconservatives are not the only ones looking to develop alternative international institutions. In keeping with their preference for multilateralism some liberals and even some realists propose a "Concert of Democracies."[61] That idea has also found its way into a major report on American national security, growing out of a series of conferences at Princeton University,[62] a post-Bush Doctrine strategic option to address the threat of weapons of mass destruction,[63] and also in the McCain presidential campaign[64] as an alternative to international institutions on which it is too dangerous to rely.[65]

That idea is tempting, but raises many issues. Who would define democracy?[66] How would different interests, views and strategies even among democracies be resolved? To take a current example, Britain, France and Germany have different views on confronting Iran. Would adding Turkey, Mexico, and India, and all democracies, help the group to reach consensual ground that would be effective? Will countries like Iran be any more cooperative if a Concert of Democracies tells them to desist from their nuclear ambitions? That seems unlikely. Then, there are the consequences of dividing the world into the good guys (us) and the rest of the world.

As Brooks and Wohlforth argue:

> The existing [international] architecture is a relic of the preoccupations and power relationships of the middle of the last century – out of sync

with today's world of rising powers and new challenges, from terrorism and nuclear proliferation to financial instability and global warming. It is one thing to agree that change is needed, but quite another to settle on its specifics. As soon as the conversation shifts to brass tacks, competing visions begin to clash. In an anarchic world of self-interested states – that is to say, in the real world – the chances that those states will cooperate are best when a hegemon takes the lead. There are, of course, good reasons to question whether the United States, the only contender for such a role today, is up to the task.[67]

Van Evra agrees with that last point, writing that "American ability to execute a concert strategy is limited by the insularity of American culture ... The federal government is unready for the task of global political manager."[68] This of course assumes that the United States will be asked to occupy that position, a questionable premise given that some of our allies have demonstrated their desire to assert their own leadership both before, during and after the Bush Administration.

While critics have focused on Mr. Bush's skepticism regarding international institutions, less attention has been paid to his efforts to reform old institutions and develop new ones. The administration attempted to transform existing institutions and their practices, including the U.N., World Bank, foreign aid, and the North Atlantic Treaty Organization (NATO), to name just a few.[69] The Bush Administration invested tremendous resources and political capital in an effort to help these institutions modernize and operate more effectively.[70] Of course, more effective international institutions would then help shoulder the burden that the United States carries as the chief defender of the liberal international order. However, critics miss the irony of the fact that Mr. Bush's efforts were consistent with the views of both "realists" and "liberal internationalists."

The administration's attempts to reform international institutions led to the development of new international institutional initiatives; the Proliferation Security Initiative[71]; a new international climate pact among the United States, Japan, Australia, China, India, and South Korea that bypasses the Kyoto accords[72]; and possible alternative multilateral structures such as the 2000 Community of Democracies initiative launched by the administration. Few have noticed, most likely because few have read the document, that the National Strategy to Secure Cyberspace lays out a profoundly multilateral strategy.

I term this the "New Internationalism." It is a little noticed but important part of the Bush Doctrine. What critics saw as American "unilateralism" was in fact the first stage of an attempt to build a new international institutional order, or at least modernize the old one. As Jervis notes, "the United States is a revisionist hegemon seeking a new and better international system rather than a status quo power continuing the order in which it now wields significant power and exercises great influence."[73]

Jervis finds it "ironic" that the power who has done most to develop the liberal international system and benefits from it the most would want to change it.[74] However, the reasons are not hard to discern. The status quo, as desirable as it might be in overall terms to the United States, has become both antiquated and dangerous. It is dangerous because the status quo does not address important changes in the nature of the international system like the rapid fluidity of people, capital and information that places national security threats in a new context. It is antiquated because many of the institutions that the United States helped develop after World War II either must find new missions (such as NATO), must address new problems (such as global warming), or must find better, more effective ways to address old ones (such as poverty).

Obama seems more like the president of a "status quo" rather than a "revisionist" hegemon. He has written that "The United Nations requires far-reaching reform," but he has not suggested how he proposes to accomplish that. He has argued that,

> Today it's become fashionable to disparage the United Nations, the World Bank, and other international organizations. In fact, reform of these bodies is urgently needed if they are to keep pace with the fast-moving threats we face. Such real reform will not come, however, by dismissing the value of these institutions, or by bullying other countries to ratify changes we have drafted in isolation. Real reform will come because we convince others that they too have a stake in change – that such reforms will make their world, and not just ours, more secure.[75]

Democratic Transformation

Finally, there is the issue of spreading democracy. The Bush Doctrine is rhetorically front and center behind the idea of expanding democracy, often in difficult and inhospitable places. In so doing it appears to depart from its realist heritage. Yet, in doing so it is also following a well-worn path in American diplomatic and strategic history.[76] The United States re-imposed democracy in Germany and instituted it in Japan after World War II. Then as now, these democratic impulses were hardly altruistic and there is a strong realist element in those efforts and in Mr. Bush's as well. What Mr. Bush has signed on to is the closest finding there is in political science to a validated law. Mature democracies do not fight wars with each other. They don't terrorize each other either. Why this is so remains a matter of some debate,[77] but the fact remains.

Mr. Bush understands this and has repeatedly made very clear that, "elections are only the beginning of democracy, not the end,"[78] a point that President Obama either missed or ignored. President Obama, like every other modern president, has signed to the virtues of democracy: "We have heard much over the last six years about how America's larger purpose in the world is to promote the spread of freedom – that it is the yearning of all who live in the shadow of tyranny and despair. I agree."[79] Yet, he then added, "But this yearning is not satisfied by simply deposing a dictator and setting up a ballot box."

The president reaffirmed his rhetorical commitment to democracy in a major address at Cairo University,[80] although consistent with one of his leadership strategies that allows him to claim that he firmly stands on either side of an issue, he is also strongly on record as being against the expectations of building "Jeffersonian democracies."[81]

President Obama's agreement with at least one premise of the Bush Doctrine must be seen alongside some major differences. He said,

> The true desire of all mankind is not only to live free lives, but lives marked by dignity and opportunity; by security and simple justice. Delivering on these universal aspirations requires basic sustenance like food and clean water; medicine and shelter. It also requires a society that is supported by the pillars of a sustainable democracy – a strong legislature, an independent judiciary, the rule of law, a vibrant civil society, a free press, and an honest police force. It requires building the capacity of the world's weakest states and providing them what they need to reduce poverty, build healthy and educated communities, develop markets, and generate wealth. And it requires states that have the capacity to fight terrorism, halt the proliferation of deadly weapons, and build the health care infrastructure needed to prevent and treat such deadly diseases as HIV/ AIDS and malaria.

These are all laudable goals, and certainly consistent with the spread of democracy. However, who will undertake these tasks? Some of the governments that are most in need of this kind of help, are the most likely to resist it. What if governments demand "local control," and those projects become a funnel for leaders' ambitions and power?

These issue arise because candidate Obama pledged, "As President, I will double our annual investments in meeting these challenges to $50 billion by 2012 and ensure that those new resources are directed towards these strategic goals."[82] That is generous by some measures. However, the issue is not how much money is given, but the competence, honesty, and the adequacy of the delivery structures and personnel involved.

In championing democracy, the Bush Doctrine presented a twist on the "root causes" of political instability argument by using an old solution to solve a new problem. It takes an innovative conceptual step of redefining the issue of "root causes" by suggesting that at their core, the ills of "failed" and "rogue" states alike are that they lack freedom and democracy. In his view, problems of poverty, infrastructure failure, authoritarianism, and dictatorship would all benefit from a healthy dose of democracy. President Bush is not the first president to want to make the world safe for democracy. He is, however, the first to use democracy to make the world safe for America.

Some argue that democracy cannot be imposed.[83] However, it can and has been. Yet, the conditions for doing so are quite distinctive. In Germany and Japan it took a devastating military defeat, long years of allied occupation, and the building up over time of democratic institutions and practices. At the same time, it is clear that invasion and occupation is an expensive route to democratization. Here again the Bush Doctrine confronts more of the dilemmas and paradoxes of America's role in the world. It is criticized if it doesn't push authoritarian allies like Egypt towards democracy. Yet, in attempting to do so, it often runs into roadblocks. An international conference intended to advance democracy in the Middle East was derailed because Egypt demanded the right to control what groups would get funding from a new aid fund.[84] As the United States has learned in Palestine and Iraq, elections do not guarantee the emergence of liberal democracies.

How far to push, how to push, and when to push are not easy questions to answer. Yet Washington does sometimes push. One analyst noted that during the Bush Administration, "Washington has stepped up pressure on repressive regimes in countries such as Belarus, Burma and Zimbabwe where the costs of a confrontation are minimal while still dealing gingerly with China, Pakistan, Russia and other countries with strategic and trade significance."[85] And as noted, President Obama has already followed in the same path with Russia and China.

Yet, in spite of the Bush Administration's "realism" when dealing with needed, but undemocratic allies, they did make pointed statements. When Egyptian opposition leader Ayman Nour was sentenced to a five-year prison term on what the administration felt were bogus charges, the Bush Administration suspended important trade talks.[86] As Jervis notes, "all signs indicate that Bush and many of his colleagues believe in what they say and even critics have been surprised (and some horrified and others heartened) by the unprecedented extent to which Washington has pressed friendly and probably unstable regimes such as Egypt and Saudi Arabia to democratize, even if it has not used the most forceful instruments at its disposal."[87]

The key problems for strategies of democratic transformation are that it is almost always a process that is most prudently measured in decades, that there is little solid knowledge about why or how they occur or can be brought about,[88] and that imposing democracy by force, as Iraq has demonstrated can be costly and its outcome uncertain.[89] Still, allowing the now more easily transportable problems of poor, failing, dictatorial or radical states to fester is a recipe for disaster.

There is only so much that the Bush Administration, or any other administration, can do to foster democracy. And some of the things it can do are going to be internationally unsettling. The United States has a long history of both covert and overt intervention in the internal affairs of sovereign states. The United States was involved in the overthrow of possibly pro-Soviet governments like Iran and Argentina at the height of the Cold War. Yet, they gave covert aid to Solidarity in Poland, intervened against a former ally Ferdinand

Marcos, helped force Jean-Claude (Baby Doc) Duvalier into exile, pressured Augusto Pinochet to hold a referendum which he lost, and pushed Taiwan's Chiang Ching-kuo to end martial law and begin the transition to democracy. Preventing dictatorships inimical to important American interests and aiding our allies to bring down hostile governments already in power are two sides of the same interventionist coin. Whether through covert aid to friendly groups within hostile countries, friendly aid to parts of the government that we want to support against others, or the whole range of economic and military aid worldwide, the United States is always intervening in the affairs of other states. One implication of this fact is that others see the United States as more of a "revolutionary" than a status quo state.[90] And in truth, it is sometimes difficult to discern which is the more accurate characterization. One wonders whether the same puzzlement will be the perceptual fate of the Obama Administration.

4 The Bush Doctrine
Myths and Criticisms

The Obama Administration's developing national security Doctrine would benefit by looking to what others have done. This is routinely done as presidents and their advisors look to history, both for policy advice and cautionary lessons.[1] And that review ought to include the Bush Doctrine.

This is a particularly difficult undertaking when a Doctrine, its derivative policies, and the administration that set them in motion are so controversial and elicit such strong feelings and views. It is difficult to know what portions of the disagreements over the Doctrine arise from partisan views, dislike of President Bush and his agenda, the difficulties of the Iraq occupation, or the specifics of the policies themselves. There is also the added element of a president who won office by very explicitly presenting himself as the anti-thesis and antidote to the policies of his predecessor. Still, national security policy is critical enough to hope that campaign rhetoric and any personal feeling they represent can be put aside for the common good in this area.

Perhaps the first place to begin is the widespread view that the Bush Doctrine was a wholly unusual departure in American foreign and national security policy. Consider the critique of two senior international relations specialists Ivo H. Daalder and James M. Lindsay who worked in the Clinton Administration, and one of whom (Daalder) served as a foreign policy advisor to Senator Kerry in the 2004 presidential campaign. They characterize the Doctrine as "revolutionary" and "radical."[2] They subtitled their book on the administration "The Bush Revolution in Foreign Affairs." The word revolution conjures up historic institutions and practices swept away but what exactly is it about Mr. Bush's foreign policy that makes it a "revolution," and "potentially even radical"?

Not the goals of American foreign policy, since Daalder and Lindsay agree that these are fully consistent with the goals of many of the presidents who preceded him.[3] Indeed, they argue, somewhat paradoxically, that the goals are thoroughly conventional,[4] and that, surprisingly, Mr. Bush could be considered a "status quo" president![5] It is quite a neat conceptual feat to be both revolutionary, almost radical, yet at the same time thoroughly conventional and an upholder of the status quo.

Three years later, the same authors proclaimed, "The Bush revolution in foreign policy is over."[6] However that very same year, the lead author lauded the revised Bush Doctrine (NSS 2006) as follows "The new strategy's twin pillars—of promoting human rights, freedom, and democracy, and of working together with our friend and allies—have been central pillars of American foreign policy for decades."[7] Yet, any fair reading of the earlier NSS 2002 clearly demonstrates that the Bush Doctrine has held this basic worldview since its inception, even if it is more clearly articulated in the 2006 revision.

There seems to be a certain selectivity at work here. The Doctrine appears to gain approval when it makes clear its commitment to multilateralism, international institutionalism, and extensive search in almost all circumstances for foreign policy options other than force. And conversely, it arouses ire when it addresses the military or other forceful actions that may be needed if these stances don't work. Yet any national security doctrine or analysis that is at all realistic, especially after 9/11, must deal effectively with both prospects.

The Realist Critique of the Bush Doctrine

The realist critique of the Bush Doctrine is especially important to assess since, realism appears to be the banner under which Obama national security policy is unfolding. The foundation of realism is an unsentimental, clear-eyed view of one's circumstances, an equally clear-eyed assessment of what needs to be done given what one hopes to accomplish, and the capacity and will to do it. However, like "rationality," this term requires more of presidents than they are often capable of. Presidents, like everyone else, interpret their circumstances through the lens of their understandings and experience. Their policy solutions reflect these elemental frames. This is no less true of realists than it is for other strategic perspectives.

Realists critique the Bush Doctrine primarily for its transformative vision. In the realist view we must act on the world as it is, not as we wish it to be. It is already clear that the Obama Administration is proceeding on the view that we must talk with our enemies, accept the limits of our power, and make strategic accommodations, as are being done with Russia's invasion of Georgia and discussing human rights with China, as necessary. The Bush Administration is remiss, in this view, because it didn't accept the status quo and sought to transform rather than manage our national security circumstances. Worse, from the standpoint of realists, it inserts decidedly loaded language like "good" or evil" into foreign policy debates which leaves us less room to accommodate the interests of those who oppose us.

There is, however, a case to be made that it is realists who are themselves unrealistic. There are profound political and moral legitimacy questions that hover over the concept of realism. Foreign policy based solely on a realism in which "interests" are unleavened by values or ideals would merely be a form of strategic narcissism. It would be a policy without real alliances or allies, only national advantage and it is inconceivable that the American public would support it, even if its advantages could be demonstrated.

Both President Bush and President Obama pride themselves on being optimistic people, but it is the idealism found in Bush's policies that surprises. Realism and idealism are considered an odd couple in foreign policy, but that needn't be the case. Ideals can temper the harsh choices that realism presents and provide a "second look" to purely self-interested, cost-benefit analysis. This is not a call to substitute ideals for realism. It is only to point out that ideals can play a constructive role in making difficult decisions.

Moreover, that gap looms larger in academic debates than in real-life policy making. As Condoleezza Rice notes, "in real life, power and values are inextricably linked."[8] One reason is that leaders often do have to act at least partially on ideals. Colin Dueck's analysis of the factors underlying America's post-World War II strategic response to the Soviet Union makes this quite clear: "liberal beliefs still acted as a crucial filter, on the consideration of U.S. strategic alternatives … "[9] Yet, even if they were not so inclined personally, American leaders would need to consider ideals to help maintain this country's international legitimacy.

On the other hand, idealism in national security policy must always be seen through the prism of the hard choices that presidents are called upon to make. The Bush Doctrine's main claim to idealism came in its support for building democratic governments in Iraq and Afghanistan, two countries in which the question, what kind of governments would develop after the invasion, was front and center. In other words, the "idealism" was less an ethereal vision than it was a solution to a very practical and critical problem.

It is unclear as yet, just where idealism plays a role in President Obama's national security worldview. His outreach to Iran, Russia and Syria seem a clear case of *realpolitik* coupled with a willingness to take the risks involved with those undertakings. How well he has assessed those is a key question.

One decision to date that gives pause along these lines is his decision announced the second day of his administration that he would close the detention facility at Guantánamo Bay within a year.[10] This action immediately, publicly and clearly emphasized his new direction in post-Bush national security policy. However, the Executive Order was signed and publicized without a detailed plan for how the implementation would be handled. Among the questions left for later consideration were what would happen to all the prisoners including those who were considered very dangerous, what kinds of judicial proceedings would be set up, where and with what standards of evidence? Also unresolved were questions of what would happen to dangerous inmates where evidence against them was circumstantial, relied on questionable witnesses or could be challenged on the basis of coercion.[11] It is hard to know how much weight to give factors that might have influenced Obama's decision, among them: his personal convictions and ideals, how he wishes himself and the United States to be viewed, the rhetorical and policy need to make a very public departure from the policies of his predecessor, or a hard-headed assessment that such a facility and the policies associated with it have no real national security purpose.

The truth about clear-eyed realism is that it is not wired into a leader's perceptual apparatus no matter how smart they are. It must be mobilized and applied in each new circumstance and in the old ones often more than once. And it is often part of a complex psychological and perceptual package. In this respect, Obama is no different than any other president. What remains to assess is how often and how weighty each of the elements that seem to have gone into the Guantánamo decision will play out in other decisions and what patterns then emerge.

Realism and the Expansion of Interests

Realists point out that as countries gain more power, they gain more interests.[12] It therefore stands to reason that the United States as *the* most powerful country has expanded its interests. So, Robert Jervis writes, "American policy towards Iraq and the Bush Doctrine in general conforms to the *standard Realist generalization* that a state's definition of its interests will expand as its power does."[13] Yet, the Bush Administration's "interest expansion" was clearly a response to 9/11 and, in essence, defensive. It was the by-product of a severe strategic shock.[14] It is not the international equivalent of manifest destiny.

Scholars, as well as lay people, use theories and often are unaware of the extent to which they are both descriptive and *prescriptive*. Jervis, himself a realist, states quite directly that his analysis of the Bush Doctrine is "partially motivated by my opposition to American policy."[15] We are therefore faced with a somewhat paradoxical situation wherein a realist criticizes a president for behaving exactly as realist theory predicts he will. The implication of the criticism is that the president ought *not* to act in accordance with the theory. In taking this position, Jervis both affirms realism's explanatory power while decrying the very policies that in his view lead to the theory's confirmation.

Actually, the dilemma in assessing the Bush Administration's behavior runs somewhat deeper because Jervis also points to a difference between "what the deterrent relationship is and can appear between the US and Iraq and how we can explain what Bush and his colleagues appear to believe." He goes on to say that, "the divergence between the two, and the ways in which the actors' beliefs affect the use and impact of threats, raises questions about how we theorize about actors who are themselves thinking about deterrence."[16] Indeed it does.

One question that immediately arises is why the actors' views of their circumstances, risks, and choices as they struggle with questions of threats and deterrence should be accorded any less weight than the views of the theorists who are analyzing their choices. Jervis answers this question rather decisively. He says that, "when states behave 'badly,' general claims may be embarrassed." More specifically, "We are theorizing about actors that have their own explanations, which may be different than ours, and we have a problem explaining behavior we think is foolish when our theories do not incorporate foolishness."[17] The problem with this view is that it makes the theorist the final arbiter of what is wise or foolish, impetuous or prudent, or pragmatic or ambitious. Not only does the president have to live up to the tenets of a particular theoretical perspective, but he must also do so in a way consistent with the theorist's views of exactly how he should do it.

In any conflict between academic theories and presidential behavior, the latter must be given due deference. Presidents are, as will soon be argued, in a different position having command responsibility. However, the issue here goes beyond that.

Academic theories of national security policy base their claims of validity on their ability to explain the behavior of states and their leaders. These theories are often grounded in studies of what leaders have done. Yet, leaders are always dealing with evolving circumstances. Their views are focused on the present and the future and its contingencies. That is, they are focused on a set of policies that they hope will bring about a particular set of future facts. The large number of factors that influence such policy decisions insure they are always likely to be more complex than the theories we have to explain them. So, perhaps it is not that leaders "behave badly" and cause embarrassment to general claims, but that general claims should be more modest in the face of the complexities that presidents face and must act upon.

The Baker Commission Critique of the Bush Doctrine

The Bush Doctrine is often compared, unfavorably, with the advice of the foreign policy realists who advised George W. Bush's father. And it is considered an indication of the Obama Administration's realistic bent that it has reached out to the most prominent advisor of George H.W. Bush, Brent Scowcroft. Exhibit A is Obama's retention of Robert Gates, a long-time Scowcroft protégée as Defense Secretary, a position he held in the G. W. Bush Administration.[18]

Critics of the Bush doctrine can point as well to one of the major public critiques to emerge of Bush's policies—the Baker Commission Report. That Commission was led by James A. Baker III, considered a certified member of the realist school. In a recent interview he recommended to President Obama that he should engage Syria (and by extension others like Iran), "but with the caveats in the Iraq Study Group report. Syria's marriage with Iran is one of convenience, and if we assured them they would get back the Golan and normalized relations with the U.S., we might wean them from Iran."[19] In the same interview he touted "pragmatism,"[20] a virtue that realism lays claim to and one that President Obama and his administration have as well.

The Baker Commission could well be a case study in the pragmatism of realism. Their assessment that Syria or Iran would be interested in helping the United States extricate itself from Iraq or want a stable Shiite-led Iraq seemed more hopeful than realistic. Critics pointed to evidence that Syria was clearly implicated in trying to destabilize Lebanon, and Iran was helping to destabilize Iraq. When asked about this criticism, Mr. Baker replied, " … based on our limited contacts with the government of Iran, authorized by the president, we don't think that they will come and sit down, but we ought to hold them up to global public scrutiny, if you will, for their rejectionist attitude if they refuse."[21]

The consequence of asking one of the countries involved in trying to defeat American policy in Iraq to help extricate the United States is a public admission of failure that would have profound impact in the Middle East and elsewhere. It would immediately raise the power and prestige of Iran with dangerous consequences. The most obvious one would be to force our allies to reevaluate our dependability and their reliance on us. This in turn would force them into an accommodation with the new regional power, Iran. Another likely consequence would be to embolden Iran in its hegemonic aspirations. This is a high price to pay for providing public evidence of Iran's "rejectionist attitude." The fact that Iran has been on the State Department's list of states that sponsor terrorism since 1984 would seem just as persuasive.[22] Moreover, it is unclear what effect "global public scrutiny" would have on Iran. Iran seems not to care very strongly about adverse international opinion regarding their refusal to circumscribe their nuclear ambitions. The fact is that many countries, both within and outside of the region, identify with Iran's stance, of defying the United States.

One of the Baker Commission's major recommendations was for a meeting with either the fifty-seven-member organization of Islamic Conference,[23] or the twenty-two-member Arab League[24] to "assist the Iraqi government in promoting national reconciliation ... "[25] A look at the disparate religious, political, regional, and national interests of all the countries that would be involved in such a conference suggests there is more than a small dose of optimistic expectation in thinking that the conference could succeed in the goal the commission has in mind for it. The *New York Times* military correspondent in Iraq wrote, "The military recommendations issued yesterday by the Iraq Study Group *are based more on hope than history* and run counter to assessments made by some of its own military advisers."[26] Just because you are touted as a realist, doesn't make you one.

The Bush Doctrine: Myth and Reality

Controversy heightens emotional responses. Extreme controversies generate strong, sometimes narrow views that lose sight of important facts. The Bush Doctrine is controversial, and not surprisingly has evoked a number of strongly held, but not necessarily accurate views.

Conspiracy Theories and the Advisory Process

One of the most widely held myths is that the Bush Doctrine is the result of, and that the real powers in the administration are, a small, highly influential group of neoconservatives. They had been supposedly agitating for Bush

Doctrine-like policies years before the Bush presidency.[27] Limited evidence for this view is to be found in the pre-Bush Administration views of several administration officials. Among them are Paul Wolfowitz and Douglas Feith, both of whom served in the Department of Defense. Others who are ordinarily included as "influential" outside advisors include Richard Perle and William Kristol, neither of whom has ever served in the Bush Administration.

The standard critical narrative runs somewhat as follows: "An intellectually lightweight president, unschooled in foreign affairs, was led by a highly motivated cabal of foreign policy advisors and mysteriously connected outsiders to embrace their controversial doctrines."[28] A particularly muddled recent addition to this view adds that the group was primarily Jewish and beholden to the State of Israel.[29] This is precisely the view that led to the resignation of Charles Freeman, Obama's nominee for head of the National Intelligence Council.[30] Francis Fukuyama, himself a neoconservative critic of the Bush Doctrine, says of these accusations, "Much of this literature is factually wrong, animated by ill-will, and a deliberate distortion of the record of both the Bush Administration and its supporters."[31]Another version of this view is found in an allegation by Lawrence B. Wilkerson, Chief of Staff to former Secretary of State Colin Powell, that "in President Bush's first term, some of the most important decisions about U.S. national security—including vital decisions about postwar Iraq—were made by a secretive, little-known cabal ... made up of a very small group of people led by Vice President Dick Cheney and Defense Secretary Donald Rumsfeld."[32]

There are a number of logical difficulties with this view however. It is true that when he entered the presidency, Mr. Bush was unschooled in foreign affairs. However, Mr. Bush is an intelligent man, though not particularly introspective or generally not interested in abstract policy or philosophical debates. He was by no means a policy pushover.[33] Indeed, the usual criticism of his leadership style was that it is "arrogant" and "imperious," two traits that are inconsistent with being a pushover. Moreover, as noted in Chapter 2, Secretary of State Colin Powell, Vice President Dick Cheney, National Security Advisor Condoleezza Rice, and Secretary of Defense Donald Rumsfeld were, if anything, conservative nationalists and more "realist" than not, but not neoconservatives. The same was true of the president before 9/11. As James Mann makes clear in his magisterial history of the Bush war cabinet, labels are not necessarily useful.[34]

The focus of this criticism is not only the president, but also the narrowness of his advice, and of his advisory process. It is likely that for many, the Bush Administration's advisors and decision structure stand in stark contrast to the Obama Administration's smart, accomplished[35] national security so-called "Team of Rivals,"[36] a term which Obama has used to encourage comparisons between his governing team and Abraham Lincoln's Cabinet.[37] That team consists of, at the top, retained Secretary of Defense Gates, General Jim Jones as national security advisor and Hillary Clinton as Secretary of State. One admiring commentator characterized this trio as "the Brilliant Brain Trust."[38]

Another said that this selection suggested that the president was sending, "an indelible signal that the President-elect is a confident fellow and absolutely intent on creating a new national unity (and sanity) in Foreign Policy and Security matters."[39]

Perhaps. That group is very senior and very experienced, but so were Bush's advisors. Obama's group is very smart and accomplished, but so were Bush's senior advisors. Presidents Bush and Obama both had little foreign policy experience, so perhaps the differences lie elsewhere. Perhaps it lies in President Obama's approach to getting and taking advice, as well as the advice he gets.

At Obama's press conference introducing his national security team there was the following exchange[40]:

Q: Thank you, Mr. President-elect. You've selected a number of high-profile people for your national security team. How can you ensure that the staff that you are assembling is going to be a smoothly functioning – a smoothly functioning team of rivals, and not a clash of rivals?

PRESIDENT-ELECT OBAMA: I assembled this team because *I'm a strong believer in strong personalities and strong opinions.* I think that's how the best decisions are made. One of the dangers in a White House, based on my reading of history, is that you get wrapped up in groupthink and everybody agrees with everything and there's no discussion and there are no dissenting views. So *I'm going to be welcoming a vigorous debate* inside the White House.

President Obama's point may well be a public reflection of the decision style he wants to showcase. In reality, the clash of "strong personalities and strong views" is not necessarily the best way or only way to come to good decisions. Regardless of the strength of the views presented or the participants' investments in them, it is the quality of the views not their strength that matter. And it is the consideration of the options available and the analyses of the premises and expectations that are their foundation that matter more than the clash of titans.

While Obama's national security team is made up of experienced members with strong and well-developed views, there is a legitimate question about the *range* of views. Most are "realists." Most are on record as favoring diplomatic outreach to countries like Russia, Syria, and Iran. All agree on the general pace of withdrawals from Iraq, that comes closer to Obama's stated preference than to drawing it out over more time. All seem to agree that Iran is a problem best dealt with by "forceful" diplomacy. All seem to agree that settling the Arab–Israeli conflict is a critical key to American Middle Eastern policy. As one skeptic asked, "What are the sharp policy disputes Mr. Obama will have to mediate and synthesize, of the kind that divided Colin Powell and Donald Rumsfeld, Paul Wolfowitz and Richard Armitage, John Bolton and Nicholas Burns?"[41]

Given what we know so far about the national security decision process in the Obama Administration, this is a legitimate question. When the Obama Administration considered whether to fully and directly participate in any negotiations with Iran over its nuclear program initiatives, a senior administration official said, "There was no internal debate over whether to fully join the negotiations if and when another round is scheduled."[42] As will be discussed in greater detail in Chapter 11, when analyzing the administration's options for Afghanistan, "*All* of the president's advisers agreed that the primary goal in the region should be narrow—taking aim at al Qaeda … "[43] And finally, Jane Mayers reports on the debate that preceded the decision to stop coercive interrogation practices. She quotes Greg Craig, Obama's chief legal advisor as saying, "there was *unanimity* among Obama's expert advisers, that to change the practices would not in any material way affect the collection of intelligence." Top CIA officials though argued that so-called "enhanced" interrogation techniques have yielded lifesaving intelligence breakthroughs.[44]A heated public debate has broken out regarding this question.[45]

The unanimity of views among Obama's advisors on these three important matters does raise the question of how seriously non-conensual views are considered. When President Obama delivered a speech in Prague committing himself to a world without nuclear weapons, he said at one point, "I'm not naïve. This goal will not be reached quickly – perhaps not in my lifetime. It will take patience and persistence. But now we, too, must ignore the voices who tell us that the world cannot change. We have to insist, 'Yes, we can.'"[46]

The president's point is fair enough. However, the question of what to do until that day arrives is one of substantial consequences. In committing the United States to new limitations by signing the Comprehensive Nuclear Test Ban Treaty, not modernizing its nuclear stockpiles and further reducing them, the president has placed a large bet. He is betting that "if the United States demonstrated a willingness to sharply reduce its atomic arsenal, and if it revived treaties that would ban all signers from conducting nuclear tests or producing new uranium and plutonium suitable for bomb-making, it would be far easier to rally nations to confront Iran's nuclear ambitions and North Korea's presumed arsenal."[47]

The bet is premised on the assumption that by taking the strategic risk of leading by example, the United States can stimulate reciprocal strategic concessions from countries like Iran, Syria and North Korea. On its face, this does not seem like a winning bet, but it would be important before reaching any conclusions to know how the administration both understood the risks and considered ways to hedge them.

Certainly President Obama's stated preference for strong personalities and strong positions stands in stark contrast to what critics perceived as the Bush Administration style. For critics, the cabal narrative is explanation enough for the many policy failures they attribute to the Bush Administration's decision-making process and its reliance on the Bush Doctrine. Yet, even a cursory examination of the evidence suggests their view is wrong.

The evidence is that Bush foreign policy principals came to agree on many things, but strongly disagreed on many others. All the administration's foreign policy principals had their way on some, but by no means all, policy issues. Secretary Rumsfeld wanted to include Iraq immediately on the post-9/11 target list along with Afghanistan, but the president overruled him. Secretary Powell insisted the president go to the United Nations (U.N.) for approval. He got his way, but not exactly in the way he had envisioned. President Bush coupled his request to the U.N. with a suggestion that it measure up to its stated ideals and principles.

On some occasions, the administration foreign policy principals agreed, only to run into opposition from Paul Bremer, Chief Presidential Envoy to Iraq from May 2003 to June 2004.[48] On the issue of quickly putting together an Iraqi "Provisional Council" to supersede the original Governing Council without elections, for example, they lost. The question of whether to delay the first interim Iraqi election (January 30, 2005) after the Hussein regime fell produced a spirited debate. The *Washington Post* reported that, "a powerful debate was raging, officials now acknowledge, among the president's top advisers over postponing the January 30 interim election in hopes of first tamping down the flaring insurgency and bringing disaffected factions to the table." National Security Advisor Steven Hadley acknowledged, "There was a good debate in front of the president." "It was a close question and if it had gone to consensus, I don't know how it would have come out."[49] Ultimately, it did not go to a consensus decision but to Mr. Bush, who opted to stick with the election. This was not the first time that the president's views settled a debate with a decision.[50]

The decision to review fundamental policy in Iraq in the aftermath of the Baker Commission report also triggered a wide-ranging administration debate. The White House debate included consultations with a large number of parties both domestically and internationally.[51] The options considered were wide ranging and fundamental. They included ending the outreach effort to insurgents,[52] "the redeployment of U.S. forces to the Iranian and Syrian borders," withdrawing U.S. troops from more vulnerable positions and starting modest draw downs of American forces in part to encourage Iraqis to take on more responsibility,[53] focusing primarily on hunting terrorists,[54] and the numerous variations of the so-called surge option.[55] And these were only the ones that were reported publicly.[56] All of these options were framed by the president's conviction that not succeeding in Iraq would have dire strategic consequences for the United States, cause severe damage to its position in the Middle East and elsewhere, those of its allies, and of course for the majority of Iraqis.[57] This dire assessment was held by a number of the wide range of those who advised the president, including the CIA[58] and the Secretary of Defense.[59]

Many of these options were clearly incompatible with each other. Each choice carried with it significant risks and many uncertainties. Advisors strongly differed with one another. Choices had to be made. In these respects, the decision as to how to proceed in Iraq mirrors, in essence, the circumstances most national security decisions entail and that critics fail to give sufficient weight. In the end, this momentous decision was reflective of other important foreign policy decisions the administration made. Bush's foreign policy advisors came to agree on many things and diverge on others. It is not surprising that smart, principled, and experienced policymakers would have disagreements, sometimes very strong ones. The fate of those advisors' policy preferences, like those in other administrations, seems best to be described by the adage: win some; lose some. The word "cabal" does not do justice to the facts.

It is to be hoped that the national security advisors of the Obama Administration will have the same intense kinds of debates. The president has expanded the membership of the National Security Council to include the U.S. Ambassador to the U.N.[60] He has instituted a review, "the presidential study directive," looking into ways to improve coordination and implementation of national security policy.[61] He is attempting to frame national security problems in a regional rather than country-by-country way, departments will be able to monitor NSC deliberations to cut down on their learning time on issues that arise, and studies of a wide range of national security issues are underway.[62] He has also merged the staffs of the Homeland Security and National Security Councils to "speed up and unify security policy making in the White House,"[63] while adding new offices for cybersecurity, WMDs, and "resilience" (response to attacks, natural disasters, or pandemics). All of these initiatives can lend themselves to more comprehensive consideration of the issues at hand. Yet, none of these initiatives, as useful as they might be, can be counted on to insure good judgments or effective policies.

It is important that a president develops a national security process with which he feels comfortable. Some presidents like Eisenhower and Nixon preferred a formal options system in which issues are debated and assessments and recommendations are passed up the line. Some like Roosevelt and Clinton preferred a more free wheeling system. George W. Bush did not like reading position papers and preferred to have his advisors carry out debates in front of him. President Obama apparently also likes to have debates take place in his presence, but also reads many policy papers. Many presidents use some combination of these systems. Eisenhower made careful notes on all the decision memos he read, but he also had extensive personal contacts within and outside of the government that he tapped into for particular issues.

Whatever the president's preference for organizing the national security process, it can be said with certainty that it will have its flaws. Obama's national security advisor General Jones said in an interview "so it's my job to make sure that minority opinion is represented. But if at the end of the day he turns to me and says, 'Well, what do you think, Jones?,' I'm going to tell him what I think."[64] This view runs the risk of having the chief national security advisor blur the line between preparing decisions for the president's judgment and giving him advice. That was one of the criticisms of Condoleezza Rice during the first Bush term. Moreover, "representing" minority views is not the same as giving them a full or fair hearing.

Jones also made it clear, "that he will run the process and be the primary conduit of national security advice to Obama, eliminating the 'back channels' that at times in the Bush administration allowed Cabinet secretaries and the vice president's office to unilaterally influence and make policy out of view of the others."[65] This seems reasonable if you are worried that the president will be particularly susceptible to powerful personalities, but the president seems to be a pretty confident and powerful personality himself. And the same was true of George W. Bush in the White House. Bush famously said that he was "the decider," and President Obama seems to have similar views about his role.

At his press conference President Obama had this to say about his own role among these powerful personalities with strong views,[66] "*But understand, I will be setting policy as president. I will be responsible for the vision that this team carries out, and I expect them to implement that vision once decisions are made.* So, as Harry Truman said, the buck will stop with me. And *nobody who's standing here, I think, would have agreed to join this administration unless they had confidence that in fact that vision was one that* would help secure the American people and our interests."

Deference is not the only decision process issue President Obama is likely to face. His advisors are quoted as saying that, "he makes decisions more confidently than anyone they've ever watched in politics."[67] The president agrees. In an interview in response to a question of how he was finding the job of president, Obama replied, "I find that the governance part of it, the decision part of it, actually comes pretty naturally."[68] Speaking to a group of White House TV anchors about his presidency he said, "and it turns out I'm pretty good at it."[69] The president's clear confidence in his own abilities and judgment may simply be a realistic assessment. On the other hand, overconfidence in one's decision-making abilities and judgments is a ubiquitous feature in decision-making on many areas, and a decided occupational hazard for presidents.[70]

Obama's quotes are a pretty strong public statement of self-confidence and determination to be in charge. The danger for every president is that even powerful advisors will shrink from telling him what they think he doesn't want to hear. An interested window on that problem emerged from an interview that President Obama gave in which he was asked[71]:

Q: Has anybody said to you, No, sir, you can't do that? Has there been a moment in these last six weeks where you tried to do something and somebody said, Sorry, sir, it doesn't work that way?

A: Well, I mean, I think what we were talking about earlier in terms of Guantanamo. People didn't have to tell me, No you can't do that. It was simply, Well, sir, here are the challenges that we face in terms of making a decision about that.

One of the lessons of presidential decision-making that it is hoped the new president can learn and retain is that his advisors will certainly want to express their views and have them adopted, but they will be equally if not more concerned to help the president accomplish what he says or indicates he wants to do.

Obama recognizes this to some degree. Speaking of the impact of his vice president on national security and other matters, Obama said, "There's, I think, an institutional barrier sometimes to truth-telling in front of the president. Joe is very good about sometimes articulating what's on other people's minds, or things that they've said in private conversations that people have been less willing to say in public."[72]

Robert Gates said of Obama's decision style that, "he makes sure he hears from everybody in the room on an issue."[73] So during the 90-minute debate that preceded the president's announcement of his new Afghanistan policy, "Mr. Obama ... went around the table to elicit the final views of his national security team."[74] While this effort at inclusiveness is useful, it is unclear how effective it is given Obama's comment about Biden's emerging role, noted above. Here, we must be careful to clearly distinguish decision process from effective policy substance. Equating the two is a common error.

This is no small matter with a president who has expressed strong confidence in his own presidential decision-making capacities. Admiral Michael Mullen, Chairman of the Joint Chiefs of Staff had this to say of Obama during an interview:

STEPHANOPOULOS: Has he surprised you in any way?
MULLEN: No, not really. I mean, I met him before the—I think a week or so after he was elected. We had very frank conversations about our positions on various issues, in terms of how we saw things. *He was very clear about what he wants to do.*[75]

High confidence regarding your abilities in what is arguably a sui generis role, coupled with strong views, unmodified by the policy learning that should take place in White House debates, should raise a cautionary flag for the president, his advisors, and us.

The Unilateralism Critique of the Bush Doctrine

Much has been written about the Bush Doctrine's "unilateralism."[76] The usual criticism is that President Bush ignored and alienated important allies, and the rest of the world because, "He prefers to build an empire on American power alone rather than on the greater power that comes from working with friends and allies."[77] This was usually accompanied by complaints about the president's "disdain for the sorts of formal multilateral arrangements," and the "arrogance of American power."[78]

Such analyses ignore a great deal of contrary evidence. There is little evidence that Mr. Bush was interested in building an "empire" in the traditional understanding of that term. There is also little evidence that he "prefers" not to work with friends and allies. Mr. Bush was on an extended search during his presidency for allies. Among these one might count are new and closer relationships with India,[79] Pakistan, and Japan,[80] among others, and attempts to bring China and Russia into the international institutional community.

The criticism of Mr. Bush's "disdain" for international agreements is premised on the assumption that international agreements that Mr. Bush rejected, accomplished their stated purposes with no significant damage to American economic or strategic interests, and that there are no better ways to accomplish these purposes. Yet, in all the cases in point presented as evidence for "disdain," for example, the Kyoto Protocol, the Anti-ballistic Missile Treaty, the International Criminal Court, and the Nuclear Test Ban Treaty, the administration has raised reasonable and legitimate arguments for its views.

Consider the widely criticized decision of the administration not to sign the Kyoto accords. At the time these were negotiated, during the Clinton Administration, the Senate went on record 95–0 opposing them, and President Clinton never submitted them to the Senate for ratification. One reason was that the treaty would have had a substantial adverse impact on the U.S. economy. Another was that it exempted two major polluting countries, China and India, from its provisions. Those reasons are still valid.

Global warming is a problem. However, exactly how much of a problem it is, what causes it, and whether the Kyoto agreement adequately addresses it in a timely, cost-effective manner are issues of genuine debate. The Bush Administration did not simply reject the Kyoto accords and do nothing else. It proposed an alternative climate warming-reduction policy. That proposal included an agreement among six nations (the United States, Japan, Australia, China, India, and South Korea) that "will build on existing bilateral agreements on technology sharing to control emissions, but will not set mandatory targets."[81] That agreement envisioned the use of technology, not mandatory caps to reduce warming, and "cap and trade" methods to further that process. Interestingly, a 2005 international panel on global warming "called for a broader version of the Kyoto Protocol, one that might include the Bush Administration's voluntary approach to combating global warming," and a "gradual and voluntary reduction of carbon-dioxide emissions, in proportion to economic output."[82]

Although it is not widely acknowledged, Mr. Bush's approach has become a respectable and legitimate alternative to mandatory benchmarks of the Kyoto Accords. Prime Minister Tony Blair said in a 2005 meeting on Global Challenges, "The truth is, no country is going to cut its growth or consumption substantially in the light of a long-term environmental problem."[83] The 2007 G-8 Conference adopted a consensus document that contained much of the administration's thinking: "global goals" instead of mandatory targets, an invitation to "major emerging economies" (that is India and China) to join these voluntary efforts, a recognition that "technology is the key to mastering climate change," a new emphasis on "the peaceful uses of nuclear energy" for power, a recognition that "over the next twenty-five years, fossil fuels will remain the world's dominant source of energy," and finally the most important point, that climate programs "must be undertaken in a way that supports growth in developing, emerging, and industrialized economies."[84] As one commentator noted, "Close your eyes, and you might think this was President Bush in the Rose Garden."[85] One may disagree with a voluntary approach that recognizes the importance of balancing the factors that Bush raised, but it is an alternative set of suggestions to be debated and assessed, not a simple negation.

Stephen Walt laments the Bush Administration stance toward the international community and asks us to,

> imagine how the United States might appear if it had behaved differently. Suppose the second Bush Administration had said it was not going to submit the Kyoto Treaty for ratification (an announcement that would have surprised no one) but had immediately added that it recognized the dangers posed by global warming and was therefore ready to place on the table a new and fair-minded proposal that showed a sensitivity to the concerns of others as well as appropriate to particular U.S. interests.[86]

Well, that's pretty much what the administration did. However, critics ignored or dismissed that initiative.

Or, consider the administration's reluctance to fully support the International Criminal Court. Critics see this as a prime example of the United States disdaining international institutions and trying to place itself above international law. Yet, as Robert Jervis points out, United States reluctance "makes a great deal of sense" because "it is the hegemon's (American) force that will be engaged in the most difficult activities, and its status makes it an obvious target for those with multiple motives ranging from jealousy to domestic policy to regional aspirations that can be furthered by embarrassing it."[87] Jervis' more provocative point is that there is some legitimacy in granting the "hegemon" some international leeway given its presently unique international role. Note this is not an argument about the inherent virtue of the United States, only recognition of its special responsibilities as the main supporter of the liberal international order.

Bush did not make this argument publicly for understandable reasons. Asking for an exemption on the basis of your country's special responsibilities would have been met with equally understandable skepticism and controversy. It is hard to be both the maintainer of the order and above it at the same time, another paradox of the United States' still unique position in the world. It is a revisionist power trying to help develop a new world status quo. It is a primary power and a primary target. And it must remain a member in good standing of the international order in order to buttress it, but find a way to temporarily excuse itself to take care of pressing national interests when necessary.

For all the complaints about the Bush Administration's unilateralism, America's allies acted as if they understood. Consider America's equivocal ally France. The French clearly opposed the United States invasion of Iraq and stymied American attempts at the U.N. to gain a resolution specifically adding force to the consequences for Iraqi noncompliance. Yet, at the same time, France has helped the United States in counter-terrorism operations,[88] and both have worked effectively together at the U.N. to pressure Syria to withdraw from Lebanon.[89] Moreover, the two countries worked very closely on counter-terrorism efforts. One report notes, "The CIA has established joint operation centers in more than two dozen countries where U.S. and foreign intelligence officers work side by side to track and capture suspected terrorists and to destroy or penetrate their networks."[90] While Germany and the United States were at loggerheads over the decision to invade Iraq, the German Secret Service's information aided the invasion.[91]

If the Bush Doctrine is synonymous with unilateralism, how does one explain the administration's Proliferation Security Initiative? It is designed to intercept weapons of mass destruction materials and now has over ninety-five members including France and Germany.[92] These states are diverse in their geography, form of government, and closeness to United States foreign policy.[93] As Barry Posen has noted, "Allies are essential to success in the war on terrorism, which helps to explain the determination of President George W. Bush and his administration to build a broad coalition."[94]

Or, consider the Society for Worldwide Interbank Financial Telecommunication (SWIFT) program designed to track terrorist funds. This program was painstakingly constructed with the United States in the lead of a consortium of European powers including Belgium, Spain and other European nations.[95] Belgium opposed the Iraq War from the start and Spain did after its conservative government was voted out of office; yet both were critical partners in this multilateral effort. Partnership clearly has more levels than critics allow.

Finally, there is the little noticed "Global Initiative to Combat Nuclear Terrorism," a partnership announced by then Presidents Bush and Putin on July 15, 2006.[96] That initiative has resulted in the sharing of information and expertise in the areas of nonproliferation, counter-proliferation and counter-terrorism. As of the end of the Bush Administration, that multilateral initiative had attracted seventy-five partner nations.[97]

Many criticisms of the Bush Doctrine contain a partisan political dimension. Disagreements with France on Iraq are emphasized; agreements with France on fighting terrorism, helping them quell rebel violence in the Ivory Coast, and containing Iran's nuclear program are downplayed or forgotten. Disagreements with Germany (before the 2005 election of Chancellor Angela Merkel) are emphasized; new and improved relationships with India, Eastern European countries, and Japan are ignored or downplayed. Even when the administration allowed its European or Asian partners to take the lead or work with the United States as part of a team, the administration was still criticized.

Hillary Clinton criticized the president for his multilateral efforts with Iran and North Korea, saying, "I believe that we lost critical time in dealing with Iran because the White House chose to downplay the threats and to *outsource the negotiations.*" "I don't believe you face threats like Iran or North Korea by *outsourcing it to others* and standing on the sidelines."[98] Yet, Ms. Clinton then went on record as demanding that the president agree to convene a regional peace conference to deal with Iraq's situation or lose funding for the prosecution of the war.[99] Such criticisms leave the impression that no matter what the Bush Administration did, or didn't do, it was subject to criticism by some.

The post-9/11 world of alliances is complicated because old allies like France are, under some of its leaders, rivals and spoilers on some issues, while they cooperate with the United States on others. Russia has both helped and stymied the United States in dealing with Iran's nuclear ambitions,[100] and has also been implicated in passing on American intelligence to Saddam Hussein at the start of the Iraq War,[101] and more recently supplying Iran with Tor-M1 air-defense missiles.[102] In fairness, the testiness of France and the limited alliance with Russia is a story that predates the Bush Administration.

New to the post-9/11 world are the partnerships that have developed and the added strains on old ones. It is a world in which new nations in Eastern Europe have become allies out of shared historical experiences and perspectives, and others like Pakistan have become allies because of military necessity. Other alliances of economic, political, and strategic necessity, such as those with Saudi Arabia and Egypt, are troubling in a number of ways, but important enough to merit continued efforts on our part.

The Bush Administration took tough stands regarding what it considered to be the security interests of the United States. It sometimes did so in a brusque, impatient, and provocative way.[103] And it certainly, in the aftermath of 9/11, relied less on diplomatic "give and take" than on stating its positions and following through on them; although this stance seems to have shifted as it has confronted the dangers of a nuclear armed Iran.[104] Perhaps instead of adding up to a "disdain" for allies, a thrust for "empire," or the "arrogance of power," it simply reflects understandable and realistic concerns born out of the 9/11 attacks and the implications that the administration drew from them.

By tone, inclination, and circumstance the Obama Administration will be very different. In important ways it can afford to be. It has not been hit with a devastating attack on American soil and faced the prospect that another could follow shortly. It has the advantage of all the institutional structures put into place as a result of the Bush Doctrine both domestically and internationally. And it has the luxury of building on the Bush Doctrine's success and seeing its errors so that it may avoid them.

The real issue is not whether the Obama Administration can publicly get along better with America's allies, but what it is willing to do when there are strong disagreements among us. Getting NATO allies to commit more troops to Afghanistan is a case in point, but not really comparable to what President

Bush faced after 9/11. It is to be devoutly hoped that President Obama never faces such circumstances, but should he do so the approval of our allies or others will hopefully not be at the top of his list of concerns.

The American Exceptionism Critique

One of the paradoxes of the Bush Doctrine is that while it is indelibly associated with American foreign policy in general, and President Bush in particular, its elements are very much in evidence in other countries as well. This makes a great deal of sense because, while the United States is the primary target of catastrophic terrorism and rogue state actors, it is not the only one. Terrorist plots have been uncovered or carried out in Canada, England, India, Spain, and Germany. Disagreements with the Bush Administration over Iraq and the war on terror proffer no safe haven.[105]

In Japan, which has been reluctant since World War II even to contemplate taking actions except in self-defense, then Japan Defense Agency Director General Shigeru Ishiba said in January 2003, "If North Korea expresses the intention of turning Tokyo into a sea of fire and if it begins preparations [to attack], for instance by fueling [its missiles], we will consider [North Korea] is initiating [a military attack]. ... Once North Korea declares it will demolish Tokyo and begins preparing for a missile launch, we will consider it the start of a military attack against Japan."[106] Ishiba later stressed that, even with Japan's Peace Constitution, "Just to be on the receiving end of the attack is not what our constitution had in mind. ... Just to wait for another country's attack and lose thousands and tens of thousands of people, that is not what the constitution assumes."[107] Japan's strong stance is likely related, at least in part, to its first-hand experience of having some of its citizens abducted by North Korean agents. In a 2009 update of this stance, Japan threatened to shoot down a North Korean satellite rocket if it showed any sign of entering its territory after launch.[108]

Other Western democracies appear to have considered the same lesson.[109] Former Australian Prime Minister John Howard observed, "It stands to reason that if you believe that somebody was going to launch an attack on your country, either of a conventional kind or a terrorist kind, and you had a capacity to stop it and there was no alternative other than to use that capacity, then of course you would have to use it."[110] And British Prime Minister Tony Blair said in a speech, "Containment will not work in the face of the global threat that faces us. The terrorists have no intention of being contained. The states that proliferate or acquire WMD illegally are doing so precisely to avoid containment. Emphatically I am not saying that every situation leads to military action. But *we surely have a duty and a right to prevent the threat materializing.*"[111]

Russian officials have also indicated their support for preventive military action, both as a matter of strategic doctrine and potential state practice. Russian Defense Minister Sergei Ivanov was quoted by *Itar-Tass* in late 2003 as telling his military commanders "we cannot absolutely rule out preventive use of force if Russia's interests or its obligations as an ally require it."[112] In September 2004, Colonel General Yuri Baluyevsky, Chief of the Russian General Staff, declared: "As for carrying out preventive strikes against terrorist bases, we will take all measures to liquidate terrorist bases in any region of the world."[113]

The French Government under Jacques Chirac was publicly highly critical of the preventive war concept, but a French government document issued in January 2003 for its 2003–8 military program addressed preemption as well: "We must ... be prepared to identify and forestall threats as soon as possible. In this context, the possibility of preemptive action might be considered, from the time that an explicit and confirmed threatening situation is identified."[114] In a 2007 poll conducted by the Open Europe Institute, 17,000 citizens of states that are members of the European Union were asked to agree or not with the following question: "We must stop countries like Iran from acquiring nuclear weapons, even if that means taking military action."[115] The results were striking. Fifty-two percent of Europeans agreed, while forty percent disagreed. The Danes gave the greatest support at sixty-eight percent and the Slovaks the least at thirty-seven percent. Support for military action amongst the "great powers" was closely divided; France fifty-three percent, Britain fifty-one percent, Italy forty-nine percent, and Germany forty-five percent.

Recently, the U.N., in recognition of the changed circumstances of international threats, issued a major report on issues facing the international community, including the use of preemptive and preventive force. The report concluded that any instances where anticipatory self-defense is seen as necessary should be presented to the U.N. Security Council. As for those states that might be "impatient" with such a course of action, "the risk to global order and the norm of non-intervention on which it continues to be based is simply too great for the legality of unilateral preventive action ... " While acknowledging that the international community is obligated to be concerned about "nightmare scenarios" of catastrophic terrorism and rogue states with weapons of mass destruction, the report concludes that only the Security Council can legally take action preventively or preemptively.[116]

These initiatives, quotes, and data underscore the point that a number of countries, not just the United States, face similar threats and must answer some of the same questions posed at the outset of this analysis. This "agreement to some degree of principle" certainly does not mean there is no problem with either the concept of preventive war or its actual use. The Iraq War certainly demonstrates that. So does the verbal exchange between India and Pakistan in which both countries suggested the other was a legitimate target for preemption.[117]

The Bush Doctrine is clearly unique in the scope of the answers it proposes in response to these questions and its ability to carry them out. However, it is not alone internationally in having reached the conclusions it has about the dangers and the stance that sometimes may be necessary for self-protection. This list of agreement statements with "preventive" stances, even though there are clearly operational differences, reflects an important fact. Many nations and institutions are arriving at a similar understanding of the difficult issues they face with regard to the tradeoffs between security, knowledge, legitimacy, and action. Premature action risks legitimacy. Tardy action risks devastation. Neither choice can take comfort in the likely state of knowledge concerning other actors' capabilities or intensions.

The Anti-American Critique

What of the fact that dislike and suspicion of the United States abroad is at an all time high? A 2007 international Pew survey reported that the image of the United States had "plummeted" in many parts of the world with mounting distrust of President Bush and U.S. foreign policy in Muslim countries, but also among traditional allies. Yet, overall, "majorities in 25 of 46 surveyed said they had positive views of the United States ... suggesting that anti-Americanism had grown deeper, but not wider."[118] Critics allege that it is almost all a function of the Bush Administration's arrogance, unilateralism, and hegemonic ambitions most noticeably reflected in the invasion of Iraq. According to this view, all that is needed is a less arrogant, more multilateral administration that will eschew military solutions to what are seen at base as "political problems" and world public opinion will rebound. The world's enthusiastic response to the Obama election suggests that a part of this hope might be true, but only a part.

In fact, anti-Americanism springs from a variety of sources, some of which have to do with Mr. Bush's policies, many of which do not. Janice Stein examined a number of such factors including: views of Mr. Bush himself, his policies, America as a hegemonic imperial power, and the use of anti-Americanism as a reference point of the development of new national identities in a number of countries worldwide.[119] She concludes, "Contemporary anti-Americanism is certainly a function in part of this president and his policies but it is also a response to a deeper global angst in the face of rapid change and structural uncertainty. We live in a time of global anxiety—an age of terror, rapid change, strained identities, global markets—and negative attitudes toward the most powerful state may be one of the few global pacifiers available."[120]

The international public doesn't like American primacy. It is probably fair to say that some of this, as Stein points out, is mixed in with the difficulties that globalization poses for modernity in many countries trying to make that transition. Here of course is one of the great ironies of "soft power." Our ideas and economy are both envied and reviled. The relentless pace of modern society, typified by the United States, is also a destroyer of many aspects of "traditional culture."[121] This leaves many worldwide caught between the world they know and the world in which they must compete, but are often ill prepared to do so. The soft power of this experience is a source of anger not support toward the United States.

Public Consensus and the Bush Doctrine

Essential to any successful doctrine are elite consensus and public under-standing. The Truman Doctrine emerged gradually over time. The Soviet Union's behavior toward Eastern and Western Europe after the end of World War II and its support of communist China and North Korea convinced all but skeptics and sympathizers that it was a profound national security threat to the United States and its allies. The American public, originally primed to consider the Soviet Union a wartime ally, gradually came to understand that it had become our enemy. Most Republican and Democratic foreign policy elites rallied to the Truman Doctrine. Over time, a bipartisan consensus emerged on the best strategies with which to deal with the threat: broadly, containment and deterrence.

The Bush Doctrine has never gained equal support among major foreign policy elite groups, especially those connected with the Democratic Party. The 9/11 attacks were almost immediately followed by the invasion of Afghanistan and the invasion of Iraq. The latter quickly fractured any bipartisan consensus and world support. As a result, the Bush Doctrine never enjoyed the foreign policy leadership consensus that had been critical to developing the widespread public support of the Truman Doctrine.

The Bush Doctrine did gain some support in the American public, among members of the foreign policy establishment and among leaders in other countries. However, that support was clearly limited by partisan, philosophical, and strategic divides. These divides, about which we will have more to say in Chapter 10, permeate almost every aspect of the Doctrine and how it is viewed. It affected how the war in Iraq was viewed, affects views about American involvement in Afghanistan, and influences views about what the United States should do about Iran. These splits are as much about foreign policy philoso-phies as they are about partisanship, although the two are strongly related.

There is then obviously no public consensus about the Bush Doctrine, its policies or its premises. There are numerous reasons for this but one surely is that although Americans knew that they had been attacked, and an attack meant war, they were unclear about just what kind of war it was. Historical memory, to the extent that it exists, conjures great land, sea and air battles of the kind fought in World War II, or perhaps the smaller version of this model exemplified by Vietnam. A fight to avoid successful catastrophic terrorism requires the public to imagine what it would prefer not to think about, and thankfully there is no model for them to use. Aspiring hegemons who use weapons of mass destruction as implicit threats while conducting subversion are also a new and complex manifestation of aggressive ambitions whose implications have not yet been fully tested in the real world. And of course being somewhat "theoretical," such threats have to jockey for notice with the more immediate concerns of political and now economic life.

Matters are not helped by the fact that the United States has yet to find and settle on an appropriate term to name our nemesis. The Bush Administration characterized their efforts in response to 9/11 as the "War on Terror." They also briefly tried out the phrase "strategy against violent extremism,"[122] but quickly reverted to the "War on Terror."[123] This prompted Senator Joe Biden and others to observe that terror was a tactic and one couldn't easily wage war on a tactic.[124] Democratic presidential contender John Edwards didn't like the phrase because, "Bush and his gang have used [it] to justify anything they want to do."[125] The committee staff of the House Armed Services Committee circulated a memo after Democrats gained control of Congress stating that the phrase "global war on terror" should not be used. Also banned was the phrase "long war."[126]

Certainly in this conflict Muslims as a group are not the enemy. Most are not radical and the United States enjoys good relations with a number of Muslim countries like Indonesia and Bangladesh. What of the term "radical Muslims" or "militant Islam"? Not all radical Muslims take up arms against the United States or its allies. Islamists can be militant without being murderous. Nor does a term like "Islamic Fascism" convey the savageness that is at the heart of the strategy to accomplish their ambitions.

Finding a fitting term is important because a name that captures essential elements acts at once to both remind the public and continue mobilizing it. Political, philosophical and strategic disagreements have been at the heart of the post-9/11 naming debates. This becomes clearer if we look back at the consensus that developed around the concept of the "Cold War," a term that was well understood and conveyed the nature and depth of the post World War II Soviet threat. No one suggested that every Soviet citizen or every communist country was equally aggressive toward and dangerous to the United States and its allies. The threat was crystallized in one country, its leaders, and their behavior in one term. The term *Cold War* was paradoxical because neither of the two words that comprised it exactly fit the nature of the circumstances. During the Cold War there were actually military engagements and the word war did not exactly fit the wide array of elements—peaceful competition, political subversion, proxy wars and so on that characterized this period. Yet most leaders and citizens understood that the Soviet Union was aggressive, expansionist, dangerous and had to be contained.

The nature of the post-9/11 threat is equally clear even if we have not yet found consensual words for it. The United States and its close allies are facing a determined group of Islamic radicals whose purpose is to expel both from all the areas it considers its territories and whose method of doing so is to produce as much carnage as possible, by whatever means they can gather in the service of advancing their hegemonic religious and political ambitions.

At the bottom of the naming debates are profound differences in worldview and strategy. Indeed, it would be fair to say that the assertive strategic stance of the Bush Doctrine is precisely the issue that has caused the split among foreign policy elites. Some time ago, Oli Hoslti found that generally, "two thirds to three quarters of Republicans were either hard liners or internationalists, the two groups that expressed support for militant internationalism," while " ... even more substantial majorities of the Democrats were *accommodationists*, a group defined as opposing militant internationalism while supporting cooperative internationalism."[127] We will take this matter up more fully at a latter point, but it is certainly clear that these profound strategic differences make it almost impossible for the Bush Doctrine to reach the level of consensus that the Truman Doctrine achieved, at least as long as the strategic premises of the two major parties remain so far apart.

The administration didn't help its cause by its bouts of public inarticulateness. Mr. Bush supported his contention that Saddam Hussein must be removed with a list of Saddam's past behaviors and weapons of mass destruction aspirations. Yet President Bush never made clear why Saddam Hussein was more dangerous than Kim Jong-Il, or why he might be more (or less) dangerous than Mahmoud Ahmadinejad, the hard-line mayor of Tehran who won the Iranian presidency in 2005,[128] and both the 2002 and 2006 National Security Strategies were noticeably silent on the circumstances in which preventive action should be considered and used,[129] a point of legitimate criticism.[130] This is a gap in the Bush Doctrine that still needs to be addressed.

The crux of the rationale as to why the Bush Doctrine or something very close to it ought to be and most likely will have to be a part of American national security doctrine so long as the post-9/11 threat environment remains has been forcefully stated by Tony Blair in discussing Iraq: "Here is the crux. It is possible that even with all of this, nothing would have happened. [It is] possible that Saddam would change his ambitions; possible he would develop the WMD but never use it; possible that the terrorists would never get their hands on WMD, whether from Iraq or elsewhere. We cannot be certain. Perhaps we would have found different ways of reducing it. Perhaps this Islamic terrorism would ebb of its own accord. But do we want to take the risk? That is the judgement."[131]

Given that intelligence is unlikely to fully resolve these issues when they arise, other means must be sought. One needed strategic tool that would *help* sort through these difficult issues is a metric by which to judge the *dangerousness* of a leader or regime. After examining the new calculus of risk and the political issues that now frame it, we will then turn to an examination of assessing dangerousness and the tools of strategic psychology available to deal with it.

Part II

The Strategic World after 9/11

5   The New Calculus of Risk

The 9/11 attacks reinforced the Bush Administration's realist view that the world was a dangerous place. They also changed the way senior administration policymakers looked at risk. It is really not possible to understand the Bush Doctrine without understanding that catastrophic terrorism introduced a new primary frame of risk assessment into the American national security decision process. In doing so, it altered both traditional baselines and assumptions.

In the past the United States could rest comfortably, somewhat assured that their size and power provided a protective buffer. As Kenneth Waltz notes,

> Strong states can be inattentive, they can afford not to learn; they can do the same dumb things over and over again. More sensibly, they can act slowly and wait to see if the threatening acts of others are truly so. They can hold back until the ambiguity of events is resolved without fearing that the moment for effective action will be lost.[1]

After 9/11, this was no longer possible because of the dangers of catastrophic terrorism. Though Robert Litwak argues that, "the September 11 attacks did not alter the structure of international relations, they did usher in a new age of American vulnerability"[2] he misses the insight that his coupling of these two matters provides. It is precisely because the United States *is*, and feels, more vulnerable that the international system has changed.

Anxious hegemons will be less likely, in Waltz's words, to be inattentive, act slowly, or await developments. Nor in such circumstances does their size necessarily give them a margin of safety and limit their vulnerability.[3] As a consequence, they will calculate and act differently. In the case of the United States, being both the most powerful nation in the world and the chief defender of the liberal international system, these changes are bound to have consequences for how it views its foreign policy options and responsibilities. One question about the Obama Administration is whether the feeling of urgency that motivated the post-9/11 Bush Administration response has receded, and if so, with what effects on their formulation of the national security issues and risk assessment they face.

Framing a World of Problems

The implications of the frame shift that occurred after 2001 are substantial. A single problem was catapulted into the role of *the* primary issue for American national security policy, and a good deal of domestic policy as well. That problem was the potential use of nuclear, biological and chemical (NBC) weapons by terrorists against the United States and its allies. In a world of problems, 9/11 imposed an instant hierarchy on the American national interest. For the first time since World War II and the Cold War there was a single central issue to organize national security focus, understanding, and frameworks. The advantage of such a focus is that it prioritizes threats. The disadvantage is that there is a world full of problems that requires attention beyond this focus. Views may differ about which of the myriad world problems should make the B or C list,[4] but the major A-list problem was very clear, at least to the Bush Administration.

One by-product of reframing is cognitive and conceptual rearrangement. As a result of the 9/11 attacks the United States and its allies became involved in a wide range of issues and geographical regions. At the same time, 9/11 also rearranged policy priorities, perspectives, and responses. Issues that were central moved to the periphery, issues that were on the periphery became more central. For example, before 9/11, immigration was primarily framed as a national culture and political issue. It has now been reframed as a national security one.

Reframing also had an effect on the reconsideration of policy alternatives. The Bush Administration started out being skeptical of "nation building." Yet, Bush ended his term in office involved in two major efforts to do exactly that in both Iraq and Afghanistan. The revised 2006 NSS, as noted, explicitly called for the development of "post-conflict stabilization capacities" which is nation building by another name. Even previously peripheral problems in other countries now impact the weapons of mass destruction (WMD) problem. Before 9/11, integrating Muslim immigrants in France and England was an issue of modest importance within these countries; after 9/11 it has become part of America's terrorism problem. Even what appeared on the surface to be a mundane bureaucratic issue of international airlines rules governing, say, flights between Bonn and New York became a different kind of issue after 9/11. The Bush Administration insisted that foreign airlines flying into the United States provide the United States with passenger information that could be run through terrorist databases.[5] Many European Union countries objected because of their own rules regarding privacy. What might have been considered a minor dispute has, in the wake of 9/11, become considerably more complicated and central.

The Cold War as Metaphor?

In having a primary frame, the post-9/11 national security setting appears, on first glance, to resemble the Cold War struggle. Then as now, the United States faced a determined enemy and a long difficult struggle. Then as now, the conflict was global and as much a war of ideas as of weapons. Then as now, the United States was drawn into new partnerships and strategic arrangements. Then as now, it was necessary for strategic thinkers to develop and refine a "grand strategy" to deal with the threat and forge a public and leadership consensus about its utility and legitimacy.

These parallels are striking, but there are important differences. Then the United States had a tangible adversary with a home address and plenty to lose. Now, the United States has a great deal to fear from non-state actors, with no home address, little to lose and who are motivated by religious zeal to die for their cause. Over time during the Cold War, the potential range of losses that would be incurred in any all-out military exchange introduced some degree of accommodation and moderation into the conflict. The revolutionary zeal and bunker mentality that were central elements of the first generation of Soviet leaders faded as a result of time and circumstance. Then, the United States developed a grand strategy, containment and its associated policies that garnered bipartisan leadership and public support. At present, however, there is no consensus on grand strategy, and indeed no agreement in political leadership circles about exactly what kind of threats we face, their nature, and their urgency. Then the public was reluctant, but eventually did accept the fact that the United States faced a dangerous adversary in the Soviet Union and that appropriate steps had to be taken. Now, owing in part to the partisan and strategic worldview split in political leadership circles, the public has reached no consensus regarding the nature of the national security problems this country faces and what to do about them. The degree of unified purpose that characterized the Cold War is little in evidence.

Cold War Risk Framing

Over the course of the Cold War the intentions and capacities of the Soviet Union came into sharper focus. It then became somewhat easier to establish a range of probabilities of loss and gain associated with alternative courses of action. Especially after the Cuban missile crisis, tensions between the United States and Soviet Union never reached apocalyptic levels because each side had so much to lose. Both sides had an investment in preserving their respective countries, their citizens, and their way of life, all of which would have been destroyed by a nuclear exchange. So, while the prospect of a nuclear exchange had to be prepared for, the risk of such an exchange was made smaller by the commitment of both sides to avoid it and the awful consequences of not doing so successfully.

Somewhat paradoxically, during the Cold War, the higher risks of catastrophic loss in nuclear exchanges appear to have heightened the risks of regional competitions and conflict between the two superpowers. The logic appeared to be this: we can afford to take more chances of conflict in places where the stakes are not central to core security concerns. The nuclear dilemma—that the weapons are too awful to use, except as a last resort to protect absolutely vital interests, left some room for mischief when such interests were not at stake. Cold War conflict between two superpowers therefore operated in very different decision frameworks. Over time, these differing frameworks became relatively easy to discern and leaders were able to apply different decision rules appropriate to each. In the area of core interests, the doctrine of massive retaliation and mutual assured destruction operated. In the area of important interests, the "normal" national security operation concepts—deterrence, containment, denial, and coercion were employed, as suitable. And the areas of peripheral interest were generally left to their own devices.

Losses, Gains, and Risks: Post-9/11

This idea of *decision domains* is an important part of understanding how decisions are actually made which in turn has implications for understanding the Bush Doctrine. Prospect theory, which was first developed in 1979 by Daniel Kahneman and Amos Tversky is a theory of how decisions are made under conditions of risk and uncertainty.[6] It rests on the assumption that the most significant "carriers of utility" are not absolute states of wealth or welfare, but changes relative to a reference point (or "reflection" point).[7]

The implications of prospect theory for the analysis of the Bush Doctrine lie in understanding just how presidents calculate risk. From there it is possible to see the impact 9/11 had for that process and for the national security policies that followed from it. Let us start first with the difference between expected utility (cost-benefit) theory and prospect theory. The expected utility model, long dominant in studies of foreign policy decision-making assumes that leaders and their advisors calculate the costs and benefits of particular policy options and then select the one that best maximizes their preferred outcomes. This model describes a rational approach in theory, but in practice it falls far short of describing what decision-makers actually do. There are many documented reasons why this model falls short as a valid description of how leaders think. Leaders often don't consider the full range of options available. Moreover, some options are unthinkable for various reasons. And everyone, including leaders, makes use of cognitive "shortcuts" that undermine the strict cost-benefit analysis that is at the core of the model.[8]

The central insight of prospect theory is that expected utility (calculating costs and benefits) is itself derived from the starting reference point of the decision, which in turn shapes how the decision is framed. Only then are calculations of relative cost benefits applied. The core discovery of Daniel Kahneman and Amos Tversky is that where you start when you make a decision affects what you see and how you calculate risk. When outcomes are uncertain, *where* individuals start the decision process (their reference point) leads to *how* individuals understand and thus frame the issues before them, and it is only then that they begin to make the traditional cost-benefit calculations. In short, framing precedes cost-benefit analysis.

The starting point, or reference point, can spring from one of four elements.[9] The most common assumption is that people start from the status quo. But this is not always or necessarily the case in national security decisions. Presidents might well use their policy goals as the starting reference point and begin the decision process there. Or they can begin with their expectations as the starting point. Finally, they can rely on previous experience, either personal or historical (or both) as the point at which they begin the decision process.

Central to prospect theory are two domains: the *domain of loss* and the *domain of gain*. Not surprisingly, individuals tend to make very different decisions when they frame a problem as one of likely losses as opposed to one of likely gains. Generally speaking, the prospect of loss generally weighs more heavily than the possibility of gain (this is termed "loss aversion"), and the prospect of certain losses leads to substantially different behavior than the response of relative or possible loss.[10] Individuals are more likely to take larger risks to avoid what they see as a certain or highly likely loss.[11] As it turns out losses carry more psychological weight in the decision process than possible gains. This is the basis for the phase "loss aversion." In experiments, the ratio is approximately 2:1.[12]

Framing National Security Losses and Gains

So the very first implication of prospect theory for appreciating the calculation of risk post-9/11 is that the most important problem facing the United States, the intersection of terrorism and technology, is absolutely in the domain of loss. In fact, this very much understates the situation. A successful WMD attack can only be viewed as being in the arena of catastrophic loss. A second aspect of prospect theory's 9/11 implications is the reciprocal relationship of reference points to framing. Recall that the beginning reference point affects the way the issue is framed and then calculated. Yet, it is also true that how the problem is framed can affect the reference point.

Consider the impact of 9/11 on the Bush Doctrine. The traumatic events that day were clearly in the domain of losses. Then consider that the central motivating premise of the Doctrine was worry regarding the critical link between technology and terror. That premise too clearly placed the core national security policy premises into the area of loss. Yet, as noted, the word "loss" hardly conveys the seriousness of prospects that the United States faced then and still faces now. Not only would a successful catastrophic terrorism attack cause enormous economic and social damage, it would very likely tear apart the United States' political culture and framework.

This suggests that while prospect theory's distinction between two general domains, loss and gain, is adequate for its theoretical purposes, it is probably prudent when dealing with national security policy to be a little more specific. I propose that we think about the domain of losses in national security theory in terms of *catastrophic*, *dire* and *tolerable* losses. The first are losses whose level would severely and adversely affect a state's basic power stature, national security, or way of life. The 9/11 attacks qualify not only because they were an unprecedented attack against the United States, but also because they were emblematic of the more devastating attacks that could follow possibly using

WMDs. It is clear that President Bush, and later such bipartisan groups as the 9/11 Commission, understood that national security threat as potentially catastrophic. Therefore President Bush's response was exactly in keeping with what prospect theory predicts that someone will do when faced with such potential losses, namely take substantial risks to avoid them.

Dire losses—those with a substantial impact on American power stature—put national security at greater risk but do not immediately threaten the country's basic existence or way of life. The loss of the Vietnam War is one recent historical example. The general agreement of the dire consequences that would be the result of an American failure in Iraq or the coming to power of Muslim radicals in Pakistan would be examples of others. Finally, there is the loss arena of *tolerable losses.* These are national security setbacks that don't specifically affect American power, put American security at grave risk, or directly threaten the country. The vast majority of losses in this range would be outcomes an administration would prefer not to see, but that if they do happen would be neither devastating nor dire. The elections of Eva Morales in Bolivia and Hugo Chavez in Venezuela fall into this category, as does the fall of the conservative government in Spain after the Madrid bombing.

Likewise, it is also potentially useful to try and more specifically frame national security gains. I propose two: triumph and success. *Triumph,* rare in national security life, occurs when major security goals are completely and convincingly achieved. The rehabilitation of Western Europe including Germany after World War II is one case, the fall of the Soviet Union another. Less rare but still highly valued is the second tier of national security gain: *success.* Here, a country achieves, on balance, a number of its important national security goals while not having suffered substantial or unacceptable losses in the process. A case that seems to fit this category is coalition success in dislodging Saddam Hussein from Kuwait in 1991. Success of course comes in degrees. In some cases, the cost may be high, but the importance of the goals obtained, even if partial, is observably higher. The decision to resist the North Korean attack on South Korea would seem to be an appropriate illustration. The United States invasion of Iraq and removal of Saddam Hussein in 2003 may yet rise to the level of at least a partial and important success.

Differences in national security framing have consequences for the sense of strategic urgency. This certainly happened during 9/11, especially because it was very possible that another attack might occur. Ordinary procedure would have to take a back seat to security imperatives. And this is exactly what happened in the formulation of some Bush Doctrine policies, like domestic wiretaps, that were later modified.[13]

Post-9/11 Risk Reconsidered

In the real world of national security policy some dictators, like Saddam Hussein, take dangerous risks, often repeatedly. Other actors like Osama bin Laden and his senior associates are willing to die in order to accomplish their purposes.

The normal model of risk aversion, in which continued life is ordinarily a very highly valued goal, does not seem highly applicable in these circumstances. How to understand and try to calculate these risks is a crucial matter.

Those calculations are made more difficult because the chances of terrorist success depend in part on American strategic behavior. If the United States does little, nothing, or bungles its preventive efforts, their chances of success are higher. If the United States does everything that can be done within reason reasonably well there will still be a great deal of uncertainty that it will be able to prevent catastrophe.

Vice-President Cheney's assertion that "deliverable weapons of mass destruction in the hands of a terror network, or a murderous dictator, or the two working together [are unacceptable] … the risks of inaction are far greater than the risk of action"[14] is a succinct statement of the Bush Administration's calculation of risk. It is a small step conceptually to the view that, "to forestall or prevent such hostile acts by our adversaries, the United States will, if necessary, act preemptively."[15] This is the new calculus of risk.

The Risk of Catastrophic Terrorism Redux

A critical question that emerges in the post-9/11 milieu is how exactly to understand the risks of catastrophic terrorism. One question that arises is whether the administration "overlearned" a traumatic but unusual event. The term "overlearning" refers to one of two specific decision distortions. The case that least concerns us here occurs when a historical lesson, not necessarily traumatically learned personally by the leader, still carries disproportionate weight in his thinking for other reasons. Phrases like "Munich" or "Never again!" illustrate historical lessons that become iconic metaphors and don't have to be personally lived through in order to weigh heavily in a leader's calculations. The case most relevant to our concerns here occurs when the traumatic nature of an event functions as a form of cognitive imprinting. In this case decision-makers learn the appropriate thing, but it is given disproportionate weight in their thinking. As a result, the leader sees all or most major problems in a domain through the prism of that traumatizing experience.

Does this model fit the dire national security assessments of post-9/11 national security policy? We can look at the broadly bipartisan conclusions of the 9/11 Commission, its follow-up reports, the testimony of the Director of National Intelligence, and the 2007 National Intelligence Estimate on the terrorist threat to the U.S. homeland,[16] all of which support the view that the intersection of radicalism and technology is an appropriate lens through which to view America's primary national security problem. They all give it heavy weight in their analysis of its catastrophic consequences. The Bush Administration was rightly shocked by the attacks, but their judgments about the meaning of these events and their importance have received independent and bipartisan confirmation.

There is another question that arises regarding the utility of framing national security risk through the lens of prospect theory. In the experiments that underlie the prospect theory, experimenters set out both the problem and the odds connected with it.[17] In real life, leaders have little idea of the odds associated with particular events. There is no real answer to the question of the likelihood of successful terror attacks and herein lies the difference between those who think the risk is "overblown," and those, like President Bush, who choose to take large risks to avoid the possibility of catastrophic loss. But this raises a very serious question. Although it seems obvious that a successful attack should be placed in the domain of catastrophic loss, we must admit that we simply don't know what the odds are of a successful attack.

John Mueller says the terrorist threat has been "massively exaggerated,"[18] and he raises such points as the fact that as of the time of his analysis: terrorists hadn't struck in five years even though this country's immigration system is still porous; that many domestic leads have not led to terrorists' convictions; that dramatic acts of destruction have proved counterproductive by massively heightening concerns about terrorism around the world; and that terrorist attacks like the Madrid and London train bombings are easy to organize and didn't take much time to plan, yet they have not been carried out in the United States. He then adds up the total number of people killed since 9/11 by al Qaeda or al Qaeda-like operatives outside of Afghanistan and Iraq and says it is not much higher than the number who drown in bathtubs in the United States in a single year. Moreover, the lifetime chance of an American being killed by international terrorism is about one in eighty thousand, about the same chance as being killed by a comet or a meteor. Further, he argues, even if there were a 9/11-scale attack every three months for the next five years, the likelihood that an individual American would number among the dead would be two hundredths of a percent (or one in five thousand).[19]

This argument however, misunderstands probability and logic. The issue is not how many Americans have been killed in the absence of a WMD attack, but how many would be. The question is not how many Americans would be killed if a 9/11 attack happened every three months for the next five years, but what would happen to American society if a nuclear device was set off in Washington or New York, or a series of disastrous explosions were set off in major American cities. Such an event according to Stephen Walt "*could easily be the most significant event in U.S. history.*"[20]

Here again we encounter one of those difficult dilemmas that saddle presidents and bypass international relations theory: if the United States does not aggressively protect itself against catastrophic terrorism, it risks unthinkable destruction to its people, culture, and way of life. If it does, it risks charges that its concern is overblown while making our allies or others insecure about our power or intentions. How a president should weigh the trade-offs is a—if not the—question facing leadership in this country for the foreseeable future.

Assessing Risk: The Great Divides

Assessing risk is not only a matter of probability but also of perspective. Professors and presidents differ not only in their vantage point and responsibilities, but also in the quality of the theory and information that they can confidently bring to bear and the consequences of being mistaken. Those differences may usefully be analyzed as gaps between any president and his advisors and the numerous other foreign policy observers in assessing risk and acting on those assessments.

Bystander Theory and Command Responsibility

One little commented upon, but critical, divide between those who developed and applied the Bush Doctrine and its critics lies in the arena of command responsibility. The president takes an oath of office to preserve, protect, and defend the Constitution of the United States. Implicit in this charge is the physical protection of the country, its institutions, its citizens, and its way of life. His critics may have strong views on what the president ought to do, but they offer their advice with the luxury of having no real, let alone ultimate, command responsibility.[21] If they are wrong, they will be forgiven and most of the country won't notice or remember what they said in the first place. A president's national security decisions, for better or worse can affect every man, woman, and child in the country—and many other parts and people of the world as well.

This gap leads to an enormous difference of perspective between those who have ultimate responsibility for national life or death decisions and those who do not. To take but one crucial difference, critics and pundits do not have to answer for any erroneous risk calculations to the extent they seriously make them at all. In decisions about Iraq, Russia, Iran, and North Korea for example, the president and his advisors must weigh the risks of a variety of possible actions, and do so in a world in which the actual level of risk for particular events is opaque.

This is one explanation for President Obama's turn to what seems to be an embrace of Bush Doctrine policies although as noted, not necessarily its assumptions. In David Broder's view, "Obama's liberal critics are right. He is a different man now. He has learned what it means to be commander in chief."[22]

It is of course, possible to carry this explanation just so far. The added weight of personal responsibility and weighty consequences doubtlessly add to the sobering burden on presidential shoulders. And certainly this distinguishes presidents from pundits and theorists. Yet, however weighty their decisions, presidents still operate in a world of theories—their own and those of their advisors.

Predicting the Future Versus Living in it

Presidents must live in an uncertain present and anticipate an unknown future. International relations theory has been of limited help in warning them about the dangers they may confront. It is not that international relations theorists haven't tried. Few have listened to Richard Betts' sensible warning that, "no forecast should be considered anything else but heuristic [and] any sensible reader should be aware of articles (like this one), that pretend to say anything about the future, since by definition they cannot really know what they are talking about."[23] Sage advice; nonetheless, the temptations are very great.

Charles Kupchan predicted in 1998 that, "an era of unprecedented peace seems to be at hand as the 21st Century draws near."[24] James Kurth wrote in 2000, shortly before 9/11,

> At the beginning of the twentieth century, two of the major strategic concepts used by Western powers were *balance of power* and *sphere of influence*; at the midpoint of the twentieth century, two of the major strategic concepts were *containment* and *deterrence*. From the perspective of postmodern and postnational American elites, who conceive of international affairs largely in terms of the global economy and the open society, these four strategic concepts are now hopelessly old-fashioned and irrelevant.[25]

Regrettably a number of actual regime leaders such as Kim Jong-il or Iranian President Mahmoud Ahmadinejad do not seem to have either a postmodern or post-national perspective.

In 1997, three scholars advocated a policy of "restraint" through the withdrawal of American forces from Europe, Asia, and much of the Middle East. They further proposed attending primarily to American domestic problems because of the lack of security threats the country faced.[26] Even Robert Jervis wrote in 1998 that, "The reason why the United States will not develop a grand strategy is the same reason why one is not necessary: *the current world*, like the one the nation lived in before the invention of heavy bombers, *presents no pressing threats.*"[27]

This is not to single out these mistakes or their authors; every active researcher, including me, who has tried to anticipate outcomes, has had similar experiences. The point here is rather different. Even smart, well-grounded, and thoughtful scholars have failed to anticipate major developments that have unexpectedly arisen for our government. Therefore, it follows that no administration can rest secure in the knowledge that the experts, or academics, it relies on, can provide any clear defense against uncertainty. This straightforward fact should lead to some humility when outsiders judge the attempts of any administration to address foreign policy issues; it should certainly be a factor in their assessment on such a profound set of circumstances as the 9/11 attacks and their implications.

Policy Uncertainty and International Relations Theory

The president cannot count on having any firm knowledge of the problems that will face him, the strategies that he or his adversaries might use, or their results. Alongside the substantial responsibility gap between persons with command responsibility and commentators without it, there is an equally substantial gap between the contributions of international relations theory and research and the necessity of actual judgments by those charged with the responsibility of making them.[28]

A major part of the international relations field, following one of its chief theorists,[29] simply excludes trying to understand the actual foreign policies of particular states. They do so because such policies do not take place within "autonomous realms," which is to say that the sources of state foreign policies are complex, being influenced by both domestic and external factors. When international relations theory does focus on and attempt to explain state foreign policies and behavior, it has rival explanations and controversies, but little if any verified and accepted theory. It does have one generally validated proposition: mature democracies do not go to war against each other. However all else is debatable and debated. This makes international relations an intellectual, exciting and fertile field of inquiry. However, presidents must make choices and do not have the luxury to await settled theory, should it ever arrive.

Many of the strongest criticisms of the Bush Doctrine come from international relations theorists who consider themselves realists. One of the most prominent has observed that, "most students of international relations, including those who see threats and the use of force as central, opposed the war in Iraq and many other aspects of Bush's policy."[30] He includes himself in that group, and is a member of the Coalition for a Realistic Foreign Policy. They signed petitions published in the *New York Times* and elsewhere criticizing the administration for moving toward empire, occupying Iraq, and failing to end the Palestinian–Israeli stalemate.[31] This group boasts some of the best-known names in the international relations field.

At first glance, the views of this dazzling group of specialists might well be considered to carry enormous weight. After all, their field of study is exactly what all the political debate is about. Moreover, they are all self-described realists, members of a school that prides itself on being able to look tough facts in the eye unflinchingly, without sentimentality, and to act accordingly in the service of national interest. Regretfully for this rosy view of realism, however, its practitioners are no more immune to debates about what they see as facts, how they weigh them, and the conclusions they draw than the rest of the world.

There are in fact, varieties of "realists." Some see the expansion of state power as a by-product of human nature.[32] "Offensive realists" argue that, "the great powers do not merely strive to be the strongest great power. ... Their ultimate aim is to be the hegemon, the only great power in the system."[33] "Defensive realists" consider the expansion of powerful states like the United States a function of strategic insecurity in a world where power and force still rule (the assumption of "anarchy"). Most recently, "Neoclassical Realists" believe that states try to maximize their power while viewing their circumstances through the lens of their own cultures, perceptions, and psychology.[34]

They argue that the nature of the international system is critical, but so are perceptions of it.

Realists examine the international system with theories that aspire to explain how states will act. However, realists of various views do not exhaust the range of international relations theorists trying to explain how the world operates while, at the same time, having strong views on what American national security policy ought to be.

Liberal institutionalists, for example, contend that in a world of power collective security institutions will prove to be a salvation from anarchy.[35] The United Nations (U.N.) is the iconic exemplar of this perspective, but it is not the only international institution that liberals put their faith in. Realists, of course, think such faith is a "false promise,"[36] or in the less polite phrasing of real-world circumstances, dangerously naïve. Here, as in other matters, the realists and the Bush Administration see eye to eye, with the caveat that the Bush Administration tried to make many of these institutions live up to their promise.

Other kinds of international relations theorists look at the same world, with different theories and different questions, and arrive at different conclusions. The ensuing academic debates are rarely fully resolved. Debates arise and fade away without any particular theory being able to claim decisive victory or an agreed upon metric by which to adjudicate conflicting claims.[37]

International Relations Theory and Advice: The Case of Reassurance

Each of the different views of realism and other general theories of how the international system operates carries with it very different implications for how states ought to act. If aggressive power expansion is the best explanation of foreign policy, then states in the real world had better plan accordingly. If states are aggressive because of insecurity, we must lessen that insecurity. In order to ensure that our allies, rivals, and enemies do not feel insecure, the realists emphasize a therapeutic term: reassurance.[38] This is a particularly important concept underlying the Obama Administration's outreach to Iran and Russia, as previously noted.

Anne-Marie Slaughter writes, "International legitimacy is the currency of reassurance"[39] and that the United States should reassure its Asian and European allies that "it would neither dominate nor abandon them by deliberately enmeshing itself in a set of regional and global institutions and that it would accept certain constraints on how it exercised its power."[40] Not surprisingly, the generally very thoughtful Princeton Project on American National Security, which she co-directed, begins with the premise that, "The U.S. commitment at the heart of the liberal order should be to work with other nations to constrain our power in order to reassure others, to be able to demand the same restraint of them."[41] Yet, what is the United States to do for example, when one of its chief allies, South Korea, longs for reconciliation with North Korea, while the latter is supplying missiles and other dangerous technology to

America's enemies? What does a president do when his allies' privacy concerns prevent them from sending the names and background information of passengers traveling to the United States so that they can be checked against a terror watch list?

There is, however, a much larger problem with the strategy of reassurance. It rarely works. As Evan Montgomery has written, "the central dilemma of reassurance is that the very actions necessary to overcome uncertainty between security seeking states will often leave those actors more vulnerable to greedy ones."[42] Reassuring potentially hostile states requires military reductions that genuinely reduce a state's offensive capabilities.[43] He is of course referring to states whose security worries might lead to conflict, not reassurance among allies. Indeed, that subject hardly comes up in the international relations literature because it seems so odd to think that you would need to "reassure" your close allies in this way.

When the Obama Administration or any other administration is trying to reassure its close allies about its intentions by subordinating strategic options to collective institutional legitimacy, it needs to be concerned about the response of aggressive or hostile powers. Our enemies also hear behavioral messages sent to allies. If reassuring allies is no easy matter, reassuring hostile and dangerous regimes is even more difficult, indeed potentially compromising. Moreover, delegitimizing brutal regimes can lead to salutary changes in the international community. Did not the Helsinki Accords begin to change Soviet behavior? The delegitimizing of the Soviet Union's expansion after World War II underpinned containment, an iconic policy for realists.

Reassurance simply is not always reassuring. It can be disbelieved. It can be used as a strategic bargaining chip to gain more concessions by continually asking for more concrete manifestations of sincerity. Reassurance may degenerate into naïveté, weakness, or both. Paradoxically, calming your allies via self-imposed constraints may ultimately embolden your enemies' risky (to them, you, and your allies) behavior.

Could versus Will

Modesty is also in order when addressing the issue of how an administration should manage specific issues. Most scholars consider American primacy a fact, but its consequences are a matter of uncertainty and dispute. Theories of balancing against the hegemon can suggest how other states *might* act, but they provide no guidelines about how other states *will* act. Serious counterbalancing is not a necessary outcome of primacy for a democratic state that tolerates policy diversity. Furthermore, even if it were more likely, it might well be considered a cost that must be borne in the service of important national security policies.

"Soft" balancing is a fact of international life against a primary power and one that is democratic tolerates a great deal of it. Looking at U.N. Assembly speeches, it is clear that the world is awash with a laundry list of criticisms of U.S.

policies.[44] However, the relationships of many of these countries to the United States are complex and not primarily oppositional. In any event, the long anticipated counterbalancing to United States primacy, especially as exemplified by the Bush Administration and Doctrine has "failed to emerge,"[45] and as a result, "scholars are exploring new concepts of balancing."[46] Christopher Layne has argued for a new form of counterbalancing somewhere between "hard" and "soft." In his theory, countries not really afraid of the hegemon's intentions toward them engage in "leash slipping." These countries build up their military capabilities to "maximize their ability to conduct an independent foreign policy."[47] Layne gives the examples of England, France and perhaps the European Union. His observations overlook that a certain degree of allied autonomy has always been the case. Even at the height of the Cold War, Willy Brandt's opening to the East (*Ostpolitik*) was worried about but tolerated by Washington.

Stephen Walt details the techniques that other powers may use to stymie or influence hegemons without necessarily balancing against them.[48] He now says that balancing may be "oppositional," similar to North Korea's attempt to use its nuclear weapons program as blackmail to extract security and economic pledges from the United States (this used to be called strategic bargaining).[49] He notes that some strategies like "bonding" are "accommodating," and can occur where close friendship is used to gain influence. It can also appear when friendship is generally more strategic, as when you recruit your friend to aid you against your enemies.[50] The reality is that almost all of America's allies pursue mixed strategies of "bandwagoning" and independence because they can and because their interests are not identical to ours.

The most obvious case of attempted balancing against the United States is one rarely mentioned by international relations theorists, the alliance of countries like Bolivia, Venezuela, Iran,[51] and Cuba. Cuba and Venezuela have recently offered Russia, another member in good standing of this group,[52] both naval and air bases for their military.[53] America's competitors and enemies try to balance against and undermine American power and interests any way they can and this is to be expected. Most balancing theory neglects the fact that states do it for their own interests and not primarily as a response to the United States. Russia as noted in the *Washington Post*,[54] has "a larger purpose: to proclaim the return of his country as a power that would 'balance' the United States. Mr. Putin, who has described the collapse of the Soviet Union as a 'catastrophe,' [has spoken] nostalgically about the Cold War." Furthermore, "With its soaring oil revenue and its hold over European energy supplies, its modernizing nuclear forces, and its willingness to provide weapons and nuclear technology to such states as Iran, Syria and Saudi Arabia, Russia would regain a status such that the United States would be afraid to make an extra step without consulting." These are matters primarily of Russian ambitions, not the results of American primacy.

Or, consider the terrible bind of states caught in the so-called security dilemma. This is said to occur when states acting to increase their security might unintentionally increase their insecurity instead.[55] That theory says that bolstering one's own security might make other states insecure and precipitate the very conflict you are seeking to avoid. It is also possible, however, that there are some states and groups that a state might wish to make think more than twice before they seriously contemplate undertaking provocative or hostile acts. How should a state balance these concerns? The theory of the security dilemma doesn't say because it's really a broad statement of possibilities. And here, as elsewhere, one person's excessive response to security concerns is another's prudence.

Should the United States build a missile defense system to guard itself and its European and Middle Eastern allies against attack or blackmail from China, Iran, or North Korea? Their development would change the strategic balance. Should the United States move to protect itself even if our improved security makes others more insecure? The security dilemma provides no specific guidelines. It offers a set of possibilities of what *might* happen; but to be fair, the president must also consider the possibility that these things will *not* happen. And finally a president must consider that being able to block missiles from a country like Iran or North Korea may well make them more insecure, but prudent, about launching them and the question then arises: is that really necessarily a bad outcome?

The Policy Dangers of Shallow Psychology

Many international relations theorists ignore precisely the issues that would be of most use to presidents and policymakers. They do so by making a very large assumption; namely, that states act "rationally." That stance is best summed up by Robert Keohane's proposition that, "the link between system structure and actor behavior is forged by the rationality assumption, which enables the theorists to predict that leaders will respond to the incentives and constraints imposed by their environments."[56] Of course leaders respond to their environments, but whether they do so in the way posited by rationality theory is quite another matter.

What is rationality? It requires leaders to see their circumstances clearly, accurately assess their options and the consequences of their choices, and then act accordingly. Unfortunately, this turns out to be the perfect description of what few decisions-makers do, in large part because they can't.[57] Circumstances are rarely crystal clear, and even if they were, are viewed through the filters of culture, history, and psychology. These various filters are rarely neutral with regard to how information is seen, what feelings it arouses, and how it is analyzed. Moreover, even if options are clear, their consequences rarely are. Underneath the assumption of rationality is a cultural conceit, namely, that others would and *should* act as I would.

There is one further dilemma that exacerbates these issues. International relations theory aspires to accurately understand and explain the behavior of states. Their dominant and preferred vehicle for doing so is the research study that results in a usable generalization. A generalization, of course, is a statement about actors or motivations, in general. National security policy on the other hand must, of necessity, be considered with the motivations and behaviors of specific actors. Given the multiplicity of international relations theories about such matters and their indeterminacy, professional theory can only hope to serve, at present, as rough guides for the kinds of specific assessments and decisions that a president must routinely make.

There is one absolutely essential area of national security policy that international relations theory is particularly unsuited to be helpful to presidents, and that is in the domain of leadership intention and motivation. One of the most crucial elements of any consequential national security decision is assessing the intentions and motivations of other actors in the system. Intentions and motivations are not, of course, synonymous with the behavior a state may choose, but it is difficult to imagine a useful strategic analysis that does not carefully consider these matters.

International relations theory is of little help here, primarily because it seeks, as noted, generalizations rather than specifics. But such theories also falter as aids because they rely on useful, but shallow, theories of leadership motivation, when they examine such matters at all. International relations theory finds it hard to integrate the harsher motives that permeate state and actor motivations in real life. George W. Bush made the decision to invade Iraq primarily because he came to view Saddam Hussein as brutal, ruthless, aggressive, sadistic, murderously revengeful, a person with poor judgment who was filled with grandiose dreams of glory and regional hegemony. As a result of all these traits he was regarded as extremely, even uniquely dangerous, but you won't read much about these elements of psychology so central to the assessment of intentions and motivation in many international relations journals. Nor is there yet much interest or work on how these leadership characteristics might affect the state level behavior generalizations that the international relations theory focuses upon. Yet, as I will argue, characteristics like these are essential in trying to make a differential policy diagnosis of *dangerousness* that might lead on one hand to deterrence or on the other to preventive force.

The question of what to do about leaders like Saddam Hussein, Kim Jong-il, or Ali Khamenei rests on deciphering their worldviews, thinking, and psychology. *If* they are sufficiently "like us" to see their circumstances and ours the way we do, see their options and ours as we do, and act accordingly, the United States and the concepts of deterrence and containment are in good shape. If not, American national security policy had better be flexible enough to consider other alternatives.

Imminence and Uncertainty

In his 2003 State of the Union Address President Bush argued, "Some have said we must not act until the threat is imminent. Since when have terrorists and tyrants announced their intention, politely putting us on notice before they strike? If this threat is permitted to fully and suddenly emerge, all actions ... would come too late."[58] Earlier in 2002 at West Point he said, "given the intersection of technology and catastrophic terrorism ... if we wait for threats to fully materialize, we will have waited too long."[59] In these and other administration statements, Mr. Bush raised, but did not really answer a very profound strategic question: how long, in any particular circumstance can the United States afford to wait, before taking decisive action? The answer to that question has enormous significance for the national security of the United States. It also has profound implications for American international legitimacy. International law has always recognized a right to self-defense. The question regarding catastrophic terrorism is: how far before an attack occurs does that umbrella of legitimacy extend?

Using "imminence" as a justification for self-defense has a long history. American reliance on that source of legitimacy goes back to the *Caroline* case in 1842. Daniel Webster argued for the right of "anticipatory self-defense" in cases in which there was "a need for self defense, instant, overwhelming, leaving no choice of means, and no moment for deliberation."[60] Webster's formulation provides a "right then and there" quality to the understanding of imminence, which has usually led to "armies massing" and "countdown to missile launch" being used as examples. The question, however, is whether these same kinds of examples and the circumstances they depict are relevant to today's particular dilemmas. The evidence is that they are not.

Part of the problem with assessing imminence has to do with uncertainty. The examples noted above actually sound more useful than they are. Kenneth Pollack points out that when Saddam Hussein's armies massed on the border of Kuwait in 1991, intelligence was still unclear whether this was a form of coercive diplomacy or the prelude to an attack.[61] It proved to be the latter. So too, launch countdowns may well be too late in the sequence of attack events to be a useful strategic Rubicon and besides al Qaeda-type attacks are not likely to be missile attacks.

Case in Point: Iranian Nuclear Weapons

The same issue of uncertainty arises more concretely with regard to Iran's acquisition of nuclear weapons. Leaving aside the debate on what it would mean for United States security interests in the region and elsewhere if Iran developed and could deliver a nuclear weapon, and what to do about that, consider the question of when they will be in that position. It clearly makes a difference to discussions concerning what to do about it.

It was of great significance when a major U.S. intelligence review projected that Iran was about a decade away from manufacturing the key ingredient for a nuclear weapon since that would provide some time for negotiation and regime moderation.[62] However, an alternative timetable was provided by International Atomic Energy Agency General Director Mohamed ElBaradei who said that Iran could be as close as two years away,[63] or "as far as five or six years away from a nuclear weapon."[64] Two years does not seem "imminent," but it is in the very near future, perhaps impending. On the other hand, five or six years give somewhat more time, and ten years real room to explore alternatives.

More recently, Obama's Secretary of Defense and his Chairman of the Joint Chiefs of Staff disagreed about the status of Iran's weapons development. Mullen thought they had enough material to make the bomb, Secretary Gates thought they were not near having a stockpile.[65] Having enough material to make one bomb is different than assembling a stockpile. Having a stockpile is different than having the means to deliver it. Yet, even having one is enough to change the calculations of other countries regarding Iranian power, status, intentions, and capacity.

To complicate matters further, Obama's Director of National Intelligence, Dennis C. Blair, testified before Congress that, "Our current estimate is that the minimum time at which Iran could technically produce the amount of highly enriched uranium for a single weapon is 2010 to 2015."[66] He attributed differences in the possible time as "a result of differences in the intelligence community about how quickly Iran could develop a weapon if it rekindled a weapons program it suspended in 2003."[67] Yet, the question of whether Iran had really stopped its weapon program was itself a matter of dispute. In testimony before Congress, Former Director of National Intelligence, Mike McConnell had testified on that issue, "Declared uranium enrichment efforts, which will enable the production of fissile material, continue. This is the most difficult challenge in nuclear production. Iran's efforts to perfect ballistic missiles that can reach North Africa and Europe also continue."[68] His point was that continuing work on dual-use technology made it possible to continue to develop infrastructure, techniques and information that could be easily applied to a weapons program.

Not only did these senior Obama national security officials disagree, but also the longer timeframe assessment ran counter to Israeli intelligence on this matter. When asked about this Blair said that, "Israel was working from the same facts but had drawn a different interpretation of their meaning."[69] He went on to add, "The Israelis are far more concerned about it, and they take more of a worst-case approach to these things from their point of view."[70]

Herein, in capsule form, is an elementary national security fact. The "facts" do not speak clearly for themselves. Assuming that Blair, Mullins, Gates and the Israelis were all looking at the "same facts," and one cannot be sure without seeing them, they clearly came to different conclusions and these were heavily influenced by the context of potential losses and gains. Thus, where you stand and the risks associated with being there influence what you see. The difficult truth of the matter was expressed by Senator Pat Roberts (R-KAN) chairman of the Senate intelligence committee, "How many years are they away from having a nuclear weapon? We don't know, and the people providing the answers don't know."[71]

The Iran example raises the question of what imminence actually means in a post-9/11 context when the danger is high, the knowledge is ambiguous where it exists at all, and therefore certainty low. That term generally refers to something "ready to take place" or "hanging threateningly over one's head."[72] William Safire says, "'Overhanging' is in essence an immediate threat, a sinister event close at hand—unlike *impending*, which is not so near in time."[73] Assessments of imminence depend partly on knowing what is taking place and the pace of its unfolding. This requires intelligence. Yet, the places where such intelligence is most needed are often the places where it is hardest to obtain. The United States had few strategic intelligence assets within the Iraqi government. As a result, assessments were forced to depend on presumption and extrapolation, which proved deficient. North Korea, al Qaeda, and Iran are all entities where the United States is forced to make critical strategic decisions without the benefit, so far as we know, of that kind of information. Certainly that was true of the Bush Administration after 9/11 and it seems no less true now of the Obama Administration.

Francis Fukuyama argues that, "*If* we had evidence that another rogue state or failed states beyond Afghanistan were harboring nuclear-armed terrorists, then the preemptive/prevention distinction would indeed collapse."[74] The problem often is that by the time the evidence is conclusive or absolute, options have narrowed and strategic risks have dangerously multiplied. Consider Donald Rumsfeld's thought experiment:

> Go back before September 11th and ask yourself this question, was the attack that took place on September 11th an imminent threat the month before, or two months before, or three months before, or six months before? When did the attack on September 11th become an imminent threat? When was it sufficiently dangerous to our country that had we known about it that we could have stepped up and stopped it and saved 3,000 lives?[75]

A mortal threat that is *gathering* is no less lethal because it is not absolutely immediate. As a result of the experiences of 9/11, it seems very likely that the timeframe alluded to by the word "imminent" has been pushed backwards in the time line and may also be fading as a matter of practicality. Massing armies or the impending missile launch are no longer the sole reliable indicators of severe intent. In the case of Saddam Hussein, the United States argued, based on the views of a large number of national security services including its own that he was dangerous and had to be removed. His WMD programs were part of that assessment. When no stockpiles were found after the invasion, but rather programs that could be restarted when circumstances allowed, the administration argued that this was just as dangerous and warranted his removal. This understanding is at the core of one of the controversies surrounding the Bush Doctrine. Yet, as Robert Jervis concedes, "This may be a political or psychological rationalization, but it does have a strong logic to it, especially if deterrence cannot cope with dedicated adversaries, most notably terrorists."[76]

Judgment, Uncertainty and Proof

The issue is not solely one of gaining access to inside information via informants or spies. Consider again Iran's quest for nuclear weapons. U.S. intelligence officials have had in their possession for some time complete sophisticated drawings of a deep subterranean shaft designed for underground nuclear tests. However, this and other evidence according to the report was circumstantial, usually ambiguous and always incomplete. This seems very clear from the differences that have emerged from top officials of the Obama Administration. However, these difficulties have been compounded by efforts by policymakers, intelligence officials and U.S. allies to reach a confident judgment about Iran's intentions and further influenced by varying degrees of confidence about a diplomatic solution to the crisis.[77]

Ultimately, given the uncertainty that is likely to accompany any such assessments, they come down to a matter of judgment and the willingness to act on it. This is the crux of Ron Suskind's sensationalized characterization of Dick Cheney's quoted remark, "If there is a one percent chance that Pakistani scientists are helping al Qaeda build a bomb, we have to treat it as a certainty in terms of our response."[78] Though Suskind tries to elevate this into a major strategic doctrine, even using it as a title for his book, it is better understood as a statement of the profound dilemma that faces the United States in the post-9/11 world. Cheney is not equating 1% with 100%. Rather, his point is that even if the chances are 1% for a WMD terrorist attack, which are very minimal for some things, we must take these threats very seriously when they involve catastrophic terrorism.[79]

George Tenent, who was present when the remark was made, understood that,

> ... the vice president did not mean to suggest, as some have asserted, that we should ignore contrary evidence and that such a policy should be applied to all threats to our national security. On the contrary, the vice president understood instinctively that WMD must be managed differently because the implications were unique – such an attack would change history. ... There was no question ... that he was absolutely right to insist that when it came to discussing weapons of mass destruction in the hands of terrorists, conventional risk assessments no longer applied; we must rule out any possibility of terrorists succeeding in their quest to obtain such weapons. We could not afford to be surprised.[80]

Neither our theories nor our intelligence capacities give us much margin for error here.

We don't know the actual probabilities of an attack. We do know there are people and groups trying to mount them. And we know that if they happen, they will be devastating.

The uncertainty dilemma is starkly framed by the response of two major powers, other than the United States, to the Iranian nuclear program. Former

French Foreign Minister Philippe Douste-Blazy said bluntly, "No civilian nuclear program can explain the Iranian nuclear program, so it is a clandestine military nuclear program."[81] His then British counterpart Jack Straw disagreed saying, "We do not have *absolute proof,* we do not have *conclusive evidence* of this. There are strong suspicions."[82]

But what form would "absolute" or "conclusive evidence" take? A regime announcement? Spikes on a seismograph accompanied by a surge of radiation level readings? This is the dilemma behind Cheney's reported remark that, "absolute proof cannot be a precondition for action."[83] It is possible that such a premise could be a rationalization for taking any action deemed necessary, regardless of the evidence as Suskind argues is the intent of the Vice President. Or it could simply be a statement of the need to make difficult judgments. Here we come to the crux of a difficult, unresolved and growing issue.

How could we tell whether a presidential assertion is a cover for actions deemed necessary but for which there is no convincing evidence or rationale or, alternatively, a statement of needed action with a strong rationale even though the information is imperfect? The answer to that question is to be found in the quality of the evidence, the strength of the rationale, and the degree of trust and credibility developed between those who make such statements and those who must evaluate them. One of the most unfortunate by-products of post-9/11 partisanship is that it has permeated questions of national security. It has been particularly evident in the use of intelligence uncertainties to undermine the credibility of the Bush Administration and in so doing blur the distinction between legitimate risks and suspect motives. We will take up that tendentious in a subsequent chapter, but we turn now from the new calculus of risk to the new calculus of national security.

6 Deterrence, Containment and Adversarial Bargaining Post-9/11

North Korea and Iran

Grand strategies alone cannot resolve pressing national security issues. Their primary purpose is diagnostic; they develop in response to important new national security issues. Thereafter, their role is to stimulate policy and organizational infrastructure, new if necessary, to address the issues they identify. Only then can any doctrine refine and apply these policies to the tasks at hand.

One critical element in the response to threats identified by grand strategies, like the Bush Doctrine, is an appreciation of adversary psychology.[1] What are they like? What motivates them? How do *they* think and calculate the risks associated with their goals? Can these calculations be modified by American initiatives, and if so, which ones?

The Bush Doctrine is often accused of having only one instrumental strategy of preventive war,[2] and of abandoning the tried and true strategy of containment. However, this is a profound misreading of the Doctrine and of the Bush Administration's actual behavior. In his 2004 State of the Union address he specifically said: "Different threats require different strategies."[3] His varied approaches to China, Iran, Syria, North Korea, Russia, Saudi Arabia, Pakistan, Venezuela, and the Sudan make it quite clear that the *diversity* of strategic psychology applied to different circumstances is one hallmark of the Bush Doctrine. Mr. Bush did argue that containment may not work against some adversaries and in this was surely correct. Therefore, it would be foolish of any administration to throw away viable strategic tools because they are associated with a controversial presidency.

That said, the post-9/11 national security environment does raise questions about the usefulness of the major strategies that have been American mainstays in the past. The questions can be framed as follows: what strategic policy tools fit in post-9/11 national circumstances? In what circumstances are different tools most effective? What role does force or the threat of it play? And, very importantly *does the post-9/11 environment require any modification of the tools that we use?*

The two most familiar American strategic tools, deterrence and containment, grew out of strategic developments during the Cold War. During that period the United States faced a primary adversary with enormous power, but also with much to lose and, over time, and increasingly, a disinclination to risk losing it. As the 2002 National Security Strategy put it, "The nature of the Cold War threat required that the United States—with our allies and friends—emphasize deterrence of the enemy's use of force, producing a grim strategy of mutual assured destruction."[4] At the level of nuclear deterrence, the theory worked.

At regional geopolitical levels, deterrence—persuading others not to start doing something—and its more forceful sibling compellence—persuading others to *stop* doing something—had decidedly mixed results. In wars in which the United States has been directly involved—Korea, Vietnam, the 1991 Gulf War, the Yugoslav Wars, and the invasion of Iraq, the two strategies designed to avert substantial military conflict failed. The 2002 NSS says simply, "We know from history that deterrence can fail; and we know from experience that some enemies cannot be deterred."[5] Distinguished scholars of international relations agree.[6]

Deterrence and containment are often thought of as separate individual strategies, and they are. Yet, in the post-World War II Cold War, both deterrence and containment were practiced and used in tandem. The Soviet Union had to be contained, but it also had to be deterred. It is also lost sight of by some that force, or the threat of it, was an important part of both strategies. The same twin strategies, along with their strategic enabler force, will be needed in Iran and North Korea should talks fail, and even to some extent if they succeed.

The Psychology of Strategic Options

Strategic option tools are abstract concepts not concrete plans of action. As Alex George notes they "do little more than to identify, as best one can, critical variables embraced by the concept."[7] They must be converted and applied to the specific circumstances for which they are being considered. Obviously this is important because circumstances differ. And one very important way in which they do is in the psychology underlying the behavior of the individual or states one is attempting to influence. It is easy enough, but misleading to cast both Saddam Hussein and Kim Jong-il as tyrants, and leave the matter resting there. Their differences, personal and situational must be considered along with their similarities if we are to gain a solid understanding of their level of regime dangerousness.

Some theorists frame the range of strategic option tools through the lens of coercion, defined as the use of threats.[8] Others break down coercion into two categories: deterrence and compellence. The first, as noted, attempts to keep its target from doing something; the second attempts to get the target to desist from an ongoing behavior.[9] Perhaps not surprisingly, the use of force in coercion holds an equivocal status in strategic theory. By definition the use of force marks the failure of deterrence, but not of compellence. Moreover, some see coercion as taking place *before* the use of force, while others see it taking place *through* force.[10] Deterrence, in the classic sense relies more on anticipation of force than on its actual use.

In the minds of many, force means military attack or the threat of it, and historically this has been mostly true. However, force need not involve military attacks as George Bush's response to North Korea, noted below, suggests. What are clearly needed in a post-9/11 world of acute international sensitivities to force are methods of coercive non-lethal forcefulness that are effective.

This is clearly a necessary assignment for the Obama Administration because they are clearly going to try their hand at bargaining with Iran and are also faced with the continuing problem of how to handle North Korea. Without doubt this will be adversarial bargaining. That kind of bargaining covers circumstances where a range of carrots and sticks are deployed without the threat of imminent force, but the possible use of force is to some degree in the background, but not really a viable possibility.

Consider the Bush Administration's six party negotiations that were undertaken with North Korea, a charter member of Mr. Bush's "Axis of Evil." All parties were well aware that the use of preventive or preemptive force by the United States was off the table because of North Korea's nuclear weapons and ability to attack South Korea. Even a victory in the latter circumstances would result in enormous problems of refugee flows and rebuilding an impoverished society on a massive scale, two problems that North Korea's closest neighbors did not want as their responsibility.

In a recent interview, President Obama's Secretary of Defense Robert Gates seems to have taken military strikes off the table in discussing Iran. Discussing the possible use of preventive force Gates said, "I think one of the biggest lessons learned in this is that if you are going to contemplate pre-empting an attack, you had better be very, very confident of the intelligence that you have." Further, he said future presidents are likely to "ask a lot of very hard questions" before using force preemptively. "I think that hurdle is much higher today than it was six or seven years ago."[11] He is right about that, and it seems clear that this view is consistent with President Obama's outlook and preferences.

Yet, where does that leave the Obama Administration with regard to dealing with a belligerent seemingly mercurial dictatorship that has made an art of brinksmanship and a tough, smart, rising regional hegemon? In the case of North Korea and Iran it seems the most likely choices for both are adversarial bargaining followed by, or more accurately coupled with, containment. The question arises in both cases, and especially in the case of Iran, whether economic sanctions like squeezing oil imports, will prove sufficient to the task.

Adversarial Bargaining: The North Korean Example

The North Korean negotiations that have taken place during the Clinton and Bush presidencies are a cautionary tale. The carrots involved in the North Korean talks were quite substantial; the actual progress reached on American goals very small.

The 2007 tentative agreement called for large amounts of economic aid and held out the prospect of diplomatic legitimacy and even a pledge not to attempt regime change. Similar kinds of reassurances, it should be added, are also on the table for Iran.

Bush's initiative was based on a reading of the regime's psychology and especially that of its leader Kim Jong-il. At a meeting in Washington, Mr. Bush asked Chinese President Hu Jintao whether he thought it possible that Mr. Kim might consider the pattern of Chinese reform initiative by Deng Xiaoping in the 1970s. Mr. Hu said he didn't know but added that a non-threatening external environment had reassured then President Deng to begin that process. President Bush was then quoted as asking, "What if I offered him [Kim] a peace treaty?"[12]

Building on a psychological assessment that suggested patience and prudence, the North Korean negotiations involved a complicated one-step-at-a-time process. That way each side would be able to assess how well the parties were adhering to the agreement before taking the next step to develop aid and diplomatic normalization. It was hoped that these steps would continue to a successful conclusion in which North Korea gradually and successfully was brought into the international community, its commercial and political ties with its neighbors strengthened, and its nuclear weapons less central to its interests. This would represent a major contribution to the prospects of East Asian and international stability, were it to occur. That was the theory.

American negotiations with North Korea have a long history. After the 1950 invasion of South Korea by its northern neighbor, there was the long negotiated Korean War armistice that required veiled threats by President Eisenhower to use nuclear weapons to bring them to a conclusion. After the Korean War ceasefire, the United States used deterrence to counter any second North Korean temptation to invade the South. It did this by stationing American troops in the demilitarized zone. If the North did decide to invade the South it would have to fight its way through the American army and of course once war was initiated, North Korea would be subject to devastating air attacks taking out its industrial base and also its nuclear facilities. It is difficult to imagine the regime surviving in those circumstances. Containment against hegemonic ambitions in the classic Cold War sense did not arise here because there was no indication that North Korea had hegemonic aspirations in East Asia and indeed it would be hard pressed to accomplish them given the power of China and Japan.

The North Korean example does, however, illustrate the limits of a strategy of isolation, a variant of containment. Both are constricting strategies that attempt to squeeze opponents into a behavior change. Isolation is not only an attempt to delegitimize a regime but to segregate it and cut it off from normal international contact. The methods vary and a regime may be isolated diplomatically, economically, or culturally. Sometimes the methods are more forceful than diplomatic,[13] but the latter can be very effective. Countries may refuse to send ambassadors or limit commercial flights. Target countries might not be invited to attend myriad international meetings, and trade with them maybe curtailed. Although it is not often discussed as an important leverage tool, it can be very effective, especially in conjunction with other allies. The apartheid regime of South Africa, for example, came to be viewed as an international pariah state. Neither their ambassadors nor their athletes were welcomed abroad and eventually, such pressures helped lead to regime change.

Like other possible inducements or disincentives, the impact of international isolation depends on how much membership and acceptance are valued. North Korea is already the most isolated state in the world, by its own choosing and behavior. Iran has been "isolated" to some degree by its "renegade" status, but it is a powerful country that others in the region must take into account and so status isolation is not likely to be a very effective punishment. In both the Iranian and North Korean cases it must be noted, the urgent hope for diplomatic breakthrough and grand bargains is inconsistent with a strategy that attempts to employ isolation.

The belligerent threats made by North Korea against South Korea over the years, the erratic and odd behavior of its leader Kim Il Sung and the 1968 bombing and seizing of the U.S. S Pueblo all suggested a mercurial leader. The development of North Korean missiles with long-range capability and the development of a nuclear weapons program made him a dangerous one.

The Clinton Administration tried offering North Korea many economic and political inducements, but discussions continued, as they had during the Korean armistice talks with little progress. At one point, fearing that North Korea might export either its nuclear knowledge or actual weapons, the United States planned an attack and conveyed the threat. At a conference, Bill Clinton revealed that, "We actually drew up plans to attack North Korea and to destroy their reactors and we told them we would attack unless they ended their nuclear programme."[14] The threat was obviously never carried out but it did result in diplomatic movement and an agreement was reached in 1994. That agreement soon unraveled however, with each party saying the other had reneged on its promises. At one point North Korea admitted it had violated the agreement by having a secret uranium project. Shortly thereafter, it retracted that admission.

Thereafter, North Korea attempted to improve its impoverished economy by selling contraband, counterfeiting currency and selling weapon components to countries the United States and others considered dangerous. Finally, it detonated a nuclear device and began testing long-range missiles. Both were accompanied by shrill threats against South Korea.

Obama's Secretary of State Hillary Clinton has expressed her doubts that "North Korea had a clandestine program to enrich uranium, and she said she will focus on getting the Pyongyang government to give up its stock of weapons-grade plutonium."[15] To do this the Obama Administration will offer a set of inducements similar to the ones offered by the Clinton Administration. These include normalized relations, a peace treaty and energy and economic incentives.[16] Two questions arise about this stance. First, what if an agreement is reached and North Korea does indeed have the secret program they admitted to; what then? The United States will have inked an agreement and left the problem in place. Second, assuming that the first issue is not a real problem as Secretary Clinton believes, what sticks will the administration have to feel comfortable in using to help negotiations move along if, as they did for the armistice and 1994 agreement, talks go on inconclusively?

Given this history, North Korea is hardly a promising candidate for successful adversarial bargaining. The Bush Administration moved not only to isolate the regime economically and politically, but also to pressure it. It did this first via United Nations (U.N.) sanctions whose ultimate effects were questionable.[17] More effective was a move of the U.S. Treasury to watch-list Banco Delta Asia in the Chinese territory of Macau because it was deeply involved in money-laundering activities and did business with Pyongyang.[18] The freeze subjected parties doing business with North Korea to public scrutiny and legal action, and the Macao Government froze 24 million dollars in North Korean funds. Mr. Kim's government complained loudly and walked out of the six party talks, a sign that economic sanctions were having an effect. Eventually, the talks produced a tentative agreement and the freeze was lifted. However the sharp stick of imposing it had preceded the carrot of lifting the freeze.

It does seem that a strategy of incentives will not be enough, on its own to gain an agreement that will be honored. The history of North Korean–American negotiations suggests that forceful persuasion is a better bet than incentives. The Eisenhower and Clinton threats of military action are one route. Actually, for all the criticism heaped on Mr. Bush's foreign policy, his use of drying up bank access to North Korea was a highly inventive, non-lethal and successful move. Clearly with North Korea, some push is going to be needed, but it is not clear what form it will take, or if the Obama Administration will find and use one. To date, they still seem to be investing hope in U.N. sanctions.

Still, even if the Obama Administration's talks don't reach a successful conclusion again, there is a still an important side benefit of working with our Eastern Asian partners on common goals. The Marshall Plan and the building of the Cold War alliance system in Western Europe is one clear example. So too, China's cooperation with closing down North Korea's banking conduit in Macao was one important benefit of enlisting China as a partner in the six party talks. Habits of cooperation can develop out of such experiences and can operate as building blocks of mutual knowledge in the search for common ground.

Containment and deterrence: Then and now

Containment and its associated strategy of deterrence have iconic status in American collective memory and among many who criticize the Bush Doctrine. That is not surprising since that dual strategy is credited with successfully leading to the eventual demise of the Soviet Union. Many credit it with both helping to avoid all out war between the United States and the Soviet Union and effectively addressing the Soviet challenge in Europe and elsewhere. Why, some legitimately ask, isn't deterrence just as viable now in dealing with Iran, and others, as it was then?

This is a fair and serious question. The answer turns on an understanding of the nature of the strategic concepts involved, but also on the psychology of the enemy for whom they were intended. As noted, the success of every tool of strategic psychology depends on an accurate reading of the target's motivations, intentions and capacities. This is no less true of the Cold War than it is of post-9/11 national security policies.

Like any iconic concept where knowledge of its actual enactment in the real world has faded with the passage of time, containment has accumulated a number of myths. One myth is that containment was a single unchanged policy. In reality containment evolved and it went through different versions and was understood at different points in its career quite differently.[19] This was in part a reflection of the fact that strategic circumstances evolved and led to changes in policy and emphasis.[20] Change also resulted from the fact that the United States learned from its attempts to apply the strategy and refined its policies accordingly.

Another myth is that containment was essentially an alternative to war. That is true if by that one means a major war between the Soviet Union and the United States. However, during the time that containment was a principal strategic tool in the Cold War, there were a number of wars (Korea, Vietnam and the spill over into Laos and Cambodia), proxy wars in a number of other parts of the world, the American invasion of Cuba and of course the Cuban missile crisis. Containment may have averted a nuclear exchange between the two superpowers, but it was by no means bloodless.

Containment's Psychology

As early as 1941 American planners were worried about the Soviet Union but torn between their worries and the need for any ally who could help win the war. Concerns about the Soviet Union grew over the course of the war and by its end had consolidated into the realization that the Soviets were a "rival," not a partner. The Soviet's end of war and post-war behavior darkened the American view considerably.[21]

It was clear Soviet expansionist strategies would have to be addressed by some kind of American policy, and the answer was found in two iconic statements of Soviet psychology, intentions, and capabilities—the so-called "long telegram" of February 22, 1946[22] and the distillation of that memo in the form of a public analysis entitled "The Sources of Soviet Conduct."[23] The father of containment theory George F. Kennan, believed the Soviet threat to be primarily ideological and political, not military.[24] He further believed that, "At [the] bottom of [the] Kremlin's neurotic view of world affairs is traditional and instinctive Russian sense of insecurity."[25] This is an early statement of a widespread view found primarily, but not exclusively in the theories of defensive realists and some liberal institutionalists, namely that if the United States "reassures" aggressive powers, they will cease to be so.

This policy was tried with the Soviet Union, but it didn't work very well.[26] The Soviet Union continued to make large demands on allies while often failing to acknowledge allied accommodation to its interests and wishes. At any rate, while "insecurity" might explain the Soviet Union's desire for "buffer states" in Eastern Europe, it didn't explain well its quest for new satellites in Western Europe, Africa or Latin America. In reality, whatever the level of insecurity that generated Soviet behavior, the end result according to Kennan was, "a political force committed fanatically to the belief that with U.S. there can be no permanent *modus vivendi*, that it is desirable and necessary that the internal harmony of our society be disrupted, our traditional way of life be destroyed, the international authority of our state be broken, if Soviet power is to be secure."[27] In this sense the Soviet Union's "insecurity," far from being reassuring, was alarming. If the only route to their security lay in the destruction of the United States, then the United States had better be prepared and act accordingly.

Writing in 1947, Kennan came to believe that, in his famous phrasing, "it will be clearly seen that the Soviet pressure against the free institutions of the western world is something that can be contained by the adroit and vigilant application of counter-force at a series of constantly shifting geographical and political points."[28] The Soviet expansionism would be stopped by an American capacity to project (but not necessarily use[29]) military power, demonstrations of resolve, and a long-term commitment to the policy.[30]

Yet, by 1948, the view of Soviet intentions, contained in National Security Council assessment 20–24 had darkened considerably.[31] The "hostile designs and formidable power of the USSR," were "the gravest threat to the security of the United States within the foreseeable future." The "ultimate objective of the leaders of the USSR is the domination of the world." The threat is "dangerous and immediate." War may come about through "Soviet miscalculation of the determination of the United States to use all means at its disposal to safeguard its security," through "Soviet misinterpretation of our intentions," or, "U.S. miscalculations of the Soviet reactions to measures we might take."

These dark views were incorporated in the National Security Council's (NSC's) successor document, the 1950's NSC-68. It specifically viewed military strength as the most important ingredient of power. This was critical to containment because, "Without superior aggregate military strength, in being and readily mobilizable, a policy of 'containment' – *which is in effect a policy of calculated and gradual coercion* – is no more than a policy of bluff."[32] It is not widely appreciated that even détente was a policy continuation of containment by other means.[33]

Containment eventually evolved into a policy of détente. On the surface, this policy was aimed at reaching some agreement on arms limitation and other issues so that the threat of war receded. Yet, there was a larger purpose. The Nixon–Kissinger policies were based on using the levers of détente, trade and diplomacy, to influence and change the nature of the regime. Their preferred vehicle was the strategic applications and rewards and punishments to induce, much like Pavlov's dog, the appropriate response.

This strategic theory of regime change holds interest because a similar hope underlies suggestions about reaching an accommodation and even a grand bargain with Iran. With the Soviet Union that policy was premised on what amounted to behavior modification and did not work for many reasons.[34] The White House shared control of the rewards and punishments with members of Congress who often acted independently of the White House plans. The Soviets resisted the premise of "linkage" which would have opened up levers of opportunity in one area to influence others. And of course, most importantly, the Soviets, unlike Pavlov's dog, were not constrained in their movement or response and still had hegemonic aspirations.

Is Containment Obsolete?

The problems raised by critics of containment during the Cold War remain with us today. Then, containment was criticized as a passive measure forcing the United States to respond to Soviet initiatives at the time and place of its choosing.[35] Now, a primarily reactive stance does not seem adequate given the contemporary intersection of terrorism and technology. There are more assertive forward-looking strategic versions of containment, but in general a wait and react stance seems too dangerous a stance today. One question for the Obama Administration is whether "smart tough" diplomacy, while appearing very active, is not with respect to the major problem at hand, hegemonic ambitions, marking time.

The post-9/11 security environment differs in several other important respects from the post-World War II circumstances that made containment a primary option. The first, as mentioned earlier, is that the Soviet Union had a home address and according to several formal analyses was focused on directing all internal and external resources on the survival and strengthening of the Soviet regime. There is simply no comparable homeland or set of assets that make the core cadres of terrorists susceptible to "calculated coercion," gradual or otherwise.

Less often observed are two other differences. First, United States security policy treated Soviet leaders, legitimately, as generally rational actors. Certainly as noted above, American officials worried about "misperception and miscalculation." However, the basic strategy followed Kennan's formulation of Soviet psychology. Soviet power, Kennan said, "does not take unnecessary risks."[36] The Russian leaders are, he added, "keen judges of human psychology"[37] and, "the Kremlin is basically flexible in its reaction to political realities." Moreover, "Caution, circumspection, flexibility and deception are valuable qualities; and their value finds a natural appreciation in the Russian or oriental mind." And finally, "it is more sensitive to contrary force, more ready to yield on individual sectors of the diplomatic front when that force is felt to be too strong, and *thus more rational in the logic and rhetoric of power*." In short, Soviet psychology was a good fit for the psychology involved in "calculated and gradual coercion," or in the more policy-specific terms deterrence and containment. The question that arises is whether dictators like Saddam Hussein or Kim Jong-il or leaders like Iranian President Mahmoud

Ahmadinejad or Chief of State Ali Khamenei can be legitimately characterized in the same way.

One final difference between the post-World War II and post-9/11 national security environments is the question of time. While the 1948 NSC 20–24 strategic assessment called the Soviet threat "dangerous and immediate" that did not mean that war was imminent. The reason for this had to do with the Soviet's view of the flow of history and the conviction that time was on their side. Kennan wrote,

> The Kremlin is under no ideological compulsion to accomplish its purposes in a hurry. Like the Church, it is dealing in ideological concepts that are of long-term validity, and it can afford to be patient. It has no right to risk the existing achievements of the revolution for the sake of vain baubles of the future ... There is no trace of any feeling in Soviet psychology that goal must be reached at any given time.[38]

Time passes for both parties in a conflict, and also has different qualities for each. While the view that time was on their side may have encouraged the Soviets toward caution, it gave the United States time to develop and adjust its strategies. The view that the United States had to adapt for a long struggle, contained in Kennan's analyses and those of NSC 20–24 and 68, was premised on the assumption of having time. That sense of having time lessened the appeal of calls to take advantage of so-called windows of opportunity to deliver a first strike against the Soviet Union.[39] Thus, there was symmetry between U.S. and Soviet views from the standpoint of imminence. Neither party thought war between them was imminent—the Soviet Union because it believed that time was on its side and the United States because it viewed the Soviets as susceptible to a strategy of calculated coercion along an axis of ever-shifting points.

The question that arises here is whether, given the intersection of terrorism and technology, time is now operating in a parallel way. Of course, terrorists with nuclear, biological or chemical intentions are a "dangerous and immediate" threat though not in the same way as the Soviet Union's large nuclear arsenal. However, can the United States afford the same long-term view with regard to such threats? Are deterrence and containment really viable strategy options, and do we have the time to develop them now with, say, Iran, as we did during the Cold War?

Ian Shapiro touting the resurrection of containment policy as a strategy in the war against "global terrorism" says of Kennan, "With time, he believed, the dysfunctional Soviet system, overextended beyond its own borders, would collapse of its own accord. History proved him right."[40] Shapiro argues that "containment is not obsolete" but that, "The Bush Doctrine is."[41] However, the central question is whether given the intersection of technology and terror and the different psychology of Muslim extremism and Soviet psychology, we have the luxury of forty-plus years of historical time.

Some serious people believe that we do not. Recall that key intelligence officials and scholars who have spent decades considering this problem have reached this conclusion. FBI Director Robert S. Mueller III said in a speech to the Global Initiative to Combat Nuclear Terrorism law-enforcement conference that it was only a matter of time and economics before terrorists will be able to purchase nuclear weapons and that the world's law-enforcement community must unite to prevent it.[42] Three Harvard researchers including the co-director of the Preventive Defense project have written, "The probability of a nuclear weapon one day going off in an American city cannot be calculated, but it is larger than it was five years ago."[43]

Mr. Shapiro lauds containment because it followed Kennan's supposed injunction to focus on behavior not rhetoric. That is only partially correct. As noted, Kennan based containment theory on his analysis of the psychology of the Soviet regime and its leaders. What they did sprang from those sources. Their behavior, however, was a reflection of their psychology, their worldview and their thinking. Concentrating on what hostile regimes do and ignoring *why* they do so and how they understand and think about their world is surely a misreading of containment theory. It is true that one cannot always deduce motivation from behavior. On the other hand, *patterns* of behavior can give helpful clues to the motivations that underlie them, and patterns of rhetoric can reflect basic strategic worldviews. Ignoring these data can be a recipe for disaster.

Constricting Strategies and Adversarial Talk: The Case of Iran

Constricting strategies like containment and isolation often go hand in hand with persuasion strategies like deterrence or coercive diplomacy. The reason is that used alone they may keep dangers bottled up, but there is always the danger of leakage. A recent example may be seen in the Bush Administration's attempt to "isolate" Iran diplomatically to help pressure it to give up its nuclear program.[44] President Bush said, "If they [Iran] continue to move forward with the program, there has to be a consequence. And a good place to start is working together to isolate the country. And my hope is, is that there are rational people inside the government that recognize isolation is not in their country's interest."[45] In an interview, Secretary of State Rice said, "… some Iranians are finally getting the message about their isolation from the international community."[46]

Some may be getting the message, but clearly not all and certainly not the most important players. Iranian President Mahmoud Ahmadinejad compared his country's nuclear program to "a train without brakes or a reverse gear"[47] and the country has ignored a U.N. Security Council ultimatum to freeze the enrichment program and instead expanded it by setting up hundreds of centrifuges. Moreover, even diplomatic isolation seems problematic because, "Russia, China and members of the European Union … are ready to reopen talks with Iran even if it does not first halt the nuclear program."[48]

Among American allies there is little evidence of a strong and unified approach. And diplomatic isolation as a strategy was undercut by the Bush Administration's stated willingness to talk with Iran in the context of multi-party talks about Iraq.[49] This means that diplomatic isolation, even limited, is not likely. And certainly the stronger versions that truly cut off a regime from institutions and benefits of the global system (trade, global product markets, prestige affirming international meetings and so on) are even more unlikely. When the Iranians seized fifteen British solders in international waters, EU countries turned a deaf ear to suggestions that it impose severe trade sanctions in response.[50] All this suggests that the United States may need to assemble an ad hoc coalition if it wants to impose sanctions, and that this "coalition of the willing," however initially robust, will suffer from substantial leakage.[51] This history is another cautionary tale for the Obama Administration efforts to reach out to Iran.

Iranian Strategic Psychology: Two Views

Some key players have very different views of the motivations of the Iranians for seeking nuclear weapons and their strategic aspirations. Here is President Bush's view expressed during a press conference with the Prime Minister of Israel:

> We discussed the Iranian issue. The Iranian regime, which calls for Israel's destruction, openly denies the Holocaust, and views the United States as its enemy, makes every effort to implement its fundamentalist religious ideology and blatantly disregards the demands of the international community. The Iranian threat is not only a threat to Israel; it is a threat to the stability of the Middle East and the entire world. And it could mark the beginning of a dangerous and irresponsible arms race in the Middle East.[52]

In this view, Iranian nuclear weapons would provide a shield and an instrument for its regional hegemony.

An alternative formulation of Iran's psychology and intentions is found in the remarks of the former International Atomic Energy Agency General Director Mohamed ElBaradei. "The US could be very helpful in providing the security assurances that obviously lay at the heart of some of the Iranian activities."[53] However, what is really at issue here for Mr. ElBaradei is respect,

> sanctions have to be coupled at all times with incentives and a real search for a compromise based on face saving, based on respect. I mean we always forget this word respect. A lot of the problems we face, fifty per cent at least if not more, is psychological. Substance is important, but fifty per cent of it is how you approach it, how you reach out to people, how you understand where they're coming from.[54]

ElBaradei believes what motivates Iranian behavior is a search for respect. It is unclear however how that motivation explains Iranian support for terrorist groups, why it has repeatedly called for Israel's destruction, why it has attempted to subvert the democratically elected government in Lebanon, and has allowed or facilitated the importation of sophisticated weapons into Iraq designed to kill American soldiers. Are all these very aggressive, even murderous behaviors to be considered part of a longing for international respect? Psychologically this seems very improbable. There is evidence that Iran doesn't just want respect, but power and regional hegemony. Nuclear weapons are a critical vehicle for achieving it. A related question that has yet to be asked much less answered is whether the Iranian leaders' strong religious convictions and rhetoric make confrontation preferable to compromising with countries they regard as infidels or even the Great Satan.

The General Director's view about the importance of respect may be true in general, but here we are dealing with a specific regime. The director, and those who share his assumptions, owe a reasonable explanation of how the search for respect explains Iran's behavior. It is unclear how seizing hostages at gunpoint in international waters and coercing "confessions" to be broadcast worldwide is a reflection of Iranians' search for respect. It is also unclear how the desire for respect fits into the clear willingness to use terrorism and murder as its instruments. Even assuming they were, is this the kind of behavior that Iran should be validated to pursue? Advocates of the respect theory of Iranian behavior should also be called upon to explain how respect would result in the mitigation of the behaviors that President Bush outlined.

Talk Hopes

Many advocates of talks with adversaries pin their hopes on any one of three outcomes. They hope that a *modus vivendi* can be reached that will settle or at least defuse the issue at hand. The risk here is that the issue will not stay settled as one or another party seeks ways to gain at least some of what they want by subterfuge and selective interpretation. Both the hopes and the risks are easily seen in the North Korean six-party talks discussed above.

A stronger version of the first hope is that the parties will make and keep some form of "grand bargain," by offering enough of what each party wants to make large overall agreements worth their while. This is the reconciliation strategy of détente. The advantages of détente, if it can be reached, are that it lessens the areas where conflict becomes a flashpoint and provides a cooling off period in adversarial relations that might lead to moderation and cooperation (see below). The risk is that détente may only appear to lessen or suspend the chance of conflict over some major issues, and does not really resolve them. If that happens, one side or the other can feel betrayed by the failure of the other side to meet its expectations.

Perhaps the key reason that advocates invest so much in talk is hope that time will result in the moderation of the regimes with whom it is attempted.

The obvious historical model is the Soviet Union especially after the ascension to power of Mikhail Gorbachev, whose policies led to self-induced regime change.

The Hope for Regime Moderation

A question that arises about moderation or mellowing is whether it is just a matter of time, and if it is, how much time. It is also important to understand just what forces were responsible for any moderation that did develop. Recall George Kennan's view of the relationship between containment, American power, and Soviet moderation,

> ... the United States has it in its power to increase enormously the strains under which Soviet policy must operate, to force upon the Kremlin a far greater degree of moderation and circumspection than it has had to observe in recent years, and in this way to promote tendencies which must eventually find their outlet in either the breakup or the gradual mellowing of Soviet power. For no mystical, Messianic movement – and particularly not that of the Kremlin – can face frustration indefinitely without eventually adjusting itself in one way or another to the logic of that state of affairs.[55]

On its face, Kennan's analysis seems to have been accurate, although "mellowing" has a large range of possible meanings. Still, it is important to keep in mind that it was the assertion of U.S. countervailing power that led to a number of proxy wars that bought the time during which the Soviet Union first mellowed then broke apart. One could make the argument that it was precisely these proxy wars that allowed the Soviet Union to feel like it was making successful efforts to expand its influence, that kept them from feeling the severe frustration that might well have resulted in a direct U.S.–Soviet conflict.

So, to the extent that the situation with Iran and the Soviet Union are parallel, moderation, if it comes, will be the end result of a rather conflict-laden process. Zealous Islamic religious belief can be seen as a "mystical, messianic movement" which when coupled with fervent nationalism, and a belief that one's rightful place is as regional hegemon is surely a recipe for conflict with any power that opposes them, especially if it is led by apostate leaders. The view that aggressive regimes will moderate their behavior over time does have some support (the Soviet Union, Libya, and perhaps China). Yet, these "success stories" also suggest a cautionary caveat.

The Russian communists came into power in 1917 and the policies that spawned containment did not really begin to moderate Soviet behavior until Gorbachev came to power in 1985, a span of 68 years. Colonel Muammar Abu Minyar al-Qaddafi came to power in 1969 and in 2003 agreed to dismantle his nuclear weapons programs, a space of 34 years. In China, the communists came into power in 1949 and appear at this point to be in the process of a transition that can be dated to the introduction of economic reforms in the 1970s. Just how this transition will play out in national security matters is unclear. It is now over fifty years since the Communists came to power there and the status of China as competitor or possible partner is not yet fully clear.[56]

In Iran, religious revolutionaries came to power in 1979 and after almost three decades the fervor of their key leaders has shown little sign of mellowing. Their standoff with the United States and other countries over nuclear development and their support of terrorism shows little tendency towards moderation. Nor does their seizure of fifteen British soldiers in international waters,[57] or the arrest of four American citizens of Iranian descent on spying charges while they were traveling or working in Iran.[58] The United States has responded with trying to isolate Iran internationally, at least with regard to nuclear power, and has also funded Iranian pro-democracy forces, all yet to little avail.

These facts raise an important distinction between *consolidation* and *mellowing*. One psychological view of internal regime change is that over time a country develops stakes as well as interests in a well functioning international system and an intact and prosperous domestic set of circumstances. In this model, revolutionary fervor leading to revisionist aspirations for the international system becomes moderated in time as the country and its leaders "mature." This is the pre-Putin Soviet model and the Chinese one.

However, there is another model based on equally powerful developmental trends and that is the model of *revolutionary consolidation*. In this situation a strand of psychological development, whether of the individual or country doesn't begin by "maturing," but rather matures by developing and consolidating its new perspectives. In psychology, a person who is raised to believe they are special, beyond the rules and ought to be the center of attention does not often "mature" into a thoughtful considerate person who takes the concerns of others seriously. More often, they continue to develop and consolidate their "narcissistic" trends in their psychology, developing skills and rationales to support them.

Nations too, under particular kinds of leaders, may become more of what they develop into. Iran shows few signs of moderation almost thirty years after the Shah of Iran was overthrown. When Saddam Hussein came into power in 1979, he began a reign of tyranny and regional confrontation that did not end until he was removed by the United States in 2003, a span of almost thirty years. Saddam did not change his basic nature or that of the regime in those years, and if anything he became more dangerous.

Why did the Soviet Union eventually try the road of reform and moderation? Surely a containment policy that increased the "pressures" on its economy, legitimacy, and expansionism played a large role. Why did Iraq under Saddam Hussein and Iran under its leadership fail to do so? The honest answer is that this question has not been studied and so we really don't know.

Similarly, in the case of Libya there are more explanations than confidence in understanding the source of their turn toward moderation. Conservatives stressed the impact of American resolve and force. Charles Krauthammer wrote of Libya's change, "In rogue states, the only diplomacy that ever works is diplomacy at the point of a bayonet."[59] Others see diplomacy as the key. Flynt Leverett writes, "Libya was willing to deal because of credible diplomatic representations by the United States over the years, which convinced the Libyans that doing so was critical to achieving their strategic and domestic goals."[60] Others point to the role that unified and effective sanctions played, but go on to emphasize that Libya's status as a pariah state contradicted Qaddafi's view of himself as a charismatic leader uniquely suited to play a large leadership role for developing countries.[61] Clearly international isolation and opprobrium were inconsistent with such a role.

Libya's decision to move toward moderation unfolded slowly, haltingly, and with many pauses and slow progress. Isolation, sanctions, military attacks, coercive diplomacy, diplomatic flexibility, economic and political inducements, and strategic reassurances were *all* part of the array of approaches that were used over time. From the standpoint of Qaddafi's calculations, there were not only these policies of external origin to contend with but his own domestic considerations as well. These included coping with the consequences of those external policies, an al Qaeda-supported attempted assassination plot against him, pressure from domestic dissidents and those wanting faster paced economic development, and his desire to clear a smooth path for leadership to his son, Seif Islam Qaddafi.

The most comprehensive analysis of this transition to date points to at least three different stages in the evolution of the decision that spanned several presidencies[62] and concludes that, "U.S. credibility on the use of force was *a* factor."[63] Elsewhere it says that, "the credible capacity to act coercively, including but not only through military force *will continue to be crucial*."[64] There were however, numerous others factors involved as well.[65] In fact, the reasons for the transition are many, their relative weight unknown, and sequences by which policies and their effects at one stage influenced the outcome are murky. Indeed, the complexities are such that the authors point out that the very same strategy can have different results at different times; "coercive diplomacy failed in the first phase, had mixed results in the second, and succeeded in the third."[66]

These complexities underscore the uncertainties about dealing with Iran. About the best that can be hoped for with Iran on the question of moderation is that over time, its leaders will see either the virtue or necessity of moderating their religious fervor and regional aspirations. However, there is little indication that this is occurring. So the reality of the hope that engagement will lead to moderation is that it anticipates future behavior for which there is little evidence and may not arrive, if it ever does, for many years. On the other hand, against the hope for moderation must be placed the strategic consequences of a nuclear-armed Iran fueled by religious conviction and regional aspirations. Obama's bet on hope carries high risks. It is a bet of hope against likelihood.

Grand Bargains: Détente with Iran?

Some analysts hope for a comprehensive détente like agreement with Iran. Chief among them is Ray Takeyh, who has recently been hired by the Obama Administration as part of its foreign policy team dealing with Iran.[67] According to Mr. Takeyh, "Washington must eschew military options, the prospect of conditional talks, and attempts to contain the regime."[68] One reason is that, "the United States has no realistic military option against Iran." Containment won't work because Iran's "growing regional influence cannot be limited." Limited talks won't work because, "the political and strategic differences between the two countries run much deeper – and require a far more comprehensive approach." These are all questionable assertions.

Military options may not be preferable, but they are certainly possible and they do not consist solely in bombing Iran's nuclear facilities. Why Iran's influence can't be retarded or contained is unclear. A number of Arab states in the region are not anxious to be under the thumb of a hegemonic Iran and have acted accordingly.[69] Containment would not be easy, but there is an enormous difference between difficult and impossible. And do not the "deep" differences between the United States and Iran raise the issue of whether a détente agreement reached would be viable? Mr. Takeyh explicitly has in mind the "understanding" reached by the Soviet Union and the United States briefly under the presidency of Richard Nixon. Henry Kissinger defined détente as encouraging "an environment in which competitors can regulate and restrain their differences and ultimately move from competition to cooperation."[70] Regrettably for this hope, the Soviets and the Americans saw détente very differently. Russis under Putin did as well.

The Soviet Union saw détente as "competitive." As Soviet Premier Brezhnev said in 1972, "The CPSU has always held, and now holds, that the class struggle between the two systems—the capitalist and the socialist—in the economic, political, and also, of course in the ideological domains will continue." This is the case because the "outlook ... of the two systems are opposite and irreconcilable."[71] President Nixon and his national security advisor Henry Kissinger downplayed the importance of regime ideology and focused instead on interests.[72]

In short, Americans saw détente as an opportunity to reduce tensions and lessen competition, while the Soviet Union saw it as a new safer environment in which to continue the struggle against the United States. Moreover, not that history has to repeat itself, but détente followed years of tension and conflict, sometimes spilling over into proxy wars.

Détente and Iranian Psychology

Mr. Takeyh says that after its war with Iraq, Iran "became quite pragmatic" having realized "the impracticality of its ambitions." He also argues that the containment of Iran "never worked." His evidence for the failures of containment are the "well documented in yearly reports by the State Department, which detail Iran's ongoing support for terrorism and warn of advances in its nuclear program." It is unclear how these reports support the proposition that Iran has "realized the impracticality of its ambitions," has become "quite pragmatic," and, "has stopped being a revisionist state long ago."

Mr. Takeyh also argues that radicals in Iran "see the United States as a declining power." One of their members high in the Iranian government is quoted as saying, "We have assessed the ultimate power of global arrogance, and on this basis there is nothing to worry about." In spite of this statement and Iranian behavior already noted, Mr. Takeyh offers Iran's "pragmatists relief from sanctions and diplomatic relations." That move, he believes, would not only "recognize its [Iran's] interests," but "also legitimize its power" and "the authority of the Islamic Republic." It seems possible that such an offer made while the United States is still fighting wars in both Iraq and Afghanistan would, along with its economic troubles, be seen as further evidence of America's overextension and decline and might very plausibly be understood as "suing for peace." This does not seem a promising foundation for a détente.

If Iranian leaders are bitter enemies of American presence and interests in the Middle East what interests should the United States give up in order to make them feel "respected"? This issue arises most dramatically with regard to nuclear weapons and Iran's proxy support of a terrorist war against Israel. What should the United States do regarding the first? Mr. Takeyh argues that "the task of negotiators working on this issue would be to devise measures that Tehran could take to win back the trust of the international community, such as submitting to a rigorous inspection regime to show that its nuclear program is not being diverted for military purposes." Mr. Takeyh admits, "Iran's ultimate goal *may* be to produce nuclear weapons" (emphasis mine). However he is reassured because "the case of Iraq demonstrates that an exacting verification process backed by the international community can *obstruct* such ambitions" (emphasis mine). Yet, both Iranian "moderates" and "radicals" are united in their belief regarding Iran's high place in the firmament of Middle Eastern countries and in their "right" to develop nuclear abilities.[73] That place appears to be as Middle Eastern powerbroker and hegemon, not as supporters of liberal internationalism. And, they are further united in the view that nuclear abilities are central to achieving their place in the sun. Mr. Takeyh goes on record as being willing to concede that Iran would be allowed to process small amounts of uranium, if they allow intrusive inspections (a large if). However, small amounts processed over time add up, and it seems implausible that Iran would not want the protection of having its own nuclear arsenal for deterrence.

Mr. Takeyh refers to the Iranian regime's "paranoia," as one reason why Washington will have to adopt its rhetoric. He is presumably describing what he sees in that government based on long experience. Iran's "paranoid" view of the enemies that surround it has the ring of truth. Other countries do oppose Iran's regional hegemony. In this sense the enemies that Iran sees arrayed against it are the enemies its aspirations have made. In that sense their paranoia is self-fulfilling.

The term paranoia has clear clinical meaning and political consequences that appear to have eluded him. To be paranoid is to be both hostile and to start with the presumption that your suspicions about others have been validated and thus are true. It is the stance toward others that is both partially projected and partially self-fulfilling. It is projected in that it attributes to others motivations that belong as much, if not more, to Iran. Iran is a radical theocracy that wishes to reshape the Middle East. Iran's support of terrorism throughout the region is both a reflection and evidence of this. So is its avowed intention to destroy Israel. It is self-fulfilling in that Iran's behavior is itself evidence to others that it is a threat.

Mr. Takeyh writes that Iran now sees "itself as the indispensable nation in the Middle East." Certainly Iran is not indispensable in the same sense that the term applies to the United States as a developer and supporter of a liberal international order. It is more likely that this term refers to Iran's view of itself as *a,* or more likely *the,* major power broker in the Arab Middle East. Iran must assert itself because it must gain its rightful place. Subservience to its wishes is desirable, but if not, violence and subversion are clearly acceptable. That is one reason why "Iran, despite its ritualistic denials, appears to be accumulating technology and expertise for the construction of nuclear weapons."[74] The purpose of that effort is to "craft an impregnable deterrent capability,"[75] and it is supported by both "moderates" and "radicals" who have voiced agreement about Iran's "right to nuclear power." It is unclear who the moderates are in this quest. We must be careful not to confuse the meaning of the word moderate or pragmatist and misapply it where it may mislead as well as label. Caution here is suggested by Robert Gates, Obama's Secretary of Defense and a certified "realist": "The American search for elusive Iranian 'moderates' is a recurring – and mostly fruitless – theme since the revolution in 1979."[76]

We must ask what a moderate leader is in the context of Iraq, which is a theocratic dictatorship. Do moderates believe that the political system should be opened up to real choice? Do moderates believe that the clerics should give up their role in the power structure? Do moderates believe that Iran should stop using or support terrorism to advance its ambitions? Do moderates believe that Iran's regional ambitions ought to be abandoned? And if they don't, do they then agree that having nuclear weapons would be worth the price of the very narrow sanctions that the United States has so far been able to craft?

Perhaps it is worth the effort, as President Obama clearly wishes to do, to explore some form of détente with Iran. However, it should be explored with a clear-eyed understanding of the regime's past and continuing behavior and its implications for Iranian strategic psychology. Moreover, it may be the case, that for Iran, détente may only come about after a period of containment and conflict, perhaps some of it in proxy military clashes and others more directly between American allies and the United States and Iraq.

In the 1990s, for instance, "the *right incentives* persuaded Tehran to stop assassinating Iranian dissidents in Europe and supporting certain terrorist activities in the Persian Gulf."[77] These incentives were coupled with forceful pushback. Isn't this exactly a description of the use of isolation, economic coercive diplomacy, and maybe a military brush back or two that well might be a prelude to a "détente" agreement?

7   Dangerous Threats and the Use of Force

For the foreseeable future, the United States is likely to be actively engaged with its allies, in a worldwide security struggle unparalleled even during the Cold War. These efforts are bound to be contentious and will be played out before a skeptical domestic and international audience. And, at the heart of these controversies will be questions regarding when and under what circumstances to use force.

The critical issue of when to use force is a longstanding one,[1] but the post-9/11 stakes have been raised considerably. There is first and primarily the intersection of terror and technology captured in the apt phrase "catastrophic terrorism." However, there is also in the not too distant second place the rise of revisionist states fueled by religious fervor and those fueled by the tyrannical or hegemonic aspirations of their leaders. The awful and not inconceivable worry is the eventual linkage of these kinds of actors with each other.

Americans have traditionally been ambivalent about the use of force and no more so than in the middle of two difficult wars, about which there was and remains little unifying consensus. Nonetheless this is an important and necessary debate and one that ought to be encouraged. Certainly it is one that the Obama Administration ought to have in spite of its view that Obama's predecessor Mr. Bush used force too quickly and not wisely.

When should the United States be prepared to use force? The easiest answer has always been, after we are attacked. In the post-9/11 world, however, this poses the risk that legitimacy will be purchased at the cost of devastation. The central question is this: on what basis can the United States decide which leaders, countries or groups are sufficiently dangerous to warrant considering the use of force? It would be helpful in answering this critical question if we were able to develop some guidelines to help clarify the distinctions between levels of risk and real danger associated with particular leaders and regimes.

The Bush Doctrine is silent about what criteria our leaders should apply in considering preventive military action,[2] and this silence is rather obvious. It is one basis of Francis Fukuyama's criticisms of the Doctrine. He argues that the National Security Strategy, "ought to be officially revised to provide clear criteria for when we believe preventive war is legitimate, and those criteria ought to be both restrictive and specific."[3] Of course, policymakers prefer ambiguity when it comes to the possible use of force because it leaves them more choices in a world of complex calculations. However, Fukuyama's concern is understandable. He is worried about the decline of American legitimacy in the aftermath of the Second Gulf War and wants to refocus American foreign policy on "good governance, political accountability, democracy and strong institutions."[4] These are laudable, even noble, goals but they do not explain how America will protect itself and its allies in the post-9/11 world.

As to the relationship of military force to legitimacy, that is a complex question. There can be no doubt that American credibility suffered a hard blow when stockpiles of banned weapons were not found in Iraq. Professionals know that intelligence is often incomplete, unreliable, subject to different interpretations, and arrives with variable levels of confidence. The international public and critics on the other hand are much more likely to focus on what they feel is the following fact: you said you were going to war because they had nuclear weapons and they didn't. This helped undermine both President Bush and his foreign policy. And as Robert Gates indicated in an interview already noted, it has left future presidents, including President Obama, with more narrow and therefore more risky and dangerous choices.

Since there are real limits as to the accuracy of intelligence and its ability to provide reliable assessments of immediate and future threats, it is almost certain that all future intelligence-based actions will be debated. This in turn will put pressures on American legitimacy. Fukuyama argues that if we can't depend on reliable intelligence to make our case for legitimacy, the United States can at least be very clear and restrictive about the circumstances under which it will consider the use of either preventive or preemptive force. In lieu of legitimacy he seems to council restraint. Yet while restraint may increase legitimacy, it also can increase risk. Related to, but prior to questions of legitimacy the question remains: on what basis is it possible to make a case for the use of force?

Deterrence and the Use of Coercive Force

The Bush Administration came to the conclusion that deterrence had limited usefulness in dealing with terrorists who welcome death in the service of their cause.[5] This is true as far as it goes, but many who enable and support terrorists prefer life in this world and thus may nonetheless still be deterred.[6] Whether the Osama bin Ladens of the world, or their associates, can be deterred is an important element in assessing the Bush Doctrine, but it is by no means the only one. Terrorists are not the only enemy that the United States faces. There are other groups and countries that simply crave more territory or regional hegemony rather than planning the destruction or crippling of the United States.

Key questions therefore for the Bush Doctrine, and the competing doctrines we will examine in some detail in the next chapter, are just what role deterrence can and should play, when is it likely to be effective, and against whom? Deterrence theory is based on the premise that means-ends rationality, clear messages being sent and understood, and strategic pragmatism will trump strong feelings like grandiosity, rage, revenge and religious fervor. Deterrence theory has traditionally had little to say about these more powerful emotional currents, except in the case of its so-called "madman" variation, wherein leaders present themselves as "irrational" when they are really not, to gain the other side's compliance.

Force, or the threat of it, is an element of a number of strategic tools. In coercive strategies, force plays a major role. Compellence occupies a transitional boundary between persuasion and coercion. On one side of that line is real and stringently applied economic or political pain as in the case of North Korea's use of the Macao bank. On the other side of that line is military force.

Critics who worry that preventive war has been elevated to a core element of the Bush Doctrine and thus American strategy can probably relax. President Obama seems much less disposed to use force in the ways that Mr. Bush did. Moreover, research suggests this tool has very limited use. As a study on first strikes by the Rand Corporation points out, "most of the considerations that have caused anticipatory strikes to be infrequent in the past continue to apply today, so it is unlikely that large-scale anticipatory attacks will become commonplace in U.S. security policy."[7]

One reason for this is that many threats cannot be recognized early enough to be averted. Political costs may easily outweigh military gains. A demonstration of resolve in circumstances like Iraq (and Afghanistan) may have a deterrence effect and thus minimize the need for future uses of military force. For this and other reasons the Rand Study concludes, "Anticipatory attack is a niche contingency."[8] Still, even in the small number of cases where it might be used it will have dramatic effects and the rationale for using it should be well thought through, understood and explained.

So we are left with the question of what kinds of threats, from what kinds of regimes and leaders should lead to force being considered and perhaps used. The traditional answer is that they should be considered on the basis of their costs and benefits.[9] So, in such calculations, "the more certain a threat is, and the greater the advantage of attacking on relatively favorable terms, the more attractive anticipatory attack becomes."[10] Or alternatively, "the costs of not acting to prevent the development or acquisition of nuclear weapons by an adversary that will be difficult to deter may be extremely high, while preventive attack may promise a far better outcome – provided that it can produce decisive results eliminating (or substantially delaying) the threat."[11] This is the basis upon which Israel attacked Iraq's nuclear reactor at Osiraq in 1981, it was the general calculation behind the U.S. invasion of Iraq in 2003 and it was part of the consideration about what to do regarding Iran's nuclear program.

However, the analysis of costs and benefits puts the cart before the horse. The question of whether a preventive attack is worth it leaves unexamined and unanalyzed a crucial prior question: on what basis should the United States even consider the use of "anticipatory force"? Costs and benefits are a proper decision exercise only *after* a decision has been made that a regime merits such consideration. The question is then: on what basis should this determination be made?

The Concept of Dangerousness

I propose the concept of *dangerousness* to help guide discussions of whether a regime even merits a cost-benefit analysis for possible anticipatory force. This analysis of the elements that might go into an assessment of dangerousness makes no claim to be either a complete or comprehensive list of the factors that should be considered. Nor does it take up the important issue how the individual elements that constitute dangerousness should be analyzed or weighted in relation to each other. Its value, if any, lies in reframing such discussions away from premature cost-benefit analysis to a consideration of exactly what it is about a state, leader or group that makes them legitimate candidates for preventive or preemptive military force on one hand or forceful tools of strategic coercion on the other. It is a term designed to bring together psychological, political, historical, geo-political, and strategic considerations in an attempt to provide a well-grounded answer to one critical question: how dangerous is this state (leader, group) to vital American interests? For the sake of this discussion some agreement about what vital interests are, is assumed.

Assessments of what a regime or leader may, or may not, do are implicit in many national security discussions. Occasionally, the term dangerous itself is used. Mr. Bush clearly believed Saddam Hussein was dangerous. At a presidential news conference, the president was asked about the relationship between Saddam Hussein and al Qaeda and he responded,

> I never said there was an operational relationship. I was making the point that Saddam Hussein had been declared a state sponsor of terror for a reason, and, therefore, he was *dangerous*. The broader point I was saying – I was reminding people why we removed Saddam Hussein from power. He was *dangerous*. I would hope people aren't trying to rewrite the history of Saddam Hussein – all of a sudden, he becomes kind of a benevolent fellow. He's a *dangerous* man. And one of the reasons he was declared a state sponsor of terror was because that's what he was. He harbored terrorists; he paid for families of suicide bombers.[12]

Mr. Bush's Q & A response is not of course a formal analysis and indeed the list of factual elements underlying his conclusion turns out to be quite a bit longer.[13]

Clearly, not everyone agreed that Iraq should have been invaded, but what is interesting is that some, including reputable scholars, thought Saddam wasn't dangerous. Anne-Marie Slaughter, Dean of the Woodrow Wilson School at Princeton University argued that Saddam Hussein was "sadistic and brutal, but not dangerous."[14] The basis of her conclusion was that Saddam Hussein had been and was being contained. This, however, confounds the assessment of dangerous with the efficacy of the strategic tools meant to deal with it.

It is to be anticipated that one objection to attempting to develop a metric for dangerousness is that such assessments are likely to be subjective and thus suspect. If, by subjective one means that there is a perceptual element in "seeing facts," and that inferences can be influenced by beliefs, that objection is correct. Yet that very same objection applies to any attempt to develop metrics of assessment, be they "capabilities," "intentions," or even so-called factual matters like whether there really was a Soviet–American missile gap.

In fact, the psychological theory on which this chapter draws has a long history and has been refined over many decades of clinical work and observation. That no consensus has been reached makes it no different than the many variations of international relations or deterrence theory. The way in which subjectivity is reduced in all these cases is by testing competing arguments against each other and by testing theory against cases. But first, theory needs to be developed.

In undertaking an analysis of dangerousness it is inevitable that one will have to address the charge that it is the United States that is dangerous. This is clearly the view of those who charge the Bush Doctrine with aspirations for empire. It is also a view held by some world leaders. Vladimir Putin, when in office, charged that the world is now unipolar: "One single center of power. One single center of force. One single center of decision." Furthermore, "the United States has overstepped its national borders, and in every area." As a result, "Today we are witnessing an almost uncontained hyper use of force in international relations – military force."[15] And, "They (the United States) bring us to the abyss of one conflict after another." His views accord with some international public opinion[16] and even opinion among American faculty members[17] that rate the United States as a "dangerous country." It is likely to be a criticism that President Obama will hear as well should he ever have to order the use of American force should a threat requiring it arise.

It is therefore worth asking on what substantive grounds is it appropriate to consider Saddam Hussein and Iraq under his rule as dangerous and reasonably exclude George W. Bush and the United States. I will take up that differential assessment of dangerousness at the conclusion of this chapter, but first let us begin a discussion of what the term means in practice.

Dangerousness: Psychological

In 1945, the United Nations Educational, Scientific and Cultural Organization (UNESCO) declared in its constitution that, "wars begin in the minds of men."[18] Following up on that insight we can say that dangerousness originates in the psychology of leaders, their strategic worldviews and behaviors that spring from it, and from the quality of their thinking and judgment. This is no clarion call for the primacy of psychology over political and strategic factors, but rather a simple reflection of the fact that for most of the countries, leaders, and groups that the United States must worry about, the psychology of their leaders is an indispensable assessment element. We are not interested here in every element of a leader's psychology, only those that have demonstrated relevance for assessing how dangerous they are. Of these a number stand out.

One is ruthlessness; another is amorality. The two are often clinically related. Ruthlessness literally means that the ruler will stop at no established boundary, political or ethical. His ruthlessness is directed at enemies both at home or abroad and they are shown no quarter. The ultimate purpose of such ruthlessness is to maintain power at all costs. Its purposes are not tied primarily to the interests of the state but to the leader who, in his own mind defines those interests. Amorality is one of the boundaries that ruthlessness transgresses. Such leaders more often adhere to Old (an eye for an eye) rather than New (thou shall not kill) Testament psychology, but with one psychological twist. The ruthless leader's murderousness is not defensive as it is in Old Testament psychology, but rather a consequence of the rage felt in response to any real opposition to the leader's narcissism and grandiosity and the resulting view that opponents are getting what they deserve. Clinically amorality translates into no guilt, no shame and no regret or remorse. Guilt is what you feel internally when you have violated one of your own or society's internalized standards. Shame is what you feel when that transgression has been exposed to others. If you are incapable of either guilt or shame, you cannot be expected to feel either regret (you wish you hadn't transgressed that boundary) or remorse—a more powerful feeling of regret.

Leaders who murder vast numbers of their countrymen as Mao Tse-tung and Joseph Stalin have done and Kim Jong-il is doing through mass starvation to achieve their political purposes, qualify. So do leaders who level whole cities in reprisal as Hafez al-Assad did in Hama in 1982 and as Saddam Hussein did in Halabjah in 1988 using poison gas. These leaders generally make *repeated* use of murder and torture to insure their rule and the taking of lives for personal and political purpose becomes a habit that generates neither shame nor guilt. Such rulers have the psychology of cold-blooded killers, which of course, is what they are.

Heightened narcissism and revenge are two other intertwined elements of leaders about whom it is prudent to be strategically cautious. Many leaders are accustomed to assuming their own self-importance, but for tyrants and despots the evidence of their importance is never less than always validated. They may "win" one hundred percent of the vote, have monuments erected to their glory and murder anyone who dissents. Since they can do no wrong, setbacks or challenges cannot be acknowledged and must above all be avenged. This cycle lies behind the murderous response to dissent domestically. Stalking and murdering dissents abroad as both Iran and Iraq (under Saddam Hussein) did represent another level of murder as tool of control and revenge. The decision to murder in other countries as a matter of policy represents an escalation of audacity, another key differential marker.

Perhaps the highest, if that is the proper term, expression of this element was Saddam Hussein's involvement in the attempt to assassinate then ex-president Bush in 1993.[19] It is worth pausing momentarily here to consider how audacious, how powerful the rage was, and how normal inhibitions both internal and strategic were bypassed in the service of revenge for the narcissistic injury of defeat. Saddam did after all try to assassinate the ex-president of the most powerful country in the world. Obviously the need to get even overwhelmed the calculations that theories of deterrence depend upon. Since Saddam Hussein had a history of working with and supporting terrorists, this incident could not help but raise the issue of whether he might well cross other lines, with catastrophic consequences for the United States, in the search for revenge. As Richard Betts points out, "Deterrence offers less confidence for preventing state sponsorship of terrorism; it did not stop the Taliban from hosting Osama bin Laden."[20]

Especially in cases in which the single leader is the primary state actor, the leader's basic lens of perception and strategic calculation is filtered through the frame of his own self-importance. This does not mean that such leaders cannot become adept at clever strategy and tactics to get more of what they want from the outside world. It simply reflects that narcissism is a very heavy thumb on the scale of ordinary means-ends calculations. This is in addition to whatever strong religious or ideological beliefs may shape a leader's strategic worldview.

Grandiosity is another key psychological element in dangerousness. One can think of grandiosity as narcissism on steroids. Here the leader or the group not only sees everything through the lens of their own importance but believes themselves to be specially chosen and entitled to a large and glorious historical place which ought to be represented here on earth by regional hegemony. Saddam Hussein had very strong dreams of glory, imagining himself variously as, "Nebuchadnezzar, the King of Babylonia who conquered Jerusalem in 586 B.C., and Saladin, who regained Jerusalem in 1187 defeating the Crusaders."[21] The import of these dreams lies in their motivating power, if the leader is in a political position to act on them and the regional circumstances allow them leeway. In this, as in other analysis, degree is important. Saddam's dreams of glory were rooted in identification with leaders whose military victories were of historic proportions. By contrast, Libya's Colonel Muammar el-Qaddafi's identifications and aspirations were more inspirational. He thought his *thinking* encapsulated in his "Green Book" provided rhetorical inspiration and would serve as a model for the world's disenfranchised. It was the power of his thinking not his armies or hegemonic status that would prove decisive.

Dangerousness: Strategic Worldview, Thinking and Judgments

Ever since the seminal work of Nathan Leites on the operational code of the Soviet Politburo,[22] it has been clear that what leaders believe and how they view the world has enormous implications for their strategic motivations and choices. George Kennan's theory of containment, as noted, drew on a detailed assessment of Soviet strategic belief.

Beliefs about the nature of the international system and the best national security stance toward it constitute a leader or nation's *strategic worldview.*

This is, at its most basic level, a combination of psychological assumption and strategic analysis. It is both factual and inferential. It is factual for example, in the observation that there is really no superordinate power or institution in the international system that can be counted upon to restrain other powers. It is inferential in its assumptions about what constitutes the best strategic stance given such facts. Leaders operate with a set of strategic assumptions. As decision-makers think about the national security issues they face, their basic cognitive frameworks lie somewhere between psychological assumptions and tactical considerations.[23] They reflect what leaders see as they look out at the world in which they must operate. These worldviews operate as strategic premises.

What then is a "dangerous" worldview or set of beliefs? One way to answer that question is to say that they are beliefs that make unprovoked attacks, or attacks in the service of a leader's narcissistic or hegemonic ambitions more likely. One key aspect would be the belief that conflict or war is "inevitable." It is one thing to view the world as a dangerous place and to acknowledge the possibility of conflict; it is another to draw from that view the assumption that conflict with your enemies is inevitable. Embedded in that view is the assumption that your enemies are ruthless and implacable and no real accommodation is possible. The first was a key element of the Soviet strategic worldview when George Kennan penned his famous long telegram. It is also implicit in the view of America as the "Great Satan."

Another "dangerous belief" is that one's system or one's ideology, religious or secular, must be given its "rightful" central place and that anything short of that requires remedial steps. This demand is a form of national narcissism in which the country at issue combines an inflated sense of its own virtues and importance and links this with a demand for hegemony. One can see both elements very clearly in Saddam Hussein's view of himself and Iraq and in the behavior and rhetoric of Iranian leaders. Finally, with regard to allies and nature of the international system, a dangerous country's relationships are primarily filtered through its aspirations for hegemony and the demand for validation for one's primary role and leadership. For such states or groups there are no larger responsibilities to the order and functioning of the international system and no effort to cede advantage in pursuit of common ground. If such states were persons they would always be asking privately: what's in it for me?

I placed the terms dangerous beliefs and worldview in quotes above to underscore the point that neither automatically nor necessarily translates into the need for military response. Other analysis must be done. However, it is prudent to flag such behavior and take the next analytical step. The Soviet Union avoided direct military clashes with the United States, but not indirect ones. The Iranians have also avoided direct military clashes with the United States, but have been willing to further their bid for regional hegemony by taking on the United States covertly in Iraq, and through their proxy allies elsewhere. And of course, Saddam Hussein twice launched wars, both against Iran in 1980, and the invasion of Kuwait in 1990 to reinforce and obtain the greater glory he thought was due to him as regional hegemon.

It must also be emphasized here that it is the *combination* of dangerous individual leadership traits and dangerous thinking or belief systems that make circumstances in which they appear particularly troubling. Many narcissistic grandiose leaders are satisfied with domestic validation of their worth. Some political leaders, Joseph Stalin and Nikita Krushchev come to mind, have aspirations of regional and even world hegemony without necessarily having the personal psychology of a Saddam Hussein. And of course even if these two elements are combined there remains the question of whether a state's power can support their intentions and how effectively opponents will respond.

How Dangerous Leaders Think

How a leader thinks is often as important as *what* he thinks. When a leader is the primary or sole decision-maker, has absolute power and has no one to correct fatal flaws in his views or assumptions, dangerousness increases. Saddam Hussein, for example, was ruthless and cruel and had risen and remained in power in a volatile political and regional environment. He was a survivor, but he was one because he learned what it took to survive and became very adept at it. He was smart, but his psychology and his isolation repeatedly impeded his judgment.

One aspect of dictatorship is that such a leader has few personal and political barriers to carrying out his whims. Moreover, when the slightest hint of dissent can lead directly to a torturous death, others around the leader are not inclined to take on that role. Paul Bremer reports in his book that Adnan Pachachi, a Sunni legislator and onetime foreign minister once asked Saddam Hussein why he had invaded Iran (a clear miscalculation of American resolve and response). Saddam Hussein replied, "When I get something in my head, I act. That's just the way I am."[24]

We have already noted in Chapter 1 that a Department of Defense after action analysis (The Iraqi Perspective Project) found that Saddam Hussein had so isolated himself, both structurally and psychologically, from the realities of his decaying position that it was impossible to use his military assets to save his rule.[25] The Woods study embodies the dilemma of those who rely on rational actor models in the post-9/11 world.

A close associate once described Saddam Hussein as a deep thinker who would remain awake at night, pondering problems at length before inspiration came to him in the form of dreams. These dreams became dictates the next morning, and invariably those around him would praise Saddam's great intuition.[26] The report concluded that Saddam's "conception of the world beyond his country's border was particularly distorted."[27] His understanding of his opponents was based on the belief that "none possessed the ruthlessness, competence or ability to thwart his aims over the long run."[28] This is very close to an operational definition of grandiosity. And of course, Saddam's wildly inflated views of his own virtues guaranteed that his judgment and the reasoning that supported it would be faulty. The report also notes, somewhat chillingly, "It is clear that his opponents in the West, did not fully understand the implications of Saddam's perceptions of reality."[29]

The Leader's Developmental and Political History

Leadership traits like those described above have developmental histories that are intertwined with the person and country's own political history. One purpose of such analyses is to establish whether the observed traits have a long or short developmental history and to gain some sense of how and why they developed. This is not an interest in psychological biography for its own sake. Generally, the longer the history of the trait, worldview, or way of thinking the more consolidated it becomes; that is, the more it becomes integrated into the leader's psychology, worldview, and information processing preferences.

The importance of this information also lies in trying to understand the situations that give rise to the development of these characteristics, information that can provide leverage for making strategic tools more effective. The focus of such analysis is on "early development" as it helps understanding of adult leadership. It is important to know that Kim Jong-il was the son of his father Kim Il Sung and that Bashar al-Assad is the son of Syrian dictator Hafez al-Assad. The importance of these facts is not only that such leaders inherit their power, but rather that every effort is made to prepare them for power and that means political "lessons." These lessons are not only those that are picked out by the father to emphasize, but also those that both have lived through and been the subject of parent–child discussion and lessons about how to view these circumstances. These experiences are the beginning of worldview and information processing preferences, and a simple comparative timeline of leader and son (or daughter) in the context of the country's history would be very revealing.

Other leaders of concern gain power rather than inherit it. Their formative experiences in power too are worth examining for clues as to how they did it and what they learned while doing so. Mao Tse-tung began his political life as a student and then revolutionary. His "cultural revolution" was many things but it was certainly the assertion of the revolutionary conviction that had carried him to power against bourgeois recidivism. Saddam Hussein began his adult political life as an assassin and ended it convicted as a mass murderer. Here too, experiences lived through and the lessons they imparted can be very useful information. Hashemi Rafsanjani, considered a moderate Iranian leader by some, had this to say, "The war has taught us that international laws are only scraps of paper." After becoming president, and alluding to a double standard in international politics where the powerful are given leeway, he was even more explicit, "We should fully equip ourselves in the defensive and offensive use of chemical, bacteriological and radiological weapons."[30] Did other Iranian leaders draw similar lessons while in power? It would be worthwhile to know.

History in Power

What leaders do, once they are in power, is an essential element of assessing their dangerousness. The reason is straightforward. Behavior is not synonymous with a person's psychology, worldview or thinking, but it is reflective of it. A behavioral choice, say, Saddam Hussein's decision to invade Iran and Kuwait or Kim Jong-il's decision (unlike his father) not to invade South Korea, reflects the end point of a confluence of elements—psychological traits (aggressiveness, sense of grievance, entitlement, or both), strategic premises (you take what you want, if you can; better to be in power than to undertake regional aggression), and premises underlying strategic thinking (no one is more ruthless than I am; I can outlast or buy them off; South Korea and the United States will respond and this time China won't come to my aid). The same is true of Iranian assassination policies against dissidents in Western Europe, the smuggling of Improvised Explosive Devices for use against American troops (we must make our enemies pay a steep price), and the support of terrorism as a subversive tool against governments in the Middle East (the indirect approach is more prudent and effective than invasion). A look back can also clarify preferred bargaining tactics and how the leader or group deals with opposition.

Among the facts that led George W. Bush to consider Saddam Hussein dangerous was his history in power which included two invasions of other countries, brutal tyranny at home and defiance abroad, his support of terrorists and terrorism, his determination to acquire weapons of mass destruction, his implication in an attempt to assassinate a former American President, and so on. These choices, it should be kept in mind, represent the *end* result of a process that includes the intersection of a set of psychological dispositions (character elements), a strategic worldview put into action, and a set of tactical calculations. At each stage in the leader's calculation process, whatever that is, he or she has the chance of modify or moderate. So a choice to use poison gas against your enemies, attempt the assassination of a former American president and so on all attest to a murderous intent carried to fruition bypassing the inhibitions that ordinarily moderate such impulses. For that reason, they carry within them a psychological reality whose weight cannot and should not be ignored.

Gathering that kind of evidence over the course of a leader's personal and political history provides invaluable information for estimations of dangerousness. However, the point of any such list is not that each item alone, or even taken together provides irrefutable evidence, that a leader or regime is dangerous and therefore must be replaced, by force if necessary. Rather, they are only a part of a composite analysis that also must include an assessment of the political structure of the regime, the dangers that the leader or regime poses and the options available given those dangers.

The Political Structure of the Regime

In some cases like Saddam Hussein's Iraq, Libya's Colonel Muammar el-Qaddafi, or North Korea's Kim Jong-il, the leader is the primary if not the final decision-maker. In other states like Iran primary leaders sit at a decision table with other influential actors. The first circumstance presents more potential danger than the second since the leader's inclinations, strategic and psychological are, at least in theory, unchecked by other power centers. The fact that one leader can clearly and solely speak and act for the state does not mean there are not other factions or interests to be considered. Most states of concern have military, economic, political, and security services that are players in the decision process. However, their influence is difficult to gauge, at best in states like Saddam Hussein's Iraq or Kim Jong-il's North Korea.

Some regimes of concern on national security grounds are more noticeably run by a group than a single individual. Sometimes the members, though not their level of influence, are clear as in the case of the Soviet Politburo. In other regimes like Iran who, exactly, is in the primary decision councils, what their views are and the weight given to them is entirely unclear. The Iranian president, Mahmoud Ahmadinejad is clearly an outspoken "radical," but how much power he actually yields in decision councils, or whether he even takes part, is unknown. Another observer of Iranian politics writing about the decisions being made about pursuing nuclear weapons says, "such a decision would be tightly held in a small circle of regime insiders."[31] Who are they and what do they think on these issues? We don't know. When Robert Gibbs, Obama's White House Spokesman, was asked about who in Iran the president's advisors would talk with under his outreach initiative, he replied, "It is unclear who exactly that dialogue would be with in Iran."[32]

In the absence of knowledge, speculation reigns. However, it is best to be prudent in such circumstances. In the past, outsiders have framed Iranian debates as occurring between "moderates" and "hard-liners" which has not proved informative or helpful. More recently, there has been speculation that the dividing line is between "young and old."[33] Yet even those calling for talks and even détente with Iran acknowledge that, "the debates gripping Tehran today focus on how the regime can consolidate its sphere of influence and best exploit its status as an emerging regional hegemon."[34] It may well be that the internal layering of power in Iran is more Byzantine than dichotomous.[35] But the deeper truth seems to be that on some matters critical to American national security interests in the area and those of its allies, these distinctions may not make much of a difference.

Ali Larijani, the head of the Supreme National Security Council, has said, "We may be sure that the Americans are our enemies," but "working with the enemy is part of the work of politics."[36] That sounds mildly moderate, but raises the question of what goal Mr. Larijani has in mind here. One clue comes from the reported views of other moderates, "that Iran's predominance cannot be guaranteed without a more rational relationship with Washington." They worry that, "the U.S. presence in the Middle East is bound to diminish, but … that it could continue to block Tehran's resurgence. In their view, smoothing relations with the United States would pave the way for Iran to increase its influence in the region." This seems to suggest that the more "hard-line" elements want to push assertive regional behavior to accomplish its purposes as the United States tires, while the more "moderate" side wants to "soothe" relationships with the United States thus helping to hasten its departure. This is a difference to be sure, but not one that is likely to become the basis of a serious scaling back of Iranian regional objectives.

The Rule of Law

One important subset of regime political structures has to do with the restraint and dispersal of power in a society. Obviously, tyrants like Kim Jong-il and Saddam Hussein rule by fiat, or close to it, and there is no rule of law, except theirs. However, many of the world's dictators often sit atop societies that do have civic and political institutions that function, but they are either weak or compromised and thus cannot provide restraint to the leader's power. In between tyranny and democracy lie a number of countries in which leaders or ruling groups are powerful, even potentially dangerous, but also have fewer functioning institutions that could mediate executive power. One thinks here of Russia's Vladimir Putin or his handpicked successor Dmitriy Medvedev, Venezuela's Hugo Chavez, China's Hu Jintao, Egypt's Hosni Mubarak, Libya's Moammar Kadafi and a number of others. All these individuals lead countries that are not democratic, could represent some possible problems for American interests but govern in countries that have identifiable and functioning and competing power institutions.

One line of defense against aggressive external strategies of destabilization or conquest are overlapping and individually effective centers of power. Independent legislative, judicial, and executive functions can impede such tendencies, although the histories of many democracies on this score suggest it is far from a fool proof hedge. In this respect one need only consider India and Pakistan. Still established legitimate and independent sources of power and debate are barriers to assertive impulse and help to insure that diverse points of view will at least be heard.

Peaceful transitions of power are also an important diagnostic tool. Samuel Huntington had proposed two consecutive transfers as one key indicator of the stability of power sharing arrangements.[37] The importance of the more than one successful transition lies in the acceptance of any opposition power that the party that they replaced is still a legitimate alternative. Consolidating the norm of peaceful transitions is related to estimations of dangerousness in that it reflects a consensus about democratic process, the assumption that different views should be argued out before the country and decided peacefully, and the results should be respected.

Institutional, constitutional, and power sharing constraints can operate to force a level of decision discipline on a leader. Whims cannot be easily or quickly translated into action. Decision frames are subject to debate. And judgments made have to withstand the scrutiny of others whose perspective and understanding of the circumstances differ. This is, again, no guarantee that bad judgments won't be made, implementation errors will be avoided, or the balance between risk and restraint successfully assessed. But such arrangements can provide a check on the leader's more questionable psychological tendencies.

Diversity of power centers and peaceful power transition are no guarantee that the parties won't coalesce around views that lead to conflict. Hugo Chavez won office in a democratic election and supports the Revolutionary Armed Forces of Columbia insurgency in Columbia. Hamas recently won a democratic election but is still committed to destroying Israel. And Iran held "democratic" elections in which all the candidates had to obtain government approval to run, and the number of votes exceeded the number of voters.[38]

Strategic Capacity and Tools of the Group or State

States differ in the kinds of power they have, can project, and where and against whom it is likely to be used.[39] Standard military, clandestine, economic and political capacities are part of the strategic capacity mix as are a range of psychological factors (ruthlessness, determination, will). These capacities must be filtered though an assessment of the strategic importance of the region in which they are located and capacities of the other actors in the region. Saddam Hussein's army was no match for the U.S. Army, more than a match for the army of Kuwait and a rough match for Iranian armed forces. North Korea's conventional and strategic arsenal is matched and checkmated by other regional powers and alliances.

Groups like Hezbollah represent less of a conventional cross-state offensive threat than a subversive one. Their dangerousness on this dimension must be measured as a function of the adversary they face. In the case of the internal jockeying for power in the Lebanese state Hezbollah's discipline, weapons and political support make them formidable. In cross-border conflict defensive operations the same holds. As a cross-border offensive force, its power is limited.

Catastrophic terrorist groups represent a whole different magnitude of threat. Their chief resource is an unrelenting determination to inflict damage on their enemies, by the most lethal means at their disposal. Their global reach, the scope of their ambitions, and their demonstrated abilities in their chosen pursuits accentuate their dangerousness. Other, less catastrophically inclined terrorists groups are more regional in their reach and ambitions, but also use carnage as a strategic tool.

Distorted judgments and dangerous worldviews do not mean that such a leader cannot be adept at strategic bargaining. States, like people who specialize in their own self-interest can become very "canny" when it comes to making other states respond favorably to their needs. Among the best examples of this is the strategy of North Korea developed over many decades and clearly transmitted from father to son. That strategy consists of blood curdling rhetoric, military saber rattling, and a stream of threats coupled with demands for concessions, economic and political incentives, and excruciating bargaining over the smallest matters. Negotiations with North Korea over the cease-fire that ended the Korean War were marathon sessions in frustration. From the negotiations during the Clinton Administration to the 2004 accord, the world has endured a long-drawn out process, and the current six party talks show evidence of being much the same.

Strategic Dangers

The analysis of the dangers that a state or group poses is an important element in assessing dangerousness. A state or a group is not dangerous only because its leader(s) receive a high score on such an assessment. They must be capable, as well as inclined to cause the kind of local, regional, or strategic trouble that merits a closer look. In order to do so we need to ask about the range and exact nature of the dangers that the regime represents. Consider in this respect, the level of danger associated with the North Korean and Iranian regimes.

North Korea is a country led by a singular dictator with a large standing army, increasingly sophisticated missile technology, and demonstrated nuclear weapons capacity. The conventional concerns regarding such a regime are that it might bid for regional hegemony or, as it did before, try to reunite North and South Korea through military means. The presence of a well-equipped South Korean army, the American alliance with South Korea and very remote likelihood that China would again support such action make this very unlikely. So too, given the fact that several major powers—China and Japan are in the region and also well equipped militarily to deal with North Korea, the chances of a successful regional hegemonic push are small.

What then is the major threat? One is that North Korea because of some regime crisis would, in the future, launch an attack against South Korea, Japan or the United States. This is possible, but again for the reasons cited not very likely. We are then left with the most present danger of the North Korean regime, its possible role as a nuclear proliferator. Information, especially nuclear, biological and chemical information is lucrative and tempting for a regime with an economy operating at minimal levels. This is one aspect of a larger present danger. The real issue may not be found in one country giving a bomb to another, but in well-trained and devout scientists feeling a religious responsibility to help their fellow believers develop a "Muslim bomb."

Iran represents quite a different set of potential dangers. It is a country with regional hegemonic ambitions. In order to secure them it will have to neutralize the support of the United States to key regional allies. It actively seeks nuclear weapons. And it is the sworn enemy of Israel and now has a president who had threatened to wipe that country off the map. It is run by religious believers, some of whose millenarian views are cause for concern. Given these aspirations and their implications, a very serious threat is that if Iran acquires nuclear weapons capacity it will increase their incentives to pursue these ambitions by lessening the risks they face with major adversaries. A nuclear weapons capacity can be used as shield for military or economic aggression, self-deterring potential adversaries, or intimidating weaker states. More dangerous and plausible scenarios can be easily imagined.

Caroline Glick gives voice to what she calls a "moderate scenario" in which Iran allows nuclear technology or knowledge to be given to one of the many extant terrorist groups, or creates a new one, for the purpose of unleashing a clearly deniable nuclear attack on Israel. In her view, many Iranian leaders hold the view that the possible retaliation would be worth it.[40] Alarming? Yes. Impossible? No. Improbable? Maybe. It certainly cannot be dismissed out of hand.

There is the risk that "worst-case" scenarios will dominate such assessments. In matters of critical national security dangers worst-case considerations are clearly prudent. Yet it is important not to overestimate an adversary's power. Fouad Ajami notes, for example, "Iran is a radical player in the world of states, to be sure, but we should not overstate its power."[41] Decision-makers tend to be more aware of their own countries' vulnerabilities and thus weight them more heavily, while unknown adversaries' vulnerabilities cannot carry quite the same weight.[42]

Strategic Options

The level of strategic danger that a country or group represents, coupled with analysis of the leader's psychology, history in power and other elements of the overall dangerousness assessment have implications for the range of strategic options that might be brought into play. Levels of dangerousness do not automatically translate into more muscular strategic tools. For the sake of illustration, assume as a thought experiment that a dangerousness scale had been developed in which we could place states or groups with some confidence. Assume further that a regime with an overall rating of seventy out of one hundred possible points. It wouldn't follow that reconciliation strategies like adversarial bargaining or even détente were out of the question or that strategies of "forceful persuasion"[43] like coercive diplomacy and compellence were necessary starting points.

Rather an assessment of dangerousness would seem to entail the following in considering possible strategic psychology options:

- The more dangerous the regime or group, the tougher the ultimate level of strategic options that must be considered. Softer strategies can, and should be tried, but they should be tried with the understanding that stronger measures may be necessary and prepared for accordingly.
- If less forceful strategic tools are to be tried first, with the possibility that other more powerful tools might be used later, each step will require its own separate independent assessment. Often in a multi-step decision process, the tendency is for leaders to concentrate on the final step and skip over the question of the actual chances of having to move from first steps to more forceful steps.
- The more dangerous the regime or group, the shorter the time frame in which to try softer measures. Long drawn-out bargaining negotiations while the other side continues in the very behavior that gave rise to heightened levels of dangerousness stacks the deck against satisfactorily addressing and

resolving the national security issues involved. This was the rationale behind the Bush Administration's approach to both North Korea and Iran. With the first it involved a sixty-day period after which North Korea had to take a decisive step in the direction of real deal making. In the case of Iran it was reflected in Bush's insistence that Iran stop, even if temporarily, their enrichment activities.

- The more dangerous the regime or group, the more effort should be placed in fielding several complementary strategic options. True dangerousness is too potentially damaging to rely on a single strategic tool.

America as a Dangerous State?

The United States has all the military capacities to be a dangerous state. It has a large and effective army, the capacity to project its power abroad, a role as a protector of the international liberal order as well as its allies, and its own strong national security interests as a chief target for those with hegemonic or murderous intentions. Moreover, it had as its leader George W. Bush, a president who strongly believed in an assertive stance toward national defense and protecting core American interests abroad. Furthermore, the history of nationalist or liberal internationalism makes clear that the use of force is not an isolated theme in American foreign policy.[44] On what basis therefore, to put the matter bluntly, can we distinguish between America under say George W. Bush and Iraq under Saddam Hussein?

This may seem a silly question to ask and it is tempting to simply reply: of course we can distinguish them. However, the exercise is worth doing because it forces us to consider just what those differences are in a concrete, empirical way. The ability of facts and theories to distinguish different classes of phenomenon, in this case dangerousness of leaders and regimes, is an important theoretical development. The more adequate our theory is in successfully assessing real instances, the more confidence we can have in making use of it as an aid and policy tool.

One less useful approach to answering this question is to point to the different values that the two countries and leaders represent. Approaching the issue from this perspective would award merit stars to the United States because of its professed commitment to democracy and the rule of law. That's not convincing because many dictators speak highly of democracy and some, including Saddam Hussein, gain overwhelming election victories. We know from both social and clinical psychology theory that it is easy to believe the best of ourselves, and discount the legitimate doubts and objects of others. So it is best to stick to a range of facts and allow them to provide some perspective on self-perceptions.

Differentiating Leadership Psychology

Let us begin with leadership psychology. Ruthlessness and amorality are dangerous traits in the leader of a state with hegemonic ambitions. Evidence of Saddam

Hussein's ruthlessness and amorality are found in the mass graves of his victims and the testimony of survivors. Of Mr. Bush it might be said that he is determined, even stubborn, but it cannot be convincingly argued that he is ruthless. A critic might raise the issue of Iraq and ask whether the sacrifice of Americans' and Iraqis' lives for what they see as a lost cause, isn't evidence of ruthlessness and amorality. This of course requires accepting the premise of the argument that Iraq is a lost cause, but also suffers from the deficiency of raising the question of whether any commitment of American soldiers doesn't then always lead to the same charges.

That view suffers from two other defects as well. The Iraq War, whatever its ultimate outcome, was not undertaken to increase either the president's power, American hegemony, or to confirm the president's view of his own self-importance. On the contrary, the war diminished the president's standing and damaged his legacy, yet he continued to believe that ultimately success is in America's best interests. As to increasing American hegemony that would have been more easily and better accomplished by installing a strong man of our choosing from the start in Iraq as some advised and Mr. Bush refused to do, rather than rely on the uncertain prospects of allowing real democracy to develop.

The question of amorality is important here as well. There is no evidence that Saddam felt any regret or remorse about his murderous behavior towards his enemies. Until the end, he justified it all as "necessary." President Bush was clearly anguished about the loss of American life and has not been indifferent to the suffering of Iraqis. As one reporter recently noted, "Bush is not blind to the realities in Iraq. After all, he lives through the events we're not supposed to report on: the trips to Walter Reed, the hours and hours spent weeping with or being rebuffed by the families of the dead."[45] Bush felt that the war in Iraq was necessary, but his necessity and Saddam's bear no resemblance. American troops operate under strict rules of engagement; Saddam's ruthlessness was subject to no rules, but his own. The purpose of Americans in Iraq was not empire (see above) and certainly not to keep Mr. Bush in power. He left office as scheduled in 2009.

Two other character elements, heightened narcissism and the rage that fuels revenge, also present a marked contrast between the two leaders. The evidence of Saddam Hussein's grandiose sense of self can be seen in his identification with the master military conquerors of his region. These are men who forged empires, changed history and were accorded the glory that is appropriate to their accomplishments. Mr. Bush has much more modest aspirations and identifications. He is most likely to identify with presidents who have been forced to make hard decisions and suffered politically as a result. His most frequent references are to a small town haberdasher who followed an iconic president into office and was thought to never measure up while he occupied it. It's an understandable identification, but hardly the grandiose psychology reflected in identifying with a Saladin or a Nebuchadnezzar. Indeed as Bob Jervis pointed out, "it was Bush who prevented the Pentagon from doing all that was possible to put Chalabi in power as the war was coming to a conclusion" and did so because it would be contrary to democratic rule.[46] This is not to say that Mr. Bush was devoid of ambition; he wasn't. However, ambition and narcissism are not synonymous. They are fused in some presidents, but Mr. Bush's personal ambitions appeared to be in the service of his policy aspirations for the country, not the reverse.

The rage that fuels revenge is also a dangerous element in a leader's psychology, especially if there are not institutional mechanisms available to moderate or shape it. Saddam's wrath for those who questioned or otherwise opposed him is well known. Less appreciated is its boundlessness. It takes an enormous amount of rage, or narcissistic injury, and very poor judgment, to try and assassinate the former president of the most powerful country in the world. Yet, this is precisely what Saddam attempted with former President George H.W. Bush. The only evidence of any similar feeling of wanting to get even for something is found in Mr. Bush's right hand drawer of his desk where he kept pictures of those responsible for 9/11 and put an x through the pictures of those captured or killed. Note that the feelings of wanting to get even are concentrated on those who harmed America, not him. Mr. Bush has a temper, and can show flashes of annoyance at the pointed and sometimes hostile questions he is often asked. Yet, he showed a remarkably resilient temperament for someone who has been repeatedly mocked, caricatured, and patronized. A true narcissist could not have withstood the constant vilification.

Differentiating Regimes

The second level of differentiating dangerousness focuses on the comparative characteristics of the countries involved. Here again, it seems unnecessary to make much effort to compare the United States with Iraq, but again the effort is worthwhile because it makes clear some important distinctions.

To begin with the most obvious, the United States is a mature democracy with effective and independent civic institutions, effective and independent political parties that voice diverse views both within and between them, and has overlapping and effective executive, legislative and judicial centers of power. The rule of law is firmly established.

And debate about a variety of policy issues is the expected norm and the reality of American political life. As a result of all of these factors, power is dispersed and fractionalized. The combination of the separation of power, checks and balances, periodic elections and the overlapping of powers insures that accumulating power is very difficult. Policy will be subject to repeated reviews, and the public's voice will be heard and felt on a regular basis. None of these things was true of Saddam's Iraq.

In Iraq, there was only one effective political party and it had a monopoly on political power. Elections were rigged and no one could complain about that and live. Public debate was stifled and large areas of political, economic, and social life were off limits to it. Power was maintained by force, not legitimacy. The legislature was hand picked and a rubber stamp for Saddam Hussein. The same was true of the judiciary. There was not rule of law, but rather rule by fiat. The democratic structures described above simply assure that normal societal decision-making will be broadly shared, moderated or sharpened by diverse perspectives, and enacted in a context of repeated and multiple public, legislative, and judicial review. None of this can be claimed for countries like (Saddam's) Iraq, Iran, China, Russia, or others. On these limited grounds alone such countries are potentially more dangerous because they lack the wide-range and free consultative process that leads away from decisions to use force being made either quickly or lightly.

One objection to these general statements is likely to be lodged by those who claim we were and have been in the past in the grips of an "imperial presidency." They ask: is not this kind of presidency exemplified by the Vietnam War, and is not the War in Iraq precisely the kind of behavior that makes most of the above moot and the United States truly dangerous? The answer to this question seems fairly clear. During Saddam's rule, he started two wars. One was with Iran; the other he started by invading Kuwait. Both were over regional power and territorial spoils. The United States never wanted or tried to annex either Vietnam or Iraq. There are arguments that the United States invaded Vietnam for its mineral resources and Iraq for its oil. But these claims confuse side benefits with major causes. In both cases, the United States became involved for strategic reasons. In the first as a defense against communist expansion during the Cold War and in Iraq as a result for the post-9/11 reframing linking catastrophic terrorism with aggressive regimes ruled by tyrants with large ambitions and poor judgment. One may not agree with these reasons but they are plausible, supportable, and legitimate (though not because of this necessarily correct) given the circumstances.

When Saddam invaded Iran and Kuwait there was no debate, anguished or otherwise. There was no attempt to enlist the support of the United Nations and Congress. There were no teach-ins, academic, or Congressional debates. In the United States all of these things preceded and continued to occur as the wars were being fought. No one challenged Saddam in a presidential primary, as Lyndon Johnson was when elements of the Democratic Party began to turn away from our involvement in Vietnam. Lyndon Johnson was forced to withdraw from considering running for the presidency; Saddam Hussein had no such worries. The Iraqi people were not given the chance to replace their legislature with people of different views when the Iran War stalled into a bloody stalemate, as was the case when Americans became disillusioned with our strategy and progress in Iraq. In both wars, Congress played an important role in shaping the conduct of the war and its conclusion. No such role was possible in Iraq. Those opposed to the war can argue that "checks and balances" weren't sufficiently robust or effective, but it cannot be argued that they weren't exercised.

Where there are not viable effective alternatives institutionally established and legitimate centers of power, the errors that spring from a leader's psychology are hard to shape much less restrain. Where the range of basic governing premises is very narrow alternative framings and understanding do not have much chance to develop. Some claim that President Bush, and presumably other presidents who preceded him, are both powerful and isolated when it comes to making the foreign policy decisions that lead to the United States being seen as dangerous by some. It is true that American presidents have more discretion in foreign than domestic policy, but like all other governmental powers in this country, that one too is shared. Historically, issues of American foreign policy are debated between the executive and legislative branches; there are debates within different executive agencies, public debates, polls, and no lack of commentary. Within the Bush White House, as was already noted, there were a number of very robust foreign policy debates in which it is clear no one faction dominated. These discussions certainly mirrored and addressed to some degree the questions that are being debated in the larger public debates.

None of these debates are a guarantee against decision insularity or myopia. Nor do they provide a guarantee against errors of judgment or choice. However, they do suggest that differing perspectives are available and argued. And they further suggest that the use of force is strongly debated both within and outside of the halls of government and thus such decisions while possibly mistaken are rarely rash, unexamined, or not subject to public debate and review. None of these elements were characteristic of Iraq, or many of the other less democratically developed countries about which the United States has to worry.

Conclusion: Dangerousness in Perspective

The formulation of dangerousness presented herein is meant to further the process of thinking more systematically about the circumstances favoring the use of more forceful strategic tools. In this we are aided by a basic psychological fact. Countries, like individuals, develop patterns of behavior over time and these are relatively easy to discern. Many dangerous regimes develop long histories of troubling patterns. They try to subvert other countries, support terrorists, defy or violate international prohibitions, and engage in provocative acts. They are sometimes adept at the rhetoric of reasonableness and often adopt a two steps forward one step back approach to testing international limits and tolerance. Iran demonstrated this by seizing fifteen soldiers in international waters, loudly broadcasting obviously coerced admissions of wrongdoing and then in a "generous" gesture, releasing the captives. The recent arrest of several Iranian–American citizens on espionage charges reflects the same aggressive, limit-testing behavior. The difficulty is in assessing their overall meaning and making a judgment about what to do about it.

That is why a well-grounded understanding of dangerousness and its elements is useful. Key to this assessment is an appreciation of the leader's psychology, ways of thinking and worldview, but such an assessment cannot rest on psychology alone. Clearly one question that arises here is whether there are any other elements that might be helpful in making such judgments. Should a leader's or a state's relationship with like-minded partners be given more weight or perhaps its own category? Questions arise as well as to the weighting of each of the categories. Which are more important? My own view is that the leader's psychology, worldview and patterns of thinking coupled with an assessment of past behavior (which is itself an indication of the ways in which psychology shaped choice) are very important. This is, at this stage, a hypothesis.

It seems likely that degrees of dangerousness will be arrayed along a continuum, and that the elements that place a country or group at the more dangerous end of the continuum might well change. The United States, for example, might develop a new working partnership with another country that will ease the danger. Or, alternatively, a country might develop new military capabilities that will elevate its dangerousness. In the end of course, each situation must be judged on its own unique configuration of factors. Such analysis may aid as well in helping people, both at home and abroad, to better understand the concerns and risks with which American national security policy must deal. This is no guarantee of increased support. However, such analysis is likely to contribute to the public's understanding and thus acceptance of the legitimacy of national security concerns with particular countries or groups.

This suggests that there needs to be a public face to the analysis of dangerousness presented in accessible and understandable terms to alert the public to the issues at stake and build on that understanding as the country or group's behavior unfolds. Dangerousness is an easy concept to intuitively understand and thus a useful building block for the very important function of public education to the nature of the threats that face this country. Presidents will need to learn to speak in ways that go beyond the beltway if they are to develop policy legitimacy and the analysis of dangerousness is one very useful way to do this.

8 Strategic Options and the Future of the Bush Doctrine

A central question for American national security is what will take the place of the Bush Doctrine if President Obama decides to retire it. The answer to that question is not easy or obvious. Most "Grand Strategy" replacement doctrines bypass much of the Bush Doctrine's detailed conceptual work, preferring to focus on a few elements. Critics of the Bush Doctrine want the United States to be more selective and focused in its overseas commitments. Some want to withdraw from almost all of them; others simply caution that more prudence is needed. All of them criticize *aspects* of the Bush Doctrine, but none have put forward a replacement doctrine with anything near its comprehensiveness, range and depth.[1]

The Bush Doctrine, as it has developed over Bush's two terms, lays out specific policies and strategies on homeland security, terrorism, cyberspace, public diplomacy, counterinsurgency doctrine, intelligence reform, and weapons of mass destruction. And these are only the visible tip of the strategic iceberg. Mr. Bush has initiated a number of programs by executive order, some of which are known through leaks,[2] others of which are not,[3] and some of which while known and very important are rarely credited, much less discussed. For example, Mr. Bush's 2004 order to the Central Intelligence Agency to increase its human intelligence resources by fifty percent[4] is critical to improving our post-9/11 security circumstances, but it is rarely mentioned in discussing the contributions of the Bush Administration to U.S. national security.

Any replacement of the Bush Doctrine ought to include, at minimum, a clear statement of what problems it is addressing and how it proposes to do so. If the replacement doctrine does not address issues of catastrophic terrorism, groups or leaders against whom conventional deterrence is unlikely to work, or other key issues addressed by the Bush Doctrine, an explanation of why not would be in order. A serious replacement proposal would also address questions of how this strategy would work in practice, and look to provide evidence.

Many replacement doctrines avoid the issue of force, preferring instead to place their focus on the many steps they believe will keep force from needing to be used. When they do in theory endorse the use of force they add "restraining" qualifications that make its legitimate use (by their criteria) unlikely.[5] The Princeton National Security Project for example boldly states, "At their core, both liberty and law must be backed up by force." But then it almost immediately adds, "the following conditions should be met before it is seriously considered: 1) it should be a last resort; 2) we must have overwhelming confidence in the intelligence and in the prospects for success; 3) we must be prepared to deal adequately with the aftermath; and 4) we must gain approval from the U.N. Security Council or at least from another broadly representative multilateral body, such as NATO."[6] As has been noted, the idea of "overwhelming confidence" in intelligence reports is a standard unlikely to be met given the nature of the issues and regimes involved, the requirement for U.N. approval a highly unlikely if not impossible standard, and the legitimacy conferred by a U.S.-led alliance assuming it could be obtained—questionable. Given the security issues that face the United States, the willingness to use force is a regrettable but necessary element in the ability to defend vital, indivisible national interests. Measured against these standards, many of the proposed replacements for the Bush Doctrine fall far short.

Strategic Worldviews and Grand Strategies

A strategic worldview is, as noted, a set of premises about the nature of the international system, the kind of national security issues that arise given its nature, and the best response to them. These kinds of assumptions are not only to be found in a leader's operational thinking but in the theories that international relations scholars propose as well.

Offensive realists see states that are driven by aggressive expansionist urges. Defensive realists see states as motivated by insecurity. Liberal institutionalists view states as amenable to cooperation in at least some areas, and think that such experience can be generalized. The problem is that advocates of these different premises are seldom explicit about these matters and the many disagreements among them can be traced to these differing premises.[7] Are states motivated by expansive urges, insecurity, or a desire for cooperation? The implications of the answers lie at the heart of the inferential aspects of strategic worldview. Is a good offense the best defense? Is reassurance better than forceful diplomacy or even force?

The major grand strategies that are offered as replacements for the Bush Doctrine answer each of these strategic worldview questions differently, when they answer them at all. Each of the replacement doctrines also frames domains of national security losses and gains very differently and arrives at different risk calculations. Framing post-9/11 circumstances within the domain of catastrophic loss led the Bush Administration to propose and enact a wide range of national security policy initiatives. None of the possible Bush Doctrine replacement strategies seems to place the national security threats facing the United States into the domain of *catastrophic loss*. Mostly they appear to see the threat as *dire*, perhaps even *tolerable*.

Ideas and Doctrines

Between American primacy and isolation lie a range of grand strategies that seek to define, focus, and limit the temptations brought about by America's crusader tradition and current world primacy. They go by different names including: realistic Wilsonianism,[8] progressive realism,[9] ethical realism,[10] neo-isolationism,[11] selective engagement,[12,13] integration,[14,15] and offshore balancing.[16] The reader should be forewarned that in some cases the conceptual labels may or may not actually reflect the content. Calling a set of ideas "progressive realism," for example, does not make them realistic.

Strategic doctrines, especially those with a president's name attached, are leadership driven. They reflect a president's sometimes-unique understanding and perspective on the security issues that give rise to the doctrine in the first place. And it is also true that every strategic doctrine, presidential or not, requires leadership action to enact. It is not really possible to consider the Bush Doctrine, for example, without also considering the leadership qualities that are necessary to apply it. This is a somewhat overlooked aspect of presidential security doctrines that has become quite obvious given the relation between Mr. Bush's Doctrine and his leadership psychology.[17] The focus here, however, is with the conceptual and substantive aspects of the proposed Bush Doctrine replacements or strategic formulations. This will allow us not only to assess their adequacy, but also to further examine some of the post-9/11 security dilemmas that face the United States.

Not all the proposed replacements for the Bush Doctrine qualify as "grand strategies," or even as strategic theories for that matter. Some are little more than concepts awaiting serious development. Others are particular sets of policy proposals that qualify as substitutes only for specific limited Bush Doctrine policies.

Realistic Wilsonianism

Francis Fukuyama's suggested replacement for the Bush Doctrine, "Realistic Wilsonianism," might be called "Bush Doctrine lite." It is based on certain "neo-conservative premises" that it shares with that policy, including the premise that the nature of regimes and their leaders do count, and that, "American power is often necessary to bring about moral purposes."

However, the differences between the two are illuminating. Mr. Fukuyama sees his doctrine differing from that of the Bush Administration, because "it takes international institutions seriously."[18] In so saying, he fails to credit the Bush Doctrine with efforts to develop these new international institutions and trying to reform old ones. He writes, "We do not want to replace national sovereignty with unaccountable international organizations. The U.N. is not now nor will it ever become an effective, legitimate seat of global organization." However, "we don't now have an adequate set of horizontal mechanisms of accountability between the vertical stovepipes we label states—adequate, that is to match the intense economic and social interpenetration that we characterize today as globalization." Fukuyama looks forward to a multi-institutional world but acknowledges that we are not yet there. He identifies weak and/or failed states as a major security threat,[19] and suggests, following the work of Stephan Krasner, the idea of "shared sovereignty"[20] in which, "states accept the long term help of the international community."[21]

Yet, therein lies a problem. The states that represent the most severe threats are exactly those states that are unlikely to accept the long-term help of the international community. Would Somalia operating under the control of either the armed and very dangerous tribal clans and warlords or Somalia's Islamists (Union of Islamic Courts) "accept" such help? That seems very unlikely. Mr. Fukuyama's one concrete illustration is a Chad–Cameroon gas pipeline project,[22] in which Chad would allow money derived from the pipeline to be put in a U.N. trust fund. Chad later reneged on this agreement which raises the question of whether this is an adequate model for questions concerning raw political power complicated by ethnic, tribal, or religious differences.

Preventive War as Non-proliferation Policy?

"Realistic Wilsonianism" is ambivalent when it comes to the question of the use of force. "Preventive strikes," Mr. Fukuyama writes, "would have to be at least considered if Pakistan, with its nuclear weapons, fell into chaos or was taken over by radical Islamists at some future date."[23] And for this reason, and presumably similar reasons and circumstances, "preventive war is not ruled out."[24] And though this echoes the Bush Doctrine, Fukuyama criticizes it for, "failing to distinguish between preemptive/preventive war designed to stop catastrophic terrorism and the use of the same policy as a means of stopping proliferation by rogue states." It is unclear whether he is referring to the acquisition of such weapons, the transfer of information, components, or the weapons themselves to other parties, or both. He says, "the possibility of a rogue state giving a bomb to a terrorist organization for use against the United States," may be of a "considerably lower order of magnitude" than the "acquisition of nuclear weapons by rogue states."

Presumably, if the United States discovers evidence that will convince the "international community," it will be free to bomb. Aside from the question of what would constitute convincing evidence, it is unlikely that countries would simply hand over a bomb. A more likely scenario, as noted, would be one where countries or groups would provide information or dual-use items that dangerous countries or groups could then use. Acquisition of weapons of mass destruction by rogue states is a "serious problem that deserves a strong response by the international community."[25] Yet given the failed efforts at the U.N. to agree on sanctions against Iran's nuclear program, one is forced to ask: what do you do if the international community fails to make a strong response?

Mr. Fukuyama says that the question that should have been raised then about invading Iraq and should be discussed now is, "whether preventive war ought to be the *key* instrument in dealing with nuclear proliferation now that the earlier restraints posed by the Nonproliferation Treaty have broken down."[26] This question however, appears to have been decisively answered in part by the development, already noted, of the administration's Proliferation Security Initiative that now enlists over ninety-five countries in an effort to stop the spread of dangerous technology, components and information. It seems quite clear that preventive war is not the "centerpiece" of the Bush Doctrine either with regard to rogue states or nuclear proliferators.[27]

America and the World

Fukuyama has little to say about America's relationship with its allies in the aftermath of 9/11 except to say that the Bush Administration failed "to anticipate the hostility of the global reaction to the war before undertaking it, particularly in Europe."[28] It is of course, possible that they did anticipate it, and decided they needed to go ahead nonetheless. This possibility is certainly raised by his observation that, "On the eve of the war, it was clear that a majority of public opinion around the world opposed the American invasion ... "[29] But whatever the truth of that matter, a very serious question is being raised here regarding the use of force, American legitimacy, and adverse international opinion.

Should world opinions have dissuaded the United States from securing what the administration felt was an important national security interest? Though Fukuyama does not answer that central question he does say that public opinion "would not have mattered if the United States had been able to demonstrate ex post the logic and the necessity of the intervention—for example by uncovering a vigorous underground weapons program."[30] Here, however, we are back to the problem of legitimacy—would discovery of a weapons program necessarily confer more legitimacy on a preventive war against a country that had no intention of attacking the United States?

Mr. Fukuyama's explanation for the world's adverse reaction to the Iraq invasion actually has little to do with Iraq's nuclear weapons programs found or not. Among other things, he blames the Bush Doctrine and America's self-perception. The Doctrine's contribution is the assumption of American exceptionalism contained in the preventive war policy. By "granting itself a right that it would deny to other countries" the United States "relied on the implicit judgment that the United States is different than other countries and can be trusted to use its military power justly and wisely in ways that other powers cannot."[31] However, America's long historical perception of its own disinterested virtue was no longer believed, he writes, if it ever was.

America's belief in its own good intentions might strike some as arrogant or naïve. Yet, it has some basis in fact. Fukuyama mentions the creating of democracies in Japan and Germany, helping Western Europe recover, and the establishment of the liberal international order. Isolation and stinginess were unselected options back then, although clearly American interests were served by all these policies. But it is worth asking what made these decisions "wise" and "just"? Was it a matter of success? Are Vietnam, Cuba and American interventions in a variety of countries over the years somehow unwise or unjust, and if so, is it because they failed? If South Vietnam had maintained its independence would that war have been just and wise? Mr. Bush has occasionally publicly envisioned a future president of the United States meeting with the president of a democratic, peaceful Iraq who is an ally in the Middle East. Such an outcome looks possible at this point, but were it to come to pass would that make the Iraq War wiser and just?

Selective Engagement

The array of Bush Doctrine replacement proposals that falls under the categorical term "selective engagement" ranges from neo-isolationism through offshore balancing. Most, but not all, set their stance in opposition to American primacy or hegemony, which they see as requiring too much unnecessary American presence in the world. Let us begin with the concept of selective engagement.

This seems to be a congenial strategic stance for President Obama. Asked during the second presidential debate about humanitarian interventions when the United States had no national interests involved, recall he replied, "And so I do believe that we have to consider it as part of our interests, our national interests, in intervening *where possible*. But understand that there's a lot of cruelty around the world. *We're not going to be able to be everywhere all the time.*"[32]

Selective engagement promises at once that the United States will be both fully engaged where it counts and substantially restrained where it doesn't.[33] The trick is to locate exactly where those points are. As is the case with other "grand strategies," selective engagement theorists do not agree with each other and the implications of their perspective for acceptance or rejection of the Bush Doctrine vary.

Basic Strategic Premises

The basic premise of selective engagement is that great powers matter, and the United States matters a great deal. The United States therefore must be involved, albeit selectively to insure that the great powers, real and aspiring, (Japan, China, Russia, India, Iran, and the European Union) don't stumble into a war.[34] These theorists believe that (especially) great power states balance against each other, that deterrence generally deters, and that extended deterrence in which the U.S. power acts as a shield and a barrier against more aggressive and ambitious states remains viable.[35] However, they also recognize that, "balancing may be tardy, statesman may miscalculate, and nuclear deterrence could fail."[36] What then?

Consider dangerous states acquiring nuclear, chemical or biological weapons (NBCs). Well, "depending on the pace of their weapons programs and the extent of their bellicosity, strong measures *may* be warranted." However, "there is no consensus on the use of force." That is because, "advocates of selective engagement are always sensitive to costs; preventive attacks may not be feasible."[37]

Selective engagement requires criteria for making choices. Some use national interest, a notoriously slippery term, to make those choices.[38] Robert Art for example has a very specific list of national interests. They include preventing NBC attacks on the United States, preventing "great power" war, securing an adequate oil supply by keeping any power from controlling access to that important resource, preserving an open international economy, fostering the spread of democracy, and protecting the global environment.[39] The first three are "vital," the second three "desirable."[40] It is easy to see from the extensiveness of this list and the myriad ways that it involves the United States worldwide why some critics think that selective engagement isn't selective enough.[41]

Still, the most important set of comparisons with the Bush Doctrine have to do with the use of force in the arena of vital interests. Art's version of selective engagement shares a major premise with the Bush Doctrine namely that there is no threat more "vital" to national interest than protecting the country against catastrophic terrorism.[42] He details why the danger of this threat has grown, an analysis that puts him into direct conflict with the "terrorism threat is overblown" view. Art thinks military force remains "a useful and fungible instrument of statecraft,"[43] but provides no details about its use.

So how then can the United States prevent dangerous states or groups from acquiring them? One way is a "no-exception" policy to NBC spread, coupled with "a gradient punishment scheme" that distinguishes between "normal states" and "rogue states and terrorists." However, because "normal states are less dangerous than rogue and terrorists, the sanctions imposed on them should be less severe."[44] How to specify the differences behind those labels is obviously a very important matter. Dangerous states and groups are committed to expanding their borders, have a track record of using force, and also are known sponsors of terrorism.[45] Art names Iran, Iraq (writing in 1998/99), Libya, Syria, and North Korea, but significantly not China.[46] Rogue states and fanatical actors are the greatest worry because of the possible consequences of a successful attack against the United States or its allies. Such states or groups are highly motivated and thus more difficult to deter, they are indifferent to suffering of their own allies and certainly their enemies, and they are "poor calculators, making them more likely to misperceive or ignore signaled threats."[47]

His other recommended policies in this area are: to adapt measures to strengthen existing institutions like the Atomic Energy Agency, develop better intelligence to uncover and sabotage covert NBC programs, sign treaties that publicly commit states to forgo acquisitions, and offer soft incentives to states that abandon their nuclear and biological weapons and also threaten adverse political–economic results for states that don't comply.[48] He also recommends using American military power to support the anti-NBC spread regime.[49] What this means exactly, is not clear, but some sense of what it might entail is found in looking at another version of "selective engagement" with a decidedly less interventionalist stance.

Offshore Balancing: The Neo-isolationism Version

As the term implies, neo-isolationists envision a wholesale reduction in American leadership worldwide. Neo-isolationists are at pains to point out that they are not like the 1920s variety of isolations who wanted to retreat behind "fortress America," hence the adjective "neo."[50] For the most part, they supported American entry into World War II, and support the American decision to contain the Soviet Union.[51] A minority have supported a strike in Afghanistan as a measured, necessary response to 9/11.[52] However, their essence is found in the title, "Come Home America,"[53] a phrase that echoes George McGovern's campaign theme in 1972 and in the observation that, "rather than lead a new crusade, American should absorb itself in the somewhat delayed task of address imperfections in its own society."[54]

Robert Art establishes two main criteria for concluding that an argument falls into the isolationist category: if it advocates the end of the American international security alliance system and if it calls for minimal American military involvement overseas.[55] The neo-isolationist group does not advocate, "total withdrawal from the world," but rather advocates a "vigorous trade with other nations" and a "thriving commerce of ideas."[56] So when neo-isolationists refer to "restraint," it is specifically military and national security restraint.

This strong version of restraint is a tempting theory. *If* advocates are right, the United States can halve its defense budget immediately, enjoy another "peace dividend," and remove the stimulus to balance against or even attack the United States because it would no longer be a world player. At the same time, neo-isolationists contend that Asia and Europe would enjoy regional peace as a consequence of a post-hegemonic (American) balance of power. Only in the Middle East do the authors say the United States will have to station military forces and these would be minimal, a few hundred airplanes and some naval elements.

Primary Strategic Worldview Assumptions

The primary assumptions of the neo-isolationists are twofold. First, "America's physical security does not demand much in the way of defense spending or overseas deployment."[57] Likewise the key to America's second primary interest, economic prosperity, lies in maintaining a well-educated workforce and addressing its problems at home, not in stationing troops overseas.[58] The authors admit that their proposals to "cut the defense budget by 50 percent and to withdraw from long-standing alliances in Europe and Asia *may* seem radical ... "[59] In the post-9/11 security environment their plan would certainly appear so. However, they are confident that the risks are worth it, can be managed, and will lead to the desirable results they advocate. In fact, they are so confident that they write that the core economic and strategic interests of the United States can be achieved "effortlessly."[60]

Two members from the same school of neo-isolationism recently wrote that, "America will best serve its interests in the Persian Gulf by withdrawing its ground-based military forces not only from Iraq, but from the entire region."[61] Similarly, one of those authors has written "Our traditional national security goals in the Persian Gulf – protecting the flow of oil and preventing conquest of the entire region by a single country – are best served by getting rid of America's military 'footprint' there."[62] Elsewhere they write that because America's principal enemies are no longer powerful countries with large armies poised to conquer U.S. allies and because of America's ability to project its military power, "the United States can protect its key interests—with military force if necessary—*without peacetime deployments* in hostile regions."[63] As a result of this, "the United States should," withdraw U.S. forces from hostile regions—particularly the Persian Gulf—and "defend key U.S. interests with 'over the horizon' military power."[64] They have also recently reasserted their view that there are very few circumstances in the Middle East regarding the supply of oil that would require American military intervention because the world and American markets would adjust.[65] Years after 9/11 the proponents of this neo-isolationist version of offshore balancing still believe that America should withdraw almost all its troops from abroad, abrogate its defense commitments with allies worldwide and depend on massive firepower projected from places very far away from regional trouble spots.

It is clear neo-isolationists do not see American national security policy operating in the domain of potential *catastrophic loss*. Indeed, it is not even clear that it sees threats to American national security as operating in the domain of loss at all. After all, America is the most powerful country, there are no enemies with powerful armies able to take over our allies, and defending America's interest will be achieved "effortlessly." The authors appear to believe that threats to American security are minimal and that on balance we have more than enough military power to handle them. This view of grand strategy seems to see America operating in the *domain of gains*, at least the domain of overall *success*.

Writing in 2002, they assert that no "peacetime deployments" of American troops in hostile regions are needed. This is their view just nine months after the 9/11 attacks. This is consistent with their emphasis on powerful states as the key threat to the United States rather than terrorists with catastrophic aspirations, the use of nuclear-backed intimidation, or attempts at subversion. The evidence of recent experience suggests the United States needs to worry about all of these issues.

Unanswered Questions

Aside from saving American money and lives, neo-isolationists believe that strategic withdrawal "has other benefits."[66] They include the fact that Allies "would be forced to accept political responsibility for their own affairs."[67] It would lessen allied military "risk taking" since the United States will not be committed to rescuing failed gambles.[68] And it would force allies to bear the economic costs of their own security.[69]

These are of course, *possible* benefits. One general problem with many critics of the Bush Doctrine is that they simply assert the benefits of their preferences without considering the arguments against their views. So, for example, it is quite possible that allies may not fully accept responsibility for their own affairs, or if they did that they would do so in a way inconsistent with American interests. For the authors, the latter is just a cost that the United States would have to bear, so "long as no outcome can threaten the core American interests of security and prosperity."[70] So their strategy could be summed up as follows: America withdraws from its primary European and Asian alliances, partially withdraws from the Middle East keeping just enough forces to slow an attack that would jeopardize our oil access, and let our allies fend for themselves, unless they do something that threatens our core strategic or economic interests in which case we would then take unspecified steps.

Of course allies who are left to fend for themselves by their former partners are not likely to remain allies. The neo-isolationist version of offshore balancing undercuts the premises of alliances. Alliances are partnerships that work together over time, establish routines of consultation and try to meet common problems. Neo-isolationism essentially leaves our former partners on their own until we think our interests are at stake and then expects those same countries to be helpful. Aside from the likelihood of former allies bandwagoning with powerful regional rivals, very likely at the expense of U.S. interests, a more likely response to this policy stance would be resentment.

A number of other questions present themselves as well. What if our allies are attacked? These authors bluntly say that South Korea, Japan and Israel can take care of themselves.[71] What if India and Pakistan have a war, or even a nuclear exchange? Best not to be in the middle of that one anyway.[72] What of the dangers of a nuclear arms race? Not to worry; South Korea and Japan "*might*" be restrained by the chance that proliferation would scare their neighbors."[73] Moreover, even if they do decide to develop nuclear weapons, both countries, "are good candidates for safe proliferation."[74]

It is perhaps in the Middle East, among the world's most volatile areas, that this strategy raises the most questions. The neo-isolationists argue that, "American military policy in the Gulf must be designed to insure that significant amounts of Saudi, Kuwaiti, Iraqi, and other Middle East oil are not monopolized by a regional hegemon."[75] On the other hand, they argue that the United States should withdraw all its ground forces from the Middle East.[76] How is this strategic national interest circle to be squared? Easily apparently because the United States defending "its Middle East oil interests, luckily is not a very demanding job."[77]

The authors argued back in 1978 that if Iraqi troops head for their borders, they should be immediately attacked.[78] Whether that would be done with or without a U.N. resolution is not made clear. Of course, Iraq is no longer the problem that it was when this was written. Would the same apply if Iran mounted an internal Shiite coup against an American-sponsored "unity" government in Iraq? Once the United States had left, would it reintroduce American troops? That does not seem likely. Along similar lines, two of the authors want the United States to withdraw and, "allow Iraq to govern itself, so long as it does not support terrorism or attack its neighbors."[79] It is very unclear what this means. What would happen if a Shiite-led Iraq helped with money, arms and advice to its religious brethren elsewhere in the Middle East? That would not be an "invasion," but it would certainly be invasive and subversive. And what does "support terrorism" mean? Does it mean contributing money to another known terrorist organization like Hamas that has both a social and armed wing? Would we insist that the money be documented to being going to the social wing? And would that matter given that finances are fungible?

In their focus on states attempting to become major regional hegemons at the expense of their neighbors, neo-isolationists focus on cross-border invasions. That is a danger, especially with a number of very weak, oil-rich states in the immediate area. But invasion is not the only way to secure compliance. Threats, intimidation and subversion work too. Massed armies do not have to cross borders in either of these cases. That is one of the legitimate fears of a nuclear-armed Iran in the region if the United States goes home.

Another big fear in the region is the fate of Saudi Arabia. And a large part of that fear is not cross-border invasion, but internal destabilization. For all their talk about the ways in which oil markets would adjust, thus requiring no American troops to secure access, these authors do say, "The one scenario in which intervention would probably make sense would be to prevent a group that actively supported al Qaeda from *winning* a civil war."[80] On the other hand, immediately before making that assertion they say, "it is unlikely, though, that if a Saudi civil war were to begin, American military intervention would restore stability."[81] This is because of "complicated local politics," so, as a result, "many of their [American] actions [would be] at least ineffectual, if not counterproductive."[82]

In their view no American troops should be anywhere in the area, because airpower will suffice, except in the kind of important situations, like subversion, where it is useless. Then we should intervene with troops, but doing so will be ineffective and counterproductive. It is very difficult to reconcile the inconsistencies of such an analysis.

Defining Terrorism Down?

Neo-isolationists have little to say about catastrophic terrorism then or now. About conventional terrorism, they are clear: "There will of course still be terrorist attacks, and their sponsors should feel America's wrath."[83] It is however, unclear what kind of wrath is being urged and against whom. Iran and

Syria are official state sponsors of terrorism. It is unclear just what kind of "wrath" these states have experienced or should expect from the United States. More recently, their argument has been that, "Terrorist groups who are *not* targeting America should be opposed, but not by force."[84] They should only be responded to by "sharing intelligence, freezing terrorists' assets, and discrediting their violent ideologies."[85] If this policy were followed American forces would not be available to help allies track down and kill terrorists like the Abu Sayyaf group in the Philippines that is linked with al Qaeda, has targeted Americans for kidnappings, but is not engaged in plans to directly attack the United States.[86] And our allies both major and minor would have to look elsewhere for help.

Among the major benefits touted for this strategy is that "Restraint should reduce the incentive of terrorists to attack the United States."[87] As the authors note, "the presence of U.S. forces incites anti-American sentiment among many Muslims around the world." Moreover, "Osama bin Laden declared war on the United States, resulting in the September 11 attacks, in significant part because of the U.S. presence."[88] Herein lies another fundamental, but unanalyzed problem for neo-isolationism as a Bush Doctrine replacement strategy. The authors seem to be arguing for an accommodation to terrorist demands. If we don't engage in the behavior that Osama bin Laden said made him attack the United States, we can avoid another 9/11. This stance assumes that acquiescing to such demands is the key to reducing terrorist incentives. However as Richard Betts points out, "There is no reason to assume that terrorist enemies would let America off the hook if it retreated and would not remain as implacable as ever."[89] Indeed, an alternative, and psychologically more viable view is that terrorists who have their tactics and power validated by accommodation (capitulation is a stronger, but still accurate term) will not simply call it a day. On the contrary, a prudent "rational" terrorist would surely ask for more.

Neo-isolationism: An Antiquated Perspective?

In keeping with its pre-9/11 perspectives, neo-isolationism is concerned with powerful states that might rapidly become dangerous regional hegemons. The demonstrated existence of such a state is one of the three tests that must be met before the neo-isolations would reengage.[90] The other two are the ability of a new hegemon state to either "mount an attack across oceans or threaten U.S. property by denying America access to the global economy." Lastly, "in order to *agglomerate the world's power under one empire*, a challenger would have to overcome the nuclear capacities of the other great powers ... "[91] Notice that requirements for involvement have risen from the rise of a regional hegemon who must be able to rapidly take over a region to one that is "able to agglomerate the world's power under one empire."

These are unrealistic bars to American engagement. They would literally require the emergence of another Nazi Germany or Soviet Union out to conquer the world before the United States could gain neo-isolationist approval to reengage with the world. In this view, North Korean missiles capable of reaching the United States would not trigger "reengagement" because North Korea could not conquer Japan, South Korea, and China. Along similar lines, an aggressive Iranian theocracy armed with nuclear weapons would not be of concern so long as their missiles could not reach the United States. Another major problem with these litmus tests is that we won't know we have to deal with them until they have happened. It is this fact that leads to Art's criticism that neo-isolationism is essentially "a passive strategy."[92] In an age of catastrophic terrorism this is a recipe for disaster.

The Bush Doctrine has adopted a diametrically different approach. It has recognized that allies are the essence of a protective strategy. Therefore it doesn't abandon its partnerships, but tries instead to build on and extend them. Pakistan, Ethiopia, and India are state examples. The Proliferation Strategy Initiative, NATO's new mission in Afghanistan and the extremely multilateral and institutionally National Strategy to Secure Cyberspace are all policy manifestations of this stance. The Bush Doctrine takes the position that in an age of catastrophic terrorism, national security passivity is a form of suicide.

Varieties of Selective Engagement

Between supremacy and isolation lie numerous efforts to develop a mix of engagement and restraint. These strategies differ on America's role in the world, the role of American power, the circumstances and limits of that power's usefulness, how the United States ought to relate to its allies, and the psychological premises that underlie its strategic stance. To complicate matters, there are different accounts of this same basic strategy, and depending on the versions, the practical policy differences can be very profound.

Over time, these differences have made for provocative debates that have been a mainstay of professional books, conferences and journals. However, the many similarities of these strategies coupled with their profound differences and the lack of anything resembling a professional consensus about their utility make it hard to say just which strategy, or which version of it makes the most sense, if any, as a replacement for the Bush Doctrine.

The Nature of Primacy

The stance against which selective engagement takes issue is variously defined as hegemony, primacy, or preponderance. All three terms reflect the same basic fact: that the United States now enjoys enormous superiority over a range of strategic attributes, and no modern presidency has sought to do otherwise. That is certainly the thinking behind the Bush Doctrine's idea that U.S. military and economic power will discourage potential rivals from acquiring the means to challenge, and perhaps threaten, American interests.

In discussions about primacy a common confusion arises between the acquisition of power and its use. American primacy is consistent with a wide variety of political and partnerships arrangements. Primacy is consistent with empire, in which the hegemon simply rules the geography over which it has power. It is consistent with hegemony, defined as control or a dominating influence, which is used for enforcing "hegemonic stability."[93] It is, in theory, also consistent with a form of neo-isolationism that one could envision in which the United States maintains its military primacy but chooses to stand apart from the balancing strategies of other countries and regions unless they are direct threats to American national interest. It is also consistent with voluntary concerts of power, extensive multilateralism, military restraint and offshore balancing of various sorts.

The Clinton Administration tried combining primacy with a strategy of "engagement and enlargement,"[94] that encouraged rhetorical and practical efforts to further cooperative security with its allies. Those efforts floundered on the shoals of some difficult facts. Even cooperative security requires American leadership and this in turn requires substantial commitment of time, energy, and resources. The alternative to American leadership, robust and effective international institutions, was and remains an unaccomplished fact. Even before the Bush Doctrine, the Clinton Administration "discovered that international cooperation is not easy to arrange."[95] Issues such as economic policy toward Japan, the ethnic wars in Bosnia that splintered allied solidarity, and the issue of economic sanctions against Cuba, Iran and Libya made clear there are limits to "cooperative security."

Offshore Balancing: Three Versions

A chief candidate in any discussion about the future of U.S. foreign policy is offshore balancing. There are at least three different versions of this strategy. One is Stephen Walt's position that encourages robust American international leadership, applauds primacy noting that it is "the taproot of America's international influence, and the ultimate guarantor of its security."[96] However, he also urges various forms of restraint in the use of American power.[97] The major problem for Walt is how the United States can reconcile primacy with legitimacy.

The second version of offshore balancing is exemplified by the work of Christopher Layne. He views American primacy as an unnecessary historical legacy of World War II and the Cold War.[98] According to Layne, present American policy is based on the assumption that, "the international order will remain stable if the United States defends others' vital interests and would become disorderly and unstable if others acquired the means to defend their own interests."[99] In his view the United States plays the role of sheriff, but mostly for its allies and this leads to a major problem—overextension.[100]

The third version of selective engagement is put forward by Barry Posen.[101] Of the three major versions of selective engagement, Posen's version of it is much closer to the Bush Doctrine. In his view:

> Resources must be ruthlessly concentrated against the main threat [which is] the extended al-Qaeda organization and the states that support it. Al-Qaeda is an imminent threat. Other terrorist organizations, however, must be kept under surveillance and attacked preemptively if they seem ready to strike the United States or its allies in mass attacks, or if they appear intent on aligning themselves with Al-Qaeda.[102]

However, he has also recently argued that, "The United States needs to be more reticent about the use of military force; more modest about the scope for political transformation within and among countries; and more distant politically and militarily from traditional allies."[103] Thus Rosen seems to be trying to combine aspects of the Bush Doctrine for terrorists and their supporters and a version of selective engagement for other issues.

Basically, offshore balancing is a strategy that rests on the view that the United States need not have a military presence in every place in which it might have interests. Instead, Walt proposes that American troops be withdrawn from some places where they are no longer needed (Europe) and redeployed "over the horizon" in areas where they might be. In some cases, like Western Europe, that strategy makes sense because there is no longer the major threat of either a major great power war or a hegemon who would control the region through military occupation. In other areas like East Asia, American military presence would consist primarily of naval and air forces, while in the Persian Gulf, the United States would pursue a balance of power strategy "relying on local allies."[104]

. Just which state(s) would be America's local ally to contain and restrain a country like Iran is not clear. Certainly, it is unlikely to be Israel since Walt believes the United States should lean hard on Israel to settle the Arab–Israeli conflict on a resolve-it-or-else basis.[105] Saudi Arabia and Egypt are too domestically fragile and countries like Jordan are simply not strong enough. Moreover, it is not clear that being America's designated proxy is a large improvement, from the standpoint of reducing local tensions.

A similar problem arises elsewhere as well. In Asia, as in other regions, a smaller American footprint might be "reassuring," but states located in dangerous neighborhoods might be made quite anxious. Would Japan or South Korea prefer more autonomy to deal with China and North Korea? Japan is slowly reemerging from its constitutionally required defensive military stance, while South Korea has been extremely reluctant to lean on North Korea to keep it from further developing its offensive nuclear weapons potential. The idea of proxies or surrogates is appealing, but there are some regional and international interests that the United States has to take the lead in helping to secure.

Offshore Balancing and Strategic Threats

The three versions of offshore balancing view America's major strategic threats very differently. Walt sees catastrophic terrorism as the major threat facing the

United States and his assessment is worth underscoring. Recall his warning that, "the repercussions for America's economy, civil liberties and foreign policy would be incalculable."[106] Note too his observation that, "*we might have little idea where or how to retaliate* … "[107] From the standpoint of prospect theory Professor Walt's theories, like President Bush's strategic worldview, are clearly operating in the domain of *catastrophic loss.* Walt believes that the chances of a regime giving or selling nuclear weapons to a terrorist group are "extremely remote."[108] On the other hand, he thinks the problem of catastrophic terrorism "may be America's single greatest foreign policy priority."[109] We have returned full circle here to the dilemma of the intersection of risk, uncertainty and consequences. The irony and the paradox here is the United States must focus on a low-magnitude high-consequence problem with policies that stir worldwide anxieties, opposition, and distrust.

Neither Walt nor Layne directly take up the strategy of "offensive realism" as a response to catastrophic terrorism that has placed military elements in a large number of countries worldwide pursuing terrorists and their allies. Walt seems ambivalent about force. He titles one of his sections "Mailed fist, Velvet Glove."[110] He is concerned that the United States use its power judiciously, "asking questions first and shooting later" and "abandoning" the policy of prevention.[111] He is keen to do this and more to reassure our allies, but he leaves the question of when the United States might need to use military force unexamined. He focuses on the second invasion of Iraq not only as a cautionary tale, but also as providing ample reason that, "preventive war will rarely (if ever) be a viable policy option."[112] One can certainly agree with the "rarely" part of his advice; it's the "if ever" that seems to foreclose an option that although difficult may become necessary.

Layne also seems ambivalent about force. On one hand he writes about offshore balancing post-9/11 that "international politics is also a self-help system in which each actor must rely primarily on his own efforts to ensure its survival and security and in which each can employ the means of its choice, *including force* to advance its interests."[113] Further, "the United States must retain its capacity of acting unilaterally in defense of its national interests."[114] This sounds like the analysis of "offensive realists" who see international politics as at bottom a life and death struggle. So, given his stance the question arises: what should the United States have done about a defiant Saddam Hussein in 2002? Layne recommends that instead of a "sledgehammer approach," the United States adopt "a finely calibrated strategy to remove Iraqi threats to U.S. security."[115] What does that entail? Well, "if the United States has good intelligence, these targets [Saddam's weapons programs facilities] can be destroyed in precision air and missile strikes." Moreover, "by developing a full range of intelligence and covert operation capabilities, the U.S. can sabotage Iraq's (or any other hostile state's) weapons of mass destruction program by interdicting the flow of key components and materials, destroying plants and facilities, and eliminating the scientists and engineers without whose expertise such weapons could not be developed."[116]

Layne the realist appears to have succumbed here to some wishful thinking. As noted, good intelligence is hard to come by in closed societies, as the mistakes of many intelligence agencies worldwide demonstrated before the 1991 and 2003 Iraqi invasions. And, even assuming that facilities could be found, an attack or a series of attacks would constitute an act of war. It seems unlikely that the United States would be able to muster international legitimacy for military force by appeal to the anarchic nature of the international system.

There is also the problem of stopping the flow of NBC materials. The Proliferation Defense Initiative has attempted to fill this gap, but it is far from leak proof. The United States stopped and was forced to release a ship carrying missile components because it did not have legal authority to impound them. More difficult, are countries that provide dual-use technology or even nuclear plants that give critical technical knowledge and experience, as well as fuel by-products that can be used for weapons purposes. A "full range of intelligence" won't be of much help here. Finally, there is Layne's suggestion that we "eliminate" the scientists and engineers that work on such projects. It is unclear how Pakistan would react to the United States reaching in and "eliminating" scientists like A.Q. Kahn, but one suspects not well. Countries worldwide are likely to have an adverse reaction to such a policy and the targeted country may well consider this an act of war.

Layne's post-9/11 recipes for offshore balancing are based on "burden shifting," rather than "burden sharing."[117] He does not want the United States to discourage the rise of new regional great powers because not discouraging them will reduce the "perception of U.S. threat."[118] On the other hand, many of our allies are likely to be more threatened by the rise of hegemons in their region coupled with a withdrawn United States. Here we come to another crucial distinction. Critics often recognize only the negative perceptual and emotional effects of American power. But that power cuts both ways. While the citizens of many countries disagree with American policies and in some cases are angry with them, it does not necessarily follow that they want less American presence. What they want is an American presence that supports their views of what ought to be done in one or another situation. Designing American foreign policy on the basis of what others would have the United States do to advance their interests would, in a number of circumstances, be very imprudent. Moreover, it is just as likely that the United States will garner criticism for doing too little (defined by others' expectations) as for doing too much. And as noted, in some dangerous regions the withdrawal of the United States will create anxiety not reassurance.

Layne mentions that China, the European Union and Japan are rising great powers. Further he argues that, "Russia, China, Iran and India have a much greater long-term interest in the regional stability in the Persian Gulf/Middle East than the United States."[119] So, we should withdraw and let a "hundred great powers bloom." But this is a recipe for conflict and instability as those nations jockey for a better "balance of power." Layne says that one of the benefits of offshore balancing, allowing regional powers to rise and letting them sort through a balance of power without U.S. involvement is that it will make the United States less of a target of hostility. After all, "Iran and Iraq aligned against the United States" "because they resented intrusion into regional affairs."[120] That may be true but the United States became regionally involved because of its own clear national security interests and those still exist. And it does seem somewhat inconsistent to argue that the United States should leave the matter to others, while at the same time proposing air and missile strikes on the facilities of a country and assassinating their scientists and engineers if we feel such actions are warranted.

Posen, as noted, has few qualms regarding the tough measures needed given the threat. He writes "while diplomacy looms large in this struggle … The United States must be prepared to bypass national governments should they fail to cooperate." Given its ruthlessness, "the United States can't allow al-Qaeda sanctuary *anywhere*."[121] And what about states that support our enemy, either covertly or overtly? He writes, "to deter national armed forces from getting in the way, or to foil them if they try, the United States must maintain a strong conventional military capacity." In one among a number of bold statements Posen argues that "direct support of terrorists who try to kill large number of Americans is tantamount to participation in the attack."[122] So in that sense, such states are perhaps "either for us or against us" in the war on terror.[123]

He also argues that, "*Occasionally, it may be necessary to engage in conventional wars with such countries.*"[124] Moreover, "when a regime has close relationship with terrorists, it is reasonable to treat the host nation as an ally of al-Qaeda and an enemy of the United States." The United States "must be prepared to wage war against such states to destroy terrorist groups themselves, to prevent their reconstitution by eliminating the regimes that support them, and to deter other nation states from supporting terrorism." This is strong policy medicine for difficult times. Surprisingly, it is one of the only such *direct* statements on the sometimes necessity of force that one finds in discussions of Bush Doctrine replacement strategies.

Conclusion

Critics are unanimous that the Bush Doctrine must go, but the proposed substitutes are many and their recommendations contradictory. Walt and Layne, while both selective engagement theorists remain far apart in their views of the risks that face the United States and what to do with them. Posen identifies as a selective engagement theorist, but his views seem to fit very comfortably with the strategic assumptions of the Bush Doctrine.

Seeking a viable replacement for the Bush Doctrine is no easy matter once you get past the generalities. Stephen Walt is absolutely right about the importance of restraint in the use of force, but restraint is a paradoxical policy. It can reassure some of our allies some of the time, but there are likely to be circumstances when they will wish us to be more forceful than circumspect. On the other hand, as noted, the Saddam Husseins of the world see withdrawal and hesitation as weakness.[125] For leaders with this psychology, reassurance acts to affirm that the United States lacks the will that underlies staying power.[126] Far from leading to a more hospitable world, such a posture invites threatened allies to accommodate and make their own peace with our enemies. In so doing they can hardly, at the same time, be counted upon to be our regional proxies.

Offshore balancing is an attractive option, but some versions require the United States to incur high costs. Among them the dismantling of partnerships that have taken decades to develop. Liberal institutionists focus for the most part on economic and political international institutions, but military grouping like NATO and SEATO also serve political community building functions as well. In abandoning them, the United States would be leaving the balance of power in dangerous regions to the dynamics of great power competition, a dangerous policy by itself. It would also be abandoning the decades of partnership that hold out the hope and occasionally reflect the reality of, a number of countries coming together with common interests to protect and expand the liberal international order. Offshore balance theorists seem divided between dismantling and enhancing our regional alliances. They also seem not to have resolved the dilemma of what to do about catastrophic terrorists and very dangerous regimes that aren't amenable to persuasion, reassurance, or even deterrence.

It is certainly necessary to be cautious about the use of force. It exacts terrible costs on the society that uses it, those against whom it is directed, and those countries and people caught in these circumstances. The United States is caught between the sometimes-strategic necessity of force and the moral and legitimacy dilemma that always arises with force's use. One can view the ambivalence that results as a sign of moral strength and no society, least of all a democratic country that aspires to international leadership, can or should use force lightly. But use it sometimes they must.

Neither selective engagement nor off-shore balancing theorists reached any accord regarding these critical questions. Neo-isolationists seem very out of touch with the strategic realities that face the United States. None of these theories provide comprehensive alternatives to the Bush Doctrine. All of these grand theories suggest prudence and restraint in varying degrees, but only Posen and Walt address the hard questions of when restraint is dangerous.

It is unlikely that controversies surrounding the Bush Doctrine will be resolved by academic debates. They will be resolved, if at all, at the level of America's political leadership. And here the disagreements are very deep. Such disagreements are very worrisome because political leaders are, after all, the ones charged with the actual stewardship of American national security and also play a critical role in explaining and developing public consensus. It is to these great political divides that we now turn.

Part III
The Politics of Post-9/11 National Security

9 The Politics of Risk Assessment

The continued safety of the United States depends on assessing the risks of dangerous regimes and non-state actors. It also requires being able to make that case, if necessary, both domestically and abroad. The quality of the available evidence is important in being able to effectively do so, but so is the credibility of those making the case. Here the United States in general and President Obama are swimming against a very strong perceptual tide. The Bush Administration's credibility was badly damaged by the failure to find hidden stockpiles of weapons of mass destruction (WMDs) in Iraq, even though that intelligence error was not the United States' alone. The administration's judgments regarding post-Saddam Iraq War policies were also badly mistaken though, as noted in Chapter 1, positions on both sides of the key debates had their merits. Others have charged the administration with intentionally distorting intelligence data to further its war aims As a result, the administration has been opened up to charges of poor judgment, bad policy, avoidable error, and misrepresentation. Yet, it would be a serious mistake to conclude that this country's international credibility problems can all be laid at the doorstep of the Bush Administration.

The Bush Administration found itself at the center of ferocious domestic and international debates about every aspect of its assessments of strategic risk and the information used to reach them. There have been controversies over the prelude to the 9/11 attacks, over pre-war intelligence regarding Iraq, and about post-invasion judgments. These controversies have definitely damaged the credibility of the administration. However, they have also damaged the credibility of this country more generally. The first was an intended target, the second collateral damage.

Similar charges of having manipulated and misused pre-war intelligence data have also been made about American's two closest allies, Tony Blair and John Howard. In both cases, the charges led to formal parliamentary inquiries. In all three cases, the formal inquiries did not support the charges made.[1] The fact that the same charges of misrepresenting evidence were made against all three leaders who strongly supported the war effort, though the specific charges differed, suggests that opponents of assertive national security stances that include the use of force when necessary, regardless of the administration in office, are trying to develop a new, powerful, and effective rhetorical weapon. It consists of requiring high levels of certainty that go well beyond the ordinary capacity of intelligence and analysis. Debates about presidential decisions regarding the use of force now turn on the standard of "smoking guns" rather than a preponderance of evidence and presidential judgment. Neither of the latter is exempt from error, but given that such evidence rarely exists in the circumstances where such judgments are likely to be made, this unrealistically high barrier is likely to cause continuing trouble for the United States.

The debates surrounding prewar intelligence are instructive not only because judging the various claims allows us to gain some traction on the question of the president's credibility on these issues. They are also important because they throw some light on the nature of intelligence assessments and the appropriateness of the new smoking gun standards. These new standards fuel skepticism that distorts the assessment of issues that we will examine shortly like the intervention of Iran in Iraq, or the state of North Korea's nuclear program. Yet, even in cases where the intelligence evidence and agreement about it is very strong, as is the case for the National Intelligence Estimates on the consequences of prematurely leaving Iraq, strategic perceptions and the politics that accompany them, still play an important and distorting role. All of these in turn have implications for the United States that will last well into the Obama Administration.

An Avalanche of Explosive Charges

Before the invasion of Iraq, Democrats and Republicans agreed that Saddam Hussein was a dangerous man and had to be removed.[2] As time passed the charge was made that the Bush Administration misrepresented, hyped, fabricated, misused, and otherwise misled Congress and the American people in the run-up to the war. These accusations in turn rested on numerous other accusations. Among them were that Mr. Bush was "obsessed" with Iraq from the earliest moments of his administration and thus determined to go to war regardless of the evidence; that Congress did not have access to all the information the president had (with the attendant implication that the president held back information that would have indicated there was no need for a war); that the Vice-President repeatedly and inappropriately visited the CIA and intimidated their analysts to come up with views that supported the administration; that there were important disagreements among intelligence analysts about such things as the possible use of aluminum tubing which, had they been sufficiently emphasized, would have changed Congressional support for the war; that documents about Iraqi attempts to obtain yellowcake from Niger were fakes and were known to be so early on but that Mr. Bush still said that Iraq had tried to obtain it in Africa; that Mr. Bush hyped the relationship between Saddam Hussein and al Qaeda; that he had said Saddam was an "imminent" threat; and that the administration tried to "smear" critics like Joe Wilson who (in Wilson's words) had "debunked the lies that led to war."

The main charge that Mr. Bush intentionally misled the country, the Congress and tried to pressure American intelligence assessments is simply not supported by the available facts. An exhaustive review in 2005 by the *Washington Post* found, "The administration's overarching point is true: Intelligence agencies overwhelmingly believed that Saddam Hussein had weapons of mass destruction, and very few members of Congress from either party were skeptical about this belief before the war began in 2003. Indeed, top lawmakers in both parties were emphatic and certain in their public statements."[3] The bi-partisan Robb-Silverman Committee "did not find any evidence that administration officials attempted to coerce, influence, or pressure analysts to change their judgments related to Iraq's weapons-of-mass-destruction capabilities."[4]

Nor did Mr. Bush inflate the threat posed by Saddam by claiming it was imminent. As noted in his 2003 State of the Union address, the president specifically rejected "imminence" as a justification for the Iraq invasion saying, "Some have said we must not act until the threat is imminent ... If this threat is permitted to fully and suddenly emerge, all actions, all words, and all recriminations would come too late." There are legitimate grounds for worry here. A gathering threat can become imminent very quickly, especially if it is unchallenged while it gathers.

There is ample evidence that members of the Bush Administration were wrong, or at least not on solid evidentiary ground in at least one of their assertions. It was not possible to verify from multiple independent sources the early intelligence that one of the hijackers Mohammad Atta had met with Iraqi officials in Prague.[5] Other administration assertions were factually true, but their implications were disputed. Mr. Bush did call attention to Saddam Hussein's support for terrorists (Abu Nidal) and terrorism (contributing large amounts of cash to the family of every suicide bomber who died killing Israelis). He also pointed out the possibility that Saddam had a cooperative relationship with al Qaeda. This view was inconsistent with the assumption held by some academics and intelligence analysts that Saddam was a secular ruler who distrusted Islamic revolutionary movements, and was unlikely to support groups he could not control.[6] The administration was skeptical that Saddam would not help a radical Muslim group because of ideology or issues of control. Their skepticism receives some support in view of Iran's aid to a wide variety of anti-American groups in Iraq including those that are antithetical to its fervent religious beliefs. The enemy of my enemy can be a useful ally, and given Saddam's grandiosity it is not clear he thought he couldn't control them.

Bob Jervis has made the point that, "Bush frequently used Saddam and 9/11 in the same sentence, which implied the former's involvement." "How else," he asks, "would something like half the country have come to believe – and still believe – that Saddam was involved in 9/11?"[7] An alternative explanation is that Mr. Bush was trying to draw the link between 9/11 dangers and the dangers of Saddam as the leader of a state that aspired to regional hegemony. At any rate, when the president was asked directly several times whether he thought Saddam was implicated in 9/11, Mr. Bush replied: "No." Yet, in spite of point-blank statements by the president half the public "still believes that to be true." Doesn't this suggest the American public reached its view for reasons other than administration insinuations?

These and other questions over the build-up to the war have led Chaim Kaufman to argue that, the administration knowingly "inflated the threat" of an Iraq–al Qaeda connection in its efforts to "sell the war."[8] However, his rhetoric here is itself somewhat inflated. He says that the administration argued that, "Hussein was personally responsible for assisting in the 9/11 attacks," and that it "invented" links between Saddam and al Qaeda.[9] The administration did note the (ambiguous) intelligence regarding the Atta meeting but never made the accusation Kaufman claims. Nor were the links between Saddam and al Qaeda "invented." The bi-partisan Congressional 9/11 Commission, the bi-partisan Silverman-Robb Commission, the British Butler Commission, and CIA Director George Tenant in testimony before Congress and in his book, *At the Center of the Storm*,[10] have detailed Iraq's many points of contact with al Qaeda and thus provided support for this assertion. The nature of that relationship remains elusive. Saddam did provide sanctuary to some al Qaeda elements and that was of course helpful to the terrorist group, but it also allowed Saddam a means of monitoring (and controlling?) it.

The Cognitive Sources of Pre-war Intelligence Errors

The errors that American intelligence agencies made, occurred not because of political pressure, suppression of facts, or fabricated evidence, but rather because of erroneous assumptions, confidence in the predictive power of past behavior, failures to consider alternative explanations, or to put aside favored ones. This is the conclusion of scholars who have examined the prewar intelligence assessment and the formal Senate investigation of the matter as well.[11]

These kinds of errors are well known to political scientists familiar with cognitive psychology and decision theory,[12] and can easily be found in numerous historical examples. To cite one example among many, in 1962 as the Soviets were shipping their missiles into Cuba, strategic assessments simply could not fathom that the Soviets would do such a risky thing. By solely concentrating on the risks, analysts neglected the possibility that the Soviets would see the move more as one of large potential gains.[13] Cognitive errors are ubiquitous and difficult to guard against, but they are of quite a different character than willfully manipulating intelligence to start a war under false pretenses.

One can take the view that the Bush Administration lied, manipulated, hyped, and invented threats to sell the war. An alternative and more plausible view, given the evidence, is that the Bush Administration came to an important and for them central insight into the catastrophic threats that faced the United States after 9/11 linking dangerous leaders and WMD technology. As a result, they came to the conclusion that Saddam was a very dangerous man, and had to be removed. The intelligence assessments about the state of Saddam's then current WMD programs we now know (but didn't know then), were in error. But the reports of documented contacts with al Qaeda, his aggressive behavior over decades in the region, and murderous behavior towards Iraqis, all led in the same direction.

No single piece of evidence was unequivocal. Every fact and claim had its critics. For the Bush Administration the clear preponderance of evidence— some of it partial, some of it put forward with high confidence, and much of it based on the facts of the historical record of Saddam's decades'-long history of aggressive behavior abroad and murderous behavior at home all led to the same judgment: Saddam's continuation in power represented unacceptable risks to the security of the United States. In those circumstances it is not surprising that information like that of the Atta meeting was not dismissed out of hand because it could not be verified by multiple sources. Nor did the administration have to believe that Saddam and al Qaeda had an operational relationship to worry about the implications of their history of contacts. Finally, the whole concept of "threat inflation" assumes that the "real threat" is much lower than presented, and this in turn relies on assumptions, inference, and counterfactuals.[14] Arguments that Saddam could be contained were inconsistent with evidence that sanctions were eroding, and in any event the possibility that Saddam *could* be contained was no guarantee that he *would be*.

Abundant evidence suggested that Saddam was dangerous and that doubtlessly exerted a strong inferential pull on the process of reaching a judgment that he had to be removed from power. However, the administration's behavior should not be assessed solely as a matter of perception and judgment, but a matter of command responsibility and leadership. Mr. Bush reached a judgment about Saddam and his sworn responsibility as President required him, after due consultation and debate, to act on that determination. Once that bridge was crossed, Mr. Bush did what most, though not all, presidents have done when they have reached the conclusion that the country faced a dire threat; they argued their case.[15]

That Mr. Bush did not give a nationally televised speech highlighting the specific caveats entered in the appendices of the overall intelligence judgments does not mean that he deliberately and dishonestly inflated a small threat into a much larger one.[16] Rather, he was a president trying to mobilize the country and the international community to a possibly lethal danger based on what he felt was a preponderance of evidence.

The analytical errors that led to faulty prewar intelligence are clear, as are their consequences for future American credibility. However, these difficulties have been compounded by the ways in which intelligence errors and the uncertainties of analysis have been utilized as a political weapon. Fred Hiatt, editorial-page editor of the *Washington Post*, writing about the charges of manipulating pre-war intelligence, notes something important enough to quote at length[17]:

> ... the more they dominate the public debate, the harder it is to sustain public support for the war. ... many Democrats would view such an

outcome as an advantage. Their focus on 2002 is a way to further undercut President Bush, and Bush's war, without taking the risk of offering an alternative strategy—to satisfy their withdraw-now constituents without being accountable for a withdraw-now position. Many of them understand that dwindling public support could force the United States into a self-defeating position, and that defeat in Iraq would be disastrous for the United States as well as for [Iraqi Vice President Adel Abdul] Mahdi and his countrymen. But the taste of political blood as Bush weakens, combined with their embarrassment at having supported the war in the first place, seems to override that understanding.

Hyatt's analysis suggests that a major political purpose of many charges made against Mr. Bush was to destroy the administration's credibility on its conduct of the war, from the decision to invade Iraq to how the invasion and its aftermath were carried out. The first set of charges were factually unfair, but succeeded in their political purpose.[18] The second set of criticisms were substantially merited and in combination with the first set of charges sent the president's approval rating plummeting.

Smoking Guns and the Assumption of Duplicity

We have entered a period in which any presidential assertion that is not capable of being backed up one hundred percent and has full consensus about it, is deemed an example of a pattern of already demonstrated bad behavior. We must honestly acknowledge the fact that this kind of evidence does not often exist in intelligence assessments. It is easy to ask many questions that have no definitive answers. Those unanswered questions can easily lead to doubts about accuracy. For some loud voices, the stance seems to be: if we can't say that it's totally true, it is likely to be false. For others, such doubts fuel suspiciousness and the imputation of nefarious motives. Chaim Kaufman's worry about threat inflation and the failure of the marketplace to stop misleading ideas seems to have a counterpart—a tendency to downplay real threats and avoid taking strong evidence seriously.[19] We can see both these dynamics at work in two contemporary examples: the debate over Iranian involvement in Iraq and assessments of North Korea's cheating on the agreement reached with President Clinton.

Iranians in Iraq

In December 2006 American forces captured several Iranians along with computer disks and emails that implicated them in helping to plan attacks on American forces.[20] The United States then announced that Iran was implicated in helping to make the most sophisticated and deadly roadside bombs. The evidence included, "an analysis of captured devices, examination of debris after attacks, and intelligence on training of Shiite militants in Iran and in Iraq by the Iranian Revolutionary Guard and by Hezbollah militants believed to be working at the behest of Tehran." Additional evidence came from the interrogation of "One of the detainees [who] has identified an Iranian operative as having supplied two of the bombs."[21]

The United States then presented physical evidence of its assertions when, "officials spread out on two small tables during a news briefing an array of mortar shells and rocket-propelled grenades with visible serial numbers that the officials said link the weapons directly to Iranian arms factories."[22] The report then added, "Because the elite [Iranian] Qods Force is involved, a senior military analyst said, the American intelligence community believes that the weapons shipments have been approved at the highest levels of the Iranian government."[23] In a preview of what actually happened, the story said, "Today's presentation of evidence is bound to generate skepticism among those suspicious that the Bush Administration is trying to find a scapegoat for its problems in Iraq and, some political analysts and White House critics believe, is looking for an excuse to attack Iran."[24]

With clockwork predictability, the next news story announced, "Skeptics Doubt U.S. Evidence on Iran's Actions in Iraq."[25] The *New York Times* reported that, "Representative Silvestre Reyes of Texas, the Democratic chairman of the House Intelligence Committee, suggested that the White House was more interested in sending a message to Tehran than in backing up serious allegations with proof." Nothing was said about the physical evidence that Iran was supplying deadly bombs into Iraq that were being used against American forces. Others didn't dispute the physical evidence, but rather its implication. George Perkovich, a nonproliferation specialist at the Carnegie Endowment for International Peace was quoted as saying, "I'm not doubting the provenance of the weapons, but rather, the issue of what it says about Iranian policy and whether Iran's leaders are aware of it."[26] In order for his view to be correct, a military arm of the Iranian government charged with carrying out highly sensitive missions like the training of Hezbollah and other terrorists groups, political assassination and subversion would have to be mounting a "rogue" operation against the United States providing the latter with a pretext for military action against Iran, a prospect that seems very unlikely. The United States government had already let the Iranian government know through third parties that it was aware of Iranian involvement in Iraq including the shipment of men and weapons. If the Iranians didn't know before then, it would certainly seem prudent on their part to find out after the United States issued "protests." Still, skepticism was not quieted.

The next line of skepticism to emerge focused on the relative contribution of the Iranian government involvement in making and shipping roadside bombs, if true, to strengthen the insurgency raging in Iraq. Wayne White a member of the Iraqi Study group was quoted as saying the two main engines of violence in Iraq were Sunni jihadists and Shiite militias and that, "whatever the Iranians are doing has to be like 1 percent of the problem."[27] Paul Pillar, called the physical evidence presented "anecdotal," and opined that, "Iran was not in back of particular attacks but rather supplied materials which was then used by others."[28] Lawrence Korb, of the progressive Center for American Progress said, "If Iran were to go away today, the situation in Iraq would not change dramatically."[29] However, roadside bombs had been directly responsible for the deaths of 170 Americans and wounded over 600 in the 2005–2007 period.[30] At the time they accounted for seventy percent of U.S. troop casualties.[31] As of 2007, two thousand seven hundred and fifty-five American solders had died in combat,[32] with a staggering two thousand and four killed by roadside bombs. Substantially decreasing the availability of these would seem to be a dramatic and important contribution to the war effort and to saving American and Iraqi lives.

In another news story that delved into the technical complexity of the roadside bombs anonymous critics were quoted as saying, "that *nearly* all the bomb components *could* have been produced in Iraq or somewhere else in the region."[33] One component however, clearly wasn't manufactured in Iraq or the region. The same article reported that, "the use of precision copper discs combined with passive infrared sensors amounted to 'a no-brainer' that the explosive components were of Iranian origin, because no one has used that sort of configuration except Iranian-backed Shiite militias."[34]

Joseph Cirincione, described in the article as a "senior vice president for National Security at the Center for American Progress, a liberal research and advocacy organization" was quoted as saying, "Iran may well be involved in the supply of these weapons, but so far they haven't proved it."[35] This quote directly raises one of the most difficult and increasingly politicized questions: what, exactly, is it that constitutes credible proof? The United States provided a wide variety of evidence—serial numbers linking the bombs with Iranian arms factories, specific engineering configurations that identify the bombs, the capture and interrogation of a captured insurgent who said he got his bombs from the Iranians, and captured computer disks and emails attesting to Iranian help to anti-U.S. forces. This seems like a very reasonable amount of evidence, and so it is unclear what the assertion "so far they haven't proved it" means, or what it would take, in the real world, to prove it.

The Revised North Korea Intelligence Assessment

One of the most vexing problems that will face the Obama Administration is what to do about dangerous countries that have acquired nuclear weapons. There are a number of countries that fit or in the future will fit into that category, although each country's degree of dangerousness must remain a matter of specific assessment.

Whether and to what degree one can trust those with whom one makes an agreement is a critical question. How reliable is the information on which you base your decision to go forward is another crucial matter. The nature of the regime and its history adds to the mix. All of these factors, and others played out in the controversy over the North Korean Nuclear assessment. It is a narrative with some lessons for the Obama Administration that would clearly like to reach some agreement with Iran concerning its nuclear program.

North Korea is a brutal dictatorship in which most power is in the hands of a mercurial leader. It is a poor country but one that nonetheless bristles with military hardware including medium-range ballistic missiles. It has exported missiles and other weapons to dangerous regimes; it is a country with a history of aggression, criminal activity, and has developed nuclear weapons. Its belligerent rhetoric is a standard tactical tool, but it would be imprudent to summarily dismiss it.

In 1994, the Clinton Administration signed an Agreed Framework in which North Korea pledged to freeze and "eventually dismantle" its plutonium-producing nuclear facilities—the United States was to provide five hundred thousand tons of heavy fuel oil every year through a consortium, largely funded by Japan and South Korea. At the time, North Korea was *believed* to have only a small supply of plutonium, enough for perhaps one or two weapons.[36] That same year, the CIA gave the President and Congress an assessment and said that North Korea had begun constructing a plant that would increase production to two per year.[37]

In 2002 the Bush Administration charged that the North Korean government had violated the agreement it had reached with the Clinton Administration by developing a secret program to produce enriched uranium. This was distinct from the plutonium-based nuclear weapons program that the CIA had focused upon in their assessments for the Clinton Administration. One difference between the two methods is that plutonium requires large, easily detected reactors, while the technology for enriching uranium is much smaller and easier to hide. Bush Administration officials said North Korea admitted to having the program,[38] but later denied doing so, but the Clinton-forged agreement collapsed. North Korea then reprocessed spent fuel rods—which had been monitored by U.N. inspectors under the 1994 agreement—to obtain the weapons-grade plutonium and exploded a nuclear device in 2006.

All parties agree that Pakistan sold North Korea upwards of 20 centrifuges to produce highly enriched uranium, a main fuel for atomic bombs. The North Koreans also tried to buy thousands of aluminum tubes in the early 2000s that CIA analysts thought suitable for building more centrifuges.[39] In May 2002, two Germans were convicted in Stuttgart for trying to ship twenty-two million tons of aluminum tubing to North Korea.[40] North Korea also bought one hundred and fifty tons of aluminum tubes from Russia in June 2002.[41] Richard Armitage, then Deputy Secretary of State, and a protégé of Colin Powell, said at the time that North Korea was "intent on going to a full-up production program" starting from "at least" February 2000.[42] Others thought this was not a "smoking gun" because the aluminum tubes "weren't strong enough and were very easy to get and not controlled."[43] Others believed that the United States was to blame for the breakdown of the agreement because it had never followed through with its responsibilities under the accord.[44]

The central question was not whether the North Koreans were trying to diversify their sources of fuel for nuclear weapons, which was a violation of the agreement, but "how far they had gotten."[45] John E. McLaughlin, a former director of central intelligence and the deputy CIA director in 2002 said, "At the time we reported this, we had confidence that they were acquiring materials that could give them the capability to do this down the road, but no one" he added, "said they had anything up and running. We also made clear that we did not have a confident understanding of how far along they were."[46]

It was with this background that the Bush Administration turned to six party talks to try once again to induce North Korea to give up its nuclear weapons production facilities. In briefing Congress about the administration's view of such talks, the chief U.S. intelligence officer for that country, Joseph R. DeTrani testified that the agency had "high confidence in what it said" that North Korea had acquired materials that could be used in a "production scale" uranium program, but had only "mid-confidence that such a program exists."[47] This differed from a statement President Bush had made in a 2002 presidential news conference, "And then we discovered that, contrary to an agreement they had with the United States, they're enriching uranium, with the desire of developing a weapon. They admitted to this."[48]

That difference sparked heated debate and accusations. *New York Times* reporters wrote, "But now, American intelligence officials are publicly softening their position, admitting to doubts about how much progress the uranium enrichment program has actually made."[49] The phase "but now" suggests there were no doubts when Mr. Bush made his statement, but that is inaccurate in two ways. The 2002 CIA report to the president and Congress, highlighted the uncertainty, reminding readers that North Korea's nuclear program was "a difficult intelligence collection target."[50] The central question, though, was not *whether* North Korea has a nuclear weapons program, but the amount of progress it was making on it. At the time that this story broke, the office of the Director of National Intelligence declassified a portion of the then most recent, one-page update circulated to top national security officials regarding the status of North Korea's uranium program. That assessment said that the intelligence community still had "high confidence that North Korea has pursued a uranium enrichment capability, which we assess is for a weapon."[51] The administration had made a detailed presentation of its evidence to North Korea in 2004.[52]

Administration critics were quick to assume the worst. The *Los Angeles Times* wrote an editorial urging the administration to "come clean on North Korea"[53] which portentously noted, " ... for the second time, serious questions have been raised about the credibility of U.S. assessments of the potential nuclear threat posed by an enemy nation." Echoing the critics' view of Iraqi pre-war intelligence, they further asked, "Did the Bush administration rush to provoke a crisis with North Korea on sketchy evidence, trashing a flawed but workable arms-control agreement? Did they 'spin' the intelligence to justify preordained policies?" And Selig S. Harrison, writing in *Foreign Affairs,* accused the administration of "misrepresenting and distorting the data"[54] basing his charges on what he felt was " ... the important distinction between weapons-grade uranium enrichment (which would clearly violate the 1994 Agreed Framework) and lower levels of enrichment (which were technically forbidden by the 1994 accord but are permitted by the nuclear Nonproliferation Treaty [NPT] and do not produce uranium suitable for nuclear weapons)."[55] He accused the administration of exaggerating and blurring the distinction between making weapons grade uranium (a clear violation) and "lower" levels of enrichment that were "technically forbidden" by the accord.

In the end Mr. Harrison did concede that, "Pyongyang clearly did violate that accord by pursuing uranium-enrichment efforts (however limited they may turn out to have been) and thus, technically, violated the 1994 Agreed Framework as well."[56] Mr. Harrison's phrasing here suggests that he had little real information on how limited these efforts were, but what are clear are his attempts to downplay the violations. Another anonymously quoted source minimized the breach this way, "it made no sense for the energy-starved North – which is to get the equivalent of up to 1 million tons of heavy fuel oil under the nuclear disarmament deal – to run such a program consuming record amounts of power at a time it was making good progress on its plutonium-based arms program."[57] In other words, since North Korea was making good progress on cheating on the agreement using plutonium, it made no sense for them to also cheat by developing a uranium-based program.

Democratic Senator Jack Reed was quoted as saying that, "The administration appears to have made a very costly decision that has resulted in a fourfold increase in the nuclear weapons of North Korea."[58] His accusation reflects the view that since North Korean did not have, or get very far, with a secret uranium program, calling off the accord reached by the Clinton Administration was wrong. He added that if the decision to stop implementing those accords, "was based in part on mixing up North Korea's ambitions with their accomplishments, it's important."[59] It is unclear why a finding that North Korea cheated on its agreement obligations should have been ignored because they didn't get as far as they were trying to get at the time they were caught.

While the administration never publicly articulated its strategic reasoning, it is easy enough to surmise. Cheating on this agreement undermined the development of trust and confidence necessary for any such accord to succeed. Moreover, given that the agreement covered issues with very strong national security implications the most pressing issue was clearly not whether the North Koreans would continue to be rewarded with the benefits required by the agreement in spite of failing to keep their side of the bargain. A much more serious matter was the potential for North Korea to clandestinely develop and expand their nuclear arsenal altering the regional and perhaps the international balance of power. It is important to keep this in mind when dealing with the Iranians and Syrians.

Part of the real story embedded in the North Korean assessment is an old one. The ability of intelligence agencies to discern "the precise status of foreign weapons programs" is extremely limited.[60] These barriers are most likely to be present in the very societies that are the chief countries of concern. As another analysis put it, "Broad assessments often hinge on detailed information about equipment, which can be difficult to prove."[61] The failure to "prove" detailed information can cut two ways. It can push presidents to undertake higher risk operations as the Bush decision to invade Iraq demonstrates. Or it can be the rationale for not taking action when other policies are preferred. Secretary of State, Hillary Clinton, in discussing why North Korea's possible secret uranium enrichment program should not stand in the way of diplomatic engagement said in an interview, "I think that there is a sense, among many who have studied this, that there may be some program somewhere, but no one can point to any specific location nor can they point to any specific outcome of whatever might have gone on, if anything did."[62] It seems clear that the essentially ambiguous nature of intelligence lends itself not only to taking too much risk when less would be prudent, but also taking on more risk by downplaying information that may interfere with preferred policy options.

Critics did not inquire *why* the intelligence estimate about North Korean progress on developing uranium enrichment facilities had changed from "high" to "mid" confidence. A number of reasons might be possible including: the lack of inspectors in the country, the effectiveness of administration sanctions or the Proliferation Security Initiative in helping to dry up such activities, or the improved ability of North Korea to hide its efforts.[63] It is also very possible that North Korea ran into technical difficulties that forced them back on their more successful plutonium-based weapons. It was clear that North Korean purchases from Pakistan and other efforts were designed to circumvent the agreement reached with the Clinton Administration. Critics never addressed the issue of how an administration ought to approach a regime like North Korea after it was found to have substantially violated such accords. Treating such a violation as "technical" has the effect of defining compliance down. In blaming Mr. Bush for North Korea's nuclear test, critics seem to be blaming the victim. It was the United States after all that was cheated on.

It is certainly possible for the administration to have continued fulfilling its part of the agreement in spite of the breach. However, to do so North Korea would have had to admit and cure it. Since it never did the first, it would have been difficult for the United States to assume the second. Moreover, to continue the breached agreement would have put the United States in the paradoxical position of supporting the regime's secret efforts by providing fuel and freeing up North Korea's small foreign currency reserves to go nuclear shopping. As was the case with prewar Iraq intelligence and the meddling of Iranians in Iraq, the North Korea intelligence debate underscores a number of tendencies that are corrosive to both national security debates and American legitimacy.

The first is the failure to acknowledge the limits of intelligence assessment in countries that it is very difficult to penetrate. These difficulties are common knowledge among professionals and they ought to be the guiding underlying frame of any reporting and analysis of such debates. Analysis of these issues should also be framed by the reality that faces those charged with protecting the United States and its interests. They often *must* make decisions. They often do not have the luxury of time or a large margin of error, especially after 9/11. What is striking about the Iranian and North Korean examples is how little attention is paid to the strategic or national security implications of different courses of action—the risks and advantages involved in different possible strategic interventions. Instead, words are noted and compared and differences become the focus, not what might well be very legitimate reasons for reassessment. Or, differences between the evidence presented and the questions that still could be raised are treated as if the latter automatically discredit the former.

Exiting Iraq: Politics, Judgment, and the National Intelligence Estimate

We can see the dysfunctional mix of partisan differences, the limits of intelligence and analysis, and the need to make important national security judgments in spite of these limitations in the case of the administration's surge plans in Iraq. With public discontent with the conduct of the war in Iraq mounting, Congress requested that the National Security Council provide it with a formal National Intelligence Estimate on the conflict. Portions of that 2004 report were leaked before it was officially delivered. The portion of the estimate that was leaked said that, "The Iraq conflict has become the 'cause celebre' for jihadists, breeding a deep resentment of US involvement in the Muslim world and cultivating supporters for the global jihadist movement."[64] As the news article describing this information put it, "Democrats seized on the intelligence assessment for new ammunition to criticize the Iraq war and Mr. Bush."[65]

The leaked estimate however, turned out to have reported only one small part of the overall National Intelligence Estimate (NIE) assessment, the part that would be most damaging to the administration. The assessment did say that the war had "increased Islamic radicalism, worsening the terror threat."[66] However, when the president declassified the full report, it turned out that the very next sentence said: "Should jihadists leaving Iraq perceive themselves, and be perceived, to have failed, we judge fewer fighters will be inspired to carry on the fight." That is, a defeat of the jihadists and their allies in Iraq would result in a decrease in the number and motivation of recruits. That finding is important because it is linked to another namely, "that activists identifying themselves as jihadists, although a small percentage of Muslims, are increasing in both number and geographic dispersion."[67] As a result, if this trend continues, "threats to US interests at home and abroad will become more diverse, leading to increasing attacks worldwide."[68]

However, the heart of the NIE assessment concerned the consequences of failure in Iraq. It read:

> **Coalition capabilities, including force levels, resources, and operations, remain an essential stabilizing element in Iraq.** If Coalition forces were

withdrawn rapidly during the term of this Estimate, we judge that this almost certainly would lead to a significant increase in the scale and scope of sectarian conflict in Iraq, intensify Sunni resistance to the Iraqi Government, and have adverse consequences for national reconciliation.

If such a rapid withdrawal were to take place, we judge that the ISF would be unlikely to survive as a non-sectarian national institution; neighboring countries—invited by Iraqi factions or unilaterally—might intervene openly in the conflict; massive civilian casualties and forced *population displacement would be probable;* AQI would attempt to use parts of the country—particularly al-Anbar province—*to plan increased attacks in and outside of Iraq;* and spiraling violence and political disarray in Iraq, along with Kurdish moves to control Kirkuk and strengthen autonomy, could prompt Turkey to launch a military incursion.[69]

The major consequences that the NIE estimate points to are the likely disintegration of Iraq into warring factions backed by outside parties leading to outside interventions and the massive destabilization of the Middle East. It would be a humanitarian disaster of the highest order, and the Sunni heartland would be used to launch terrorists attacks "in and outside" of Iraq. Every one of these consequences has enormous implications for American national security and those of its allies both in the Middle East and elsewhere.

It is relevant to note that the 2005 NIE Iraq assessment was derived from a new and much more rigorous analytical process taking into account past criticisms.[70] And, given the controversy that has surrounded caveats on other NIE estimates regarding Iraq, it is also important to note that the finding was reached and presented with a "high degree of confidence," code words for substantial and deep interagency agreement. Nonetheless, issues regarding the analysis were raised.

Democrats complained in Congressional hearings about the lack of alternatives in the NIE estimate.[71] Senator Feingold wrote to Mr. Negroponte about, "Setting up a false choice between indefinite military involvement and a rapid, unplanned withdrawal distorts the current debate in Congress and in the country about how best to defend our national security interests in Iraq."[72] Mr. Negroponte replied that the analysis had come from analysts developing the questions posed to his office by Democrats, namely, whether the presence of coalition troops was a major cause of violence in Iraq.[73] Senator Rockefeller complained that there was no definition of "rapid" and added that the inclusion of the effects of rapid withdrawal, "took us back to days we are trying to get away from," when the White House was accused of "misusing intelligence."[74] National Intelligence Council Chairman Thomas Fingar, who supervised production of the NIE, responding to pointed questions from Senator Bayh, told the Senate panel that "unquestionably and categorically" there had been no political pressure to shape the estimate.[75]

The formal NIE Iraq assessment was not the only one to reach this conclusion about the dangers of withdrawal. In a report published by the left-center

Brookings Institution, Daniel Byman and Kenneth Pollack, two Middle East analysts with long intelligence assessment experience, developed a detailed analysis of some consequences of an American withdrawal and failure in Iraq.[76] The report states unequivocally "We found that much of what is considered 'conventional wisdom' among Westerners about how to handle civil wars is probably mistaken. For instance, we found little to support the idea that the United States could easily walk away from an Iraqi civil war—that we could tell the Iraqis that we tried, that they failed and that we were leaving them to their fates. We found that 'spillover' is common in massive civil wars; that while its intensity can vary considerably, *at its worst it can have truly catastrophic effects; and that Iraq has all the earmarks of creating quite severe spillover problems.*"[77] Finally General Barry McCaffrey (Ret.), a strong critic of administration policies in Iraq said, "Failure in Iraq at this point could generate a regional war among Iraq's neighbors that would imperil U.S. interests for a decade or more."[78] The consensus among national security professionals on this matter could hardly be clearer.

The Brookings report dealt primarily with the concrete consequences of a rapid redeployment of American troops out of Iraq before stability has been achieved. Neither report however, dealt with the psychological consequences of failure. It can be reasonably assumed that a rapid American departure from Iraq resulting in any number of the dire consequences that were predicted by the NIE and the Brookings Institution studies would have had very adverse effects on the United States, its allies, and the region. Certainly regimes and groups would take note of America's decision to leave Iraq before establishing minimum stability. They would have known that the United States had been warned about the consequences of premature withdrawal and decided to do so anyway. And this would have had negative implications for American credibility and the range of strategic tools that depend on credibility that includes not only capacity, but also will, and staying power.

A premature withdrawal leading to the difficulties described above would have affected the American public as well. Many would have been relieved that the United States was no longer heavily involved in a brutal and complex war. Yet, given the likelihood of humanitarian disasters, regional conflict spillover, and the implications for instability in this vital region, feelings of relief would likely have been accompanied very quickly by anxiety and calls to "do something." Though once a country disintegrates, it is very hard, if not impossible to reconstitute it, as the United States learned on occupying Iraq after Saddam Hussein's decades of allowing his country to decay.

Conclusion: A Divided Future for American National Security

On March 20, 2007 the Democratic Congress passed a bill in the House requiring the end of the major U.S. mission to Iraq by August 31, 2008.[79] Two hundred and sixteen Democrats of all ideological persuasions voted for the bill, fourteen Democrats voted against it. A number of Democrats who voted against the bill (cf. Kucinich, Lewis, Waters) did so because it didn't go far enough in immediately cutting off funds for the war. It is therefore legitimate to say that the bill and the provisions within it represent the "center of gravity" of the Democratic Party on this vital national security issue.[80]

The NIE and Brookings assessments about the damaging consequences of a failure in Iraq had been circulating in Congress and elsewhere for some time. Yet, this powerful analysis did not become the basis for a bi-partisan agreement for staying committed to the continued stabilizing of Iraq because of American national security interests in that country and in the region, and therein lies its lesson.

The Bush presidency is over, but the deep divides surrounding national security worldviews are not. President Obama takes office with a clean slate regarding his national security decisions. And he begins his presidency, unlike how Mr. Bush ended his, with the presumption of good faith. Yet, the underlying differences in strategic views still are prevalent and powerful between the two parties and in the public at large and that is a topic to which we now turn.

10 The Politics of Post-9/11 National Security
A Profound Worldview Divide

That the United States faces dangerous and difficult national security choices seems obvious and finding the right strategic stance is of critical importance. Yet, for the most part our national debate about national security has been episodic, disjointed, and highly partisan. One result has been relatively little in-depth discussion and public education of the difficult choices that faced the Bush Administration after 9/11, choices that will also face President Obama.

The political arena is an essential, but less than ideal, forum for these kinds of debates. Public debates could function to lay out the basic choices the United States faces and the risks and advantages of the options that are reasonably available. When such debates occur, the public has a better understanding of the issues, the stakes, and what, if anything can be done about them. They would then be able to make more informed choices, cognizant of the dangers, risks, and opportunities involved in alternative broad policy initiatives. That is the theory, but not the fact.

The reality is that public debate often centers on the rise of this or that specific national security circumstance, during which the president is trying to explain *his* view of what should be done, and why. Strongly held national security convictions mixed with deep partisan attachments add to a toxic mix. Rarely do the debates over specific issues add up to a discussion of the overall perspective.

Mr. Bush had to respond quickly to a direct attack on the United States. There was little time to debate first principles or policies. That came later, over time, and the debate was heated, partisan and often nasty. Mr. Bush was a sometimes effective, on occasion eloquent, articulator of his policy reason. But that was the exception, not the rule. He was, as every president is, caught in the need to explain specifics, with the result that his general premises were lost from view for long periods of time. This created the gap that allowed others to articulate their premises which were basically that the Bush policies, almost each and every one of them were wrong. As a result, over time, President Bush and his policies suffered, but so did public understanding of some very essential issues.

President Obama takes office with a presumption of intelligence, good faith and moderation, characteristics never attributed to his predecessor. He has begun the national security part of his presidency by rhetorically distancing himself from the more controversial policies of Mr. Bush, while keeping options to make use of them open. He has also begun by articulating a declared policy of engagement and outreach. The discussion to date on that general initiative has been on the issue of whether it is ever prudent to talk with adversaries, but on that there is really no debate. Of course it is.

The real questions concern the risks, possible advantages, and limits of accommodation. The real questions concern just how hard the president is willing to push, if engagement doesn't bring about the hoped for results. And the questions underlying all of these issues are just how tough the president is willing to be on the issues that matter, and what he thinks those issues are. These questions cannot be adequately addressed until there is more of an administration record on these matters. Until that time debate will center on the specifics and they will be read as indicating more basic national security views and premises.

In trying both to develop and gain support for his national security policies President Obama will have to contend with many obstacles. Among them is the fact that the Bush years left the public exhausted by the harsh partisanship of the many debates surrounding his national security policies and left the public yearning for relief in the form of real bi-partisanship. That promise is one of the bases on which Obama won the presidency. But the tough reality is that the public itself is divided on many of the Bush Administration policies and on the premises that underlie them.

All presidents have a strategic worldview that heavily influences the policies they prefer. Yet, so does the American public and they have been and remain deeply divided. One of the things that presidents must do is to try to find a fit between their national security worldview and policies and the public's. Presidents try to accomplish this in different ways. They can try to achieve a rhetorical match that edits out or downplays important differences. They can try to match their policies with the range of what's publicly acceptable. Or, they can try to unequivocally state their views, the reasons for them and hope to bring the public along. Mr. Bush chose the last with some efforts to make use of the first. It is too soon to say anything definite about President's Obama choices here except that he has started out with a heavy initial emphasis on his rhetorical bridging skills.

What is clear is that he starts his presidency with a long-standing and deep public split on national security matters, one that echoes loudly within the confines of the two major national parties.

A Profound National Security Divide

Unlike the long and informative debates that accompanied containment policy after World War II, the Bush Doctrine has not been a vehicle for any bi-partisan consensus. Quite the opposite. The reasons can be traced to several factors: the urgent necessity for formulating a doctrine and translating it to action after the

9/11 attacks; the president's leadership style; partisan considerations; and the fundamental chasm between the basic national security worldview, framing, and understanding of the nature of risk post-9/11 by Democrats and Republicans. In that bubbling cauldron of discussions of the Bush Doctrine and its policies, are some of the most contested areas of contemporary American political life. They remain so, and it is useful to understand how they developed.

The First Fissures

Mr. Bush assumed the presidency in 2001 after a close and bitterly contested election that was only settled by the intervention of the Supreme Court. As a result, many felt that his presidency was illegitimate and became determined to oppose his policy initiatives. The result was a brutal, public and ongoing assault on Mr. Bush personally, and his administration, by those who doubted his capacity, competence, honesty, and motives. This group of Bush rejectionists found allies in the Democratic Party on a number of national security issues.

The center of gravity of the Democratic Party in national security matters has been solidly left center for many years. That leftward migration began when Democrats began to turn away from the Vietnam War and repudiated the president of their own party. It only increased with the nomination of George McGovern, whose campaign theme "Come Home America," perfectly captured the preference of many Democrats and the foreign policy theorists who supported them. They wanted to take care of pressing domestic needs rather than become involved in foreign wars that squandered precious resources that they thought were better used at home. That theme, as noted, has found a voice in academic grand theories that advise withdrawal from all of America's military alliances in favor of a focus on domestic needs.[1]

To the extent that Democrats in positions of national responsibility did support American engagement in the world, their preferred stance was liberal internationalism. They saw America's strength as resting on its relationships with its allies and in building strong international institutions. America might take the lead, but always as a member in good standing of its alliances and international obligations. Force is a last resort for liberal internationalists. In the past, when it had to be used, Democrats insisted that it must be used sparingly, precisely, and legitimately. Talking and reaching agreements were always preferable.

Not surprisingly then, Democrats had strong objections to a number of Mr. Bush's foreign policies pre-9/11. They objected to his withdrawal from the Anti-Ballistic Missile Treaty and his determination to build a missile defense system. They objected to his refusal to commit the United States to the treaty establishing the International Criminal Court and they criticized his refusal to sign on to the Kyoto Climate Accord. From the liberal international perspective, these criticisms made sense. After all, arms control agreements like the

Anti-Ballistic Missile (ABM) treaty, in their view, helped to stop wars. Signing on to agreements like the International Criminal Court and Kyoto accords demonstrated America's commitment to being a good international citizen.

The Bush Administration saw all these matters differently. The ABM treaty was not effectively preventing North Korea or Iran from developing missiles that could reach the United States or its allies. Being a good international citizen by taking the lead during natural disaster relief or helping to develop international institutions, did not keep the United States from becoming a target of politically motivated accusations and investigations. Such suits were not without precedent and indeed were filed as a consequence of American involvement in the Iraq War.[2] Giving others the ability to try and convict American field commanders and government leaders would inhibit the United States from its security responsibilities abroad, precisely the result that some hoped to obtain by making its action subject to the judicial judgment of the international community.

From Fissure to Chasm

Mr. Bush would have had a difficult foreign policy path even if 9/11 had not happened, but when it did his response exacerbated the deep strategic tensions between the two parties. The 9/11 attacks brought a brief truce between the administration and its Democratic critics, but it was inevitable that it wouldn't last given the president's response, leadership style, and strategic conclusions about the meaning of the attack.

Mr. Bush's leadership style, even in normal circumstances, is assertive, but 9/11 was anything but normal. In times of crises, leaders don't have time to consider or develop new styles. Mr. Bush's response, not surprisingly, was in that respect "typical" of his style but only more so. The administration operated on war footing. Plans and policies were developed and developed in a rush. Congress was informed and sometimes consulted, but not engaged, especially its Democratic minority. They soon began to complain about executive overreach and excess, and as early as June 2003, critics began to publicly complain about another "imperial presidency."[3]

Democrats and Republicans have battled over almost every aspect of Bush's policies. Democrats accused the president of not paying enough attention to terrorism before 9/11, with the implication that had he done so 9/11 could have been avoided.[4] They argued over the pace of progress during the invasion of Afghanistan. They disagreed over whether Saddam Hussein could have been contained by "smart" sanctions. They quarreled about whether the administration misled Congress and the American public in the run-up to the Iraq War. They have disputed dozens of specific policies having to do with the aftermath of the invasion, and they bitterly clashed over a timetable for the withdrawal of American troops. Since 9/11 they have repeatedly disagreed over what the United States should (and should not) do to protect itself, including the use of domestic spying on terrorist suspects and giving the rights that American citizens enjoy to enemies captured abroad.[5] Some Democrats argued that Bush should be censured,[6] others that he should be impeached.[7] Obama's AG says Bush officials may face criminal charges.

It is easy to attribute the national security divide to the Democrats' view that Mr. Bush was illegitimate, incapable and incompetent. However, this would be a mistake. The foundation of the divide is not to be found primarily in the close election of 2000, Mr. Bush's assertive leadership style, or even his trans-formational agenda—though these matters counted. The real differences reflect strategic worldviews.

The two views give different weight to the nature and level of post-9/11 risk. They have different views on the nature and importance of alliances and world opinion. They differ in the willingness to heavily count on international institutions for American national security. They differ in the amount of stock they place in negotiations and formal agreements. And differ in the degree of reluctance, ambivalence and the circumstances under which they would consider and use force.[8]

Liberal Internationalism: Strategic Worldview Premises

More than policy preferences separate Democrats and Republicans, liberals and conservatives, and hawks and doves. They are separated by quite different ways of seeing the world, different ways of framing what they see, and very different sets of risk calculations associated with them.

Clashing Strategic Worldviews

Stretching back for many decades it is clear that our two political parties have simply coalesced around very different strategic worldviews. Oli Holsti's land-mark study of foreign policy opinion made this very clear. Examining a variety of surveys and groups going back decades, Holsti confirmed that public and leadership opinion on foreign policy had become "far more partisan and ideo-logical."[9] Moreover, generally Republicans took positions consistent with the Bush Doctrine view of the importance of *assertive realism*, while Democrats took positions consistent with cooperative internationalism.

The specific strategic tools that each group favored were also clear. Repub-licans accorded their highest ratings to an approach with a strong *realpolitik* flavor, whereas Democrats favored liberal strategies for peace.[10] One of the most striking differences between the two groups concerned whether Amer-ican military superiority was an effective or ineffective approach to securing peace. Over half of the Republicans rated military superiority as a "very effec-tive" path to securing peace, while Democrats as a group rated military super-iority as the "*least* promising strategy for peace with only 15 percent of them giving it a 'very effective' rating."[11]

In some ways these distinctions mirror those between the grand strategies of liberal internationalism and traditional realism, or national realism. That is,

"Liberalism denies that conflict is an immutable element of relations between nations."[12] And, "it emphasizes the potential for cooperative relations among nations; institutional building to reduce uncertainty and fears and antagonisms based on misinformation and misperception, and the positive sum possibilities of such activities ... [to] mitigate, if not eliminate, the harshest features of international relations emphasized by the realists."[13] The center of gravity of the Democratic Party retains those premises to this day.

Realists of course see the world differently, but that is not really the core of the issue. The world is not all of one piece. It is not either inclined toward cooperation or, alternatively toward war. Which set of basic strategic world-view premises fits depends on the geography, circumstance and specific issues. Cooperation as a premise fits better in Western Europe than it does in the Middle East; is more easily applied to trade than deterrence, and seems very much less prudent as a premise post-9/11 than pre-9/11.

A Difference of Framing Perspectives

The Bush Administration started out pre-9/11, framing national security in the domain of loss, somewhere between *dire* and *undesirable*. In essence, it began by framing national security issues with the cognitive premises of the realist position: the world is a dangerous place, alliances are useful but not always dependable, and reliance on the international community on matters of important national security issues is naïve, foolish and dangerous. From this perspective an ABM system made good sense, an ABM treaty didn't. There are risks associated with such a view. Some countries may resent us, others may seek to counter our policies in a variety of ways, and our assertiveness may wind up provoking the insecurities and possible rash actions of the very countries we seek to dissuade. These risks are balanced by the consequences of being caught unprepared or unaware.

Pre-9/11, Democrats and their liberal allies seemed to frame national security issues somewhere between the domains of *success* and the domain of undesirable, but *tolerable loss*. That is, national security risks were present, but not dire and America's many advantages could be leveraged through reliance on our allies and the strengthening of international agreements and institutions to mitigate, if not overcome them. Our adversaries could be induced to give up their aggressive aspirations by a combination of discussions, reassurance and carrots.

This view too carried risks. Signing treaties might not really bind dangerous countries or leaders. Allies might have interests other than ours. And a less assertive national security stance might heighten the dangers of another attack. Yet, all these risks were considered manageable and worth taking. In prospect theory, as noted, potential losses carry more psychological weight than potential gains and the increased likelihood of certain losses stimulates risk-acceptant behavior to avoid them. The realist perspective, adapted by the Bush Administration, framed national security matters in terms of potential loss and most certainly did so to an even greater degree after 9/11. Naturally, they are willing to take the risks associated with a more assertive stance to help insure that damaging losses didn't occur.

Perhaps less obvious is the fact that liberal internationalists and Democrats who put their faith in allies, treaties, and accommodation are also apparently quite willing to accept substantial national security risks, although their position is rarely framed that way. Their primary risk is that their optimism will prove unfounded or naïve and United States security will suffer.

The 9/11 Reframing

The 9/11 attacks didn't change Mr. Bush's national security worldview but they did reframe it. The attacks validated a central realist premise by proving, once again, that the world not only *could be* a dangerous place, but also *was* in fact dangerous. As the intersection of terror and technology came into sharper focus, it became clear that being caught unaware and unprepared was not only dangerous but also potentially lethal. Certainly, it was a possibility that the United States could not afford to ignore.

The 9/11 attacks also modified and reframed Mr. Bush's assessment of risk. In a world that now had demonstrated itself to be very dangerous and perhaps lethal to the United States, the level of the domain of risk that the United States operated in changed dramatically as well. In Chapter 5 I suggested there were three levels in the domain of loss for national security issues: *catastrophic*, *dire* and undesirable, but *tolerable losses*. Before 9/11 the general default position of the national security realists, like Mr. Bush, could be said to range between dire and undesirable but tolerable. The 9/11 attacks pushed the basic setting of the president's cognitive framing directly to catastrophic.

The 9/11 attacks also seem to have dramatically softened, if not reversed, the president's opposition to nation building. His conclusion that more democracy was an antidote to the more radical strains of Muslim thought and anti-Americanism led naturally to the idea that democratic transformation, a form of national development if not nation building, was a viable and important strategy. I am *not* arguing here that Mr. Bush viewed every foreign policy issue through the lens of catastrophic risk, only that he viewed the risk of catastrophic terrorism as an absolutely essential element in the quest to preserve American national security. And he then acted in ways consistent with that view of the risks and stakes involved.

A degree of reframing took place as well in Democratic and liberal circles. Most foreign policy professionals and political leaders in this group supported the regime change in Afghanistan. Where they began to draw a line of debate was over the wider war on terrorism, the assertive rhetoric of the administration, domestic security issues, and increasingly after most Democrats had voted for it, regime change in Iraq.

A clear illustration of those differences in risk framing and assessment between the strategic center of gravity of the Bush Administration and those of the Democratic Party can be seen in the views of presidential candidate John Kerry. In an interview on foreign policy given by Mr. Kerry during the 2004 presidential campaign to Matt Bai of the *New York Times*, Kerry said that to make America safe "requires destroying terrorists and I'm committed to doing that."[14] Yet Mr. Bai goes on to point out that the differences between Bush and Kerry were "profound."[15] "Bush casts the war on terror as a vast struggle that is likely to go on indefinitely, or at least as long as radical Islam commands fealty in regions of the world." Kerry "displayed a much less apocalyptic worldview." He said of terrorism,

> We have to get back to the place we were, where terrorists are not the focus of our lives, but they're a nuisance. As a former law-enforcement person, I know we're never going to end prostitution. We're never going to end illegal gambling. But we're going to reduce it, organized crime, to a level where it isn't on the rise. It isn't threatening people's lives every day, and fundamentally, it's something that you continue to fight, but it's not threatening the fabric of your life.

One way to understand the differences between Kerry and Bush is to see how they frame the problems with regard to potential risks and where in the domains of losses or gains they place it.[16] Mr. Bush clearly is placing the threat in the domain of *catastrophic losses*, while Mr. Kerry seems to place it in the category of undesirable but *tolerable losses*, or perhaps given his use of the word "nuisance" in the gains domain of possible *success*. These different domain placements reflect different strategic worldviews as well for both the individuals involved and the center of gravity in national security matters for their respective political parties. They also have important implications for the stance taken to address these threats.

National Security: Democrats Tilt Left

Democrats have, since the Vietnam War tilted left on national security matters. Evidence of this can be found not only in the political rhetoric of their presidential candidates but also in examining the views of core voters who support them. For example, an in-depth study of those who supported Howard Dean for president showed that eighty-two percent of the activists said they were liberal, 16 percent were moderate, and just 1 percent were conservative.[17] Activists, of course, are the core supporters of a political party and accordingly exert a disproportionate pull on the party. This tendency becomes quite pronounced when major establishment figures in the Democratic Party who occupy high political offices are themselves from the liberal branch of the party.[18]

Survey data underscore the distinction between "left" and "liberal" on national security matters. Eighty-one percent of Dean supporters say preemptive war is rarely or never needed, while fifty-two percent of rank-and-file

Democrats chose those options.[19] Asked whether U.S. foreign policy should heed allied interests or be based mostly on U.S. interests, seventy-eight percent of Dean supporters and forty-nine percent of the rank and file chose allied interests. Asked whether diplomacy or military strength was the best way to ensure peace, ninety-six percent of Dean supporters and seventy-six percent of all Democrats chose diplomacy.[20]

What seems clear from these data is that liberal Democrats do differ from "all Democrats"; they are clearly more left leaning. Yet, it is also the case that Democrats as a whole (and remember that this sample includes conservative Democrats) are decidedly left-center. One gets a stronger sense of this by examining some further data on foreign policy. In August 2004, the Pew Center in collaboration with the Council on Foreign Relations published a comprehensive survey of American foreign policy views.[21] They found that for Republicans, terrorism was the number one problem, while the economy was the number one problem for Democrats (p. 7). So from the perspective of framing risk, Republicans frame foreign policy as primary, while Democrats saw domestic issues as primary.

Asked in late September 2001 whether U.S. wrongdoing might have motivated the 9/11 attacks, forty percent of Democrats said yes. By July 2004 that number had risen to fifty-one percent (p. 7). Asked whether the United States should either be the single world leader or the most active among nations sharing leadership, only twenty-nine percent of Democrats chose the single world leader option (p. 15). In October 2001, eighty-one percent of Democrats thought it very important to reduce the spread of nuclear weapons; by July 2004 that number had declined to sixty-three percent (p. 23). This finding perhaps owed something to the administration's rationale of stopping Saddam Hussein's further nuclear development.

When one examines the differences between Democrats and Republicans on a variety of national security issues, the differences are stark. In a 2005 Pew Research Center poll those differences were evident.[22] Asked whether the United States will succeed in Iraq, eighty-three percent of Republicans and forty-five percent of Democrats said "yes." Asked whether troops should be kept in Iraq until it is stabilized seventy-five percent of Republicans and thirty-eight percent of Democrats said troops should be kept. Asked whether the war in Iraq has reduced the chances of a terrorist attack fifty-nine percent of Republicans and fifteen percent of Democrats said "yes."[23]

Not surprisingly, strong partisan differences emerge over the administration plans to commit more troops to Iraq to stem the violence there.[24] A January 2007 Pew poll found that seventy-five percent of Republicans and twenty-nine percent of Democrats supported keeping American troops in Iraq. As to the need for more troops, forty-seven percent of Republicans and eleven percent of Democrats backed the president's "surge" plan. Strikingly, sixty-two percent of Democrats thought that Congress ought to try to block administration plans by withholding funding for additional troops. And even more strikingly, another poll asked respondents: "Do you personally want the Iraq Plan of President Bush to succeed?" Overall, thirty-four percent of Democrats said "no" as compared to eleven percent of Republicans and nineteen percent of independents.[25]

And finally, in a 2009 Pew poll, respondents were asked which would have the greatest effect on reducing the terrorist threat, military operations or diplomacy. Sixty-two percent of Republicans chose military operations, twenty-two percent of Democrats did so. A majority (sixty-two percent) of Democrats said *decreasing* the U.S. military presence overseas would have a greater impact in reducing the terrorist threat; half of independents agreed. By contrast, forty-eight percent of Republicans said that *increasing* the U.S. military presence abroad is the more effective way to reduce the threat of terrorist attacks.[26]

These are not novel findings, and that is precisely the point. In a period when America is clearly a target for terrorists who want to attack this country, most Americans wish to be protected.[27] The question that arises from these data is whether the stance of the Democratic Party and its allies on a range of specific national security issues are out of step with the general public.

A New Generation of Democratic Realists?

The first generation of neoconservatives started political life as strong defense Democrats. Intellectually, that group gathered around Henry "Scoop" Jackson (D-WA), a strong supporter of national defense and of containing the Soviet Union during the Cold War. The Democratic Party migrated leftward on defense issues during the 1960s, the presidential candidacy of George McGovern in 1972, and thereafter. Whether it was the migration of their party leftward, their own movement rightward, or a combination of both, neoconservatives as individuals and as a group found themselves political orphans within the Democratic Party.

Some members and supporters of the Democratic Party have been quite clear that the party has a "national security problem." George Packer, writing in the *New Yorker* about the Democratic Party's failure to be seen as seriously concerned with national security has characterized the dilemma as follows:

> The two complementary tendencies that doomed his [Kerry's] effort on Iraq have characterized Democrats since the war on terrorism began: on one side, the urge to take cover under Republican policies in order not to be labeled weak; on the other, a rigid opposition that invokes moral principle but often leads to the very results it seeks to prevent. Neither posture shows a willingness to grapple with the world as it is, to do the hard work of imagining a foreign policy for the post-September-11th era.[28]

Tough Talk is Easier than Hard Decisions

That failure to more completely understand the nature of the 9/11 experiences for most Americans and its implications for the Democrats is well captured in another *New Yorker* article on "toughness." In it, Senator Biden was asked what advice he would have given John Kerry. He replied, "I would say to John, 'Let me put it to you this way. The Lord Almighty, or Allah, whoever, if he came to every kitchen table in America and said, 'Look, I have a Faustian bargain for you, you choose. I will guarantee to you that I will end all terror threats against the United States within the year, but in return for that there will be no help for education, no help for Social Security, no help for health care.' What do you do? 'My answer,' Biden said, 'is that seventy-five per cent of the American people would buy that bargain.'"

Asked whether Democrats have a seriousness or toughness problem, John Kerry had another view, "Look, the answer is, we have to do an unbranding." By this he meant that the Democrats had to do a better job of selling to the American people what he believed was already true—that the Democrats are every bit as serious on the security issue as Republicans. "We have to brand more effectively. It's marketing."[29]

Some Democrats and their supporters recognize that beneath the problems of branding and marketing lie real problems of substantive policy choice. That is why several recent books have been written extolling the virtues of strength and forcefulness when necessary and urging Democrats to recognize that fact and integrate it into their policies. The titles are the message: *Hard Power: The New Politics of National Security*[30]; *With All Our Might: A Progressive Strategy for Defeating Jihadism and Defending Liberalism*[31]; and *The Good Fight: Why Liberals—and Only Liberals—Can Win the War on Terror and Make America Great Again.*[32] When Democratic Party pragmatists, progressives, and liberals make common cause with at least some of the underlying tenets and strategic worldview of the Bush Doctrine there is some cause for hope that a bipartisan consensus may emerge.

Still, as Peter Beinart, a senior editor at the *New Republic* and an author of one of the above-mentioned books has written, "Three years after September 11 brought the United States face-to-face with a new totalitarian threat, liberalism has still not 'been fundamentally reshaped' by the experience." Further, he argues, "there is little liberal passion to win the struggle against Al Qaeda."[33] Beinart traces the national security splits in the Democratic Party back through the beginnings of Cold War anti-communism. He believes that it is possible for the left to embrace the global fight against Islamic extremism without sacrificing, and perhaps even advancing, their progressive views. However, he offers no specific theoretical rationales or policy prescriptions other than investing in international institutions.[34]

The problem for the Democrats is that tough talk can only take the party and the country so far. The public gets its stance about the national security center of gravity by listening to the party's senior leadership and their proposals for specific national security issues. Candidates for major elective office help to define the party's stance. A clear illustration that tough talk is easier than hard decisions is provided by John Edwards, Democratic Vice Presidential candidate in 2004 and a presidential candidate in 2008. At a major national security conference in Israel, Mr. Edwards said:

At the top of these threats is Iran. Iran threatens the security of Israel and the entire world. Let me be clear: Under no circumstances can Iran be allowed to have nuclear weapons ... To a large extent, the US abdicated its responsibility to the Europeans. This was a mistake. We have muddled along for far too long. To ensure that Iran never gets nuclear weapons, we need to keep ALL options on the table, Let me reiterate – ALL options must remain on the table.[35]

"All options" in presidential discussions of national security issues is a code-word for military force, and Mr. Edwards seems quite clear. There are "no circumstances" under which Iran can be allowed to have nuclear weapons. The direct implication of that is also clear. If Iran went ahead and tried to develop such weapons it would be subject to military attacks. He also criticized and rejected Mr. Bush's multilateral approach to the issue. It would be hard to issue a more unequivocal threat.

A little over a week later Mr. Edwards gave a clarifying interview to the liberal opinion journal *The American Prospect*.[36] Asked about Iran, he said, "America should be negotiating directly with Iran, which Bush won't do. Second, we need to get our European friends, not just the banking system, but the governments themselves, to help us do two things – put a group, a system of carrots and sticks on the table." The carrot side is peaceful nuclear energy and an economic package. The stick side is, "to say if you don't do that, there are going to *be more serious economic sanctions than you've seen up until now. Now of course we need the Europeans for this,* cause they're the ones with the economic relationship with Iran."

What of the "all options on the table" assertion? Edwards rhetorically asks in that interview,

> what happens if America were to militarily strike Iran? Well you take this unstable, radical leader, and you make him a hero ... The second thing that will happen is they will retaliate. And they have certainly some potential for retaliating here in the United States through some of these terrorist organizations they're close to, but we've got over a hundred thousand people right next door ... And the third thing is there are a lot of analysts who believe that an air strike or a missile strike is not enough to be successful. To be successful we'd actually have to have troops on the ground, and where in the world would they come from?

The interview concludes as follows:

AP: So, I just want to get it very clear, you think that attacking Iran would be a bad idea?

JE: I think [it] would have very bad consequences.

AP: Can we live with a nuclear Iran?

JE: I'm not ready to cross that bridge yet.

There is a obvious similarity between Mr. Edwards' view and President Obama's view at least with regard to the tough talk about Iran. President Obama's view on Iranian nuclear weapons was very clear during the campaign. At the April 27, 2007 Democratic Debate he said that, "have no doubt, Iran possessing nuclear weapons will be a major threat to us—and to the region … " and further "But I think it is important for us to also recognize that if we have nuclear proliferators around the world that potentially can place a nuclear weapon into the hands of terrorists, that is a profound security threat for America and one that we have to take seriously."[37] At the Democratic Debate on September 26, 2007 he said, "I make an absolute commitment that we will do everything we need to do to prevent Iran from developing nuclear weapons," and further that "all of us [speaking of the other democratic candidates] are committed to Iran not having nuclear weapons."[38] In his first debate with Senator McCain on September 26, 2008, he said "Senator McCain is absolutely right, we cannot tolerate a nuclear Iran. It would be a game changer."[39]

At the Democratic Debate in Philadelphia on April 16, 2008 he repeated his pledge and could not have been clearer[40]:

> … our first step should be to keep nuclear weapons out of the hands of the Iranians, and that has to be one of our top priorities. And I will make it one of our top priorities when I'm president of the United States. I have said I will do whatever is required to prevent the Iranians from obtaining nuclear weapons. I believe that that includes direct talks with the Iranians where we are laying out very clearly for them, here are the issues that we find unacceptable, not only development of nuclear weapons but also funding terrorist organizations like Hamas and Hezbollah, as well as their anti-Israel rhetoric and threats towards Israel. I believe that we can offer them carrots and sticks, but we've got to directly engage and make absolutely clear to them what our posture is. Now, my belief is that they should also know that I will take no options off the table when it comes to preventing them from using nuclear weapons or obtaining nuclear weapons, and that would include any threats directed at Israel or any of our allies in the region.

President Obama's Stance on Iran

Yet, the president is also clearly in agreement with Mr. Edwards' preference for talking directly with Iran in order to reach some specific or overall agreement. In the January 31, 2008 Democratic Debate, Obama said that if we offer Iran "both carrots and sticks, they are more likely to change their behavior and we can do so in a way that does not ultimately cost billions of dollars, thousands of lives, and hurt our reputation around the world."[41] To what, specifically, did that phase "carrots and sticks" refer? One indication comes from an unusually detailed set of policy ideas that he gave in response to a question about Iran during the second presidential debate[42]:

> *if* we can work more effectively with other countries diplomatically to tighten sanctions on Iran, *if* we can reduce our energy consumption through alternative energy, so that Iran has less money, *if* we can impose the kinds of sanctions that, say, for example, Iran right now imports gasoline, even though it's an oil-producer, because its oil infrastructure has broken down, *if* we can prevent them from importing the gasoline that they need and the refined petroleum products, that starts changing their cost-benefit analysis. That starts putting the squeeze on them.

There are many conditionals in that statement. They rely on bringing to successful conclusion initiatives that have already been tried, but have yet to produce results. The new administration is certainly on solid ground in making efforts to avoid an outcome it has repeatedly said is unacceptable. It is clearly willing to offer major inducements to Iran and hope that some of its allies like Russia and strict sanctions-avoiding helpers like China can be turned. Certainly, it's worth trying. However, it raises the question of what limits the administration is willing to place on its incentives, and what it contemplates doing if its efforts fail. On those key elements, the Obama Administration's thinking is very opaque.

The Consequences of America's Strategic Divide: Less Legitimacy, Less Security

The charges and countercharges leveled against the Bush Administration, its Doctrine, and resulting debates at home have had a profound effect on America's international position. Writing in 1991, Richard Rose coined the phrase the postmodern presidency,[43] one aspect of which was that the presidency and the international system had become interdependent. What Rose had in mind was that the president's foreign policy decision-making was increasingly constrained by the views and interests of other international power centers. In some respects our new national security circumstances promise more of the same but with an additional twist.

The technological forces that give rise to and support interdependency also make possible unprecedented alliances of like-minded groups with the capacity to make use of media vehicles to amplify their power and their points. Contentious and acerbic American domestic debates about all aspects of national security, of which there have been many since President Bush took office, are picked up, transmitted, interpreted, and used to further the agendas of groups hostile to the United States and its interests. Such use is stripped of context or perspective and enlisted in efforts to delegitimize the policies and strategic concerns of the United States. Irresponsible accusations and hyperbolic language made in the course of domestic debates bring about a de facto alliance between enemies of the Bush Doctrine at home and enemies of America abroad. This is why both sides to the national security debate have to be exceedingly careful about the terms they use and the characterizations they make. It is one thing to say the United States effort in Iraq is in danger of failing, another to say that it already has while an effort to salvage it is under-way. It is one thing to say that you disagree with the president's policies, another to call them a concocted fraud.

And recall this is taking place in a world in which skepticism about the United States and its national security claims are rife. We live, after all, in a world in which fifty-six percent of British Muslims denied that Arabs had car-ried out the 9/11 attacks. Forty-six percent of French Muslims answered similarly, as did forty-six percent of German Muslims and thirty-five percent of Spanish Muslims. These numbers only increased when Muslims with no experience of living in Western society were polled.[44] And in the United States, twenty-two percent said that they did not believe that Arabs carried out those attacks, while thirty-two percent said they didn't know or refused to answer.[45] It is also a world in which in December 2001, an amateur tape sur-faced showing Osama Bin Laden sitting on a floral mattress entertaining visi-tors and exulting about the unexpectedly lethal results of his 9/11 attack. News reporters immediately searched out foreign reaction and reported as fol-lows, "Viewed around the world Thursday, the much-awaited video that the U.S. calls proof of Osama bin Laden's responsibility for the Sept. 11 attacks met with sharply divided, but predictable, reaction: Those who already believed in the guilt of the Saudi exile felt their convictions confirmed; the doubters, especially in the Middle East, dismissed the tape as a fabrication."[46]

Conclusion

The post-9/11 split on national security has damaged both the Democratic and Republican Parties, but its more serious effect is to damage the American ability to shoulder the burdens of post-9/11 national security. The Democrats and their allies who argue that the "War on Terror" is a misnomer because you can't declare war on a strategy have a point but miss the larger reality. They also need to remind Americans that the war is really against the possibility of catastrophic terrorism. It should be possible to criticize the war, while under-lining the threat. Similarly, Republicans who think talks are always a trap would do well to keep in mind, as seems to be the case with North Korea, that negotiations *can* lead to steps that defuse conflicts, even if their path is fraught with future uncertainties that must be guarded against. In six nation talks, North Korea agreed to the first steps along the path to give up its nuclear weapons[47] and took the first steps to fulfill its part of the agreement.[48] How-ever, that agreement too has unraveled.[49] Still, given the alternatives, agree-ment was worth exploring.

Yet, it is clear that talking and dealing with such regimes will involve hard trade-offs. One of these is that a regime that has allowed mass starvation will be given new international standing and its domestic political arrangements legitimized. The incentives that are being discussed will prop up an odious regime with sad consequences for its citizens. These are the facts of international life and it would be beneficial if, instead of having criticized the administration for holding six-party as opposed to bilateral talks, those in a position to know the issues, frankly and fairly discussed them.

In this way, Americans would learn that in the post-9/11 world, as it has to some degree always been the case, there are no easy answers to many difficult foreign policy questions; only, for the most part, tough choices. In the post-9/11 world, the United States needs *both* parties to adopt the most basic tenets of "realism"—that the world *is* a dangerous place, that there are groups and states that wish us harm, and that while it is often preferable to talk, it is sometimes necessary to fight. Yet the Obama administration has, with a few policy exceptions, positioned itself in opposition to the basic premises of the Bush Doctrine for understandable but still questionable reasons. Iraq has become disillusioning. There is much political traction to be gained by criticizing the former administration. And successful new presidents always bring the promise of new beginnings.

Yet international realities and campaign tactics are often discordant. As a candidate it's easy to criticize, but as president it is much harder to execute successful policy. Just what is the right balance between supporting Iranian demonstrators protesting what they say is a stolen election[50] and not challenging a regime with whom you wish to dissuade from acquiring nuclear weapons?[51] Is it possible for a policy premised on *realpolitik* to reflect and advance America's long tradition of supporting freedom and democracy, while overlooking a regime's brutality and hegemonic aspirations in the hope of reaching a deal? Couldn't a smart realism find a way to do both?

The hope of reaching a nuclear deal that also curtails Iran's regional ambitions appears increasingly untenable. Yet, the Obama Administration seems determined to play out this hope against accumulating evidence that they will be dashed against the hard reality of the nature of the Iranian regime and those in it who hold power. When does actual reality begin to trump hope? At what point do Obama's advisors, who were again (see p.62) apparently unanimous in the view that Obama responded to the Iranian election crisis with exactly the right blend of strength and nuance,[52] reconsider the element of wishful determination that appears to be part of what they see as their realism?

It is clear that the end of the Bush Administration does not herald a new era of tranquillity. The world has not become safer. And President Obama is facing the same kind of tough decisions that earned Mr. Bush the enmity of his critics. America desperately needs two major parties that are firmly committed to the long struggle against groups, and their state allies that want to catastrophically harm the United States and its allies. Right now they don't have that.

11 Obama's National Security Tasks
Worldview, Leadership and Judgment

The United States is caught in a *legitimacy dilemma*. The anarchic self-help nature of the international system and American responsibilities for the liberal international order insure that the United States will be called upon or occasionally required to use its power. However, many worldwide worry about and fear the United States because of its power. They would like it used only for the purposes of which they approve and these are unlikely to always be a good match for American national security requirements. Others would like to curtail American power to further their own ambitions.

President Obama clearly hopes to escape this dilemma by making use of the enormous good will that has greeted his election, rhetorically distancing himself at every opportunity from his predecessor and embarking on national security outreach initiatives that are likely to result in international and domestic support and approval, at least in the beginning. Yet, unless President Obama is willing to abandon assertive self-defense or the world somehow dramatically changes he will face many of the same dilemmas that confronted Mr. Bush and perhaps some that are worse.

While the Bush Administration's push to further democracy worldwide has faltered,[1] the impulse remains. The belief that "a world of liberal democracies would be a safer and better world for Americans and all people to live in" is one of the few widely shared premises of foreign policy analysts on both sides of the national security debates.[2] The further development of that liberal world order both requires American leadership and furthers American interests, but for these very reasons is likely to stimulate concern and opposition in some quarters.

Critics are fond of pointing out there are limits to American power, and they are right. The unipolar world is over. The return of "great power" rivalries is an increasingly evident fact. The United States faces the revival for the first time in many years of traditional "great power" politics being played out across of the globe from China in the Far East and Pacific Rim to a newly resurgent and assertive Russia in Eurasia. America's ideological opponents are straining to produce the counterbalancing that international relations theorists have been long searching for.

A New World Order and its Challenges

The unipolar world is devolving a three-tiered system. There is the resurgence of "great powers," the rest of the world, and the United States. Paradoxically, the United States retains its primacy in this newly evolving three-tiered system, while at the same time being one of those "great powers." As a result, the United States is both very much a part of but in some ways outside of the power system that is emerging. It will have to contend with rising great powers like China and those who aspire to that status like Russia and Iran. It will have to play a balancing role there depending on its allies like India, Japan, South Korea, Australia, members of the European Union and others.

At the same time it has a unique position of leadership in supporting and further developing the liberal world order. It is also a chief target of catastrophic terrorists. This dizzying national security load puts enormous and conflicting responsibilities on the shoulders of the United States. The world paradoxically demands our involvement and our prudence as the price of legitimacy. It is unclear that the answer to these many challenges and tasks is that "the United States must lead by restraining itself."[3]

The United States cannot substantially reduce or avoid many of its commitments without downgrading its leverage. And if we do that prematurely, before other structural elements are in place, the liberal international order in which both liberals and conservatives have an enormous stake will be in danger.

That means that the United States will have to protect itself and to do so it will have to take a strong and assertive stance towards those who are clearly, at least at this point, its enemies. While the brutality and difficulty of the Iraq War have doubtlessly made Americans weary of military involvements, there was after 9/11 strong support for the assertive national security stance that is *a* foundation of the Bush Doctrine.

A 2005 PSRA/Pew survey asked: do you think that using military force against countries that may seriously threaten our country, but have not attacked us can often be justified, sometimes be justified, rarely be justified, or never be justified? Fourteen percent said often, thirty-eight percent said sometimes, twenty-seven percent said rarely and fifteen percent said never. In a Gallup/CNN/USA Today poll taken a year after 9/11 a set of questions posed situations,

> in which a country has not attacked the United States, but is considered a threat. For each of these situations, please tell me whether you would favor or oppose the United States using military action against the country if there were strong evidence that: the country was aiding terrorists who were making plans to attack the United States (justified = 87 percent); the country was planning to attack the United States in the future (justified = 81 percent); the country was an enemy and was developing chemical/biological weapons (justified = 79 percent); the country was an enemy and was developing nuclear weapons (justified = 75 percent).

Finally, a 2003 PSRA/Pew poll asked: do you think that using military force to remove dictators of countries that may threaten the United States, but have not attacked us, is usually the right thing to do, sometimes the right thing to do, rarely the right thing to do, or never the right thing to do? Fifteen percent said usually right, fifty-one percent said sometimes right, and twenty percent said rarely right.[4]

No more recent poll numbers on these specific issues appear to be available, but it would be a good bet that Americans continue to want to be protected and are willing to accept strong measures to do so. Of course, force is obviously not the only vehicle for self-protection. The United States must do everything it can to forge alliances, but it must be prepared to act when necessary even when some allies choose not to join us. It must invest in a new generation of international institutions, reform old ones, and try through patient, often frustrating efforts, to make them more effective and relevant. And finally, it must remain committed to the long-term effort to bring the benefits of democratic government and economic wellbeing to all those places still in need of it. These seem like prudent basic goals for the United States in the post-9/11 world and represent one set of reasons why the Bush Doctrine, in some form is likely to be with us for some time and ought to be.

Mr. Obama takes office eight years into what is likely be a long war against Muslim extremists and their allies worldwide. He will have to deal with groups and countries that would like to destroy us, countries that aspire to dominate their regions—by violence if necessary, countries that are organizing with others so inclined to frustrate and impede us, a small number of like-minded allies who nonetheless must worry about their own domestic politics and a world with high expectations about what the United States ought to be doing and strong views about any failure to do so. It is not a world suited to the tender minded, the weak willed, or those with a wish to be popular or to please.

It is also not a world conducive to the success of the strategic worldview of liberal internationalism, cooperative liberalism and certainly not the political and strategic premises of liberals in the Democratic Party. These views and premises have their place. However, that place should not be as *the* dominant national security framework for the post-9/11 world. This does not mean that the United States should resort to threats and force at the first sign of trouble. It does not mean that the United States should discourage the development of international institutions and alliances. It does not mean that the United States should ignore world opinion.

It does mean that given the dangers of the post-9/11 world President Obama would be wise to recognize, and act upon, the knowledge that there are real limits to what these efforts can accomplish. The United Nations (U.N.) does have "unique legitimacy," but also grave problems in confronting issues that may occasionally become matters of life or death for the United States and its allies. Developing agreement regarding sanctions against Iran reflects both the U.N.'s importance and its limits. In matters of grave national security concerns a president must always be ready to ask and answer the question: what if they don't agree to allow me to act, and I must?

President Obama will certainly have the job of repairing the damage done to international perceptions by the assertive response of the United States after 9/11 and the charges of its critics. In a pre-election survey, seventy-four percent of respondents said that the next president "should take a different approach than George Bush has."[5] When asked what traits they were looking for in a new president the quality most picked by respondents was "strong leadership."[6] On the other hand, in a survey taken the preceding month the respondents chose "working well with leaders of other countries" as the most important characteristics (thirty-two percent) while "bringing unity to the country" was a close third (twenty-five percent).[7] To some degree just being a new president will go some way toward that goal. If President Obama can speak reassuringly and convincingly about American aspirations to be a good neighbor in the world, it will probably help, but only to a degree. Senator Chuck Hagel was recently quoted as saying: "The greatest challenge for America in the next 25 years is to place a new emphasis on how the rest of the world sees us."[8] With all due respect, it is not.

The greatest challenge for America in the next twenty-five years is to keep terrorists from unleashing nuclear, biological and chemical weapons on American soil or the soil of our allies. The next most important challenge is to check and manage the rise of aspiring regional hegemons in the Middle East, Eurasia, and South America. It is also important to reform the old institutions of the liberal international order and develop new ones to help manage the forces of globalization and the transitions to modernity. A focus on providing such transitional leadership will help America's standing in the world, but the assertive self-defense necessary in a post-9/11 world coupled with the role of checking aspiring hegemons is likely to undercut it. Liberal pundits like E.J. Dionne envision a new "Morning in America" and a glorious "Post Bush Awakening" as a result of his leaving office.[9] However, the world of danger for America and its allies has not disappeared because George Bush left office.

President Obama Faces the World

As president, Obama will still have to stand up to regional and international bullies, aspiring hegemons and dangerous groups and regimes. The first and only response to such circumstances cannot be: let's talk. Threats of force, and force itself have their place in strategic life, and may paradoxically be the basis for being able to successfully talk.

And, President Obama will still face the dilemma of making profound national security decisions without the benefit or comfort of smoking guns. Recently, Israeli fighter planes attacked a target inside Syria that was said to be part of a developing nuclear weapons program. The Israeli Government presented its evidence for this to the United States, but there were debates in the administration about how convincing the evidence was, whether it ought to lead to a change in the U.S. diplomatic strategy, or the degree to which the nascent Syrian program represented a threat.[10]

The treacherous terrain of national security policy abroad is matched by the dire circumstances of our domestic national security debates. The country is split—actually fractured is a more accurate term—regarding our national security circumstances and what to do about them. Strategic and partisan divides reinforce and deepen the chasm that has developed at the highest levels of foreign policy assessment. This divide has, in turn, stimulated, been stimulated by, and reinforced partisan and strategic divisions in the public at large. President Obama has taken office in a country where its citizens are exhausted and discouraged by the brutal war in Iraq. Yet, the post-9/11 dangers of the world persist and that will require an assertive stance towards these issues along the lines framed by the Bush Doctrine.

At a time when national unity is a strategic advantage, and even necessity, there is no general consensus about the nature of the problems that the United States faces and what to do about them. In terms of the center of gravity of their respective strategic worldviews, Democrats and Republicans look out on different worlds.[11] The brutal war in Iraq seems to have become the major proxy issue through which the larger issues that confront this country are argued, with the result that the larger strategic issues have been lost to view. This is the well-known effect of the cognitive heuristic of availability in which the most prominent element of a series of factors is elevated at the expense of others for precisely that reason—its prominence. This is often a psychological recipe for poor decisions, and the current status of American debate on its national security circumstances seems no exception.

President Obama has already made his decision on the timetable for leaving Iraq. It is war he is able to leave behind with some prospect of success because of the determination and perseverance of his predecessor. Decisions about Iran are looming and likely to be President Obama's version of the hard Iraq decisions that George Bush faced. How focused and tough he will be in dealing with this wily and determined adversary is a critical question.

Questions

Character is a president's stance as he confronts his circumstances. It reflects his ambitions, his ideals and values and how he approaches his many relationships and responsibilities. The definition of character integrity is not only to have convictions, but also in having the courage of them.

At this point we know a great deal about Mr. Bush's character, worldview and judgment, and its relation to being able to carry out his Doctrine, but very little on these matters relating to President Obama. We know that President Obama is ambitious and talented. We know he is smart but inexperienced in national security issues, but this does not mean that he has not developed views on them.

He spent a long presidential campaign being asked about his foreign views and being tutored to be able to answer them with some conviction and authority. However, it is hard to discern much difference between candidate Obama and what any other smart presidential candidate critical of the man he wishes to replace, but also wanting to appear to have balanced nuanced views on every matter, would say. In fairness, presidential campaigns give a hint, and only a hint of the response that a president will actually make in tough circumstances.

What they can do is provide an indication of a candidate's thinking. Whether this is what the candidate really thinks and will follow through with it or whether it is an amalgam of the candidate's views wrapped up in a palatable package whose purpose is to emphasize distinctions that seem fair and acceptable is hard to discern. This is particularly the case with candidates as smart and verbally fluent as President Obama.

As a candidate Mr. Obama stressed his desire for bi-partisan policies, a domestic parallel to his international search for agreements with countries like Syria and Iran. Yet, when it came to his actual practice the president reached out symbolically, but pretty much tried to have his way. Domestic politics are not foreign policy, yet by underscoring his wish and intention to be bi-partisan, and then not seriously considering the Republican Party ideas in the processes leading up to the first economic stimulus measure and his first budget, he raises the question of what, if anything, this implies for his foreign policy dealings.

In foreign policy he will be dealing with a world that does not have the equivalent of a Democratic Congress. Moreover, none of America's competitors, adversaries or allies will begin with the assumption that he was elected *their* president. His outreach to Syria and Iran may conceal a wish to get things accomplished his way, as he is trying to do with his stimulus and first major budget. But of course, Russia and Iran have more power than Republicans have votes and so if that is his stance, he is in for some frustrations.

On the other hand, it is possible that Mr. Obama sees the two spheres very differently and thus approaches each with a different bargaining style and plan. In domestic politics it might be that he tries to set the agenda, frame the debate and by thus doing gets most of what he wants. In foreign policy that approach isn't possible. In a multi-tiered world, especially with rising great powers that expect some degree of deference to their wishes if their help on other matters is to be forthcoming, more give and take is ordinarily necessary. How much give and how much take remains an open question.

Glimmers of a Worldview, but ...

Still, regardless of his preferences, he will have to pay some attention to foreign policy and especially national security. There, the indications are that he is at home and comfortable with the premises of liberal internationalism. These are to repeat, the view that: America's strength rests on its relationships with its allies and in building strong international institutions; America might take the lead, but always as a member in good standing of its alliances and international obligations, and force is a last resort and must be used sparingly, precisely, and legitimately. Talking and reaching agreements is always preferable. Yet, at times he sounds as if he could find a comfortable spot in the George W. Bush White House.

In *The Audacity of Hope*, Obama wrote,

> it was in America's interest to work with other countries to build up international institutions and promote international norms. Not because of a naïve assumption that international laws and treaties alone would end conflicts among nations or eliminate the need for American military action, because the more international norms were enforced and the more America signaled a willingness to show restraint in the exercise of its power, the fewer the number of conflicts that would arise—and the more legitimate our actions would appear in the eyes of the world when we did have to move militarily.[12]

This is one of those points that is absolutely fair in the making but carries within a series of questions whose answers will truly define any Obama Doctrine. When Obama says that fewer conflicts would arise, it is to be assumed he means with our allies, and not international conflicts in general. The major question here is exactly what Obama means by the words "show restraint" in the exercise of our power. Granted Obama feels that the Bush Administration overstepped its restraint in invading Iraq, but what are the restraints that President Obama will abide by?

In that same chapter he also wrote,

> the United States has the right, as do all sovereign nations, has the unilateral right to defend itself. As such our campaign to take out Al Qaeda base camps and the Taliban regime that harbored them was entirely justified … It may be preferable to have the support of our allies in such military campaigns, but our immediate safety can't be held hostage to the desire for international consensus; if we have to go it alone, then the American people stand ready to pay any price and bear any burden to protect this country.[13]

This is a statement that no president could publicly disagree with, and thus is not very informative. The number of times the United States has been directly attacked as it was on 9/11 has been small, but the American military has been directly involved in dozens of wars and operations in the last decade. It is reassuring to know that he will respond forcefully to direct attacks, but as a practical matter that doesn't cover very much territory.

Along similar lines, Mr. Obama reserves the right to "take unilateral action to eliminate any *imminent* threat to our security—so long as an imminent threat is understood to be a nation, group or individual that is actively preparing to strike U.S. targets (or allies with whom the United States has mutual defense agreements) and has or will have the means to do so in the immediate future."[14] Here again, is a statement with which no president could disagree, though it does seem to answer Dick Cheney's thought experiment about how far imminence went back in time for the 9/11 attacks. Obama's answer seems to be that if we know what they were going to do two or three years earlier, he would take them out. That's a perfectly sensible answer, but prior knowledge of intentions, capacity and results are not a typical feature of national security circumstances.

Obama has written that,

> once we get beyond matters of self-defense, though, I'm convinced that it will almost always be in our strategic interest to act multilaterally rather than unilaterally, when we use force around the world. By this I don't mean the U.N. Security Council – a body that in its structure and rules too often appears frozen in a Cold War-era time warp should have a veto over our actions. Nor do I mean we should round up the United Kingdom and Togo and then do what we please. Acting multilaterally means doing what George H.W. Bush and his team did during the first Gulf War—engaging in the hard diplomatic work that resulted in most of the world's support for our actions, and making sure our actions serve to further recognized international norms.[15]

Leaving aside not too thinly veiled criticism of President George W. Bush, and the allies who supported and helped remove Saddam Hussein (particularly Great Britain), some questions occur. Do we really need "most of the world's support" to use force? Must its use always serve to further international norms? And which norms require a fight to uphold? From the example it would appear that invading another country violates recognized international norms.

This brings to mind Mr. Obama's response, as a candidate, to the Soviet invasion of Georgia. At the time he issued a statement that the McCain campaign criticized as too cautious. He said, "I strongly condemn the outbreak of violence in Georgia, and urge an immediate end to armed conflict. Now is the time for Georgia and Russia to show restraint and to avoid an escalation to full-scale war. Georgia's territorial integrity must be respected."[16] This somewhat bland, even-handed statement is less interesting and revealing than its rationale which was given by one of Mr. Obama's foreign policy advisors, Ben Rhodes. Rhodes said Obama was deliberately measured in response to the conflict, balancing his disapproval of Russia's "troubling behavior in its near-abroad region" with *"the fact that we have to deal with Russia to deal with our most important national security challenges."*[17] Here is the realist putting aside upholding recognized international norms in consideration of anticipated Russian help. Choices like these have a long history in American foreign policy and seem to undercut the view of President Obama as a naïve internationalist.

Yet, it does return us to the question of what principles operate for Mr. Obama beyond the realistic accommodation to and with power.

The emerging "Obama Doctrine" is, like its presidential author, a set of not wholly consistent policy initiatives. This has led some to the view that, "For all the perception of a major course correction, Mr. Obama so far appears to be presiding over a foreign policy that may seem more different than it really is" and then to conclude that "Most noticeable has been the shift in tone and the promises of engagement."[18] Another commentator asks: can one begin to talk of an "Obama doctrine"? and concludes, "If style and temperament can constitute a doctrine, the answer is yes."[19]

Consistent with an emphasis on atmospherics has been the noticeable change in language. Words like "democracy" are fading from administration pronouncements.[20] "The Global War on Terror" has been replaced by the term "Overseas Contingency Operation."[21] Terrorist attacks are now designated "man-made disasters."[22] Terrorists will be decisively dealt with, but tyrants will be engaged.

Beyond tone and language, however, lies a deeper strategy premised on Obama's apparent view of our competitors' and enemies' psychology. It is a bet that these countries—China, Iran, North Korea, Syria, Venezuela, and others really, underneath their bluster and regional ambitions, want respect.[23] And President Obama has repeatedly demonstrated that he is willing to give it.

Sometimes this has taken the form of platitudinous truisms as when speaking of Islam as a great religion, or when he said, "The Iranian people are a great people and Persian civilization is a great civilization." Sometimes, it takes the form of singling out a particular accomplishment like Obama's statement, "that he felt the United States could learn a lesson from Cuba, which for decades has sent doctors to other countries throughout Latin America to care for the poor."[24]

In no case are these expressions of respect and policy initiatives coupled with any public acknowledgment of the more odious or problematic aspects of a regime's behavior. To take but one example, the policy of sending Cuban doctors to care for the poor is laudable but also strategic. Sending Cuban political and military cadres throughout South America is less praiseworthy.

More controversially, Obama has coupled his sometimes overly effusive[25] offerings of respect with equally public criticisms of the United States—aspects of its history and its foreign policies in the last eight years before he became president. Included in his criticisms aired during his 2009 foreign tours, in varying degrees of specificity, were American race relations, arrogance, dismissal of our European allies, engaging in torture, holding enemy combatants in Guantánamo, being the first and only country ever to use a nuclear bomb on another country, showing insufficient respect for the Muslim world, and just not listening to others. These criticisms have inflamed conservatives,[26] but in Obama's view "if we occasionally confess to having strayed from our values and our ideals, that strengthens our hand; that allows us to speak with greater moral force and clarity around these issues."[27] Whether the force of our moral virtue will move countries like North Korea, Iran or Venezuela is questionable.

The calculus behind this approach is interesting. In Obama's words, "Countries are going to have interests, and changes in foreign policy approaches by my administration aren't suddenly going to make all those interests that may diverge from ours disappear. What it does mean, though, is, *at the margins*, they are more likely to want to cooperate than not cooperate."[28] One supposes that if one can change the odds for agreement, even at the margins, it may be worth the effort. Yet, one must ask, again: does modesty, public recognition of American faults, a willingness to publicly overlook the others' strategically problematic behavior and an emphasis on respect whether fully deserved or not lead states to put aside their core strategic interests? Obama's words suggest they don't. Yet, if that is true one is still left to ask what role force or its variants like coercive diplomacy play when listening, respect, and engagement fail to protect vital interests.

Beyond this question though, the expression of Obama's public criticisms seems to reflect a deeper stratum of Obama's thinking. Asked about his own foreign policy doctrine, Obama replied by giving a few general principles; among them: "[T]here are a couple of principles that I've tried to apply across the board: Number one, that the United States remains the most powerful, wealthiest nation on Earth, but we're only one nation ... " His point here was one he has made repeatedly, that we need others to help us solve the world's problems, which is fair enough.

Still, Obama's view of his own country would seem to be in some respects equivocal. At his press conference in Strasbourg, France the following exchange took place:

Q: Thank you, Mr. President ... could I ask you whether you subscribe, as many of your predecessors have, to the school of American exceptionalism that sees America as uniquely qualified to lead the world, or do you have a slightly different philosophy? And if so, would you be able to elaborate on it?

PRESIDENT OBAMA: I believe in American exceptionalism, just as I suspect that the Brits believe in British exceptionalism and the Greeks believe in Greek exceptionalism ... Now, the fact that I am very proud of my country and I think that we've got a whole lot to offer the world does not lessen my interest in recognizing the value and wonderful qualities of other countries, or recognizing that we're not always going to be right, or that other people may have good ideas, or that in order for us to work collectively, all parties have to compromise and that includes us.[29]

One might characterize this as the view that America is special, but not that special.

Another major principle that does seem clear is Obama's belief in the efficacy of engagement, and this appears based in part on his view of his own unique historical standing and talents. In an interview with Richard Wolffe he said, "If I had a Muslim summit, I think that I can speak credibly to them about the fact that I respect their culture, that I understand their religion, that I have lived in a Muslim country, and as a consequence I know it is possible to reconcile Islam with modernity and respect for human rights and a rejection of violence. And I think I can speak with added credibility."[30]

That would seem to depend on what, exactly, he says. Certainly, his historical stature as the first American president of African descent doubtlessly adds to his "credibility," but it is unclear just what that word means here, or how far, as noted above, it can take him or American national security interests.

There is a deeper issue here as well. Well before Mr. Obama became president he "portrayed himself as a moral leader."[31] In a December 2003 interview, he named Gandhi, Lincoln, and King as the men he most admired because they were able "to bring about extraordinary changes and place themselves in a difficult historical moment and *be a moral center.*"[32]

The exact origin and nature of these identifications as well as a fuller examination of the implications of Obama's view of himself as a moral center for the United States and the redeemer of its moral and political standing will be the subject of a future analysis.[33] However, this much can surely be said. Such a view, psychologically, clearly reflects a fusion of substantial self-regard and self-confidence coupled with the view that America has much to atone for.

It is clear that Obama views his moral role as requiring the expiation of what he sees as America's moral and policy failings before he assumed office. He seems to believe that publicly naming these errors and promising not to repeat them will increase America's stature in the world, and his ability to capitalize on it.

Long before he was criticized for going on a "world apology tour,"[34] Mr. Obama had written, "we dismissed European reservations about the wisdom and necessity of the Iraq war."[35] A fairer description would have been that the Bush Administration did consider European objections, but decided it had to act in spite of them. Obama had also said, "In Asia, we belittled South Korean efforts to improve relations with the North."[36] A more accurate statement would have acknowledged that the Bush Administration worried that such overtures would reward provocative North Korean behavior and not result in any policy changes, a worry that seems prudent given recent North Korean military threats to attack South Korea,[37] its second nuclear bomb test[38] and the testing of new missiles.[39] These and other examples, already noted, raise the question of whether Obama's plan to increase America's moral stature might be based on fair as well as critical assessments of his predecessors.

Obama seems to believe very strongly that his efforts to redeem America's moral stature will provide him with the leadership leverage to resolve tough, even seemingly intractable international and strategic problems. On his April 2009 European trip, he had this to say: "And I had an excellent meeting with President Medvedev of Russia to get started that process of reducing our nuclear stockpiles, *which will then give us greater moral authority* ... to say to North Korea, don't proliferate nuclear weapons."[40] In Turkey, he said,

If we want to say to Iran, don't develop nuclear weapons because you develop them then everybody in the region is going to want them and you'll have a nuclear arms race in the Middle East and that will be dangerous for everybody – if we want to say that to Iranians, it helps if we are also saying, 'and we will reduce our own,' *so that we have more moral authority in those claims.*[41]

Perhaps Mr. Obama really means to say that reducing American stockpiles of nuclear weapons can be translated into a *claim* for greater moral authority. And perhaps he is right. However, it is very unclear given the psychology and aims of the leaders and countries where he hopes it will count, that it will really matter. And, there is always the danger that it will be misinterpreted as a sign of weakness or a policy of accommodation.

Another of Obama's basic premises underlying his strong belief in engagement came into focus in Turkey, where he was asked what actions he would take to insure peace in the world. Obama replied,

I think the most important thing to start with is dialogue. When you have a chance to meet people from other cultures and other countries, and you listen to them and you find out that, even though you may speak a different language or you may have a different religious faith, it turns out that you care about your family, you have your same hopes about being able to have a career that is useful to the society, you hope that you can raise a family of your own, and that your children will be healthy and have a good education—that all those things that human beings all around the world share are more important than the things that are different.[42]

In other words, beneath the differences that divide states lie core human aspirations that will help make dialogue successful. It's an admirable but surprisingly naïve sentiment for someone who prides himself on being a by-product of diverse cultural experiences. It sounds as if Obama subscribes to the view that culture and history, not to mention politics, have no consequences for how people think and view the world. Does Kim Jong-il base his national security strategies on the hope that he can have a career that is useful to his society? He and others like him would certainly say yes, but that doesn't improve our chances to reach agreement with them.

Risk, Judgment and Leadership

One thing that President Obama's budget revealed is that he is a president of vast domestic ambitions. He wants to address healthcare policy, entitlement policy, and environmental policy to name three of many. It is not clear whether he has such large ambitions internationally, and if so what they are. His domestic agenda would seem to indicate a president who thinks big, and in foreign policy this could translate to the search for "grand bargains." But it is also possible that his thinking and his ambitions, like his personal and government experience are focused on domestic issues. Time will tell.

There is another element that has emerged clearly in President Obama's domestic leadership that has implications for national security stance, and that is his propensity for large-scale risk taking. The first and most obvious instance of this was running for the presidency at all given his age and experience. Equally telling are the high expectations he is willing to generate for his ambitious agenda. As one reporter put it, if Obama wasn't comfortable with a high level of risk, "he would not have sought $1 trillion from affluent Americans and a similar sum from businesses to finance health care, education and energy initiatives. All that while simultaneously trying to save the auto industry, revive financial markets, end the Iraq war and redouble efforts to battle Islamic extremists in Afghanistan."[43] His closest aid and campaign manager David Plouffe said given the circumstances, "Political calculation and risk aversion really have to take a back seat."[44]

This remark seems to suggest that the administration views their circumstances in both domestic and foreign policy as operating in the arena of potential catastrophic loss; hence, the willingness, indeed the need, to take big risks. Yet, this view is inconsistent, both with the facts and with the administration's own behavior. The fast pace of troop withdrawals from Iraq, and the administration's decision to commit far fewer numbers of troops in Afghanistan than commanders wanted, do pose a risk, one of committing too few resources. And these actions are certainly not consistent with the high stakes commitments that follow from giving "risk aversion a back seat."

Domestically, the freezing up of credit lines is arguably in the arena of potential catastrophic loss, and the steep recession would certainly seem to qualify as dire. The first issue would certainly qualify for the bold initiatives to unfreeze liquidity that Mr. Bush initiated before leaving office and Mr. Obama built on when he became president. Obama's response to the recession was forceful, but almost purely Keynesian in conception, relying on Congress to appropriate and spend money on projects it chose. This was a conventional Democratic policy response which pitted projects supported by their constituents against the need to get money quickly pumped into the economy. This was one reason the stimulus produced tepid economic results.[45]

The administration's climate control and health care initiatives are in another risk domain altogether. Both issues are extremely complex and highly contentious. In both cases, it is not entirely clear what the core problems are, how serious they are, what can or should be done about them, and the costs and consequences of proposed actions. Is the health care problem one of rising costs, the number of uninsured, or the quality of health care? The first is a by-product of medical innovation and more use. How can we encourage the first, while discouraging the second?

Global warming has similar problems. Is carbon dioxide the chief villain? Industrialized countries are reducing their CO_2 footprint via new technology while "green" solutions are not yet economically viable. What of developing countries that have neither the technology nor the interest in cutting back on their much-needed development? Should a there be a government-imposed cap on manufacturing and public consumer choices to curtail consumption? This would seem problematic. One reason the results of the stimulus proved so tepid was that consumers saved part of their government rebates, rather than spend it.[46] Dampening consumption would have serious structural effects on American economic life and culture.

These questions only touch on the many complexities of these issues, but one thing seems clear. Neither issue represents an imminently catastrophic problem in the way that the 9/11 attacks did, or even a dire issue as the acquisition of nuclear weapons by Iran would. Therefore, the Obama Administration's efforts to rapidly push these initiatives through seem more a reflection of presidential high-risk choice and ambition than the dire nature of the circumstances. Does the same hold for his foreign policy initiatives?

President Obama's cool, analytical, and often ironic stance gives few clues of his passions, the convictions that fire him. What policy or leadership issues really move him? What does he feel passionately about? Which foreign policy and national security issues, if any, is he willing to go to the mat for?

In the debate between the two Democratic candidates while discussing Iran's nuclear ambitions, Obama was asked about extending a nuclear shield to Israel against an Iranian attack. He never answered that question. However, using minimalist language, he did say he would find a direct attack on Israel or one of our allies "unacceptable."[47] If an attack on Israel is unacceptable, what about Iranian support of elements in Iraq killing American soldiers? Is that also "unacceptable," and what would he do about it? Obama did say, "I will take no options off the table" when it comes to Iran's obtaining or using nuclear weapons. However, he has also promised high-level presidential talks with Iran, without preconditions, to offer "carrots and sticks." Is Obama ready to accept a nuclear Iran? And if so, what would he do about its behavior? Would he take the same position with Iran that he took with Russia, expressing a willingness to overlook some of its aggressive behavior in return for help in other areas? We don't know, but there are grounds for asking.

President Obama has gained a reputation as a dispassionate decision maker. One reporter noted, "Obama arrives at the presidency Tuesday after a transition that betrayed little if any perspiration and no hint of nervousness. Throughout the months since his election, he has been a font of cool confidence, never too hot, never too cold, seemingly undaunted by the magnitude of troubles awaiting him and unbothered by the few setbacks that have tripped him up."[48] Perhaps, but it is prudent to suspend early judgment, as often what you see is not all there is.

For example, one anomaly to President Obama's seemingly deliberative cool decision-making style occurred when he announced two days after taking the oath of office that he was shutting down the facility at Guantánamo. At the time he made that announcement, he had not yet had a formal review completed about what his options were on the major issues that remained, of which there were a number. He could have chosen to handle the matter differently.

He could have announced his intention to close it down after those reports were given to him and reviewed. Or (less likely) he could have waited to say anything definitive. He chose to make a bold statement, without the underlying analysis that would help resolve the issues involved. One can summon up many explanations for acting so quickly, the most obvious of which is to make a dramatic, immediate break with the policies of his predecessors (while retaining some latitude to act as his predecessor had). Whatever else one may say about this decision it does not appear to have been deliberative. When one couples that impulse with Mr. Obama's propensity for risk taking and large ambitions, you arrive at a national security intersection worth our continuing attention, and his.

A similar dynamic unfolded regarding his reversal in releasing dozens of Bush era photos alleged to show prisoner "abuse." At first, the administration said they would be released,[49] but then completely reversed itself and said they would not.[50] The precipitously announced decision to close the Guantánamo Detention Camp within a year without a detailed plan, the decision to release some of the memos surrounding the Bush Administration's debates on "enhanced interrogation," the reversal on the release of the "abuse" photos, and the reinstatement of military tribunals[51] which Obama had called a "failure," and said could not be fixed "because you can't put lipstick on a pig," after saying he would "reject the Military Commission Act passed by Congress during the Bush Administration." These all raise questions about the "conventional wisdom."[52]

All suggest that the president is able to change course and his mind. But the question arises on such important matters: why did he get himself in the position where he had to do so? For a president who prides himself on his cool, detached, and nuanced decision-making style, these certainly seem to be anomalous. In these and other circumstances, he seems to have adopted a leap-before-you-look decision stance. Whether this is simply the result of normal missteps on the sometimes bumpy road of presidential learning, a result of strong moral convictions and self-image trumping balanced assessment, or over-confidence in one's judgment is not possible to really judge at this point.

There is also the question of judgment. Obama has repeatedly touted the high quality of his own and rests that case on what he sees as his prescient opposition to the war: "on the most important foreign policy issue of a generation, I got it right and others did not."[53] It is somewhat unclear, however, just how strategically accurate the basis of his opposition was.[54] He argued that Saddam posed no imminent threat to the United States or its neighbors, but what about a gathering threat? His opposition was premised on the view that Saddam could be contained; others made strong arguments that containment was failing.[55] That argument rests on plausible analyses that either side could marshal, not on the superior judgment of Obama's side of the debate.

Obama also framed his criticism of the war with direct personal attacks on members of the administration and their motives. "I am opposed to … the attempt by political hacks like Karl Rove to distract us from a rise in the uninsured, a rise in the poverty rate, a drop in the median income—to distract us from corporate scandals and a stock market that has just gone through the worst month since the Great Depression."[56] So is the basis of his good judgment prescient geo-strategic analysis or a progressive's animus toward a conservative agenda?

Mr. Obama was also in error in opposing the surge that did, along with the new counterinsurgency doctrine and new generals, bring some substantial measure of stability to Iraq. When President Bush first announced the surge Obama said: "I am not persuaded that 20,000 additional troops in Iraq is going to solve the sectarian violence there. In fact, I think it will do the reverse."[57] This was a position he maintained throughout 2007.

The point of this is not to highlight error; no president is free of it. It is rather to point to how little we really know about Obama's decision-making process. He is smart, and very ambitious. His domestic ambitions are coming into focus but his foreign policy and national security goals remain opaque. He is willing to take large risks domestically, but how much he is willing to risk on talk and engagement is unclear.

And he has an enormous amount of self-confidence, as perhaps befits someone who has taken such large risks and won. In decision-making this is both an advantage and a source of worry. Too little confidence can leave a president insecure and at the mercy of his advisors. Too much confidence can leave a president committed to his own views, regardless. During the presidential campaign, he made the somewhat startling statement that in picking a Vice Presidential nominee he didn't have to worry about foreign policy experience because, "Ironically, this is an area—foreign policy is the area where I am probably *most* confident that I know more and understand the world better than Senator Clinton or Senator McCain."[58] This fits in well with Obama's expressed view that he is the sole author of the vision of his presidency. How much of this is presidential rhetoric or its underlying psychology remains to be seen.

He has begun with a policy of engagement and outreach, but it is unclear where, if anyplace that will lead. He has assembled a group of foreign policy advisors who mostly fit in comfortably in the realist camp. Yet, where they and Obama stand on specific issues beyond the platitudes of more concern for allies and respect for international opinion and institutions has yet to emerge.

The president appears to believe in the special responsibilities for American world leadership as well as in exercising that leadership in conjunction with allies. NATO troop contributions to Afghanistan not withstanding, relations with core European allies are generally likely to be smoother. Whether this happens because they think they have found an American president with a European worldview, or whether it is because they believe he will be less demanding with them is a matter of some import.

The president also believes that it is America's responsibility to help the world. Other presidents have thought this as well, and even acted on it. It is clear that Obama will add his name to that list but the interesting question concerns how he intends to do it. Given Obama's background as a social worker and redistributive domestic policy initiatives it seems safe to say that his presidency will be more likely to see a surge in American-led social work internationally than it will a surge of troops. Yet, he seems wiling to let bygones be bygones with Russia's invasion of its neighbor in the service of future help. In this he counts either on their gratitude or the ability to keep a *quid pro quo*.

Decision Point: The Withdrawal of American Troops from Iraq

It is impossible to assemble an accurate picture of what actually goes on in President Obama's national security debates at this early date. However, some very preliminary understandings may be possible. Consider the debate about the rate at which America would leave Iraq.

The Iraq withdrawal decision covered a relatively narrow segment of presidential choice, at the very end of a difficult and divisive war. An agreement had already been reached during the Bush Administration to remove all American troops from Iraq by the end of 2011. So, by the time President Obama took office, the window for all troops' withdrawals, barring an additional independent agreement by both parties, was approximately thirty-four months.

Obama had campaigned on a policy of quick troop withdrawal covering a period of sixteen months, pulling out approximately one combat brigade a month.[59] The president decided to remove the bulk of American troops in nineteen months, longer than the period that he has campaigned upon, but shorter than the twenty-three months which was one of the three options that presented to the president and then debated. His decision was presented as "The compromise between commanders and advisers who are worried that security gains could backslide in Iraq and those who think the bulk of U.S. combat work is long since done."[60]

The obvious take on this decision is that it represents a prudent hedge between too fast (sixteen months) and too long (twenty-three months) a withdrawal period. And that is accurate to some degree, though three additional months do not seem to be a particularly bold or brave decision. This take is consistent with Obama's persona as a pragmatic, relatively cool and unemotional decision-maker. Yet, it is interesting to inquire a little further about his choices.

One report called it a "split the difference" decision, and given the range of choices that the president received, it almost is.[61] However, note that the range of reported options presented to the president were sixteen, nineteen and twenty-three months,[62] yet it would have been possible to propose that the withdrawal for the bulk of American troops be thirty-five months taking that process right up to the end of the legal time period for American troops to be in Iraq, a thirty-nine-month withdrawal timetable. That timetable would have allowed an extra sixteen months as a hedge.

There are numerous reasons that such an extended withdrawal date might not have been considered, not the least of which is that commanders were certain it wouldn't be needed. Perhaps the need to find additional troops for Afghanistan played a role, but Obama initially committed seventeen thousand new troops there, many fewer than the more than ninety-two thousand troops that will be withdrawn under the new timetable. So too, the target date selected did leave approximately thirty to fifty-five thousand troops left after the bulk of American troops had left until the final cutoff time of December 2011. Whether these remaining troops would have their mission changed from combat to training and advising and what the actual difference in practice between these two would be is somewhat unclear.

Still, the fact that the longest withdrawal period possible was not among the three recommendations considered is interesting, and even puzzling. Why was it not considered? Perhaps, as noted it was viewed as militarily unnecessary. However, other reasons also suggest themselves. Obama's senior advisors are quoted as saying, "they had reached an accommodation that would satisfy both the military and a public eager to get out of Iraq, while relieving the strain on the armed forces and freeing up resources for Afghanistan."[63] It seems fair to say some of the military and public were anxious to get out of Iraq, but others in the military and among the public were concerned to do so only after it was clear that the investment made there had been consolidated and secured.

There is another possible explanation for the missing thirty-nine-month withdrawal option; that the White House made it clear that sooner was better, thus the maximum option was a non-starter. This possibility suggests itself because the president had so strongly gone on record against the decision to invade Iraq, was highly critical of the conduct of the war including the results of the "surge" and had campaigned on ending the war and withdrawing American troops quickly. Obama's policy preferences were then well known, had been repeatedly expressed publicly, and may have been strongly held.

Recall (see page 68) that in an interview President Obama was asked whether anyone ever said no to him, that he couldn't do something. He replied that people "didn't have to tell me, No you can't do that."[64] Rather, they pointed out the challenges involved in doing what he wanted to get done. Leaving aside the implication that the President never asks for anything for which the response is "No, you can't do that," that Q&A only underscores the built-in desire to accomplish presidential purposes that permeate and can distort the advisory system.

Finally, it is worth noting that the narrow question of how quickly American troops would be withdrawn was coupled with another arguably more major, much less commented upon decision. Senior administration officials confirmed that, "Obama does not plan on asking Iraqi officials to allow any to remain in the country after that [December 2011] deadline."[65] A senior administration official said, "The path is not toward the Korea model."[66] This decision would preclude the criticism that the Iraq War was fought to establish American bases and hegemony, and would not rule out mutually agreed upon basing of personnel or materials in the future. Yet, it might also represent a decision to truly step away from America's role and investment there. No explanations of the nature and range of debates on this important issue were provided by the Obama Administration.

Decision Point: Afghanistan

It is perhaps in Afghanistan that President Obama's stance regarding the use of force has become most immediately engaged. That war dates back to the Bush Administration's decision to topple the Taliban Regime in the aftermath of 9/11 and the refusal of that regime to hand over those responsible for planning that attack. In keeping with the premises of the Bush Doctrine, the president attempted to both eradicate al Qaeda and replace Afghanistan's Taliban government that had allowed them to operate.

That war, like its counterpart in Iraq, began with some strong initial successes followed by difficulties in consolidating those gains, and the reemergence of a lethal and to some degree successful insurgency against the democratically elected government and its American allies. In 2009, American and allied commanders were calling the situation in Afghanistan dire[67] and the administration undertook a wide-ranging review.

Military commanders had requested a major upgrading of the allied commitment there in terms of combat troops, the training of Afghan military forces, and economic development aid. They requested thirty thousand new combat troops.[68] The president responded shortly after taking office by committing seventeen thousand new American combat troops and doing so before he had a chance to formally meet with his NATO allies in Europe. In announcing the results of his review and his new policy, the president added four thousand additional troops for training not combat purposes, a commitment that the president said had been previously unfulfilled because of the war in Iraq. He also announced plans for several hundred more reconstruction workers and up to one point five billion dollars a year for five years to support Pakistan's military and economic development. Military commanders readied a request for ten thousand more combat troops.[69]

A number of things stand out about this decision, in so far as we know them. First, the president, as Robert Kagan approvingly noted, did not opt as "many of his supporters, and some of his own advisers, calling either for a rapid exit or a 'minimal' counterterrorist strategy in Afghanistan."[70] His first point is definitely true, though his second is nowhere near as clear.

One other striking element of Obama's Afghanistan strategy is the focus on having an exit strategy. In the *CBS 60 Minutes* interview he said, "There's got to be an exit strategy. There's got to be a sense that this is not perpetual drift but in fact we are making measurable progress with benchmarks in order to achieve our central goal."[71] Just what those benchmarks were, the president didn't specifically say.

What is clear is that Obama and his advisors chose the very narrow, though not necessarily limited goal of routing al Qaeda, not defeating the Taliban.

Paralleling the decision to engage Iran (see pages 64–65), "*All of the president's advisers agreed* that the primary goal in the region should be narrow— taking aim at al Qaeda, as opposed to the vast attempt at nation-building the Bush administration had sought in Iraq. The question was how to get there."[72]

That question apparently produced two groups. The first group, which included Hillary Clinton and Richard Holbrook, "favored wide-ranging coordinated efforts which would concentrate on corruption in Afghanistan as well as focus on training local officials and transforming agriculture in the country away from the notorious poppy fields that have been used to fuel the Taliban insurgency." The second group (Mr. Biden and Deputy Secretary of State James B. Steinberg are mentioned prominently as members[73]), "sought to put strict parameters on the size of the additional force deployed to Afghanistan and to ensure there was a specific mission for them."[74]

It might seem at first glance that the second group "won" that policy debate. New troops were limited to four thousand trainers and the president announced a narrow, though as noted, still ambitious goal. In the president's words, "So I want the American people to understand that we have a clear and focused goal: to disrupt, dismantle, and defeat al Qaeda in Pakistan and Afghanistan, and to prevent their return to either country in the future."[75] Noticeably absent were references to building democracy as one part of a more general strategy stabilizing Afghanistan. Indeed Secretary of Defense Gates said, "if we set ourselves the objective of creating some sort of central Asian 'Valhalla' over there, we will lose, because nobody in the world has that kind of time, patience and money."[76] Along similar lines President Obama said, "We are not going to be able to rebuild Afghanistan into a Jeffersonian democracy."[77] Hyperbole aside, the administration seems to be placing its short-term bets on economic rather than democratic development, though the two obviously have some relationship to each other.

On the other hand in his public remarks introducing his new strategy, Obama vowed to:[78]

> focus our military assistance on the tools, training and support that Pakistan needs to root out the terrorists; help Pakistan weather the economic crisis; pursue constructive diplomacy with both India and Pakistan; make clear that our relationship with Pakistan is grounded in support for Pakistan's democratic institutions and the Pakistani people; and provide $1.5 billion in direct support to the Pakistani people every year over the next five years – resources that will build schools, roads, and hospitals, and strengthen Pakistan's democracy.

Regarding Afghanistan, he said he would

> take the fight to the Taliban in the south and east, and give us a greater capacity to partner with Afghan Security Forces and to go after insurgents along the border ... At the same time, we will shift the emphasis of our

mission to training and increasing the size of Afghan Security Forces, so that they can eventually take the lead in securing their country ... this push must be joined by a dramatic increase in our civilian effort, including efforts to fight corruption, replace illicit narcotics production with other crops, an infusion of state department and foreign assistant funds to help Afghanistan develop, encourage reconciliation, support basic human rights of all Afghans, including women and children and a new Contact Group for Afghanistan and Pakistan that brings together all who should have a stake in the security of the region, our NATO allies and other partners, but also the Central Asian states, the Gulf nations and Iran; Russia, India and China.

So, it would seem that what we have here is a narrow goal, defined by an array of policy initiatives reflecting vast ambitions. The Clinton–Holbrook position seems to have won decisively in the president's list of stated objectives. However, the Biden–Steinberg position of limiting the number of combat troops needed also seems to have won. It would appear that in saying yes to both groups, Obama runs the risk of trying to accomplish extraordinarily ambitious goals without committing the military resources needed to accomplish them. This was a problem in Iraq as well before Mr. Bush successfully pushed for more troops.

The issue, to be clear, is whether the president envisions a stabilize/train/ withdrawal strategy or a clear/hold/build strategy. In Iraq the Pentagon started out with the first strategy and that alone proved unsuccessful. In conjunction with the surge and a new counterinsurgency doctrine it switched to the second and as a result, after a time was able to more successfully implement the first policy. In short, stabilize, train and leave strategies depend on first successfully clearing, holding and building strategies.

And for Obama, as for every president, the most consequential decisions will involve the use of force—when, why and how to use it. Obama's decision to add seventeen thousand troops in Afghanistan suggests at least some willingness to make that hard judgment, in this case to keep a deteriorating situation from getting worse. Afghanistan is President Obama's Iraq, at least with regard to obvious responsibility. Iraq was not his, and he made a decision for a fairly prompt troop drawdown while the situation there had become more stable, but not fully stabilized.

Yet he also made the strong executive decision to replace the commander of U.S. forces in Afghanistan with a general who had more counterinsurgency experience.[79] This decision seems to contrast with George W. Bush's too long-delayed replacement of his top commander in Iraq as the war effort faltered. Yet, it is well to keep in mind that before Bush's chosen replacement General Petraeus wrote it, there was no counterinsurgency doctrine to send in a new commander to implement. New personnel carrying out old doctrine is no recipe for success. And General McChrystal, Obama's new choice for Afghanistan commander, was head of a program approved by President Bush to use American commandos to strike at Taliban sanctuaries in Pakistan.

So there are in Obama's national security presidency so far diverse signals whose meanings we can not yet fully understand. Over time, we will learn and he will reveal more. Obama has said of himself, "I am like a Rorschach test."[80] In the case of Obama's national security strategic worldview and policies, that blank space will be filled in soon enough.

Even smart, thoughtful, and verbally fluid presidents like Mr. Obama, or perhaps one should say here especially presidents with those characteristics, can be seduced by the power of their words in domestic political contexts. There, eloquence, nuance, calmness, charisma, and celebrity carry great political weight. There's some international carryover to this president's star-power, but he is dealing with many regimes and leaders who carry their own strong views of their place, and the status of the country they rule or represent in the world. They tally Obama's clout, not so much by the adoration of his supporters at home or abroad, but rather by the concrete decisions he makes, avoids, or tries to straddle. They are the president's international and truly "attentive public."

Miranda rights for terrorists? The Obama Justice Department, "has determined that detainees tried by military commissions in the U.S. can claim at least some constitutional rights, particularly protection against the use of statements taken through coercive interrogations."[81] The problem here is that once the Justice Department concludes that terrorists are entitled to some constitutional rights, on what basis can they legitimately be denied others, say the right to a fair and speedy trial?

During his presidential campaign and after he had been elected President, Obama had scoffed at the idea of Miranda rights for terrorists,[82] but he is now squarely faced with a critical dilemma of his own making. Having denigrated the Bush policies of using military tribunals and holding dangerous terrorist prisoners indefinitely, Obama has been forced by the lack of viable alternatives to adopt similar policies including military tribunals[83] and indefinite detention.[84] How he will *substantively* be able to reconcile these policies with enforcing constitutional rights for captured terrorists is difficult to see.

The Bush Doctrine, as noted, is not only a set of policies, but also a stance toward the problems, and the leadership strengths to carry them through. Obama's reluctant embrace of some, but by no means all, of the Bush's Doctrine's policies, runs strongly counter to his liberal internationalist preferences and worldview. It will not be easy for the two to peacefully co-exist, and that may prove to be the decisive permeating national security tension in the Obama Administration.

What is clear at this point is that in some ways, in spite of his rhetoric, President Obama, by adopting several key Bush policies, has already weighed in on the question to which we now turn: Has the Bush Doctrine helped to make the United States safer?

Has the Bush Doctrine made the United States Safer?

We come now, in conclusion to an essential question. If the answer on balance is yes, then it would be prudent to keep the strategic premises and policies that have helped protect us. If not, then we had better peruse the grand theories analyzed in Chapter 8 more carefully and hope we can find a substitute.

Yet, obviously the question cannot be answered with a simple yes or no. There are at least three strategically related but distinctive questions that must be addressed. Did the Bush Doctrine and its general set of policy premises provide a sound template for addressing the major concerns of America's post-9/11 security dilemma? Has the Doctrine and its associated policies helped to secure the American homeland from further attack? And finally, have the policies pursued by the Bush Administration abroad, most notably the war in Iraq but also in Afghanistan and the push for democratization helped the national security position of this country? At this point the answers to all three questions must remain provisional, but let us at least begin to address them.

The question of whether the Bush Doctrine provides a viable framework for addressing American post-9/11 security concerns is a vital one. If it doesn't, the policies conducted under its rubric begin with a basic and perhaps irremediable flaw. I have argued throughout that the Bush Doctrine has strong conceptual framing and policy answers to the very basic post-9/11 strategic questions outlined at the beginning of this book. As I have suggested, no other "grand theory" put forward as a successor to the Doctrine comes close to providing such a comprehensive framework. More importantly, they do not provide plausible answers to the most bedeviling questions that face American strategic policy. "Selective engagement" doesn't tell us where to draw the line and under what circumstances. Neo-isolationism is a dangerously passive policy when others have vowed to continue their attacks. Realist accommodation also has its dangers when your sworn enemies threaten to obliterate one of your primary allies and gain hegemony over a vital region. None of the replacement strategies suggested really answer the question of when you might need to employ preventive or preemptive strategies, build policy specific coalitions, or even go it alone. Of course, talk is preferable to fighting, when possible. Having many allies is preferable to having fewer allies. And having the respect and appreciation of the world community is preferable to its opposite, though not if obtained at the cost of being vulnerable. To date, replacement strategies for the Bush Doctrine have not advanced concrete policies that tell us how they will address, much less resolve, these issues.

On the second question, there can be little doubt that the United States is better prepared today than it was before the 9/11 attacks to respond to an unprecedented set of threats. That fact is a direct result of the Bush Doctrine and the policies developed as a result of it. These policies both formal and informal were detailed earlier (Chapters 2 and 3) and will not be repeated here. This is not an argument that nothing more needs to be done; no defense is fool proof. However in terms of infrastructure protection and domestic security policies the administration has put into operation a wide variety of initiatives designed to protect Americans at home.

And what of the Iraq War and democratization? Has the pursuit of those policies increased or decreased the overall threat to the United States? The very first step in answering this question is asking whether it was prudent to remove Saddam Hussein instead of tolerating or trying to contain him. There is ample evidence that sanctions against Saddam were eroding and there was little international appetite for even more stringent policies. Moreover, a very strong case can be made for assessing Saddam as an extremely dangerous tyrant on psychological and strategic grounds, and with regard to his poor judgment. So there remains a strong case for removing him that is difficult to measure factually against optimistic scenarios of containment.

Assuming that case is persuasive, the next question that arises is whether the Iraq War and efforts to develop a democracy there after the removal of Saddam Hussein have increased or decreased the threat to the United States. It is clearly difficult to argue that the war has, to date, unquestionably increased the security of the United States. That is because the United States has yet to adequately achieve any of its strategic purposes there like the development of a relatively democratic and competent government that commands national loyalties and is able to take care of itself militarily.

Did the invasion of Iraq make matters worse? Some think so. The critic's view is that Iraq has diverted resources that could have been used to fight terrorism, that Iraq has become a rallying cause for radical recruitment, inflamed elements of world opinion against the United States, proved a theater of training for and allowed al Qaeda to reconstitute itself. The counter considerations are that America and its allies have dramatically bolstered their efforts against al Qaeda worldwide even while fighting in Iraq, that any action against al Qaeda would be used for propaganda purposes, that some world opinion would be inflamed by anything short of American quiescence and maybe a less-assertive defense, that every terrorist effort whether in Bali, Madrid, London or elsewhere provides terrorists operational experience, and that reconstitution efforts by replacing dead leaders and search for new safe havens are what groups do when they suffer losses during war. They are a reflection of determination on their part and equally the need for determination on our part and are by no means an equivocal sign that we have "failed." Finally, all the admitted costs of battling al Qaeda and other insurgent groups in Iraq must be seriously weighed against the costs of defeat.

The National Intelligence Estimate and Saban Center studies we reviewed pointed to catastrophic consequences should the United States fail in Iraq, all of which would lead to serious repercussions for American national security. There is no doubt that the war in Iraq, though winding down for American troops, was brutal and difficult and progress was gradual and obtained at a high cost to American soldiers and Iraqis alike. Democratization is proceeding in Iraq at a slow pace, and might still be undone, but the country appears to be reaching a fair level of political and strategic stability.

The emergence of a relatively stable Iraq with a functioning government able to deal with its most pressing security concerns (with American assistance as for example reaching a possible agreement for American fighters to provide air defenses for Iraq until such time as the Iraqi air force can be developed[85]) now seems to be within reach. Success by this standard would clearly not measure up to the "beacon of democracy" rhetoric heard early on in the Bush White House, but it would still represent a substantial and successful outcome.

Overall then the accomplishments of the Bush Doctrine are mixed, but hardly the unmitigated failure depicted by its critics. Conceptually, the doctrine has provided answers to post-9/11 strategic security concerns that other possible replacement strategies have failed so far to match. The Doctrine and its associated policies have put into place a framework both domestically and abroad designed for a long struggle on many fronts. Granted, these policies have caused strains with some allies on some matters and inflamed "world opinion," but not everywhere or equally. Clearly we need to do better on this score.

The Bush Doctrine is clearly not without its faults, but it is not without its virtues either. And President Obama, having chosen to keep a number of its policies, would do well to retain many of its premises as well.

Notes

1 The Obama Presidency and the World he Inherits

1 For a range of the issues that do face the Obama Administration now see Walter Pincus and Joby Warrick, "Financial Crisis Called Top Security Threat to U.S," *Washington Post*, February 13, 2009, A14. That story is based on the prepared statement of Dennis Blair, Director of National Intelligence, "Annual Threat Assessment of the Intelligence Community for the Senate Select Committee on Intelligence," February 12, 2009. Available from: www.dni.gov/testimonies/20090212_testimony.pdf (accessed May 17, 2009).

For an assessment of possible future threats see National Intelligence Council, "Global Trends 2025: A Transformed World," November 2008. Available from: www.dni.gov/nic/PDF_2025/2025_Global_Trends_Final_Report.pdf (accessed April 25, 2009).

2 Quoted in Thom Shanker, "China Harassed U.S. Ship, Pentagon Says," *New York Times*, March 10, 2009.

3 Paul McGeough, "Warning That Pakistan is in Danger of Collapse within Months," *Sidney Morning Herald*, April 13, 2009.

4 Bryan Bender, "US Weighs Tough Action on Pirates," *Boston Globe*, April 14, 2009; Editorial, "A Solution for Somalia: What it Will Take to Stop the Threats of Piracy and Terrorism," *Washington Post*, April 14, 2009.

5 Barack Obama, "Renewing American Leadership," *Foreign Affairs*, July/August 2007.

6 Editorial, "The World Reacts," *Washington Post*, January 26, 2009.

7 Jan Cienski, "Nato Allies Spurn US Troops Plea," *Financial Times*, February 19, 2009.

8 Quoted in John Burns, "Obama Promises the World a Renewed America," *New York Times*, January 21, 2009.

9 Timothy Garton Ash, professor of European Studies at Oxford quoted in John Burns, "Obama Promises the World a Renewed America."

10 For a view of a new international system that he describes as "post-American," see Fareed Zakaria, "The Future of American Power: How America Can Survive the Rise of the Rest," *Foreign Affairs*, May/June 2008.

11 Robert A. Pape, "Empire Fall," *The National Interest*, January/February 2009, 24.

12 Transcript Obama's interview with Al Arabiya, January 27, 2009. Available from: www.alarabiya.net/save_print.php?print=1&cont_id=65096&lang=en (accessed February 1, 2009).

13 Review and disposition of individuals detained at the Guantánamo Bay Naval Base and closure of detention facilities, January 22, 2009. Available from: www.whitehouse.gov/the_press_office/ClosureOfGuantanamoDetentionFacilities/ (accessed January 30, 2009).

14 *Ensuring Lawful Interrogations*, January 22, 2009. Available from: www.whitehouse.gov/the_press_office/EnsuringLawfulInterrogations/ (accessed January 30, 2009).

15 *Executive Order: Review of Detention Policy Options*, January 22, 2009. Available from: www.whitehouse.gov/the_press_office/ReviewofDetentionPolicyOptions/ (accessed January 30, 2009).

16 Diana Priest, "Bush's War on Terror Comes to a Sudden End," *Washington Post*, January 23, 2009, A01.

17 Christina Bellantoni, "Obama's Exec Orders Have Loopholes," *Washington Times*, February 2, 2009.

18 Greg Miller, "Obama Lets CIA Keep Controversial Renditions Tool," *Chicago Tribune*, January 31, 2009.

19 Tim Starks, "Intelligence Policy: New Perspectives of Familiar Approach," *Congressional Quarterly*, February 16, 2009; see also Eli Lake, "Small Change," *The New Republic*, March 4, 2008.

20 Keith Perine, "Justice Department Again Defends Bush on State Secrets," *CQ Politics*, February 20, 2009; see also Josh Gerstein, "Obama Defends Bush-era Secrets," *Politico*, February 21, 2009.

21 David G. Savage, "Solicitor General Nominee Says 'Enemy Combatants' Can be Held without Trial," *Los Angeles Times*, February 11, 2009.

22 Adam Liptak, "Justices Limit Authority of President on Detainees," *New York Times*, March 7, 2009.

23 *New York Times*, "Obama to Appeal Detainee Ruling," April 11, 2009.

24 Del Quentin Wilber and Peter Finn, "U.S. Retires 'Enemy Combatant,' Keeps Broad Right to Detain," *Washington Post*, March 14, 2009, A06; see also William Glaberson, "U.S. Won't Label Terror Suspects as 'Combatants,'" *New York Times*, March 14, 2009.

25 Peter Finn, "Obama Set to Revive Military Commissions Changes Would Boost Detainee Rights," *Washington Post*, May 9, 2009, A01.

26 Richard A. Oppel, Jr., "Strikes in Pakistan Underscore Obama's Options," *New York Times*, January 24, 2009.

27 Mark Mazzetti and David E. Sanger, "Obama Expands Missile Strikes Inside Pakistan," *New York Times*, February 21, 2009.

28 Helene Cooper, "Putting Stamp on Afghan War, Obama Will Send 17,000 Troops," *New York Times*, February 18, 2009.

29 Lara Jakes, "U.S. Commander: 55,000 Troops Needed in Afghanistan," *Associated Press*, February 18, 2009.

30 Associated Press, "Obama Says Future Afghan Troop Levels Uncertain," February 19, 2009.

31 Charlie Savage, "Obama's War on Terror May Resemble Bush's in Some Areas," *New York Times*, February 18, 2009.

32 Robert Kagan, "Foreign Policy Sequels," *Washington Post*, March 9, 2009, A15.

33 Robert Dreyfuss, "Obama's Evolving Foreign Policy," *The Nation*, July 1, 2008.

34 Spencer Ackerman, "The Obama Doctrine," *The American Prospect*, March 24, 2008.

35 Some exceptions include Timothy J. Lynch and Robert S. Singh, *After Bush: The Case for Continuity in American Foreign Policy*. New York: Cambridge, 2008; see also Stanley A. Renshon and Peter Suedfeld (eds) *Understanding the Bush Doctrine: Psychology and Strategy in an Age of Terrorism*. New York: Routledge, 2007.

36 Melvyn P. Leffer and Jeffrey W. Legro, "Introduction," in Melvyn P. Leffer and Jeffrey W. Legro (eds) *To Lead the World: American Strategy After the Bush Doctrine*. New York: Oxford, 2008, p. 2.

37 Jonathan Freedland, "After a Flurry of Early Activity, the Obama Doctrine is Taking Shape," *The Guardian*, March 11, 2009; see also Ackerman, "The Obama Doctrine."

38 Transcript, Second McCain–Obama Debate.

39 John F. Kennedy, "Address at the University of Washington's 100th Anniversary Program," Edmundson Pavilion, Seattle, Washington, November 16, 1961. Available from: www.learner.org/channel/workshops/primarysources/coldwar/docs/jfk.html#questions (accessed March 5, 2009).

40 Barack Obama. "Speech to the Chicago Council of Global Affairs," April 23, 2007. Available from: www.thechicagocouncil.org/dynamic_page.php?id=64 (accessed March 5, 2009).

41 Michael Grunwald, "Obama Power Will be in the White House, Not Cabinet," *Time*, December 16, 2008.

42 Jonathan Martin, "West Wing on Steroids in Obama W.H.," *Politico*, January 25, 2009.

43 Gerald F. Seib, "Obama Will be a Hands-On Chief," *Wall Street Journal*, January 13, 2009.

44 Athena Jones, "Obama: Change Comes from Me," *MSNBC*, November 26, 2008.

45 The quotes that follow are drawn from, "Transcript, Barack Obama's Inaugural Address," *New York Times*, January 20, 2009. Available from: www.nytimes.com/2009/01/20/us/politics/20textobama.html?_r=1&em=&pagewanted=print (accessed February 20, 2009).

46 John F. Burns, "Obama Promises the World a Renewed America," *New York Times*, January 21, 2009.

47 At the signing ceremony for the three presidential directives, President Obama said, "It is precisely our ideals that give us the strength and the moral high ground to be able to effectively deal with the unthinking violence that we see emanating from terrorist organizations around the world." Steven Thomma, "Obama Sends a Message: the United States Will Not Torture," *McClatchy Newspapers*, January 22, 2009.

48 Transcript, "First Presidential Debate," *CNN*, September 26, 2008. Available from: www.cnn.com/2008/POLITICS/09/26/debate.mississippi.transcript/ (accessed February 8, 2009).

49 Peter Baker, "Obama Offered Deal to Russia in Secret Letter," *New York Times*, March 3, 2009.

50 Karen DeYoung, "Obama Team Seeks to Redefine Russia Ties," *Washington Post*, March 4, 2009, A11; see also Jay Solomon and Jonathan Weisman, "U.S. Willing to Roll Back Missile-Defense Plans in Europe," *Wall Street Journal*, March 3, 2009.

51 Robert M. Gates, "A Balanced Strategy: Reprogramming the Pentagon for a New Age," *Foreign Affairs*, January/February 2009.

52 In his first presidential news conference Obama said of Iran, "their development of a nuclear weapon or their pursuit of a nuclear weapon, that all those things create the possibility of destabilizing the region and are not only contrary to our interests, but I think are contrary to the interests of international peace." "Transcript: Obama takes questions on the economy," CNN, February 9, 2009. Available from: www.edition.cnn.com/2009/POLITICS/02/09/obama.conference.transcript/ (accessed March 5, 2009).

53 Greg Miller, "U.S. Now Sees Iran as Pursuing Nuclear Bomb," *Los Angeles Times*, February 12, 2009.

54 Daniel Dombey, "Iran Holds Enough Uranium for Bomb," *Financial Times*, February 19, 2009.

55 "Transcript-State of the Union with John King; Interview with Admiral Mullen," *CNN*, March 1, 2009. Available from: www.transcripts.cnn.com/TRANSCRIPTS/0903/01/sotu.01.html (accessed March 5, 2009).

56 "Transcript: Meet the Press, Robert Gates-Secretary of Defense," *NBC*, March 1, 2009. Available from: www.msnbc.msn.com/id/29453052/ (accessed March 5, 2009).

57 In his Al Arabiya interview, Obama was asked about being able to live with a nuclear-armed Iran and he replied, "But I do think that it is important for us to be willing to talk to Iran, to express very clearly where our differences are, but where there are potential avenues for progress." See also David S. Cloud, "Obama Team Looks for Opening in Iran," *The Politico*, January 31, 2009.

58 Mark Lander, "Clinton Wants to Include Iran in Afghan Talks," *New York Times*, March 6, 2009.

59 Sheryl Gay Stolberg and Marc Santora, "Bush Declares Iran's Arms Role in Iraq is Certain," *New York Times*, February 15, 2007.

60 Editorial, "Burma's Clenched Fist," *Washington Post*, February 20, 2009.

61 Glenn Kessler, "Clinton Criticized for Not Trying to Force China's Hand," *Washington Post*, February 21, 2009, A08.

62 John K. Wilson, *Barack Obama: This Improbable Quest*. Boulder, CO: Paradigm, 2007, pp. 117–18.

63 Richard Cohen, "Moralism on the Shelf," *Washington Post*, March 10, 2009, A13.

64 Jay Solomon, "Clinton Says 'Eyes Wide Open' on Iran," *Wall Street Journal*, March 3, 2009.

65 Mark Lander, "Clinton Pledges Tough Diplomacy and a Fast Start," *New York Times*, January 13, 2009.

66 Freeman wrote, "[T]he truly unforgivable mistake of the Chinese authorities was the failure to intervene on a timely basis to nip the demonstrations in the bud, rather than – as would have been both wise and efficacious – to intervene with force when all other measures had failed to restore domestic tranquility to Beijing and other major urban centers in China. In this optic, the Politburo's response to the mob scene at 'Tian'anmen' stands as a monument to overly cautious behavior on the part of the leadership, not as an example of rash action. ... " Quoted in Jon Chait, "Obama's Intelligence Blunder," *Washington Post*, February 28, 2009.

67 Mark Mazzetti and Helene Cooper, "Israel Stance Was Undoing of Nominee for Intelligence Post," *New York Times*, March 12, 2009.

68 Adam B. Kushner, "A Return to Realism," *Newsweek*, January 26, 2009.

69 Justine A. Rosenthal, "A Sit-down with Brent Scowcroft," *The National Interest*, January/February 2009, 5.

70 The lack of plans criticism, is in retrospect, inaccurate. The problem seems not to be dearth of plans, but too many plans that were not well integrated into a set of overall plans. The rosy scenarios criticism is much more on target. The Pentagon was planning a very quick operation based on premises that turned out to be wrong. The Iraqi Army disintegrated and was unavailable to help maintain order. The economy and the infrastructure was in a shambles because of decades of neglect and abuse by the central government. And perhaps above all the Iraqis at almost every level of society were traumatized by decades of brutal rule. A number of articles and books have explored aspects of the controversies, among them: Michael R. Gordon, "The Strategy to Secure Iraq Did Not Foresee a 2nd War," *New York Times*, October 19, 2004; Michael R. Gordon, "A Prewar Slide Show Cast Iraq in Rosy Hues," *New York Times*, February 15, 2007; Kate Phillips, Shane Lauth and Erin Schenck (Editor W. Andrew Terrill), "U.S. Military Combat Operations in Iraq; Planning, Combat and Operations," Carlisle, PA: Strategic Studies Institute of the U.S. War College, April 2006. Available from: www.strategicstudiesinstitute.army.mil/pdffiles/PUB653.pdf (accessed March 12, 2009); George Packer, *The Assassins' Gate: America in Iraq*. New York: Farrar, Straus & Giroux, 2005; Thomas E. Ricks, *Fiasco: The American Military Adventure in Iraq*. New York: Penguin, 2006; and Rajiv Chandrasekaran, *Imperial Life in the Emerald City: Inside Iraq's Green Zone*. New York: Knopf, 2006.

71 Richard L. Armitage and Joseph S. Nye Jr., *A Smarter More Secure America: Report of the CSIS Commission on Smart Power*. Washington, DC: CSIS, 2007. Available from: www.csis.org/media/csis/pubs/071106_csissmartpowerreport.pdf (accessed January 25, 2009).

72 Smart Power Report, p. 8.

73 Transcript, "Obama's Interview Aboard Air Force One," *New York Times*, March 8, 2009 (emphasis added). Available from: www.nytimes.com/2009/03/08/us/politics/08obama-text.html?pagewanted=print (accessed March 5, 2009).

74 Karen DeYoung and Joby Warrick, "Drone Attacks Inside Pakistan Will Continue, CIA Chief Says," *Washington Post*, February 26, 2009.

75 Sabrina Tavernsise, Richard A. Oppel, Jr. and Eric Schmitt, "Militants Unite in Pakistan's Populous Heart," *New York Times*, April 14, 2009.

76 Zahid Hussain and Matthew Rosenberg, "Pakistani Peace Deal Gives New Clout to Taliban Rebels," *Wall Street Journal*, April 14, 2009.

77 Matthew Rosenberg and Zahid Hussain, "Pakistan's Leader Stirs Fresh Turmoil," *Wall Street Journal*, February 26, 2009.

78 Mark Lander and Elisabeth Bummiller, "Now, U.S. Sees Pakistan as a Cause Distinct from Afghanistan," *New York Times*, May 1, 2009.

79 Barack Obama, "Responsibly Ending the War in Iraq," prepared for delivery at Camp Lejeune, North Carolina, February 27, 2009. Available from: www.whitehouse.gov/the_press_office/Remarks-of-President-Barack-Obama-Responsibly-Ending-the-War-in-Iraq/ (accessed February 28, 2009).

80 Smart Power Report, pp. 34–35.

81 Oli R. Holsti, *Public Opinion and American Foreign Policy.* Ann Arbor, MI: University of Michigan Press, 1997.

82 Zakaria, "The Future of American Power."

83 Azar Gat, "The Return of Authoritarian Great Powers," *Foreign Affairs,* July/August 2007.

84 David S. Cloud, "Secret Report Urges New Afghan Plan," *Politico,* February 3, 2009; see also Helene Cooper, "Obama Weighs Adding Troops in Afghanistan," *New York Times,* February 12, 2009. The latter report indicates that, "Administration officials have indicated that they may seek to refocus United States military efforts in Afghanistan on counterinsurgency."

85 "Transcript, Second McCain, Obama Debate" (emphasis mine).

86 *The 9/11 Commission Report 2004,* p. 381 (emphasis in original).

87 "Report on the Status of 9/11 Commission Recommendations, Part III: Foreign Policy, Public Diplomacy, and Nonproliferation," November 14, 2005, 3 (emphasis added). Available from: www.9-11pdp.org/press/2005-11-14_report.pdf (accessed March 12, 2009).

88 John D. Negroponte, "Unclassified Statement for the Record Annual Threat Assessment Senate Select Committee on Intelligence," January 11, 2007, pp. 7, 9. Available from: www.fas.org/irp/congress/2007_hr/011107transcript.pdf (accessed March 12, 2009).

89 Al Qaeda, the now amorphous group most closely associated with the threat of catastrophic terrorism, has substantially solved the problems that have been tied to the demise of other terrorists groups historically—intergeneration mission transmission, recruitment, funding, message, capacity, and strategy. As one researcher put it, al Qaeda "has transitioned beyond its original structure and now represents a multigenerational threat with staying power comparable to the ethnonationalist groups of the twentieth century." See Audrey Kurth Cronin, "How Al-Qaida Ends: The Decline and Demise of Terrorist Groups," *International Security,* 31:1 (Summer 2006), p. 41.

90 National Intelligence Council, "National Intelligence Estimate—The Terrorist Threat to the US Homeland," July 2007, 6 (emphasis mine). Available from: www.dni.gov/press_releases/20070717_release.pdf (accessed March 5, 2009).

91 Blair, "Annual Threat Assessment of the Intelligence Community for the Senate Select Committee on Intelligence," p. 20 (emphasis mine).

92 National Intelligence Council, "Global Trends 2025: A Transformed World," p. iv.

93 National Intelligence Estimate, "The Terrorist Threat to the U.S. Homeland," July 2007, 6 (emphasis mine).

94 Transcript, "First Presidential Debate."

95 John Mueller, *Overblown: How Politicians and the Terrorism Industry Inflate National Security Threats, and Why We Believe Them.* New York: Free Press, 2006; see also Zbigniew Brzezinski, "Terrorized by 'War on Terror': How a Three-Word Mantra Has Undermined America," *Washington Post,* March 25, 2007, B01.

96 A. Trevor Thrall and Jane K. Cramer (eds) *American Foreign Policy and the Politics of Fear: Threat Inflation Since 9/11.* New York: Routledge, 2009.

97 Thrall and Cramer (eds) *American Foreign Policy* ... front inside cover, emphasis added.

98 David Albright, Jacqueline Shire, and Paul Brannan, "Has Iran Achieved a Nuclear Weapons Breakout Capacity? Not Yet, but Soon," Washington, DC: Institute for Science and International Security, December 2, 2008; Daniel Dombey, "Iran Holds Enough Uranium for Bomb," *Financial Times,* February 19, 2009.

99 Glenn Kessler, "Clinton Criticizes Bush on N. Korea," *Washington Post,* February 16, 2009, A11.

100 Richard Posner, *Law, Pragmatism, and Democracy.* Cambridge, MA: Harvard University Press, 2005, pp. 296, 298.

101 See Jeffrey M. Cavanaugh, "From the 'Red Juggernaut' to Iraqi WMD: Threat Inflation and How it Succeeds in the United States," *Political Science Quarterly,* 122:4 (Winter 2007–8), pp. 555–84; Chaim Kaufmann, "Threat Inflation and the Failure of the Marketplace of Ideas: The Selling of the Iraq War," *International Security,* 29:1 (Summer 2004), pp. 5–48.

102 Those who make these arguments do not agree on where the hype lies. See Kaufman, "Threat Inflation … ," p. 6 and compare to Cavanaugh, "From the 'Red Juggernaut' to Iraqi WMD," pp. 564–66. Kaufman includes assertions that the Bush Administration also underplayed doubts expressed by some parties in the run-up to the war. A key piece of evidence for his view is the State Department's "Future of Iraq Project" that provided an "extensive analysis of post-war Iraq." In fact that project was a set of concept papers and possible ideas for a post-war Iraq in a variety of areas and was not intended as, nor did it constitute, an "extensive" analysis. The GWU national security archives introduce the complete set of project documents as follows, "Under the direction of former State official Thomas S. Warrick, the Department organized over 200 Iraqi engineers, lawyers, businesspeople, doctors and other experts into 17 working groups to strategize on topics including the following: public health and humanitarian needs, transparency and anti-corruption, oil and energy, defense policy and institutions, transitional justice, demo-cratic principles and procedures, local government, civil society capacity building, edu-cation, free media, water, agriculture and environment and economy and infrastructure." Note that post-invasion security was not among the major working groups topics, although it was mentioned in passing. Complete documentation of the project can be found at: www.gwu.edu/~nsarchiv/NSAEBB/NSAEBB198/index.htm (accessed February 1, 2009).
103 The key findings of that report can be found at: www.cia.gov/library/reports/general-reports-1/iraq_wmd_2004/chap1.html (accessed February 20, 2009).
104 John J. Mearsheimer and Stephen M. Walt, *Can Saddam be Contained? History Says Yes*. Harvard University: Belfer Center for Science and International Affairs International Security Program Occasional Paper, November 2002.
105 Mearsheimer and Walt, "Can Saddam be Contained?" p. 4.
106 Mearsheimer and Walt, "Can Saddam be Contained?" p. 4.
107 Mearsheimer and Walt, "Can Saddam be Contained?" p. 4 (emphasis mine).
108 The report has a sophisticated methodology section that reflects the authors' under-standing of the ways in which information processes work and can either further or inhibit complex understandings. See Kevin M. Woods with Michael R. Pease, Mark E. Stout, Williamson Murray, and James G. Lacey, "Iraqi Perspectives Project: A View of Operation Iraqi Freedom from Saddam's Senior Leadership," Norfolk, VA: The U.S. Joint Forces Command, 2006. The complete unclassified study can be found at: www. jfcom.mil/newslink/storyarchive/2006/ipp.pdf (accessed February 28, 2009).
109 Robert Jervis, *Perception and Misperception in International Politics*. Princeton, NJ: Princeton University Press, 1976.

2 The Evolution of a Post-9/11 National Security Perspective

1 Ashton B. Carter, John Deutch, and Philip Zelikow, "Catastrophic Terrorism: Tackling the New Danger," *Foreign Affairs*, November/December (1998); see also, *The 9/11 Commission Report: Final Report of the National Commission on Terrorist Attacks upon the United States*. New York: Norton, 2004.
2 Francis Fukuyama, *America at the Crossroads*. New Haven, CT: Yale University Press, 2006, p. 67.
3 David Frum and Richard Perle, *An End to Evil: How to Win the War on Terrorism*. New York: Random House, 2003; see also, Angelo M. Codevilla, "No Victory, No Peace: What Rumsfeld's Memo Reveals … and Other Lessons from the War -So Far," *Clar-emont Review of Books*, November 26, 2003.
4 See for example, George Will, "Rhetoric of Unreality," *Washington Post*, March 2, 2006, A21; see also George F. Will, "The Triumph of Unrealism," *Washington Post*, August 15, 2006, A13.
5 For example, Francis Fukuyama warned, "preventive war cannot be the centerpiece of American strategy." Stephen Walt expresses a similar misunderstanding when he writes, "making preventive war a centerpiece of U.S. national security policy did considerable damage to America's national image." See Fukuyama, *America at the Crossroads*, p. 183 and Stephen M. Walt, "In the National Interest," *Boston Review*, February/March 2005, 6.

John Bolton had this to say about the matter, "I don't consider ... preemption to constitute a doctrine ... it is an element in an overall approach to the geo-strategic state of the world today ... the issue is not whether preemption has somehow assumed a higher place—or a different place—than before in the range of options that the U.S. has, but whether the nature of the threat posed by terrorists or terrorist-supporting states and WMD means that preemption necessarily fits into that different context." Interview with then Under Secretary of State, John R. Bolton, *The Fletcher Forum on World Affairs*, 29:1 (2005), pp. 5–6; see also M. Elaine Bunn, "Preemptive Action: When, How, and to What Effect?" *Strategic Forum*, 200 (July 2003), p. 7.

6 This was no small matter and we are just beginning to learn what went on behind the scenes. For example, a report submitted by the Undersecretary of Defense for Policy, Eric S. Edelman in rebuttal to a report of the Department of Defense's Inspector General on the operation on prewar intelligence contained the very interesting item that an ad hoc group was formed shortly after the 9/11 attacks, "to review all basic information about a number of international terrorist organizations with a basic focus on the question: *What does it mean to be at war with a terrorist network?*" See "Comments by the Office of the Under Secretary of Defense on a draft of a Proposed Report by the DOD Office of Inspector General" Project NO. D2006DINTOl-0077.000 Review of pre-Iraqi War Activities of the office of the Under Secretary of Defense for Policy (u) January 16, 2007, p. 13. Available from: www.fas.org/irp/agency/dod/ousd011707.pdf (accessed June 26, 2009).

7 Here the Bush Doctrine combines the first two "images" that Kenneth Waltz discussed in his classic book, an emphasis on leader images and on regime images. The Bush Doctrine takes very seriously Waltz's second image that the nature of regimes drives international politics. However, it is clear that the administration combines this with the view that particular leaders, like Saddam Hussein are also critically important and can, along with regime type magnify the strategic dangers. See Kenneth Waltz, *Man, the State and War*. New York: Columbia University Press, 1965.

8 Stephen L. Harris and Gloria Platzner, *Classical Mythology: Images and Insights*, 3rd ed. Mountain View, CA: Mayfield, 2001, p. 5.

9 Tony Smith, *A Pact with the Devil: Washington's Bid for World Supremacy and the Betrayal of the American Promise*. New York: Routledge, 2007.

10 James Mann, *The Rise of the Vulcans: The History of Bush's War Cabinet*. New York: Viking, 2004; see also, Fukuyama, *American at the Crossroads*, pp. 12–65.

11 Project for the New American Century, Letter to President Clinton on Iraq, January 26, 1998. Available from: www.newamericancentury.org/iraqclintonletter.htm (accessed April 23, 2009). Two years later, Robert Kagan and William Kristol published a book that surveyed the array of threats facing the United States and offered strong policy prescriptions to deal with them; see Robert Kagan and William Kristol (eds), *Present Dangers: Crisis and Opportunity in American Foreign and Defense Policy*. San Francisco, CA: Encounter Books, 2000.

12 Project for the New American Century, Statement of Principles, June 3, 1997 (emphasis mine). Available from: www.newamericancentury.org/statementofprinciples.htm (accessed March 5, 2009).
The statement was signed by a number of people who would play prominent roles in the administration, among them: Elliott Abrams, Dick Cheney, Zalmay Khalilzad, I. Lewis Libby, Donald Rumsfeld, and Paul Wolfowitz.

13 Steven Hurst argues that the pre-9/11 group of White House senior foreign policy advisors are best considered as "conservative nationalists," rather than neoconservatives; see Steven Hurst, "Myths of Neocons," *International Politics*, 42 (2005), pp. 75–96.
I think "nationalist realism" is a better, more descriptive term. The president and his advisors would, and have, argued that they are being clear-eyed and realistic about what needs to be done, even if accomplishing their purposes is a large reach. However, in any event, the use of the term "neoconservative" for this early group is a misnomer.

14 George W. Bush, "A Distinctly American Internationalism," Ronald Reagan Presidential Library, Simi Valley, CA, November 19, 1999. Available from: www.mtholyoke.edu/acad/intrel/bush/wspeech.htm (accessed March 5, 2009).

15 Here are some key phrases: "The empire [Soviet Union] has passed, but evil remains"; "America has determined enemies who hate our values"; "We must protect our homeland and our allies against missiles and terror"; "in defense of our nation, a president must be a clear-eyed realist"; "armies and missiles are not stopped by stiff notes of condemnation, [but] by strength and purpose and the promise of swift punishment"; "unless a president sets his own priorities, his priorities will be set by others"; and "The Comprehensive Test Ban Treaty ... is not verifiable ... it would stop us from insuring the safety and reliability of our deterrent—It is not enforceable ... it offers only words and false hopes and high intentions—with no guarantees whatsoever."

16 Joseph Grieco, "Anarchy and the Limits of Cooperation: A Realist Critique of the Newest Liberal Institutionalism," *International Organization*, 42 (1988), pp. 485–507.

17 John J. Mearsheimer, *The Tragedy of Great Power Politics*. New York: Norton, 2001, p. 36.

18 John H. Herz, "Idealist Internationalism and the Security Dilemma," *World Politics*, 2 (1950), pp. 157–80; see also Robert Jervis, "Cooperation Under the Security Dilemma," *World Politics*, 30:2 (1978), pp. 167–214.

19 John J. Mearsheimer, "The False Promise of International Institutions," *International Security*, 19:3 (1994/95), pp. 5–49.

20 *A National Strategy of Enlargement and Engagement*. Washington, DC: U.S. Government Printing Office, 1994 [revised 1995 and 1996]. The 1996 version can be found at: www.fas.org/spp/military/docops/national/1996stra.htm (accessed March 5, 2009).

21 See John Lewis Gaddis, *Strategies of Containment: A Critical Appraisal of American National Security Policy during the Cold War*. New York: Oxford University Press, 2005; John Lewis Gaddis, *The United States and the Origins of the Cold War, 1941–1947*. New York, Columbia University Press, 1972; Samuel F. Wells, Jr. "Sounding the Tocsin: NSC 68 and the Soviet Threat," *International Security*, 4:2 (Autumn 1979), pp. 116–58; John Lewis Gaddis and Paul H. Nitze, "NSC-68 and the Soviet Threat Reconsidered," *International Security*, 4:4 (Spring 1980), pp. 164–76; and Melvyn P. Leffler, *A Preponderance of Power: National Security, the Truman Administration, and the Cold War*. Stanford, CA: Stanford University Press, 1992.

22 All the quotes that follow in this paragraph are drawn from that document; emphases are added.

23 This line of strategic reasoning is consistent with Betts' finding that offensive dominant terrorist strategies are favored in the offensive–defensive balance. See Richard K. Betts, "The Soft Underbelly of American Primacy: Tactical Advantages of Terror," *Political Science Quarterly*, 117 (2002), pp. 27–31.

24 Fukuyama, *America at the Crossroads* ... , p. 82.

25 "We will extend the peace by encouraging free and open societies on every continent." See "President Bush Delivers Graduation Speech at West Point," June 1, 2002. Available from: www.nti.org/e_research/official_docs/pres/bush_wp_prestrike.pdf (accessed March 5, 2009).

26 Condoleezza Rice, "A Balance of Power That Favors Freedom," Wriston Lecture, Manhattan Institute, October 1, 2002. Available from: www.manhattaninstitute.org/html/wl2002.htm (accessed March 5, 2009).

27 Douglass J. Feith, *War and Decision: Inside the Pentagon at the Dawn of the War on Terrorism*. New York: Harper, 2008, pp. 521–22; see also Condoleezza Rice, "Promise of Democratic Peace," *Washington Post*, December 11, 2005, B07.

28 Critics see the democracy argument as a suspect compensatory rhetorical device after the failure to find WMD stockpiles. However, its presence in major speeches and documents *before* the invasion tends to undercut this position. It is also, however, indisputable that after the failure to find WMD, democracy achieved more prominence. Yet it is also true that major wars initiated by choice often have more than one strategic rationale. Indeed, it is the possibility of achieving multiple goals that often tips the scale in the direction of attack.

29 Department of Defense, Quadrennial Defense Review Report, February 6, 2006. Available from: www.comw.org/qdr/qdr2006.pdf (accessed April 23, 2009).

30 Quadrennial Defense, p. vi.
31 Lawrence Freedman, *Deterrence*. Cambridge: Polity Press, 2004, Chapter 2; see also Patrick Morgan, *Deterrence: A Conceptual Analysis*. Beverly Hills, CA: Sage, 1997.
32 Freedman, *Deterrence* ... , Chapter 1.
33 Quadrennial Defense ... , pp. 49–51.
34 "The National Security Strategy of the United States," March 16, 2006. Hereafter, NSS 2006.
35 "The National Security Strategy of the United States," September 17, 2002, p. 4. Hereafter, NSS 2002.
36 NSS 2006, p. 10.
37 George Packer, *The Assassins' Gate: America in Iraq*. New York: Farrar, Straus & Giroux, 2005; see also Michael R. Gordon and Bernard E. Trainor, *Cobra II: The Inside Story of the Invasion and Occupation of Iraq*. New York: Pantheon, 2006; Thomas E. Ricks, *Fiasco: The American Military Adventure in Iraq*. New York: Penguin, 2006; and L. Paul Bremer (with Malcolm McConnell), *My Year in Iraq: The Struggle to Build a Future of Hope*. New York: Simon & Schuster, 2006.
38 NSS 2002, pp. 12, 34.
39 NSS 2006, p. 9.
40 NSS 2006, pp. 14, 15.
41 NSS 2006, pp. 33, 45.
42 NSS 2006, pp. 9–10, 19.
43 NSS 2006, p. 19.
44 NSS 2006, p. 39.
45 NSS 2006, pp. 35, 39.
46 NSS 2006, p. 41.
47 NSS 2006, p. 12.
48 NSS 2006, p. 18.
49 NSS 2006, p. 20.
50 NSS 2002, p. 5.
51 NSS 2006, pp. 3–4, 33, 34.

3 The Real Bush Doctrine

1 Tony Smith, *A Pact with the Devil: Washington's Bid for World Supremacy and the Betrayal of the American Promise*. New York: Routledge, 2007, p. 2.
2 See for example, Stephan G. Rabe, "The Johnson Doctrine," *Presidential Studies Quarterly*, 36:1 (March 2006), pp. 48–58; Jeffrey Kimbell, "The Nixon Doctrine: A Saga of Misunderstanding," *Presidential Studies Quarterly*, 36:1 (March 2006), pp. 59–74; Dennis Merill, "The Truman Doctrine: Containing Communism and Modernity," *Presidential Studies Quarterly*, 36:1 (March 2006), pp. 27–37; and Chester Patch, "The Reagan Doctrine," *Presidential Studies Quarterly*, 36:1 (March 2006), pp. 75–88.
3 Barry R. Posen and Andrew L. Ross, "Competing Visions for U.S. Grand Strategy," *International Security*, 21:3 (Winter, 1996–97), p. 5 (emphasis mine). Robert Art asks similar questions: What are American interests in the world and what are the threats to these interests? What are the possible grand strategies to protect America's interests from these threats? Which of these grand strategies best protects America's national interests? What specific policies and military capacities are required to support the grand strategies chosen? See Robert Art, *A Grand Strategy for America*. Ithaca, NY: Cornell University Press, 2003, p. 2.
   Elsewhere, Posen emphasizes that, "A grand strategy is a political-military, means-ends chain, a state's theory about how it can 'cause' security for itself ... [and, how best to] ... devise political, economic, military and other remedies for these threats." Here the link is on goals (ends) and the means to reach them. Left unsaid here, is that novel circumstances may well require new means and the reframing of old ones and this can only be effectively accomplished if the diagnosis of the new strategic issue is adequate. See Barry R. Posen, *The Sources of Military Doctrine*. Ithaca, NY: Cornell University Press, 1984, p. 13.

4 See for example, H.W. Brands, "Presidential Doctrines: An Introduction," *Presidential Studies Quarterly*, 36:1 (2006), pp. 1–4.

5 Department of Defense, Quadrennial Defense Review Report, February 6, 2006. Available from: www.comw.org/qdr/qdr2006.pdf (accessed April 5, 2007).

6 "National Strategy for Combating Terrorism," The White House, February 2003. Available from: www.state.gov/documents/organization/60172.pdf (accessed March 1, 2009).

7 "National Strategy for Combating Terrorism," The White House, September 2006. Available from: www.cbsnews.com/htdocs/pdf/NSCT0906.pdf (accessed March 1, 2009).

8 "National Strategy for Homeland Security," The White House, July 2002. Available from: www.dhs.gov/xlibrary/assets/nat_strat_hls.pdf (accessed March 1, 2009).

9 "National Strategy to Combat Weapons of Mass Destruction," The White House, December 2002. Available from: www.fas.org/irp/offdocs/nspd/nspd-wmd.pdf (accessed March 1, 2009).

10 "The National Intelligence Strategy of the United States," The White House, October 2005. Available from: www.dni.gov/publications/NISOctober2005.pdf (accessed March 1, 2009).

11 Coordinating Committee, "The U.S. National Strategy for Public Diplomacy and Strategic Communication," June 2007. Available from: www.state.gov/documents/organization/87427.pdf (accessed March 1, 2009).

12 *U.S. Army Field Manual: Counterinsurgency*, December 15, 2006. Available from: www.fas.org/irp/doddir/army/fm3–24.pdf (accessed March 5, 2009).

13 Cf. "President Bush Delivers Graduation Speech at West Point," June 1, 2002. Available from: www.teachingamericanhistory.org/library/index.asp?documentprint=916 (accessed April 23, 2009); see also George W. Bush, January 29, 2002. Available from: www.archives.cnn.com/2002/ALLPOLITICS/01/29/bush.speech.txt/ (accessed April 23, 2009); Condoleezza Rice, "A Balance of Power That Favors Freedom," Wriston Lecture, Manhattan Institute, October 1, 2002. Available from: www.manhattan-institute.org/html/wl2002.htm (accessed March 12, 2009).

14 Barry P. Posen and Andrew L. Ross, "Competing Visions for U.S. Grand Strategy. ... ", p. 33; Madeleine Albright, "Interview," *New Perspectives Quarterly*, (Summer 2004). In 1992, the Pentagon drafted a new grand strategy designed to prevent the emergence of any possible global rival. That idea ran into considerable criticism, and the Clinton Administration began to describe the United States as the "indispensable" power when it took office. Being indispensable is a softer, gentler way of being preeminent. See William C. Wohlforth, "The Stability of a Unipolar World," *International Security*," 24:1 (1999), p. 5; see also, Patrick Tyler, "The Lone Superpower Plan: Ammunition for Critics," *New York Times*, March 10, 1992, A12; "Excerpts from Pentagon's Plan: 'Prevent the Re-emergence of a New Rival'," *New York Times*, March 8, 1992, A14. Substantial excerpts from the plan may be found at: www.pbs.org/wgbh/pages/frontline/shows/iraq/etc/wolf.html (accessed March 5, 2009); see also www.digitalnpq.org/archive/2004_summer/albright.html (accessed March 5, 2009).

15 For some details regarding the scope and depth of that primacy see Joseph Nye, Jr., *Soft Power: The Means to Success in World Politics*. New York: Public Affairs, 2004, Chapter 1; see also Robert J. Leiber, "Persistent Primacy and the Future of the American Era," *International Politics*, 46:2/3 (2009), pp. 119–39.

16 Samuel P. Huntington, "The Erosion of American National Interests," *Foreign Affairs*, September/October 1997, 43.

17 Posen and Ross, "Competing Visions. ... ," p. 32.

18 Robert Art, "Geopolitics Updates: The Strategy of Collective Engagement," *International Security*, 23:3 (Winter 1998/99), p. 101.

19 Charles A. Kupchan, *The End of the American Era: U.S. Foreign Policy and the Geopolitics of the Twenty-First Century*. New York: Alfred A. Knopf, 2002, p. 63.

20 Arthur Schlesinger, Jr., "The American Empire? Not So Fast," *World Policy Journal*, 23:1 (Spring) 2005, 43–46.

21 Sebastian Mallaby, "For a New Imperialism," *Washington Post*, May 10, 2004, A25.
22 George W. Bush, "A Distinctly American Internationalism," Ronald Reagan Presidential Library, Simi Valley, CA, November 19, 1999. Available from: www.fas.org/news/usa/1999/11/991119-bush-foreignpolicy.htm (accessed April 23, 2009).
23 Bush, "A Distinctly American Internationalism."
24 Bush, "A Distinctly American Internationalism."
25 Rice, "A Balance of Power That Favors Freedom."
26 Robert Jervis, "International Primacy: Is the Game Worth the Candle?" *International Security*, 17:4 (Spring 1993); see also Samuel P. Huntington, "Why International Primacy Matters," *International Security*, 17:4 (Spring 1993).
27 NSS 2002, p. 1.
28 Walter A. McDougall, *Promised Land, Crusader State*. New York: Houghton Mifflin, 1997.
29 Richard E. Neustadt, *Presidential Power and the Modern Presidents: The Politics of Leadership from Roosevelt to Reagan*. New York: Free Press, 1990, Chapter 1.
30 For analysis of the roles that others see the United States as occupying, see Francois Heisbourg, "American Hegemony? Perceptions of the US Abroad," *Survival*, 41:4 (1999–2000), pp. 8–14.
31 John F. Kennedy, "Address at the University of Washington's 100th Anniversary Program," Edmundson Pavilion, Seattle, Washington, November 16, 1961. Available from: www.learner.org/channel/workshops/primarysources/coldwar/docs/jfk.html#questions (accessed March 5, 2009).
32 "Transcript, President-elect Obama Fifth Press Conference," *Chicago Tribune*, December 1, 2008. Available from: www.blogs.suntimes.com/sweet/2008/12/presidentelect_obama_fifth_pre.html (accessed March 5, 2009).
33 Obama, "Renewing American Leadership."
34 Transcript, Remarks of Senator Barack Obama to the Chicago Council on Global Affairs, April 23, 2007.
35 Obama Remarks to the Chicago Council on Global Affairs.
36 Obama Remarks to the Chicago Council on Global Affairs.
37 Glenn Kessler and Thomas E. Ricks, "The Realists' Repudiation of Policies for a War, Region," *Washington Post*, December 7, 2006, A01. All quotes in this paragraph are drawn from this story.
38 Obama Remarks to the Chicago Council on Global Affairs.
39 Obama Remarks to the Chicago Council on Global Affairs.
40 Obama, "Renewing American Leadership."
41 Transcript, Democratic Debate CNN/YouTube, South Carolina, July 23, 2007.
42 Transcript, First McCain-Obama Presidential Debate.
43 Jack L. Snyder, *The Ideology of the Offensive: Military Decision Making and the Disasters of 1914*. Ithaca, NY: Cornell University Press, 1989.
44 Donald Rumsfeld, "21st Century Transformation of U.S. Armed Forces." Remarks as delivered at the National Defense University, Fort McNair, Washington, DC, January 31, 2002. Available from: www.defenselink.mil/speeches/2002/s20020131-secdef.html (accessed March 12, 2009).
45 Robert Jervis, "The Confrontation between Iraq and the US: Implications for the Theory and Practice of Deterrence," *European Journal of International Relations*, 9:2 (2003), p. 316.
46 Transcript, First Democratic Debate, April 27, 2007.
47 Obama, "Renewing American Leadership."
48 Remarks of Illinois State Sen. Barack Obama Against Going to War with Iraq, October 02, 2002. Available from: www.barackobama.com/2002/10/02/remarks_of_illinois_state_sen.php (accessed March 5, 2009).
49 Transcript, Second McCain-Obama Presidential Debate, October 7, 2008.
50 Transcript, First Presidential Debate, 2008.
51 Jay Solomon, "Obama Weighs Reviving Nuclear Pact as NATO Moves to Engage Russia," *Wall Street Journal*, March 6, 2009.

52 "We are also guided by the conviction that no nation can build a safer, better world alone. Alliances and multilateral institutions can multiple the strength of freedom-loving nations ... coalitions of the willing can augment these permanent institutions." See NSS 2002, p. 5.

Mr. Bush is not the only leader to make use of situation-specific alliances. After the 9/11 attacks, Sandy Burger, President Clinton's National Security advisor said, "what we need now is a coalition of the willing that is organized for a long term purpose." Quoted on Jim Lehrer, *On Line News Hour*, September 12, 2001. Available from: www.pbs.org/newshour/bb/military/july-dec01/terror_response_9–12.html (accessed March 12, 2009).

Well before 9/11, the U.N. Secretary General speaking of the situation in East Timor said, "The deployment of these two forces – first a coalition of the willing, and then a United Nations peacekeeping operation – shows the difference rapid deployment can make." See The Secretary General Briefing to the Security Council on a visit to the U.N., February 29, 2000. Available from: www.un.org/peace/etimor/docs/BSG.htm (accessed March 12, 2009).

53 J.M. Goldgeiger and P.E. Tetlock, "Psychology and International Relations Theory," *Annual Review of Political Science*, 4:67 (2001), p. 78.

54 Robert Kagan, "Strategic Dissonance ... "

55 Walter Russell Mead, *Power, Terror, Peace, and War: America's Grand Strategy in a World at Risk*. New York: Knopf, 2004, pp. 141–46.

56 Kagan, "Strategic Dissonance," p. 138.

57 Michael R. Gordon, "Cheney Asks Yemen to Join the Pursuit of Al Qaeda's Remnants," *New York Times*, March 15, 2002; see also Alan Sipress, "Cheney, in Yemen, Notes Improved Ties U.S. to Aid Effort Against Armed Groups," *Washington Post*, March 15, 2002, A16.

58 Alan Cullison, "Kyrgyzstan Hesitates on Plan to Close Base," *Wall Street Journal*, March 6, 2009.

59 Tom Rachman, "Europe and U.S. Agree on Air Passenger Data," *New York Times*, October 6, 2006.

60 Ivo Daadler and James Lindsay, "Democracies of the World Unite," *The American Interest* (November-December 2006).

61 In fact, there has been for some a "Community of Democracies" in operation. It was first convened in Warsaw in 2000. See the State Department's Community of Democracies site. Available from: www.state.gov/g/drl/c10790.htm (accessed March 12, 2009).

62 See John Ikenberry and Anne-Marie Slaughter, Co-Directors, "Forging a World of Liberty Under Law: U.S. National Security in the 21st Century," Final Report of the Princeton Project on National Security Forging a World of Liberty Under Law: U.S. National Security in the 21st Century, September 27, 2007, pp. 11, 29–30. Available from: www.princeton.edu/~ppns/report/FinalReport.pdf (accessed March 12, 2009).

63 Stephen Van Evra, "A Farewell to Geopolitics," in Leffer and Legro, *To Lead the World: American Strategy After the Bush Doctrine*, pp. 23–26.

64 John McCain, "An Enduring Peace Built on Freedom," *Foreign Affairs*, November/December 2007.

65 Ikenberry and Slaughter, "Final Report of the Princeton Project on National Security," pp. 23–26.

66 The Princeton document says that membership, "would be selective, but self-selected. Membership would be predicated not on an abstract definition of liberal democracy or on the labels attached by states to other states, but rather by the obligations that members are willing to take on themselves. Members would have to: pledge not to use force or plan to use force against one another; commit to holding multiparty, free-and-fair elections at regular intervals; guarantee civil and political rights for their citizens enforceable by an independent judiciary; and accept that states have a 'responsibility to protect' their citizens from avoidable catastrophe and that the international community has a right to act if they fail to uphold it." See Ikenberry and Slaughter, "Princeton: Final Report," p. 30.

67 Stephen G. Brooks and William C. Wohlforth, "Reshaping the World Order: How Washington Should Reform International Institutions," *Foreign Affairs*, March/April 2009; see also Stephen G. Brooks and William C. Wohlforth, *World Out of Balance: International Relations and the Challenge of American Primacy*. Princeton, NJ: Princeton University Press, 2008.

68 Van Evra, "Farewell to Geopolitics," p. 26.

69 Guy Dinmore, "Bush Plans Overhaul of US Foreign Aid System," *Financial Times*, December 11, 2005; See also Editorial, "Fixing Foreign Aid," *Washington Post*, May 24, 2004, A22; David Sanger, "Bush Sees Need to Expand Role of NATO in Sudan," *New York Times*, February 18, 2006, A1; see also Editorial, "NATO's New Threat," *Los Angeles Times*, February 5, 2006.

70 Drezer writes that, "the Iraq controversy has overshadowed a more pragmatic and multilateral component of the Bush administration's grand strategy: Washington's attempt to reconfigure U.S. foreign policy and international institutions in order to account for shifts in the global distribution of power." See Daniel W. Drezner, "The New New World Order," *Foreign Affairs*, March/April 2007.

71 Carla Anne Robbins, "Why U.S. Gave U.N. No Role in Plan to Halt Arms Ships," *Wall Street Journal*, October 23, 2003, A1.

72 Review & Outlook. "Sayonara Kyoto," *Wall Street Journal*, July 29, 2005.

73 Robert Jervis, "The Remaking of the Unipolar World," *The Washington Quarterly*, 29:3 (Summer 2006), p. 17.

74 Jervis, "The Remaking of the Unipolar World," p. 7.

75 Obama, "Remarks to the Chicago Council on Global Affairs."

76 Robert Kagan, "Strategic Dissonance," *Survival*, 44:4 (2002–3), pp. 135–38.

77 David Kinsella, "No Rest for Democratic Peace," *American Political Science Review*, 99:3 (2005), pp. 453–58. This issue also contains several additional responses to the "democratic peace" debate.

78 George W. Bush, "President Discusses Global War on Terror Following Briefing at CENTCOM," Tampa, Florida, February 17, 2006. Available from: www.georgewbush-whitehouse.archives.gov/news/releases/2006/02/print/20060217–4.html (accessed March 12, 2009).

79 Obama, "Remarks to the Chicago Council on Global Affairs."

80 "Remarks by the President on a New Beginning: Cairo University," June 4, 2009. Available from: www.whitehouse.gov/the_press_office/Remarks-by-the-President-at-Cairo-University-6-04-09/ (accessed June 5, 2009).

81 Quoted in Paul Koring, "Democracy Fades from Obama's Afghan Agenda," *Globe and Mail*, February 4, 2009.

82 Obama, "Remarks to the Chicago Council on Global Affairs."

83 Chris Patton, "Democracy Doesn't Flow from the Barrel of a Gun," *Foreign Policy*, September/October 2003.

84 Robin Wright, "U.S. Goals Are Thwarted at Pro-Democracy Forum," *Washington Post*, November 13, 2005, A24.

85 Peter Baker, "The Realities of Exporting Democracy," *Washington Post*, January 25, 2006, A01.

86 Baker, "The Realities of Exporting Democracy."

87 Jervis, "The Remaking of the Unipolar World," p. 12.

88 Larry Diamond, "Universal Democracy?" *Policy Review*, 119 (2005).

89 Daniel Byman, "Constructing a Democratic Iraq: Challenges and Opportunities," *International Security*, 28:1 (2003), pp. 47–78.

90 On this point see Francois Heisbourg, "American Hegemony? Perceptions of the US Abroad," *Survival*, 41:4 (1999–2000), p. 11.

4 The Bush Doctrine: Myths and Criticisms

1 Richard E. Neustadt and Ernest R. May, *Thinking in Time, The Uses of History for Decision-makers*. New York: Free Press, 1988.

2 Ivo H. Daalder and James M. Lindsay, *America Unbound: The Bush Revolution in Foreign Policy*. Washington, DC: Brookings Institution Press, 2003, p. 2.

3 Daalder and Lindsay, *America Unbound*, p. 36.

4 Daalder and Lindsay, *America Unbound*, p. 39.

5 Daalder and Lindsay, *America Unbound*, p. 40. Along similar lines, Kagan argues that the foreign policy stance represented by the Bush Administration does not reflect, "one man or one party, or one circle of thinkers. They spring from the nation's historical experience and are a characteristic response to international circumstances." See Robert Kagan, "End of Dreams, Return of History," *Policy Review*, 2007, p. 2

6 Ivo H. Daalder and James M. Lindsay, "Democracies of the World Unite?" *The American Interest*, November-December, 2006.

7 Ivo H. Daalder, "Statement on the 2006 National Security Strategy," The Brookings Institution, March 16, 2006. Available from: www.brookings.edu/views/op-ed/daalder/20060316nss.htm (accessed March 12, 2009).

8 Condoleezza Rice, "America Has the Muscle, but it Has Benevolent Values, Too," *Telegraph-UK*, October 17, 2002.

9 Colin Dueck, "Realism, Culture and Grand Strategy: Explaining America's Peculiar Path to World Power," *Security Studies*, 14:2 (2005), p. 225.

10 Mark Mazzetti and William Glaberson, "Obama Issues Directive to Shut Down Guantanamo," *New York Times*, January 22, 2009.

11 Peter Finn, "Plan to Eliminate Prison Faces Hurdles," *Washington Post*, January 22, 2009, A06; see also Josh Gerstein, "Why the Gitmo Policies May Not Change," *Politico*, January 23, 2009; Jake Tapper, Jan Crawford-Greenburg, and Huma Khan, "Obama Order to Shut Gitmo, CIA Detention Centers," *ABC News*, January 22, 2009.

12 Fareed Zakaria notes, "The classical standard realist hypothesis can be formulated as follows: *Nations expand their political interests when their relative power increases*" [emphasis in original]. Fareed Zakaria, *From Wealth to Power: The Unusual Origins of American's World Role*. Princeton, NJ: Princeton University Press, 1998, p. 19.

13 Jervis, "The Confrontation between Iraq and the US," p. 316 (italics added).

14 Kagan writes that Americans have always promoted a liberal international order abroad, although rarely fully aware of the power they project. Being "unaware" of this, they often find themselves shocked and surprised when the international political system intervenes in their lives in a dramatic and unwelcome way. See Robert Kagan, "Strategic Dissonance," *Survival*, 44:4 (2002–3), pp. 135–38.

15 Jervis, "The Confrontation between Iraq and the US," p. 315.

16 Jervis, "The Confrontation between Iraq and the US," p. 316.

17 Jervis, "The Confrontation between Iraq and the US," p. 316.

18 Yochi J. Dreazen and Siobhan Gorman, "Scowcroft Protégés on Obama's Radar," *Wall Street Journal*, November 24, 2008.

19 "'Pragmatism' should not be a dirty word. Pragmatism is getting things done, and it *can* be principled." Quoted in Kushner, "A Return to Realism."

20 Quoted in Kushner, "A Return to Realism."

21 "Transcript—Interview with Jim Baker," *Fox New Sunday*, December 10, 2006.

22 U.S. Department of State, State Sponsors of Terrorism. Available from: www.state.gov/s/ct/c14151.htm (accessed January 15, 2007).

23 The membership list can be found at: www.oic-oci.org (accessed April 27, 2009).

24 They include: Algeria, Bahrain, Comoros, Djibouti, Egypt, Iraq, Jordan, Kuwait, Lebanon, Libya, Mauritania, Morocco, Oman, Palestine, Qatar, Saudi Arabia, Somalia, Sudan, Syria, Tunisia, United Arab Emirates, and Yemen. The Group's website can be found at: www.arabji.com/ArabGovt/ArabLeague.htm (accessed April 27, 2009).

25 James A. Baker, III and Lee H. Hamilton (Co-Chairs), *The Iraq Study GroupReport*. Washington, DC: U.S Institute of Peace, 2006, p. 46. Available from: www.usip.org/isg/iraq_study_group_report/report/1206/iraq_study_group_report.pdf) (accessed March 12, 2009).

26 Michael R. Gordon, "Will Iraq Study Group's Plan Work on the Battlefield?" *New York Times*, December 7, 2006 (emphasis mine).

27　Stephan Halper and Jonathan Clarke, *America Alone: The Neoconservatives and the Global Order*. New York: Cambridge University Press, 2004.

28　Gerard Baker, "Neo-conspiracy Theories," *The Public Interest* (Winter 2004/2005).

29　John J. Mearsheimer and Stephen Walt, "The Israeli Lobby and U.S. Foreign Policy," Faculty Working Paper No# RWP06–011, March 13, 2006, Harvard University, John F. Kennedy School of Government. Available from: www.ksgnotes1.harvard.edu/ Research/wpaper.nsf/rwp/RWP06–011. This paper set off a storm of criticism on many grounds; see Alan Dershowitz, "Debunking the Newest—and Oldest—Jewish Conspiracy: A Reply to the Mearsheimer-Walt Working Paper," April 5, 2006, Harvard University, John F. Kennedy School of Government. Available from: www.ksg.harvard.edu/ research/working_papers/facultyresponses.htm (both papers accessed March 12, 2009).

30　Editorial, "Blame the 'Lobby'," *Washington Post*, March 12, 2009, A18.

31　Fukuyama, *America at the Crossroads*, p. 13.

32　Lawrence B. Wilkerson, "The White House Cabal," *Los Angeles Times*, October 25, 2005.

33　I take up these and other misconceptions about the president's psychology in relation to his leadership style elsewhere. See Stanley A. Renshon, *In His Father's Shadow: The Transformations of George W. Bush*. New York: Palgrave/St. Martin's, 2005.

34　James Mann, *Rise of the Vulcans: The History of Bush's War Cabinet*. New York: Viking, 2004.

35　Jeff Zeleny, "Obama Describes Team as Experienced Yet Fresh," *New York Times*, November 27, 2008.

36　Joe Klein, "National Security Team of Rivals," *Time*, November 21, 2009.

37　Ben Smith and Jonathan Martin, "Can Obama's Team of Egos Co-exist?" *Politico*, November 20, 2008.

38　Jacob Weisberg, "The Brilliant Brain Trust," *Newsweek*, November 24, 2008.

39　Klein, "National Security Team of Rivals."

40　Transcript, President-elect Obama Fifth Press Conference (emphasis added).

41　Bret Stevens, "Obama's Team of Conformists," *Wall Street Journal*, December 9, 2008.

42　Karen DeYoung, "U.S. to Join Talks on Iran's Nuclear Program," *Washington Post*, April 9, 2009.

43　Helene Cooper and Eric Schmitt, "White House Debate Led to Plan to Widen Afghan Effort," *New York Times*, March 28, 2009 (emphasis added).

44　Both quotes are drawn from Jane Mayer, "Behind the Executive Orders," *New Yorker*, January 25, 2009.

45　Scott Shane, "Interrogations' Effectiveness May Prove Elusive," *New York Times*, April 23, 2009.

46　Remarks by President Barack Obama, Prague, Czech Republic, April 5, 2009. Available from: www.whitehouse.gov/the_press_office/Remarks-By-President-Barack-Obama-In-Prague-As-Delivered/ (accessed April 15, 2009).

47　David E. Sanger, "Hints of Obama's Strategy in a Telling 8 Days," *New York Times*, April 8, 2009.

48　Bremmer, *My Year in Iraq*, p. 188.

49　Peter Baker and Robin Wright, "Iraq, Bush Pushed for Deadline Democracy," *Washington Post*, December 11, 2005, A01.

50　Bob Woodward, *Bush at War*. New York: Simon & Schuster, 2002.

51　This debate included consultations with among others: the Iraqi government, the Joint Chiefs, chief ally Tony Blair, the Pentagon, Baker Commission members, "diplomats and military commanders in Iraq ... retired generals, experts at think tanks and academics," and members of Congress. In addition, the president commissioned, "the 'Crouch Group,' a small group of advisers being coordinated by Jack D. Crouch II, the deputy national security adviser, to assemble alternative proposals from the Joint Chiefs of Staff, the State Department, the Treasury Department and staff of the National Security Council." See the following: David S. Cloud and John O'Neil, "Gates Says Iraqis and U.S. Are in 'Broad Strategic Agreement,'" *New York Times*, December 23, 2006; Robin Wright and Ann Scott Tyson, "Joint Chiefs Advise Change in War Strategy,"

Washington Post, December 14, 2006, A01; "President Bush Meets with British Prime Minister Tony Blair," Office of the White House, December 7, 2006; David Stout, "Bush Consults with Pentagon on Iraq," *New York Times*, December 13, 2006; Ben Feller, "Bush Meets with, Praises Iraq Panel," *Associated Press*, November 13, 2006; Rajiv Chandrasekaran, "On Iraq, U.S. Turns to Onetime Dissenters," *Washington Post*, January 14, 2007, A01; *Associated Press*, "Bush Meets with Lawmakers in Search of New War Strategy," December 9, 2006; Jim Rutenberg and David E. Sanger, "Bush Aides Seek Alternatives to Iraq Study Group's Proposal, Calling them Impractical," *New York Times*, December 10, 2006; Robin Wright, "Two Panels Urgently Seek Iraq Solutions," *Washington Post*, November 19, 2006, A22; and Ann Scott Tyson, "Pentagon to Reevaluate Strategy and Goals in Iraq," *Washington Post*, November 11, 2006, A01.

52 Robin Wright, "U.S. Considers Ending Outreach to Insurgents," *Washington Post*, December 1, 2006, A01.

53 Charles Babington, "Bush is Weighing Options for a New Strategy in Iraq, Aides Say," *Washington Post*, December 4, 2006, A05.

54 Robin Wright and Peter Baker, "Iraq Strategy Talks Focusing on Three Main Options," *Washington Post*, December 9, 2006, A01.

55 Jack Keane and Frederick W. Kagan, "The Right Type of 'Surge,'" *Washington Post*, December 27, 2006, A19.

56 Gerald F. Seib, "A Plethora of Plans About What's Next," *Wall Street Journal*, December 2, 2006, A2.

57 "A lot of Americans understand the consequences of retreat. Retreat would embolden radicals. It would hurt the credibility of the United States. Retreat from Iraq would dash the hopes of millions who want to be free. Retreat from Iraq would enable the extremists and radicals to more likely be able to have safe haven from which to plot and plan further attacks." President's Press Conference, December 20, 2006.

58 Rowan Scarborough, "CIA Exercise Reveals Consequences of Defeat," *Washington Times*, December 1, 2006.

59 Thomas E. Ricks, "Gates Warns Against Leaving Iraq 'in Chaos.'" *Washington Post*, November 29, 2006, A05.

60 Barack Obama, *Presidential Policy Directive-1*. Washington, DC: The White House, February 13, 2009. Available from: www.fas.org/irp/offdocs/ppd/ppd-1.pdf (accessed March 12, 2009).

61 Barack Obama, *Presidential Study Directive*. Washington, DC: The White House, February 23, 2009. Available from: www.fas.org/irp/offdocs/psd/psd-1.pdf (accessed March 12, 2009).

62 Karen DeYoung, "Obama's NSC Will Get New Power," *Washington Post*, February 8, 2009, A01.

63 Spencer S. Hsu, "Obama Integrates Security Councils, Adds New Offices Computer, Pandemic Threats Addressed," *Washington Post*, May 27, 2009.

64 Quoted in DeYoung, "Obama's NSC Will Get New Power."

65 Quoted in DeYoung, "Obama's NSC Will Get New Power."

66 Transcript, President-elect Obama Fifth Press conference.

67 David Ignatius, "Mr. Cool's Centrist Gamble," *Washington Post*, January 11, 2009.

68 Transcript, President Obama, Part I, *CBS News*, March 24, 2009. Available from: www.cbsnews.com/stories/2009/03/24/60minutes/main4890684.shtml (accessed April 15, 2009).

69 Quoted in Fred Barnes, "The Return of Big Government," *Weekly Standard*, March 29, 2009.

70 That evidence is reviewed in Stanley A. Renshon and Jonathan Renshon, "The Theory and Practice of Foreign Policy Decision Making," *Political Psychology*, 29:4 (2008), pp. 509–36; see also Phillip E. Tetlock, *Expert Political Judgment: How Good Is It? How Do We Know?* Princeton, NJ: Princeton University Press, 2005.

71 Transcript, Obama's Interview Aboard Air Force One, *New York Times*, March 8, 2009.

72 Mark Leibovich, "Speaking Freely, Biden Finds Influential Role," *New York Times*, March 29, 2009.

73 "Transcript - Secretary of Defense Robert Gates," *NBC Meet the Press*, March 1, 2009. Available from: www.msnbc.msn.com/id/29453052/ (accessed April 20, 2009).

74 Helene Cooper and Eric Schmitt, "White House Debate Led to Plan to Widen Afghan Effort," *New York Times*, March 28, 2009.

75 "Interview with Admiral Michael Mullen," *This Week*, May 24, 2009 (emphasis mine). Available from: www.realclearpolitics.com/printpage/?url=http://www.realclearpolitics.com/articles/2009/05/24/interview_with_admiral_michael_mullen_96652.html (accessed May 30, 2009).

76 Stephan Halper and Jonathan Clarke, *America Alone: The Neoconservatives and the Global Order*. New York: Cambridge University Press, 2004.

77 Ivo H. Daalder and James M. Lindsay, "Bush's Flawed Revolution," *The American Prospect*, 14:10 (November 1, 2003).

78 Daalder and Lindsay, "Bush's Flawed Revolution."

79 William S. Cohen, "The U.S. and India: A Relationship Restored," *Wall Street Journal*, December 22, 2005.

80 Thom Shanker, "U.S. and Japan Agree to Strengthen Military Ties," *New York Times*, October 30, 2005.

81 Reuters, "Bush Administration Unveils Alternative Climate Pack," *New York Times*, July 28, 2005.

82 John J. Fialka, "Panel Calls for Flexible Climate Treaty," *Wall Street Journal*, November 16, 2005, A16.

83 Quoted in Patrick Hennessy and James Langton, "Why Kyoto Will Never Succeed, By Blair," *Telegraph*, September 24, 2005. Available from: www.telegraph.co.uk/news/uknews/1499147/Why-Kyoto-will-never-succeed-by-Blair.html (accessed March 12, 2009).

84 G9 Summit 2007, "Growth and Responsibility in the World Economy," *Summit Declaration*, June 7, 2007. Available from: www.g8.de/Webs/G8/EN/G8Summit/SummitDocuments/summit-documents.html (accessed March 12, 2009).

85 Kimberley Strassel, "Bush a Shrewd Diplomat on Global Warming," *Wall Street Journal*, June 8, 2008.

86 Stephen M. Walt, *Taming American Power: The Global Response to U.S. Primacy*. New York: Norton, 2005, p. 231. Francis Fukuyama makes a similar error, "The Bush Administration and its neoconservative reporters have been very critical of existing international initiatives like the Kyoto Protocol … but have offered up no alternatives in their place that would legitimate and enhance the effectiveness of the American action in the world." See Fukuyama, *America at the Crossroads …* , p. 65.

87 Robert Jervis, "The Remaking of a Unipolar World," *The Washington Quarterly*, 29:3 (Summer 2006), p. 14.

88 Dana Priest, "Help from France Key in Overt Operations," *Washington Post*, July 3, 2005, A01.

89 Robin Wright, "U.S. to Put New Pressure on Syria Initiative Also Has Goal of Helping Lebanon Rebuild Politically," *Washington Post*, September 2, 2005, A06.

90 Dana Priest, "Foreign Network at Front of CIA's Terror Fight," *Washington Post*, November 18, 2005, A01.

91 Richard Bernstein and Michael R. Gordon, "Berlin File Says Germany's Spies Aided U.S. in Iraq," *New York Times*, March 2, 2006, A1.

92 Announced by the White House on May 31, 2003, it included the following original signing countries: Australia, France, Germany, Italy, Japan, the Netherlands, Poland, Portugal, Spain, the United Kingdom, and the United States. See Editorial, "The New Multilateralism," *Wall Street Journal*, January 8, 2004; see also Erin E. Harbaugh, "The Proliferation Security Initiative: Counterproliferation at the Crossroads," *Strategic Insights*, 3:7 (2004) and Report on the Status of 9/11 Commission Recommendations, p. 3.

93 Peter Dombrowski and Roger A. Payne, "The Emerging Consensus for Preventive War," *Survival*, 48:2 (Summer 2006), pp. 115–36; see also Sharon Squassoni, "Proliferation Security Initiative," *CRS Report to Congress*, September 14, 2006. Available from: www.fas.org/sgp/crs/nuke/RS21881.pdf (accessed April 27, 2009).

94 Barry R. Posen, "The Struggle Against Terrorism: Grand Strategy, Strategy and Tactics," *International Security*, 23:3 (Winter 2001/2002), p. 43.

95 Eric Lichtblau and James Risen, "Data Bank is Shifted by U.S. in Secret to Block Terror," *New York Times*, June 23, 2006; see also Barton Gellman, Paul Blustein, and Dafna Linzer, "Bank Records Secretly Tapped," *Washington Post*, June 23, 2006, A01.

96 Joint Statement Announcing the Global Initiative to Combat Nuclear Terrorism (July 15, 2006). Available from: www.moscow.usembassy.gov/st_07152007.html (accessed April 15, 2009).

97 U.S. Department of State, "Global Initiative Current Partner Nations." Available from: www.2001-2009.state.gov/t/isn/105955.htm (accessed April 15, 2009).

98 Quoted in John O'Neil, "Hillary Clinton Says White House Mishandled Iran," *New York Times*, January 19, 2006.

99 Jonathan Weisman, "Bipartisan Senate Measure Confronts Bush Over Iraq," *Washington Post*, January 18, 2007, A01.

100 Peter Finn, "Iran, Russia Reach Tentative Nuclear Deal," *Washington Post*, February 27, 2006, A09; Evelyn Leopold and Irwin Arieff, "Russia Said to Still Object to UN Iran Statement," *Reuters*, March 20, 2006.

101 Thom Shanker, "U.S. Inquiry Finds Russia Passed Spy Data on to Iraq," *New York Times*, March 25, 2006; Robert Collier and Bill Wallace, "Iraq-Russia Spy Link Uncovered, SECRET FILES: Documents Reveal Iraqi Agents Trained in Moscow," *San Francisco Chronicle*, April 13, 2003.

102 Mansur Mirovalev, "Iran Hails Military Ties with Russia," *Associated Press*, February 20, 2009.

103 At his press conference on May 26, 2006, President Bush expressed regret for some of his more provocative language, like the taunt to insurgents attacking American troops in Iraq, "bring it on." See, "President Bush and Prime Minister Tony Blair of the United Kingdom Participate in Joint Press Availability," May 26, 2006,

Q: Mr. President, you spoke about missteps and mistakes in Iraq. Could I ask both of you which missteps and mistakes of your own you most regret?

PRESIDENT BUSH: saying "bring it on," kind of tough talk, you know, that sent the wrong signal to people. I learned some lessons about expressing myself maybe in a little more sophisticated manner—you know, "wanted dead or alive," that kind of talk. I think in certain parts of the world it was misinterpreted, and so I learned from that.

104 Glenn Kessler, "Shift in U.S. Stance Shows Power of Seven-Letter Word," *Washington Post*, June 1, 2006, A13.

105 Doug Struck, "Arrests Shake Image of Harmony: Muslims in Canada Brace for a Backlash After Foiled Bomb Plot," *Washington Post*, June 5, 2006, A10.

106 "Ishiba: Japan to 'Counterattack' if N. Korea Prepares to Attack," *Yomiuri Shimbun/ Daily Yomiuri*, January 25, 2003. In 2009, they repeated that warning. See Jung Sung-ki, "South to Boost Surgical Strike Capability Against the North," *Reuters*, June 26, 2009.

107 James Brooke, "Japanese Official Wants Defense Against Missiles Expanded," *New York Times*, April 17, 2003, A13.

108 Justin McCurry, "Japan Warns it May Shoot Down North Korean Satellite Launcher," *Guardian*, March 13, 2009.

109 The quotes that follow are drawn from M. Elaine Bunn, "Preemptive Action: When, How, and to What Effect," *Strategic Forum*, 200 (July 2003), pp. 6–7.

110 John Shaw, "Startling His Neighbors, Australian Leader Favors First Strikes," *New York Times,* December 2, 2002, A11.

111 "Prime Minister Warns of Continuing Global Terror Threat," March 5, 2004. Available from: www.number-10.gov.uk/output/Page5461.asp (accessed March 1, 2006) (emphasis mine).

112 Quoted in Nicholas Kralev, "Russia Vows Pre-emptive Terror Hits," *The Washington Times*, September 9, 2004.

113 Quoted in CNN, "Russia Considers Terror Strikes," 17 September 2004. Available from: www.edition.cnn.com/2004/WORLD/europe/o9/i7/russia.putin (accessed December 1, 2006).

114 LOI n° 2003–73 du 27 janvier 2003 relative à la programmation militaire pour les années 2003 à 2008 (1), section 2.3.1 [translation: law number 2003–73, January 27, 2003, concerning military programming for the years 2003 to 2008, paragraph 2.3.1]; see also Ariane Benard, "Chirac Hints at Nuclear Reply to State-Supported Terrorism," *New York Times*, January 20, 2006, A8.

115 www.openeurope.org.uk/research/globalisation.xlis (accessed April 10, 2007). www.fas. org/sgp/crs/nuke/RS21881.pdf (accessed March 8, 2007).

116 "A More Secure World: Our Shared Responsibility," United Nations, 62–64. Available from: www.un.org (accessed February 1, 2005).

117 Dombrowski and Payne, "The Emerging Consensus ... " p. 120.

118 Tiffany Harness, "Even Among Allies, Image of U.S. Drops," *Washington Post*, June 28, 2007, A18. For region- and country-specific data, see "The Pew Global Attitudes Project, Global Unease with Major World Powers," June 27, 2007.

119 Janice Gross Stein, "Anti-Americanism: Seeing Ourselves in the Mirror of the United States," in Stanley A. Renshon and Peter Suedfeld (eds) *Understanding the Bush Doctrine: Psychology and Strategy in an Age of Terrorism*. New York: Routledge, 2007, pp. 271–87.

120 Stein, "Anti-Americanism," p. 285. Consistent with this view is the Pew finding that, "in many countries, the American people get better ratings than does the U.S. generally." Pew, "Global Unease ... " p. 4.

121 Walter Russell Mead, *Power, Terror, Peace and War: America's Grand Strategy in a World at Risk*. New York: Knopf, 2004, pp. 59–61.

122 Susan B. Glasser, "Review May Shift Terror Policies," *Washington Post*, May 29, 2005, A01.

123 Peter Beinart, "The War of the Words," *Washington Post*, April 1, 2007, B07.

124 Joe Biden, "Five Years After 9/11: Rethinking America's Future Security," Speech Delivered to the National Press Club, September 7, 2006. Available from: www.procon. org/sourcefiles/Biden20060907.pdf (accessed May 17, 2009).

125 Mike Allen, "Edwards Rejects the 'War on Terror'." *Time*, May 2, 2007. Available from: www.time.com/time/nation/article/0,8599,1616724,00.html (accessed April 27, 2009).

126 Rick Maze, "No More GWOT, House Committee Decrees," *Army Times*, April 4, 2007. Available from: www.armytimes.com/news/2007/04/military_gwot_democrats_070403w/ (accessed May 17, 2009).

127 Maze, "No More GWOT, House Committee Decrees" (emphasis in original).

128 Karl Vick, "Hard-Line Tehran Mayor Wins Iranian Presidency," *Washington Post*, June 25, 2005, A01.

129 Robert S. Litwak, "The New Calculus of Pre-emption," *Survival*, 44:4 (2003–03), p. 53.

130 Fukuyama, *America at the Crossroads*, pp. 94, 184.

131 Tony Blair, "PM warns of Continued Global Terror Threat ..."

5 The New Calculus of Risk

1 Kenneth N. Waltz, *Theory of International Politics*. New York: McGraw-Hill, 1978.

2 Robert S. Litwak, "The New Calculus of Pre-emption," *Survival*, 44:4 (2002), p. 58.

3 Litwak, "The New Calculus of Pre-emption," p. 194.

4 The terminology of lists is borrowed from Joseph S. Nye, Jr., "Redefining the National Interest," *Foreign Affairs*, 78:4 (July/August 1999), pp. 22–35. Divergent lists abound for new presidents. For some suggestions for President Bush, see Nicholas D. Kristof, "Ten Suggestions for Rescuing the Bush Legacy," *New York Times*, December 31, 2006 and Richard A. Clarke, "While You Were at War ... ," *Washington Post*, December 31, 2006, B01. For a representative list of suggestions for President Obama see Richard N. Haass, "The World That Awaits," *Newsweek*, November 3, 2008.

5 Robert Pear, "U.S. Pressures Foreign Airlines Over Manifests," *Washington Post*, November 27, 2001.

6 Daniel Kahneman and Amos Tversky, "Prospect Theory: An Analysis of Decision Under Risk," *Econometrica*, 47 (1979), pp. 263–91; see also Daniel Kahneman and Amos Tversky, "Choices, Values, and Frames," *American Psychologist*, 39 (1984), pp. 341–50.

7 Daniel Kahneman, Jack L. Knetsch, and Richard H. Thaler, "Anomalies: The Endowment Effect, Loss Aversion, and Status Quo Bias," *The Journal of Economic Perspectives*, 5:1 (Winter 1991), p. 199.

8 For an examination of the model in presidential decision-making, see Alexander L. George, *Presidential Decision Making in Foreign Policy: The Effective Use of Information and Advice*. Westview Press, 1980; see also Alexander L. George, "From Groupthink to Conceptual Analysis of Policy-making Groups," in P. 't Hart, E. Stern, and B. Sundelius (eds) *Beyond Groupthink: Political Group Dynamics and Foreign Policy Making*. University of Michigan Press, 1997; Jonathan Renshon and Stanley A. Renshon, "The Theory and Practice of Foreign Policy Decision Making," *Political Psychology*, 29:4 (2008), pp. 509–36.

9 See Jonathan Renshon, "Making Frames and Taking Chances: The Utility of Prospect Theory in International Relations," Unpublished paper, Harvard University, 2007.

10 Kahneman and Tversky, "Prospect Theory"; see also, Daniel Kahneman and Amos Tversky, "Choices, Values, and Frames," *American Psychologist*, 39 (1984), pp. 341–50.

11 Kahneman and Tversky, "Prospect Theory ... ", pp. 263–291; also Kahneman and Tversky, "Choices, Values, and Frames ... ", pp. 341–350.

12 Richard H. Thaler, Amos Tversky, Daniel Kahneman, and Alan Schwartz, "The Effect of Myopia and Loss Aversion on Risk Taking: An Experimental Test," *Quarterly Journal of Economics*, 112:2 (May 1997), p. 648.

13 Adam Liptak, "White House Shifting Tactics in Surveillance Cases," *New York Times*, January 19, 2006, pp. 315–338.

14 Quoted in Linda D. Kozaryn, "Cheney Says Grave Threats Require Pre-emptive Action," *American Forces Press Service*, August 26, 2002.

15 NSS 2002.

16 National Intelligence Council, "National Intelligence Estimate—The Terrorist Threat to the US Homeland," July 2007.

17 For example in one experiment subjects are told, "You are the manager of a large manufacturing unit in a Fortune 100 company. At the present time, you are in the midst of a year-long plan to cut costs in your unit. Your goal for this quarter is to do your best to save money during the current quarter. At present you are considering two plans: Plan M. Plan M will save $120,000. Plan N. Plan N has an 80 percent chance of saving $50,000 and a 20 percent chance of saving $250,000. Both plans are one-time options. They will not be available later in the year, and you have time to complete only one of them during the current quarter."

18 John Mueller, "Is There Still a Terrorist Threat," *Foreign Affairs*, September/October 2006. The quotes that follow are drawn from that article; see also Zbigniew Brzezinski, "Terrorized by 'War on Terror,'" *Washington Post*, March 25, 2007, B01, and Ian S Lustick, *Trapped in the War on Terror*. Philadelphia, PA: University of Pennsylvania Press, 2006.

19 All the statistics used in the above paragraph are from Mueller, "Is there still ..."

20 Walt, *Taming American Power*, p. 237 (emphasis mine).

21 When Ehud Olmert, now the Prime Minister of Israel, was asked what he had learned from his predecessor Ariel Sharon, he replied, "I learned many things ... as he [Sharon] said, 'What you see from here [as prime minister] is not what you see from there [not being prime minister].'" A Conversation with Ehud Olmert Interim Israeli Prime Minister, *Washington Post*, April 9, 2006, B04.

22 David S. Broder, "Obama in Command," *Washington Post*, May 21, 2009.

23 Richard K. Betts, "Power, Prospects, and Priorities: Choices for Strategic Change," *Naval War College Review* (Winter 1997).

24 Charles A. Kupchan, "After Pax Americana: Benign Power, Regional Integration, and the Sources of Stable Multipolarity," *International Security*, 23:3 (1998), p. 40.

25 James Kurth, "American Strategy in the Global Age," *Naval War College Review* (Winter 2000).

26 Eugene Gholz, Daryl G. Press, and Harvey M. Sapolsky, "Come Home, America," *International Security*, 21:4 (1997), pp. 6, 8.

27 Robert Jervis, "U.S. Grand Strategy: Mission Impossible," *Naval War College Review* (Summer 1998) (emphasis mine).

28 Among the most persistent and useful efforts to bridge this gap can be found in the work of Alexander L. George. See his books: *Deterrence in American Foreign Policy: Theory and Practice* (with Richard Smoke). New York: Columbia University Press, 1974; *Bridging the Gap: Theory and Policy in Foreign Affairs*. Washington, DC: U.S. Institute of Peace Press, 1993; *On Foreign Policy: Unfinished Business*. Boulder, CO: Paradigm, 2006.

29 Waltz, *Theory of International Politics*, p. 195.

30 Robert Jervis, *American Foreign Policy in a New Era*. New York: Routledge, 2006, p. 4.

31 Coalition for a Realistic Foreign Policy. Available from: www.realisticforeignpolicy.org (accessed April 23, 2009).

32 Hans J. Morgenthau, *Politics Among Nations: The Struggle for Power and Peace*, 4th ed. New York: Knopf, 1967, pp. 4–14.

33 John Mearsheimer, "The Rise of China Will Not Be Peaceful At All," *The Australian*, November 18, 2005. See also John Mearsheimer, *The Tragedy of Great Power Politics*. New York: Norton, 2002, pp. 21–22, 31–39.

34 Gideon Rose, "Neoclassical Realism and Theories of Foreign Policy," *World Politics*, 51:1 (1998), pp. 144–72.

35 Robert O. Keohane and Lisa L. Martin, "The Promise of Institutional Theory," *International Security*, 20:1 (1995), pp. 39–51; see also Charles A. Kupchan and Clifford A. Kupchan, "The Promise of Collective Security," *International Security*, 20:1 (1995), pp. 52–61.

36 John Mearsheimer, "The False Promise of International Institutions," *International Security*, 19 (1994/95), pp. 5–49.

37 See, for example, Lawrence Freedman's survey of the inconclusive attempts to validate various theories of deterrence in his book *Deterrence*, Chapter 3. Robert Jervis notes, "Although it is easy to see that various kinds of research wax and wane, explaining the pattern is more difficult. Indeed, there is an element of circularity in determining what constitutes a successful research program. In the absence of some arguably objective measure, a research program succeeds when many scholars adopt it." See Robert Jervis, "Realism in World Politics," *International Organization*, 52:4 (1998), p. 972.

38 Stephen M. Walt, *Taming American Power: The Global Response to U.S. Primacy*. New York: Norton, 2005.

39 Anne-Marie Slaughter, "Comment on Walt," *Boston Review* (February/March 2005). Available from: www.bostonreview.net/BR30.1/slaughter.html (accessed March 12, 2009).

40 Anne-Marie Slaughter, "Comment on Walt."

41 G. John Ikenberry and Anne-Marie Slaughter, "Forging a World of Liberty Under Law, U.S. National Security in the 21st Century," *The Princeton Project on National Security*, September 27, 2006, 28.

42 Evan Braden Montgomery, "Breaking Out of the Security Dilemma," *International Security*, 31:2 (Fall 2006), p. 158.

43 Montgomery, "Breaking Out of the Security Dilemma," pp. 178–81.

44 Glenn Kessler, "Anger at U.S. Policies More Strident at U.N." *Washington Post*, September 24, 2006, A23.

45 Keir A. Lieber and Gerard Alexander, "Waiting for Balancing: Why the World is Not Pushing Back." *International Security*, 30:1 (2005), p. 109.

46 Jervis, *American Foreign Policy*, p. 31. Among those doing so are: T.V. Paul. "Soft Balancing in the Age of U.S. Primacy," *International Security*, 30 (2005), pp. 46–71;

Robert Pape, "Soft Balancing Against the United States," *International Security*, 30:1 (2005), pp. 7–45; and William C. Brooks and William C. Wohlforth, "Hard Times for Soft Balancing," *International Security*, 30:1 (2005), pp. 72–108.

47 Christopher Layne, "The Unipolar Illusion Revisited," *International Security*, 31:2 (Fall 2006), p. 9.

48 Both possibilities are discussed in Stephen M. Walt, *The Origins of Alliances*. Ithaca, NY: Cornell, 1987.

49 Walt, *Taming American Power ...* , pp. 153–57.

50 Here Walt seems to adopt the position of Randall L. Schweller, "Bandwagoning for Fun and Profit: Bringing the Revisionist State Back in," *International Security*, 19:1 (1994), pp. 72–107.

51 Simon Romero, "Iranian President Visits Venezuela to Strengthen Ties," *New York Times*, January 14, 2006.

52 Editorial, "Mr. Putin's Vision," *Washington Post*, February 13, 2007, A20.

53 Ellen Barry, "Russia is Weighing 2 Latin Bases, General Says," *New York Times*, March 15, 2009.

54 Editorial, "Mr. Putin's Vision."

55 See John H. Herz, "Idealist Internationalism and the Security Dilemma," *World Politics*, 2:2 (1950), pp. 157–80; Robert Jervis, "Cooperation Under the Security Dilemma," *World Politics*, 30:2 (1978), pp. 167–214.

56 Robert O. Keohane, "Theory of World Politics," in *Neorealism and Its Critics* (ed.) Robert O. Keohane. New York: Columbia University Press, 1986.

57 The classic formulation and analysis of these issues remains Robert Jervis, *Perception and Misperception in International Politics*. Princeton, NJ: Princeton University Press, 1976.

58 George W. Bush, "State of the Union Address," January 28, 2003. Available from: www.whitehouse.gov/news/releases/2003/01/20030128–19.html (accessed March 1, 2006).

59 "President Bush Delivers Graduation Speech at West Point," June 1, 2002. Available from: www.whitehouse.gov.news/releases/2002/06/20020601–3.html (accessed March 1, 2006).

60 Quoted in Terence Taylor, "The End of Imminence?" *Washington Quarterly*, (Autumn 2004), pp. 4–5.

61 Kenneth Pollack, *The Threatening Storm: The Case for Invading Iraq*. New York: Random House, 2002.

62 William J. Broad, Nazila Fatahi, and Joel Brinkley, "Analysts Say a Nuclear Iran is Years Away," *New York Times*, April 13, 2006.

63 Review & Outlook. "Ticking Tehran Bomb," *Wall Street Journal*, December 7, 2005.

64 Dafna Linzer and Colum Lynch, "Iran Continues Nuclear Work Despite Deadline, Sanction Threat," *Washington Post*, February 22, 2007, A14.

65 Jen DiMascio, "Gates and Mullen Disagree on Iran," *Politico*, March 1, 2009.

66 Peter Finn, "U.S., Israel Disagree on Iran Arms Threat," *Washington Post*, March 11, 2009, A04.

67 Quoted in Finn, "U.S., Israel Disagree on Iran Arms Threat."

68 Eli Lake, "U.S. Spy Chief Retreats on Iran Estimate," *The Sun*, February 6, 2008; see also Editorial, "Iranian Nuclear Rewrite," *Wall Street Journal*, February 8, 2008.

69 Finn, "U.S., Israel Disagree on Iran Arms Threat," p. A04.

70 Finn, "U.S., Israel Disagree on Iran Arms Threat," p. A04.

71 Quoted in Scott Shane, "C.I.A. Chief Will Face Critical Gaps in Iran Data," *New York Times*, May 7, 2006.

72 *Webster's New Ninth Collegiate Dictionary*. Springfield, MA: Merriam-Webster, 1991, p. 602.

73 William Safire, "On Language—Imminent," *New York Times*, February 8, 2004.

74 Fuyukama, *America at the Crossroads ...* , p. 87 (emphasis mine).

75 Donald Rumsfeld, *CBS Radio*, November 14, 2002.

76 Jervis, "The Remaking. ... ", p. 9.

77 Dafna Linzer, "Strong Leads and Dead Ends in Nuclear Case Against Iran," *Washington Post*, February 8, 2006, A01.
78 Quoted in Ron Suskind, *The One Percent Doctrine*. New York: Simon & Shuster, 2006, p. 62.
79 It is quite clear that the administration treats this threat as the paramount one facing the United States and treats it differently than other threats such as global warming. This is understandable. Global warming effects are uncertain at this point, are not immediate, do not have the likelihood of disrupting or devastating American civic and constitutional structure, will not result in many tens of thousands of dead Americans and so on.
80 George Tenent, *At the Center of the Storm: My Years at the CIA*. New York: Harper-Collins, 2007.
81 Molly Moore, "Iran Working on Nuclear Arms Plan, France Says," *Washington Post*, February 17, 2006, A1.
82 Ariane Bernard, "France Alleges Iran's Nuclear Plan is for Military Use," *New York Times*, February 17, 2006 (italics added).
83 Suskind, *The One Percent Doctrine*, p. 123.

6 Deterrence, Containment and Adversarial Bargaining Post-9/11: North Korea and Iran

1 Alexander L. George, "The Need for Influence Theory and Actor-Specific Behavioral Models of Adversaries," in Barry R. Schneider and Jerrold M. Post (eds) *Know Thy Enemy; Profiles of Adversary Leaders and Their Strategic Cultures*. Maxwell AFB, AL: USAF Counter Proliferation Center, November 2002, pp. 271–310.
2 Ian Shapiro recently asked, "has containment in fact become obsolete, as the Bush administration would have it?" See Ian Shapiro, "Containment Makes a Comeback," *Los Angeles Times*, February 25, 2007. His extended argument along these same lines is found in Ian Shapiro, *Containment: Rebuilding a Global Strategy Against Global Terror*. Princeton, NJ: Princeton University Press, 2007.
3 George W. Bush, "State of the Union Address," January 28, 2003.
4 National Security Strategy 2002, p. 13.
5 National Security Strategy 2002, p. 30.
6 Alexander L. George and Andrew Bennett, *Case Studies and Theory Development in the Social Sciences*. Cambridge, MA: MIT Press, 2005, p. 322.
7 George and Bennett, *Case Studies and Theory Development in the Social Sciences*, p. 301.
8 Patrick C. Brattan, "When is Coercion Successful and Why Can't We Agree on it?" *Naval War College Review*, 58:3 (Summer 2005). In doing so, Brattan builds on Thomas Schelling's classic work. See Thomas Schelling, *Arms and Influence*. New Haven, CT: Yale University Press, 1996.
9 However, not everyone subscribes to this distinction. Alex George reserved the term coercive diplomacy for attempts at influence that are essentially "defensive." He combines efforts to both keep an adversary from doing something or undoing actions already taken, and eschews the term "compellence" because of its essentially aggressive stance. See Alexander L. George, *Forceful Persuasion: Coercive Diplomacy as an Alternative to War*. Washington, DC: USIP Press, 1991, p. 5.
10 George and Simons distinguish coercive diplomacy as a combination long on the latter and short on the former, especially when it entails military force. Compellence on the other hand can be thought of as a reverse combination, a very strong and credible threat of force, sometimes accompanied with a demonstration of its use, with a demand for compliance. Alexander L. George and William E. Simmon, *The Limits of Coercive Diplomacy: Laos, Cuba, Vietnam*. Boulder, CO: Westview, 1994.
11 Donna Miles, "Iraq Experience Likely to Affect Future Decisions, Gates Says," *American Forces Press Service*, March 13, 2009. The interview took place on the Tavis Smiley Show. Available from: www.pbs.org/kcet/tavissmiley/archive/200903/20090311.html (accessed March 12, 2009).

12 Quoted in Robert B. Zoellick, "Long Division," *Wall Street Journal*, February 26, 2007, A18.

13 A more forceful version of this strategy was used by the Israelis to isolate Yasser Arafat at his Ramallah compound. First in 2001, after a terrorist attack, the government destroyed his three helicopters. Next in 2002, after another terrorist attack, Israeli tanks surrounded his office confining him to his complex. During this time the compound's walls were torn down, along with most buildings, except for Arafat's three-story office. Then, after a third suicide bomber attack, Israeli troops occupied the city of Ramallah and most of Arafat's compound. As is often the case with the use of other strategic psychology tools, this one too was not applied by itself. The increasing isolation in this case was a form of tit for tat *compellence* in which new suicide bombing in Israel resulted in a further tightening of the isolation. Tit for tat is a form of stimulus-reward psychology in which the "you do this and we will do that" sequence is meant to behaviorally shape the target's behavior. In this case military force was applied, but very selectively. The major purpose was to take away Mr. Arafat's legitimacy as a leader and insure that he could not travel the world in support of it as he had done for decades. Presumably, this exacted a psychological price.

14 Quoted in Elaine Monaghan, "Clinton Planned Attack on Korean Nuclear Reactors," *The Times*, December 16, 2002.

15 Glenn Kessler, "Clinton Criticizes Bush on N. Korea," *Washington Post*, February 16, 2009.

16 Glenn Kessler, "Clinton to Meet Families of Abducted Japanese," *Washington Post*, February 14, 2009.

17 Jim Yardley, "Sanctions Don't Dent North Korea-China Trade," *New York Times*, October 27, 2006.

18 Review & Outlook, "Kin Jong Il's Bankers," *Wall Street Journal*, November 24, 2006, A12; see also Philip Zelikow, "The Plan That Moved Pyongyang," *Washington Post*, February 20, 2007, A13.

19 John Lewis Gaddis, *Strategies of Containment: A Critical Appraisal of American National Security Policy during the Cold War* (revised and expanded edition). New York: Oxford, 2005, p. ix and passim.

20 Indeed, somewhat paradoxically, the father of containment, George F. Kennedy began by supporting a "sphere of influence" policy acquiescing to Soviet "buffer states," before he developed the policy of containment. See Gaddis, *Strategies of Containment*, pp. 14–15.

21 The general outline of this story is developed in Gaddis, *Strategies of Containment*, pp. 4–18.

22 George F. Kennan, "Moscow Embassy Telegram #511, The Long Telegram," reprinted in Thomas H. Etzold and John Lewis Gaddis (eds) *Containment: Documents on American Policy and Strategy, 1945–1950*. New York: Columbia University Press, 1978, pp. 50–63. Available from: www.gwu.edu/~nsarchiv/coldwar/documents/episode-1/kennan.htm (accessed March 12, 2009).

23 Kennan, "The Sources of Soviet Conduct … " Reprinted in Thomas H. Etzold and John Lewis Gaddis (eds) *Containment: Documents on American Policy and Strategy, 1945–1950*. New York: Columbia University Press, 1978, pp. 84–90.

24 " … in 1946 the military aspect of our relationship to the Soviet Union hardly seemed to come into question at all." See George F. Kennan, "Containment: 40 Years Later: Containment Then and Now," *Foreign Affairs*, Spring 1987.

25 Kennan, "The Long Telegram," p. 53.

26 Gaddis argues that President Roosevelt wanted to contain the Soviet Union by integration into postwar international institutions. See Gaddis, *Strategies of Containment*, pp. 9–12.

27 Kennan, "Long Telegram," p. 61.

28 Kennan, "The Sources of Soviet Conduct," p. 87.

29 "Thus, if the adversary has sufficient force and makes clear his readiness to use it, he rarely has to do so." See Kennan, "The Long Telegram," p. 61.

30 Kennan, "The Sources of Soviet Conduct," p. 87.
31 "U.S. Objectives with Respect to the USSR to Counter Soviet Threats to U.S. Security," NSC 20/4, 23 November 1948, reprinted in "Foreign Relations of the United States," Vol. 1. Washington, DC: Government Printing Office, Department of State, 1948, pp. 663–69. Available from: www.mtholyoke.edu/acad/intrel/coldwar/nsc20–24.htm (accessed March 12, 2009). All the quotes in this paragraph are drawn from that document.
32 "NSC 68: United States Objectives and Programs for National Security," National Security Council (April 14, 1950). A Report to the President Pursuant to the President's Directive of January 31, 1950 (emphasis mine). Available from: www.fas.org/irp/off-docs/nsc-hst/nsc-68.htm (accessed March 12, 2009).
33 This is certainly Gaddis' view. See Gaddis, *Strategies of Containment*, p. 287. For a magisterial analysis of détente, see Raymond L. Garthoff, *Detente and Confrontation American-Soviet Relations from Nixon to Reagan* (revised edition). Washington, DC: Brookings Institution Press, 1994.
34 A good account of the strategy and its difficulties is found in Gaddis, *Strategies of Containment*, pp. 292–94, 309–15.
35 As Robert Tucker notes, "The initiation of the policy of containment in the late 1940s was marked by controversy; its subsequent history has been one of continuing controversy. In the thirty-five years since its adoption, containment has been given a number of quite different interpretations and has been implemented in a number of quite different ways. Yet it has seldom, if ever, been free of criticism. It has been considered either too aggressive or, more often, too defensive. It has been attacked for being too demanding of the nation's resources, or too threatening in its impact on domestic institutions and the quality of national life." See Robert W. Tucker, "Containment and the Search for Alternatives; A Critique," in Aaron Wildavsky (ed.) *Beyond Containment: Alternative American Policies Toward the Soviet Union*. San Francisco, CA: Institute of Contemporary Studies, 1983, p. 63.
36 Kennan, "Long Telegram," p. 61.
37 All quotes that follow are drawn from Kennan, "Sources of Soviet Behavior" (emphasis mine).
38 Kennan, "Sources of Soviet Behavior," p. 86.
39 For an analysis of the consideration of such strikes during the Truman and Eisenhower presidencies, see Jonathan Renshon, *Why Leaders Choose War: The Psychology of Prevention*. Westview, CT: Greenwood Press, 2006, Chapter 4.
40 Shapiro, "Containment Makes a Comeback."
41 Shapiro, "Containment Makes a Comeback."
42 Quoted in Jerry Seper, "FBI Director Predicts Terrorists Will Acquire Nukes," *Washington Times*, June 12, 2007.
43 William J. Perry, Asthon B. Carter, and Michael M. May, "After the Bomb," *New York Times*, June 7, 2007.
44 State department spokesman Sean McCormack said, "Should they choose not to proceed down that pathway, then there will be consequences. And those consequences will be diplomatic isolation from the rest of the world." Quoted in Helene Cooper, "Diplomats to Begin Drafting New U.N. Sanctions on Iran," *New York Times*, February 27, 2007.
45 Quoted in Barry Schweid, "Bush Calls for Global Isolation of Iran" *Associated Press*, November 13, 2007.
46 Condoleezza Rice, "Interview with Andrea Mitchell of NBC News," Berlin, Germany, January 17, 2007.
47 Quoted in Nasser Karimi, "No 'Brakes' on Iran Nuclear Effort President's Remarks Precede Summit on Further Sanctions," *Washington Post*, February 26, 2007.
48 Dafna Linzer and Colum Lynch, "Iran Continues Nuclear Work Despite Deadline, Sanction Threat," *Washington Post*, February 22, 2007, A14.
49 Karen DeYoung, "U.S. Open to Talking About Iraq with Iran and Syria," *Washington Post*, March 9, 2007, A15.

50 Review & Outlook, "Mahmoud's 'Gift'," *Wall Street Journal*, April 5, 2007.

51 Sanctions leakage does not necessarily mean that sanctions will prove ineffectual. Jentleson et al. argue that in the case of Libya, "U.S. unilateral sanctions were the technological key" because much of Libya's infrastructure was American based. See Bruce W. Jentleson and Christopher A. Whytock, "Who 'Won' Libya: The Force-Diplomacy Debate and its Implications for Theory and Policy," *International Security*, 30:3 (Winter 2005), p. 78.

52 "President Bush and Prime Minister Ehud Olmert of Israel Participate in Joint Press Availability," The White House, May 23, 2006.

53 Transcript, "Director General's Interview on Iran and DPRK (with Daniel Dombey)," *Financial Times* (February, 19 2007). Available from: www.iaea.org/NewsCenter/Transcripts/2007/ft190207.html (accessed March 13, 2009).

54 Transcript, "Director General's Interview on Iran and DPRK."

55 Kennan, "The Sources of Soviet Conduct," pp. 572–76, 582.

56 There is no doubt that China's increasing missile and nuclear capacity is a concern to some, but its regional and world ambitions seem focused on reclaiming what it considers to be its missing territory. On the first, see Mark Helprin, "The Nuclear Threat From China." *Washington Post*, March 4, 2007, B07.

57 Sarah Lyall, "Iran Seizes 15 Britons on Patrol in Persian Gulf," *New York Times*, March 24, 2007.

58 Ali Akabar Dareini, "Iran Claims to Uncover American Spy Ring," *Associated Press*, May 27, 2007.

59 Charles Krauthammer, "The Doggedness of War," *Washington Post*, December 26, 2003, A35.

60 Flynt L. Leverett, "Why Libya Gave Up on the Bomb," *New York Times*, January 23, 2004.

61 Dafna Hochman, "Rehabilitating a Rogue: Libya's WMD Reversal and Lessons for US Policy," *Parameters* (Spring 2006), p. 68.

62 These were Phase I: U.S. Sanctions and military force (1981–88); Phase ll: multilateral and sanctions based (1989–98); Phase 111: direct negotiations (1999–2003). See Jentleson and Whytock, "Who 'Won' Libya ... " pp. 55–79; see also Hochman, "Rehabilitating a Rogue," pp. 73–74.

63 Jentleson and Whytock, "Who 'Won' Libya," p. 75 (emphasis mine).

64 Jentleson and Whytock, "Who 'Won' Libya," p. 81 (emphasis added).

65 In addition to the articles cited above, a general listing can be found in Douglas Frantz and Josh Meyer, "The Deal to Disarm Kadafi," *Los Angeles Times*, March 13, 2005.

66 Jentleson and Whytock, "Who 'Won' Libya," p. 50.

67 Paul Richter, "Biden Warns Israel Off Any Attack on Iran," *Los Angeles Times*, April 8, 2009.

68 Ray Takeyh, "Time for Détente with Iran," *Foreign Affairs*, March/April 2007. All quotes in this section, unless otherwise sourced, are drawn from this article.

69 Hassan M. Fattah, "Arab States, Wary of Iran, Add to Their Arsenals but Still Lean on the U.S." *New York Times*, February 23, 2007.

70 Quoted in Gaddis, *Strategies*, p. 309.

71 Quoted in Gaddis, *Strategies of Containment*, p. 310.

72 Gaddis, *Strategies of Containment*, p. 287.

73 Takeyh quotes the deputy head of the Supreme National Security Council, Ali Hosseinitash, as saying, "The nuclear program is an opportunity for us to make endeavors to acquire a strategic position and consolidate our national identity." See Takeyh, "Time for Détente ... "; Ali Larijani whom Takeyh labels a "moderate" dismissed a 2004 agreement with France, Germany, and the United Kingdom to voluntarily give up its nuclear fuel enrichment efforts saying it was like exchanging a pearl for a bonbon. Quoted in William Samii, "The Iranian Nuclear Issue and Informal Networks," *Naval War College Review*, 59:1 (Winter 2006), pp. 63–89.

74 Ray Takeyh, "Wrong Strategy on Iran," *Washington Post*, September 10, 2004, A29.

75 Takeyh, "Wrong Strategy on Iran."

76 Ann Scott Tyson, "U.S. is Open to a Deeper Iran Dialogue, Gates Says," *Washington Post*, March 28, 2007, A12.

77 Tyson, "U.S. is Open to a Deeper Iran Dialogue, Gates Says" (emphasis mine).

7 Dangerous Threats and the Use of Force

1 Alexander L. George, "The Role of Force in Diplomacy," in Chester A. Crocker (ed.) *Managing Global Chaos: Sources of and Responses to International Conflict.* U.S. Institute of Peace, 1996, pp. 209–22.

2 M. Elaine Bunn, "Preemptive Action: When, How, and to What Effect?" *Strategic Forum*, Institute for National Strategic Studies, No. 200, 2003, p. 7.

3 Fukuyama, *America at the Crossroads: Democracy, Power, and the Neoconservative Legacy.* New Haven: Yale University Press, 2006, p. 184.

4 Fukuyama, *America at the Crossroads ...* , p. 185.

5 It is true that historically that deterrence has both failed and succeeded for reasons that are still debated. See Lawrence Freedman, *Deterrence*, Cambridge: Policy Press, 2004, Chapter 3.

6 Paul K. Davis and Brian Jenkins, *Deterrence & Influence in Counterterrorism: A Component in the War on al Qaeda.* Santa Monica, CA: Rand, 2002; see also Daniel Whiteneck, "Deterring Terrorists: Thoughts on a Framework," *Washington Quarterly*, 28:3 (2005), pp. 197–99.

7 Karl P. Mueller, Jasen J. Castillo, Forrest E. Morgan, Negeen Pegahi, and Brian Rosen. *Striking First: Preemptive and Preventive Attack in U.S. National Security Policy.* Santa Monica, CA: Rand Corporation, 2006, pp. xvii–xviii.

8 Mueller, Jasen J. Castillo, Forrest E. Morgan, Negeen Pegahi, and Brian Rosen, *Striking First ...* , p. xxi.

9 Mueller, Jasen J. Castillo, Forrest E. Morgan, Negeen Pegahi, and Brian Rosen, *Striking First ...* , pp. 32–42.

10 Mueller, Jasen J. Castillo, Forrest E. Morgan, Negeen Pegahi, and Brian Rosen, *Striking First ...* , p. 38.

11 Mueller, Jasen J. Castillo, Forrest E. Morgan, Negeen Pegahi, and Brian Rosen, *Striking First ...* , pp. 40–41.

12 George W. Bush, "Press Conference of the President," September 15, 2006.

13 In a speech before the American legion in 2006, Mr. Bush laid out the following facts: "He was firing at American military pilots patrolling the no-fly zones. He was a state sponsor of terror. He was in open defiance of more than a dozen United Nations resolutions. He had invaded his neighbors. He had brutalized his people. He had a history of using and producing weapons of mass destruction. Saddam defied the will of the world." See George W. Bush, "President Addresses American Legion, Discusses Global War on Terror," Capital Hilton Hotel, Washington, DC, February 24, 2006.

14 Anne-Marie Slaughter, "To Pursue Primacy for its Own Sake Seems an Odd Way to Reassure Other Nations," *Boston Review*, February/March 2005. Available from: www.bostonreview.net/BR30.1/slaughter.html (accessed March 8, 2007).

15 All quotes are drawn from Thom Shanker and Mark Lander, "Putin Says U.S. is Undermining Global Stability," *New York Times*, February 11, 2007.

16 In one opinion poll, 75% of British respondent polled thought that George W. Bush was more dangerous to world peace than Kim Jong-il of North Korea (69%). See Julian Glover, "British Believe Bush is More Dangerous Than Kim Jong-il," *The Guardian*, November 3, 2006. Available from: www.guardian.co.uk/usa/story/0,1938434,00. html (accessed March 12, 2009).

Pew reports that its 2006 survey found that the British, French, and Spanish publics were all more likely to say the U.S. presence in Iraq poses a great danger to regional stability and world peace than to say this about the current governments of Iran or North Korea. See Andrew Kohut, "America's Image in the World: Findings from the Pew Global Attitudes Project," Remarks of Andrew Kohut to the U.S. House Committee on Foreign Affairs; Subcommittee on International Organizations, Human

Rights, and Oversight, March 14, 2007. Available from: www.pewglobal.org/commentary/display.php?AnalysisID=1019 (accessed March 12, 2009).

17 When a sample of American faculty members were asked which two of a list of countries were "the greatest threats to international stability," the United States came in second only to North Korea. See Gary A. Tobin and Aryeth K. Weinverg, "A Profile of American College Faculty Vol. I; Political Beliefs and Behavior," Institute for Jewish and Community Research, 2006, p. 39. Available from: www.jewishresearch.org/PDFs2/FacultySurvey_Web.pdf (accessed March 12, 2009).

18 "Constitution of the United Nations Educational, Scientific and Cultural Organization," adapted November 16, 1945. Available from: www.icomos.org/unesco/unesco_constitution.html (accessed March 10, 2007).

19 David Von Drehle and R. Jeffrey Smith, "U.S. Strikes Iraq for Plot to Kill Bush," *Washington Post*, June 27, 1993, A01; The FBI's report on the attempt concluded, "Based on interviews of the alleged coconspirators, forensic examinations of the explosive devices, and intelligence reports, the United States Government concluded that Iraq was behind the attempted car bombing." The FBI report can be found at: www.fas.org/irp/agency/doj/oig/fbilab1/05bush2.htm (accessed March 6, 2009).

20 See Richard K. Betts, "The Soft Underbelly of American Primacy: Tactical Advantages of Terror," *Political Science Quarterly*, 117 (2002), p. 31.

21 Jerrold M. Post, "Saddam Hussein of Iraq," in Jerrold M. Post (ed.) *The Psychological Assessment of Political Leaders*. Ann Arbor, MI: University of Michigan Press, 2003, p. 337.

22 Nathan Leites, *The Operational Code of the Politburo*. NY: McGraw-Hill, 1951. This framework was refined and expanded by Alexander L. George. See his paper, "The 'Operational Code': A Neglected Approach to the Study of Political Leaders and Decision-making." *International Studies Quarterly*, 13 (June 1969), pp. 190–222.

23 There is both a descriptive and a normative aspect to these questions. The descriptive part reflects the extent to which such considerations are present in decision-makers' thinking and influence their stance towards national security issues and tactics. My research on the Bush Administrations leads me to the conclusion that such strategic perspectives are readily accessible in at least Mr. Bush's foreign policy major statements and interviews. I think it likely they will be found in the perspectives of other foreign policy decision-makers as well.

As to the normative part, it is my view that systematically examining national security issues through these frames and being aware of the inferences involved in reaching policy conclusions raised by these questions would be, overall, beneficial.

24 Quoted in Joshua Partlow, "A Dictator's Arc of Power Ends in Utter Ignominy," *Washington Post*, December 31, 2006, A01.

25 Kevin Woods, James Lacey, and Williamson Murray, "Saddam's Delusions: The View from the Inside," *Foreign Affairs*, May/June 2006.

26 Kevin M. Woods, with Michael R. Pease, Mark E. Stout, Williamson Murray, and James G. Lacey, "Iraqi Perspectives Project: a View of Operation Iraqi Freedom from Saddam's Senior Leadership," Joint Center for Operation Analysis, March 20, 2008. Available from: www.jfcom.mil/newslink/storyarchive/2006/ipp.pdf (accessed May 18, 2009).

27 Woods, Lacey, and Murray, "Iraqi Perspective Project," p. 14.

28 Woods, Lacey, and Murray, "Iraqi Perspective Project," p. 14.

29 Woods, Lacey, and Murray, "Iraqi Perspective Project," p. 14.

30 Anthony H. Cordesman, *Weapons of Mass Destruction in the Middle East*. London, Brasseys, 1991, p. 93 cited in Abbas William Samii, "The Iranian Nuclear Issue and Informal Networks," *Naval War College Review*, 59:1 (Winter 2006), p. 77.

31 Richard L. Russell, "Iran in Iraq's Shadow: Dealing with Tehran's Nuclear Weapons Bid," *Parameters*, 34:3 (Autumn 2004), p. 36.

32 Glenn Kessler, "Administration Debate on Iran," *Washington Post*, January 30, 2009, A12.

33 Ray Takeyh, "Time for Détente with Iran," *Foreign Affairs* (March/April 2007).

34 Ray Takeyh, "Time for Détente with Iran."

35 Abbas William Samii, "The Iranian Nuclear Issue."
36 This and the two quotes that follow are found in Ray Takeyh, "Time for Détente … "
37 Samuel P. Huntington, "Democracy for the Long Haul," *Journal of Democracy*, 7:2 (1996), pp. 3–13.
38 Michael Slackman, "Amid Crackdown, Iran Admits Voting Errors," *New York Times*, June 23, 2009.
39 This section and the next are meant to be illustrative and make no representations to being comprehensive.
40 Caroline Glick, "If Iran Gets the Bomb," *The Jerusalem Post*, March 7, 2007.
41 Fouad Ajami, "Maintaining Perspective," *U.S. News and World Report*, February 25, 2007.
42 Jonathan Renshon, "Assessing Threat and Vulnerability: The Role of Overconfidence and Overestimation," Unpublished paper, Department of Government, Harvard University, 2007.
43 Alexander L. George, *Forceful Persuasion: Coercive Diplomacy as an Alternative to War*. Washington, DC: U.S. Institute of Peace, 1991.
44 Tony Smith, *Pact with the Devil*. New York: Routledge, 2007, passim.
45 David Brooks, "Bush and Iraq," *New York Times*, July 18, 2007.
46 Personal communication to author, July 3, 2007.

8 Strategic Options and the Future of the Bush Doctrine

1 In the sections that follow, several strong critics of the Bush Doctrine and their preferred strategies are examined. The particular authors examined are chosen because they most clearly articulate the premises of their position or are in addition the most forceful and well-known advocates of it.
2 Eric Lichtblau and James Risen, "Bank Data is Shifted by U.S. in Secret to Block Terror," *New York Times*, June 23, 2006; see also Sheryl Gay Stolberg, "Bush Says Report on Bank Data was Disgraceful," *New York Times*, June 27, 2006.
3 The *Washington Post* reports that, "The effort President Bush authorized shortly after Sept. 11, 2001, to fight al Qaeda has grown into the largest CIA covert action program since the height of the Cold War … The broad-based effort, known within the agency by the initials GST, is compartmentalized into dozens of highly classified individual programs, details of which are known mainly to those directly involved." See Dana Priest, "Covert CIA Program Withstands New Furor Anti-Terror Effort Continues to Grow," *Washington Post*, December 30, 2005, A01.
4 John D. Negroponte, "Transcript: Hearing of the Senate Select Committee on Intelligence, Annual Threat Assessment," January 11, 2007, p. 33.
5 Ikenberry and Slaughter, "Forging a World of Liberty Under Law," p. 29.
6 Ikenberry and Slaughter, "Forging a World of Liberty Under Law," p. 32.
7 Barry R. Posen and Andrew L. Ross, "Competing Visions of U.S. Grand Strategy," *International Security*, 21:3 (1996–1997), pp. 5–53.
8 Francis Fukuyama, *America at the Crossroads: Democracy, Power, and the Neoconservative Legacy*. New Haven, CT: Yale University Press, 2006.
9 Joseph S. Nye, "A 'progressive realist' foreign policy begins with modesty," *The Daily Star*, August 29, 2006. Available from: www.dailystar.com.lb/article.asp?edition_id=10&categ_id=5&article_id = 75091 (accessed January 15, 2009); for a different use of the same term see Robert Wright, "An American Foreign Policy That Both Realists and Ideals Should Fall in Love With," *New York Times*, July 16, 2006.
10 Anatol Lieven and John Hulsman, *Ethical Realism: A Vision for America's Role in the World*. New York: Pantheon, 2006.
11 See Earl Ravenal, "The Case for Adjustment," *Foreign Policy*, 8 (Winter 1990–91), pp. 3–19; Eric D. Nordlinger, *Isolationism Reconfigured: American Foreign Policy for a New Century*, Princeton, NJ: Princeton University Press, 1995; Eugene Gholz, Daryl G. Press, and Harvey M. Sapolsky, "Come Home America: The Strategy of Restraint in the Face of Temptation," *International Security*, 21:4 (Spring 1977), pp. 1–43.

12 Barry R. Posen, "The Struggle Against Terrorism," *International Security*, 26:3 (Winter 2001/2002), p. 54.
13 Robert Art, "Geopolitics Updated: The Strategy of Selective Engagement," *International Security*, 23:3 (Winter 1998/99), pp. 79–113.
14 Richard Haas, "The Case for Integration," *The Public Interest*, 81 (Fall 2005), pp. 22–29; see also Richard Haas, *The Opportunity: America's Moment to Alter History's Course*. New York: Pubic Affairs, 2005.
15 Lawrence J. Korb and Robert O. Boorstin, "Integrated Power: A National Security Strategy for the 21st Century," Center for American Progress, June 2005.
16 Stephen M. Walt, *Taming American Power: The Global Response to American Power*. New York: Norton, 2005; see also, Christopher Layne, "From Preponderance to Offshore Balancing: America's Future Grand Strategy," *International Security*, 22:1 (1997), 86–124; Christopher Layne, "Offshore Balancing Revisited," *Washington Quarterly* (Spring 2002), pp. 233–48; and Christopher Layne, *The Peace of Illusions: American Grand Strategy from 1940 to the Present*. Ithaca, NY: Cornell University Press, 2006.
17 On the president's leadership psychology, see Stanley A. Renshon, *In His Father's Shadow: The Transformations of George W. Bush*. New York: Palgrave/St. Martins, 2005.
18 Fukuyama, *America at the Crossroads*, p. 10.
19 Fukuyama, p. 179.
20 Stephen D. Krasner, "Sharing Sovereignty: New Institutions for Collapsed and Failing States," *International Security*, 29:2 (2004), pp. 85–120.
21 Fukuyama, *America at the Crossroads*, p. 179.
22 Fukuyama, *America at the Crossroads*, pp. 179–80.
23 Fukuyama, *America at the Crossroads*, p. 88.
24 Fukuyama, *America at the Crossroads*, pp. 84–88.
25 Fukuyama, *America at the Crossroads*, p. 88.
26 Fukuyama, *America at the Crossroads*, p. 90 (emphasis mine).
27 Fukuyama, *America at the Crossroads*, p. 183.
28 Fukuyama, *America at the Crossroads*, p. 100.
29 Fukuyama, *America at the Crossroads*, p. 97.
30 Fukuyama, *America at the Crossroads*, p. 97.
31 Fukuyama, *America at the Crossroads*, p. 101.
32 Transcript, "Second Presidential Debate."
33 Robert J. Art, "A Defensible Defense: America's Grand Strategy after the Cold War," *International Security*, 15:4 (Spring 1991), pp. 5–53; see also Robert J. Art, "Geopolitics Updated: The Strategy of Selective Engagement," *International Security*, 23:3 (Winter 1998/99), pp. 79–113, and Robert J. Art, *A Grand Strategy for America*, Ithaca, NY: Cornell, 2004.
34 Posen and Ross, "Competing Visions for U.S. Grand Strategy … ," p. 17.
35 Posen and Ross, "Competing Visions for U.S. Grand Strategy … ," p. 18.
36 Posen and Ross, "Competing Visions for U.S. Grand Strategy … ," p. 18.
37 Posen and Ross, "Competing Visions for U.S. Grand Strategy … ," p. 19 (emphasis mine).
38 See Samuel P. Huntington, "The Erosion of American National Interests," *Foreign Affairs* (September/October 1997), pp. 28–49; Joseph S. Nye, Jr., "Redefining the National Interest," *Foreign Affairs* (July/August 1999), pp. 22–35.
39 Art, "Geopolitics Updated … ," p. 80.
40 Art, "Geopolitics Updated … ," pp. 84, 95.
41 Posen and Ross, "Competing Visions for U.S. Grand Strategy," pp. 22–23; see also Colin Dueck, "New Perspectives on American Grand Strategy," *Survival*, 28:4 (2004), p. 209 and Art, *A Grand Strategy for America*.
42 Art, "Geopolitics Updated," pp. 85–88.
43 Art, "Geopolitics Updated … ," pp. 80–81.
44 Art, "Geopolitics Updated … ," p. 88.
45 Art, "Geopolitics Updated … ," p. 84, fn 4.
46 Art, "Geopolitics Updated … " Posen on the other hand, would limit military action against those who allied with al Qaeda. See Barry R. Posen, "The Struggle Against

Terrorism: Grand Strategy, Strategy and Tactics," *International Security*, 23:3 (Winter 2001/2002), pp. 42–43.

47 Art, "Geopolitics Updated ... ," p. 85. Art notes that he borrows these characteristics from Stephen Van Evra, *The Causes of War: Power and the Roots of War*. Ithaca, NY: Cornell 1999, Chapter 8.

48 Art, "Geopolitics Updated ... ," pp. 88–89.

49 Art, "Geopolitics Updated ... ," p. 89.

50 As Posen and Ross point out, the new isolationists seldom refer to themselves that way and actually reject the term "isolationist." See Posen and Ross, "Competing Visions for U.S. Grand Strategy ... ," p. 9, fn 5.

51 Gholz, Press, and Sapolsky, "Come Home America," pp. 6, 47. Nordlinger, *Isolationism Reconfigured ...* is an exception to this statement.

52 This paraphrase is found in Paul Starobin, "The Realists," *National Journal*, September 15, 2006.

53 Starobin, "The Realists," pp. 24–31.

54 Gholz, Press, and Sapolsky, "Come Home America ... ," p. 5.

55 See Art, "Geopolitics Updated ... ," p. 103; also p. 104, fn 36.

56 Art, "Geopolitics Updated ... ," pp. 4–5.

57 Gholz, Press, and Sapolsky, "Come Home America ... ," p. 9.

58 Gholz, Press, and Sapolsky, "Come Home America ... ," p. 10.

59 Gholz, Press, and Sapolsky, "Come Home America ... ," p. 15.

60 Gholz, Press, and Sapolsky, "Come Home America ... ," p. 10. The actual quote is, "Unlike security and prosperity, however, American's other foreign policy goals are unlikely to be achieved effortlessly."

61 Eugene Gholz, Daryl G. Press, and Benjamin Valentino, "Time to Offshore Our Troops," *New York Times*, December 12, 2006.

62 Eugene Gholz, "U.S. Interests in the Persian Gulf," Partnership for a Secure America Website, December 13, 2006. Available from: www.blog.psaonline.org/2006/12/13/ us-interests-in-the-persian-gulf/ (accessed January 22, 2009).

63 Daryl Press and Benjamin Valentino, "A Balanced Foreign Policy," Tobin Project Research Paper, June 24, 2002 (emphasis mine). Available from: www.tobinproject.org/ welcome/downloads/NS_Balanced_Foreign_Policy.pdf (accessed May18, 2009).

64 Press and Valentino, "A Balanced Foreign Policy," p. 40.

65 Eugene Gholz and Daryl G. Press, "Protecting 'The Prize': Oil and the National Interest," Paper presented at the Annual Meeting of the American Political Science Association, Chicago, IL, 2004.

66 Gholz, Press, and Sapolsky, "Come Home America ... ," p. 15. Notice the lack of a conditional tense.

67 Gholz, Press, and Sapolsky, "Come Home America ... ," p. 15.

68 Gholz, Press, and Sapolsky, "Come Home America ... ," p. 16.

69 Gholz, Press, and Sapolsky, "Come Home America ... ," p. 17.

70 Gholz, Press, and Sapolsky, "Come Home America ... ," pp. 16–17.

71 Gholz, Press, and Sapolsky, "Come Home America ... ," pp. 22–23, 29.

72 Gholz, Press, and Sapolsky, "Come Home America ... ," p. 34.

73 Gholz, Press, and Sapolsky, "Come Home America ... ," p. 22 (emphasis mine).

74 Gholz, Press, and Sapolsky, "Come Home America ... ," pp. 22–23.

75 Gholz, Press, and Sapolsky, "Come Home America ... ," p. 27.

76 Gholz, Press, and Sapolsky, "Come Home America ... ," p. 26. Kenneth Polack makes a similar argument based on the relative weakness of Iraq and Iran and the sensitivity of populations in the area to an American presence. However Pollack differs with these authors in suggesting that the United States keeps its naval base in Bahrain and its air force base in Qatar. Moreover, he also suggests forming a NATO like defense pact in the area, or trying to establish "a security condominium," commitments that directly contradict the preferences of neo-isolationists. See Kenneth M. Pollack, "Securing the Gulf," *Foreign Affairs*, July/August 2003.

77 Gholz, Press, and Sapolsky, "Come Home America ... ," p. 29.

78 Gholz, Press, and Sapolsky, "Come Home America ... ," p. 26.
79 Press and Valentino, "A Balanced Foreign Policy," p. 41.
80 Gholz and Press, "Protecting 'The Prize ... '," p. 44.
81 Gholz and Press, "Protecting 'The Prize ... '," p. 44.
82 Gholz and Press, "Protecting 'The Prize ... '," p. 44.
83 Gholz, Press, and Sapolsky, "Come Home America ... ," p. 30.
84 Press and Valentino, "A Balanced Foreign Policy," p. 40 (emphasis in original).
85 Press and Valentino, "A Balanced Foreign Policy," p. 41.
86 Jim Gomez, "Top Al Qaeda-Linked Terrorist Killed," *Associated Press*, January 17, 2007.
87 Gholz, Press, and Sapolsky, "Come Home America ... ," p. 29.
88 Gholz and Press, "Protecting 'The Prize ... '," p. 3.
89 Richard K. Betts, "The Soft Underbelly of American Primacy: Tactical Advantages of Terror," *Political Science Quarterly*, 117 (2002), p. 34.
90 Gholz, Press, and Sapolsky, "Come Home America ... ," pp. 46–47.
91 Gholz, Press, and Sapolsky, "Come Home America ... ," p. 47.
92 Art, "Geopolitics Updated ... ," p. 105.
93 Layne, "From Preponderance to Offshore Balancing," p. 94.
94 *A National Strategy of Enlargement and Engagement*. Washington, DC: U.S. Government Printing Office, 1994 [Revised version 1996].
95 Posen and Ross, "Competing Visions for U.S. Grand Strategy ... ," p. 36.
96 Walt, *Taming American Power*, p. 219.
97 Stephen M. Walt, "In the National Interest," *Boston Review*, February/March 2005, p. 1; see also Walt, *Taming American Power*, pp. 109–179.
98 Layne, "From Preponderance to Offshore Balancing ... ," p. 91.
99 Layne, "From Preponderance to Offshore Balancing ... ," p. 98.
100 Layne, "From Preponderance to Offshore Balancing ... ," p. 99; see also Layne, "Offshore Balancing Revisited", p. 247.
101 Posen and Ross, "Competing Visions for U.S. Grand Strategy ... ," p. 17, fn 14.
102 Posen, "The Struggle Against Terrorism", p. 43.
103 Barry R. Posen, "The Case for Restraint," *The American Interest*, November–December 2007.
104 Walt, "In the National Interest," p. 3.
105 Walt, "In the National Interest," p. 12.
106 Walt, *Taming American Power*, p. 140.
107 Walt, *Taming American Power*, p. 237 (emphasis mine).
108 Walt, *Taming American Power*, p. 224.
109 Walt, *Taming American Power*, p. 140.
110 Walt, *Taming American Power*, p. 223.
111 Walt, *Taming American Power*, pp. 223–27.
112 Walt, *Taming American Power*, p. 225.
113 Layne, "Offshore Balancing Revisited," p. 242.
114 Layne, "Offshore Balancing Revisited," p. 243.
115 Layne, "Offshore Balancing Revisited," pp. 242–43.
116 Layne, "Offshore Balancing Revisited," p. 245.
117 Layne, "Offshore Balancing Revisited," pp. 245–46.
118 Layne, "Offshore Balancing Revisited," pp. 246–47.
119 Layne, "Offshore Balancing Revisited," p. 246.
120 Layne, "Offshore Balancing Revisited," p. 240.
121 Posen, "The Struggle Against Terrorism," p. 44.
122 Posen, "The Struggle Against Terrorism," p. 44.
123 Posen, "The Struggle against Terrorism," passim.
124 Posen, "The Struggle against Terrorism," p. 44.
125 Daryl Press has argued recently that in crisis circumstances during the Cold War and before whether a country had made threats it did not follow through on had little impact on whether they were taken seriously when the next major threat arose. On the other hand, a variety of America's more recent enemies have keyed in on the fact that Press

accepts, that America is casualty sensitive. Press argues that the important distinction here is between fighting effectively and keeping commitments. He concludes, "Quitting after taking a small number of casualties, may send signals about a country's power." Is this not a credibility signal that other countries take into account? See Daryl G. Press, *Calculating Credibility: How Leaders Assess Military Threats.* Ithaca, NY: Cornell University Press, 2005, p. 157.
126 Gary Rosen, "Bush and the Realists," *Commentary*, September 2005, 34.

9 The Politics of Risk Assessment

1 For Britain see, Report of a Committee of Privy Counsellors (The Butler Committee), Review of Intelligence Weapons of Mass Destruction, House of Commons, July 14, 2004. Available from: www.archive2.official-documents.co.uk/document/deps/hc/hc898/898.pdf (accessed March 16, 2009).
For Australia see, the Parliament of the Commonwealth of Australia. "Intelligence on Iraq's Weapons of Mass Destruction (Parliamentary Joint Committee on ASIO, ASIS and DSD)," Canberra, December 2003. Available from: www.aph.gov.au/house/committee/pjcaad/wmd/report/fullreport.pdf (accessed March 16, 2009).
2 Senators Levin, Lieberman, Lautenberg, Dodd, Kerrey, Feinstein, Mikulski, Daschle, Breaux, Johnson, Inouye, Landrieu, Ford and Kerry had written to the president saying, "[W]e urge you, after consulting with Congress, and consistent with the U.S. Constitution and laws, to take necessary actions (including, if appropriate, air and missile strikes on suspect Iraqi sites) to respond effectively to the threat posed by Iraq's refusal to end its weapons of mass destruction programs (October 9, 1998)." Mr. Clinton himself had said, "One way or the other, we are determined to deny Iraq the capacity to develop weapons of mass destruction and the missiles to deliver them. That is our bottom line" (February 4, 1998). On October 31, 1998 Mr. Clinton signed the Iraqi Liberation Act of 1998 that, "Declares that it should be the policy of the United States to seek to remove the Saddam Hussein regime from power in Iraq and to replace it with a democratic government."
When the Iraq War was debated in Congress, Harry Reid said that, Saddam's refusal to honor past agreements "constitutes a breach of the armistice which renders it void and justifies resumption of the armed conflict." Senator Robert Byrd said, "The last UN weapons inspectors left Iraq in October of 1998. We are confident that Saddam Hussein retains some stockpiles of chemical and biological weapons, and that he has since embarked on a crash course to build up his chemical and biological warfare capabilities. Intelligence reports indicate that he is seeking nuclear weapons ... " Al Gore said, "Iraq's search for weapons of mass destruction has proven impossible to deter and we should assume that it will continue for as long as Saddam is in power" (September 23, 2002). Carl Levin said, "We begin with the common belief that Saddam Hussein is a tyrant and a threat to the peace and stability of the region. He has ignored the mandate of the United Nations and is building weapons of mass destruction and the means of delivering them" (September 23, 2002). John Kerry said, "I believe that a deadly arsenal of weapons of mass destruction in his hands is a real and grave threat to our security (October 9, 2002). So when Dick Cheney said, "And we believe he has, in fact, reconstituted nuclear weapons" (March 16, 2003), he was by no means alone in his views.
3 Dana Milbank and Walter Pincus, "Asterisks Dot White House's Iraq Argument," *Washington Post*, November 12, 2005, A01.
4 The March 2005 report of the Robb-Silberman Commission found, "no evidence of political pressure to influence the intelligence community's pre-war assessments of Iraq's weapons programs. ... [A]nalysts universally asserted that in no instance did political pressure cause them to skew or alter any of their analytical judgments." See "The Commission on the Intelligence Capabilities of the United States Regarding Weapons of Mass Destruction," March 31, 2005, pp. 50–51. Available from: www.gpoaccess.gov/wmd/pdf/full_wmd_report.pdf (accessed March 16, 2009).

5 John Tagliabue, "No Evidence Suspect Met Iraqi in Prague," *New York Times*, October 20, 2001; Patrick E. Taylor, "U.S. Drops Last Link of Iraq to 9/11," *New York Times*, May 2, 2002.
6 Chaim Kaufman, "Threat Inflation and the Failure of the Marketplace of Ideas: The Selling of the Iraq War," *International Security*, 29:1 (Summer 2004), p. 19.
7 Personal communication to author, July 3, 2007.
8 Kaufman, "Threat Inflation and the Failure of the Marketplace of Ideas," 5–38. See also Ronald R. Krebs and Chaim Kaufman, "Correspondence—Selling the Market Short? The Marketplace of Ideas and the Iraq War," *International Security*, (Spring 2005), pp. 196–207.
9 Kaufman, "Threat Inflation and the Failure of the Marketplace of Ideas," pp. 16–17.
10 George Tenet, *At the Center of the Storm: My Year at the CIA*. New York: HarperCollins, 2007.
11 Robert Jervis, "Reports, Politics and Intelligence: The Case of Iraq," *The Journal of Strategic Studies*, 29:1 (February 2006), pp. 15–18. This was also the conclusion of the Senate Select Committee. See Senate Select Committee "Report on the US Intelligence Community's Prewar Intelligence Assessments on Iraq," July 7, 2004, pp. 24–26, 28–32, 32–34.
12 Jervis, *Perception and Misperception in International Politics*; also J.M. Goldgeier and P. E. Tetlock, "Psychology and International Relations Theory," *Annual Review of Political Science* (2001), pp. 67–92.
13 Jonathan Renshon, "Mirroring Risk: Empathetic Failure and the Cuban Missile Crisis," *Intelligence and National Security*, 24 no.3 (June 2009): 315–338.
14 Pre- and post hoc explanations must also be distinguished. The fact that no WMD stockpiles were found clearly means that a number of pre-war assessments were wrong. But it does not follow that the array of evidence and inference used to reach these erroneous conclusions could or should have been known in the absence of the conclusive proof that emerged after and as a result of the invasion.
15 Franklin D. Roosevelt thought the United States faced a dire threat from Germany but did not make this case publicly, relying instead before Pearl Harbor on an incremental approach typified by the "Lend-Lease" and "Destroyers for Bases" Agreements.
16 Chaim Kaufman says, "My charge against the administration officials is that they did not admit to any uncertainty." See Ronald R. Krebs and Chaim Kaufman, "Correspondence—Selling the Market Short?" p. 203.
17 Fred Hiatt, "The Politics of War," *Washington Post*, November 14, 2005, A21.
18 A November 2005 *Wall Street Journal/NBC News* survey found that fifty-seven percent of Americans endorsed that proposition that the president "deliberately misled people to make the case for war with Iraq," compared to thirty-five percent who thought he "gave the most accurate information he had." Five months before, those numbers were forty-four percent "misled" versus forty-seven percent "accurate information." Shortly after Bush's second term began forty-one percent thought Bush had "misled" them, while fifty-three percent credited the president with being "accurate."
19 Kaufman, "Threat Inflation and the Failure of the Marketplace of Ideas ... ."
20 Sabrina Tavernise, "U.S. Says Captured Iranians Can Be Linked to Attacks," *New York Times*, December 27, 2006.
21 Michael R. Gordon, "Deadliest Bomb in Iraq is Made by Iran, U.S. Says," *New York Times*, February 10, 2007; see also Joshua Partlow, "Iran Sending Explosives to Extremist Groups in Iraq, Officials Say," *Washington Post*, February 11, 2007.
22 James Glanz, "U.S. Presents Evidence of Iranian Weapons in Iraq," *New York Times*, February 11, 2007.
23 Glanz, "U.S. Presents Evidence of Iranian Weapons in Iraq."
24 Glanz, "U.S. Presents Evidence of Iranian Weapons in Iraq."
25 Helene Cooper and Mark Mazzetti, "Skeptics Doubt U.S. Evidence on Iran's Actions in Iraq," *New York Times*, February 13, 2007.
26 Cooper and Mazzetti, "Skeptics Doubt U.S. Evidence on Iran's Actions in Iraq."
27 Yochi J. Dreazen and Jay Solomon, "Rifts Emerge on Iran Policy Skeptics Question Extent of Role in Iraq Instability," *Wall Street Journal*, February 3, 2007, A4.

28 Interview with Paul R. Pillar, "Iran May Not Be Behind Coalition Attacks, Council of Foreign Relations," February 6, 2007. Available from: www.cfr.org/publication/12559/pillar.html (accessed March 2, 2009).

29 Quoted in Lionel Beehner, "Iran's Involvement in Iraq." Council of Foreign Relations Backgrounder, February 12, 2007. Available from: www.cfr.org/publication/12521/irans_involvement_in_iraq.html (accessed March 2, 2009).

30 Partlow, "Iran Sending Explosives to Extremist Groups in Iraq, Officials Say,"; see also James Glanz, "U.S. Says Arms Link Iranians to Iraqi Shiites," *New York Times*, February 12, 2007.

31 Ann Scott Tyson, "GAO Faults U.S. Military Over Munitions in Iraq Report Says Insurgents Took Unsecured Explosives," *Washington Post*, March 23, 2007, A07.

32 www.antiwar.com/casualties (accessed June 1, 2007).

33 James Glanz and Richard A. Oppel, Jr., "U.S. Says Raid in Iraq Supports Claim on Iran," *New York Times*, February 26, 2007 (emphasis mine).

34 Glanz and Oppel, Jr., "U.S. Says Raid in Iraq Supports Claim on Iran … ," p. A1.

35 Glanz and Oppel, Jr., "U.S. Says Raid in Iraq Supports Claim on Iran … ," p. A1.

36 Glenn Kessler, "North Korea Aims to Improve on Clinton-Era Nuclear Deal," *Washington Post*, February 6, 2007, A12.

37 Glenn Kessler, "New Doubts on Nuclear Efforts by North Korea: U.S. Less Certain of Uranium Program," *Washington Post*, March 1, 2007, A01.

38 In the state department brief, the administration reiterated that North Korea had admitted that it had violated the 1995 agreement by starting up a secret uranium production program.

   Question: As a practical matter, how would the Administration or Chris Hill get North Korea to admit to a highly enriched uranium program? I mean, they've been denying this for years.

   Mr. McCormack: Well, they already admitted it.

   Question: Yeah?

   Mr. McCormack: They admitted it back in 2002 in Pyongyang when Jim Kelly, then Assistant Secretary for East Asian and Pacific Affairs, led a delegation to Pyongyang and they asked them – they asked them about this issue, they confronted them with this issue. The North Koreans, for a period of time, admitted under repeated questioning that they had a highly enriched uranium program. See Daily Press Briefing, Department of State, Sean McCormack, Spokesman, February 28, 2007.

39 Daily Press Briefing, Department of State, Sean McCormack, Spokesman.

40 Review & Outlook, "Uranium Do-Over," *Wall Street Journal*, March 1, 2007.

41 Kessler, "New Doubts on Nuclear Efforts by North Korea," p. A01.

42 Quoted in Kessler, "New Doubts on Nuclear Efforts by North Korea," p. A01.

43 David Albright, president of the Institute for Science and International Security, quoted in David E. Singer and William J. Broad, "U.S. Concedes Uncertainty on North Korean Uranium Effort," *New York Times*, March 1, 2007, A1. See also David Albright, "Yet Another Questionable Extrapolation Based on Aluminum Tubes," The Institute for Science and International Security (ISIS) February 23, 2007. Available from: www.isis-online.org/publications/dprk/DPRKenrichment22Feb.pdf (accessed March 2, 2009).

44 Selig S. Harrison, "Did North Korea Cheat?" *Foreign Affairs*, (January/February 2005).

45 Christopher R. Hill, chief American negotiator with North Korea quoted in Singer and Broad. "U.S. Concedes Uncertainty on North Korean Uranium Effort." At the time the charge was made, there was no publicly released national intelligence addressing this issue.

46 Quoted in Singer and Broad, "U.S. Concedes Uncertainty on North Korean Uranium Effort," p. A1.

47 Kessler, "New Doubts on Nuclear Efforts by North Korea", A01; see also Editorial, "Another Intelligence Twist." *Washington Post*, March 2, 2007, A12.

48 George W. Bush, "The President's Press Conference," November 7, 2002.

49 Singer and Broad, "U.S. Concedes Uncertainty on North Korean Uranium Effort," p. A1.

50 George Jahn, "Analysis: U.S. Intel on Nukes in Doubt," *Associated Press*, March 1, 2007.
51 Singer and Broad, "U.S. Concedes Uncertainity," p. A1.
52 Kessler, "New Doubts on Nuclear Efforts by North Korea," p. A01.
53 Editorial, "Come Clean on North Korea," *Los Angeles Times*, March 2, 2007. The quotes that follow in this paragraph are drawn from that editorial.
54 Harrison, "Did North Korea Cheat?" p. 99.
55 Harrison, "Did North Korea Cheat?" p. 100.
56 Harrison, "Did North Korea Cheat?" p. 107.
57 Anonymous source quoted in Jahn, "Analysis: U.S. Intell on Nukes in Doubt."
58 Singer and Broad, "U.S. Concedes Uncertainty," p. A1.
59 Singer and Broad, "U.S. Concedes Uncertainty," p. A1.
60 Sanger and Broad, "U.S. Concedes Uncertainty," p. A1.
61 Jahn, "Analysis: U.S. Intell on Nukes in Doubt."
62 "Fox News Interview with Secretary of State Clinton: North Korea and the Six-Party Talks," U.S. Department of State, February 20, 2009. Available from: www.state.gov/secretary/rm/2009a/02/119426.htm (accessed April 13, 2009).
63 These possibilities are raised in John R. Bolton, "The North Korean Climbdown," *Wall Street Journal*, March 5, 2007.
64 Brian Knowlton, "Report Stirs Debate on Terror Fight," *New York Times*, September 24, 2006. All quotes in this paragraph are drawn from that article. See also Mark Mazzetti, "Spy Agencies Say Iraq War Worsens Terrorism Threat," *New York Times*, September 24, 2007.
65 Edward Kennedy said, "The assessment should put the final nail in the coffin for President Bush's phony argument about the Iraq war." John Kerry said, "The National Intelligence Estimate provides jarring confirmation that the disastrous policy in Iraq is a giant recruiting poster for terrorists." Nancy Pelosi said, "President Bush should read the intelligence carefully before giving another misleading speech about progress in the war on terrorism."
66 Knowlton, "Report Stirs Debate on Terror Fight," p. 1.
67 Declassified Key Judgments of the National Intelligence Estimate "Trends in Global Terrorism: Implications for the United States," April 2006, p. 1 (emphasis added). Available from: www.dni.gov/press_releases/Declassified_NIE_Key_Judgments.pdf (accessed March 2, 2009).
68 Declassified Key Judgments of the National Intelligence Estimate.
69 National Intelligence Estimate, "Prospects for Iraq Stability: A Challenging Road Ahead," National Intelligence Council, January 2007 (emphasis added, bold in original). Available from: www.dni.gov/press_releases/20070202_release.pdf (accessed March 2, 2009).
70 These changes are explicated in the National Intelligence Estimate, "Prospects for Iraq Stability: A Challenging Road Ahead," National Intelligence Council, January 2007, pp. 3–5.
71 Walter Pincus, "Democrats Criticize Lack of Alternatives in Intelligence Estimate," *Washington Post*, February 15, 2007, A05.
72 Pincus, "Democrats Criticize Lack of Alternatives in Intelligence Estimate," p. A05.
73 Pincus, "Democrats Criticize Lack of Alternatives in Intelligence Estimate," p. A05.
74 Pincus, "Democrats Criticize Lack of Alternatives in Intelligence Estimate," p. A05.
75 Walter Pincus, "U.S. Sees New Al-Qaeda Threat," *Washington Post*, February 28, 2007, A04.
76 Daniel L. Byman and Kenneth M. Pollack, "Things Fall Apart: Containing the Spillover from an Iraqi Civil War," *Saban Center Analysis*, January 2007, Number 11. Available from: www.brookings.edu/papers/2007/01iraq_byman.aspx (accessed March 2, 2009).
77 Byman and Kenneth M. Pollack, "Things Fall Apart," p. x (emphasis added). Elsewhere (p. xv) the report warns that the United States should prepare for "particularly severe manifestations of spillover."
78 Barry R. McCaffrey, "No Choice: Stay the Course in Iraq," *Los Angeles Times*, April 3, 2007.

79 Jonathan Weisman, "House Passes Iraq Pullout Timetable War Funding Bill Approved 218–212; Bush Vows Veto," *Washington Post*, March 24, 2007, A01.

80 Elizabeth Williamson and Jonathan Weisman, "Democrats Plan to Press GOP on Iraq Majority Party Frustrated on Hill," *Washington Post*, June 30, 2007, A02.

10 The Politics of Post-9/11 National Security: A Profound Worldview Divide

1 Eugene Gholz, Daryl G. Press, and Harvey M. Sapolsky, "Come Home America: The Strategy of Restraint in the Face of Temptation," *International Security*, 21:4 (1997), pp. 5–48.

2 Adam Zagorin, "Charges Sought Against Rumsfeld Over Prison Abuse," *Time*, November 10, 2006.

3 Arthur Schlesinger, Jr., "The Imperial Presidency Redux," *Washington Post*, June 28, 2003, A25; see also Editorial, "The Imperial Presidency 2.0," *New York Times*, January 7, 2007.

4 The accusation was that Mr. Bush received a specific warning in his daily briefing about the September 11 al Qaeda attack in July 2001 that he ignored. Democrat Dick Gephardt, paraphrasing a question asked of Richard Nixon said, "I think what we have to do now is to find out what the president and what the White House knew about the events leading up to 9/11, when they knew it and, most importantly, what was done about it at that time." It turned out that the briefing document said that the terrorist group had a continuing interest in attacking the United States, hardly a startling or specific statement. "Transcript: Gephardt Holds Press Conference Regarding '9/11 Blame Game'," *CNN*, May 16, 2002. http://transcripts.cnn.com/TRANSCRIPTS/0205/16/se.02.html (accessed June 24, 2009).

5 Mike Allen, "Democrats Want Gitmo Prisoners Sent to U.S.," *The Politico*, March 7, 2007.

6 Shailagh Murray, "A Senate Maverick Acts to Force an Issue," *Washington Post*, March 15, 2006, A01.

7 A report by the House Democratic Judiciary Committee staff recommended the creation of a Special Select Committee of the Congress to report back to Congress on what the report characterizes as, "charges clearly [rising] to the level of impeachable offences." According to the Democrats there is a prima facie case that the "President, Vice-president, and other members of the administration violated a number of federal laws, including (1) Committing a Fraud against the United States; (2) Making False Statements to Congress; (3) The War Powers Resolution; (4) Misuse of Government Funds; federal laws and international treaties prohibiting torture and cruel, inhuman, and degrading treatment; Federal laws concerning retaliating against witnesses and other individuals; and Federal laws and regulations concerning leaking and other misuse of intelligence." See "The Constitution in Crisis: The Downing Street Minutes and Deception, Manipulation, Torture, Retribution, and Cover-ups in the Iraqi War," Investigative Status Report of the House Judiciary Committee Democratic Staff, Washington, DC, December 20, 2005. Available from: www.house.gov/judiciary_democrats/iraqrept122005/finalreport.pdf (accessed April 26, 2009).

8 I do not imply here that every Democrat or Republican thinks alike on these issues, only that within each party, members even if they differ with regard to some specifics are still generally to be located around this mean.

9 Oli R. Holsti, *Public Opinion and American Foreign Policy*. Ann Arbor, MI: University of Michigan Press, 1997, p. 139.

10 Holsti, *Public Opinion and American Foreign Policy*, p. 143.

11 Holsti, *Public Opinion and American Foreign Policy* (emphasis added).

12 Holsti, *Public Opinion and American Foreign Policy*, p. 49.

13 Holsti, *Public Opinion and American Foreign Policy*, pp. 49–50.

14 Quoted in Matt Bai, "Kerry's Undeclared War," *New York Times Magazine*, October 10, 2004.

15 Bai, "Kerry's Undeclared War." The quotes that follow in this paragraph are drawn from that article and interview.

16 One caution here is that we know little about how leaders understand and act on their views of gains and losses.

17 Pew Research Center, "The Dean Activists: Their Profile and Prospects," April 6, 2005, 3. Available from: www.people-press.org/reports/pdf/240.pdf (accessed April 27, 2009).

18 Here one would have to count Howard Dean, elected head of the Democratic National Committee, liberal Senate icons Patrick Leahy and Ted Kennedy, as well as a host of less vocal but nonetheless reliably liberal Democratic Senators, and a very liberal House Democratic caucus headed by House Majority Leader Nancy Pelosi.

19 Pew Research Center, "The Dean Activists: Their Profile and Prospects," p. 5.

20 Pew Research Center, "The Dean Activists: Their Profile and Prospects," p. 28.

21 Pew Research Center for the People and the Press, "Foreign Policy Attitudes Now Driven by 9/11," August 18, 2004. Available from: www.people-press.org/reports/pdf/222.pdf (accessed March 16, 2009). Data in this and the next two paragraphs are drawn from that report.

22 Pew Research Center for the People and the Press, "More Say Iraq Hurts Fight Against Terrorism," July 21, 2005. Available from: www.people-press.org/reports/pdf/251.pdf (accessed March 16, 2009). Data in this paragraph are drawn from that report.

23 For additional data and analyses that confirm these findings; see Miroslav Nincic and Monti Narayand Datta, "Of Paradise, Power and Pachyderms," *Political Science Quarterly*, 122 (2007), pp. 239–56.

24 Pew Research Center for the People and the Press, "Broad Opposition to Bush's Iraq Plan," January 16, 2007. Available from: www.people-press.org/reports/pdf/301.pdf (accessed March 16, 2009).

25 Fox News/Opinion Dynamics Poll, January 16, 2007. Available from: www.foxnews.com/projects/pdf/011807_foxnewspoll.pdf (accessed March 16, 2009).

26 Pew Research Center for the People and the Press, "Obama Faces Familiar Divisions Over Anti-Terror Policies," February 18, 2009. Available from: www.people-press.org/report/493/obama-anti-terror-policies (accessed March 16, 2009).

27 A December 28 2005 Rasmussen poll found that sixty-four percent of the public (and fifty-one percent of Democrats) said that the National Security Agency ought to be allowed to intercept telephone conversations between terror suspects in other countries and people living in the United States. Available from: www.rasmussenreports.com/2005/NSA.htm (accessed March 16, 2009).

28 George Packer, "A Democratic World: Can Liberals Take Foreign Policy Back from the Republicans?" *New Yorker*, February 16/23, 2004; see also James Mann, "Think Globally: Just How Many Elections do Democrats Have to Lose Before They Deal with Their Foreign Policy Problem," *American Prospect*, November 21, 2004.

29 Both quotes are drawn from Jeffrey Goldberg, "The Unbranding," *New Yorker*, March 21, 2005. For a plea that Democrats exercise more "message management," see Matthew Yglesias, "Message Management," *American Prospect*, December 13, 2005.

30 Kurt M. Campbell and Michael E. O'Hanlon, *Hard Power: The New Politics of National Security*. New York: Basic Books, 2006.

31 Will Marshall (ed.) *With All Our Might: A Progressive Strategy for Defeating Jihadism and Defending Liberalism*. Lanham, MD: Rowman & Littlefield, 2006.

32 Peter Beinart, *The Good Fight: Why Liberals—and Only Liberals—Can Win the War on Terror and Make America Great Again*. New York: HarperCollins, 2006.

33 Peter Beinart, "A Fighting Faith: An Argument for a New Liberalism," *The New Republic*, December 12, 2004. For some skeptical responses to his argument from fellow liberals see, Joshua Micah Marshall, "Talking Points Memo," December 9, 2004; John B. Judis, "Purpose Driven," *The New Republic On-line*, December 12, 2004; and Kevin Drum, "Political Animal," *Washington Monthly*, December 2, 2004.

34 Peter Beinart, "Don't Be a Control Freak (Ask for Help)," *Washington Post*, June 11, 2006, B05; see also Peter Beinart, *The Good Fight*.

35 John Edwards, "Remarks to Herzliya Conference," January 22, 2007. Available from: www.herzliyaconference.org/Eng/_Articles/Article.asp?ArticleID=1728&CategoryID=223) (accessed March 16, 2009).

36 Ezra Klein, "Edwards on Iran," *The American Prospect*, February 2, 2007. Available from: www.prospect.org/cs/articles?articleId=12434 (accessed March 16, 2009). The quotes in the next three paragraphs are drawn from that interview; emphases are mine.

37 Transcript, "The Democrats' First 2008 Presidential Debate," April 26, 2008. Available from: www.nytimes.com/2007/04/27/us/politics/27debate_transcript.html?pagewanted=print (accessed February 18, 2009).

38 Transcript, "The Democratic Presidential Debate on MSNBC," *New York Times*, September 26, 2007. Available from: www.nytimes.com/2007/09/26/us/politics/26DEBATE-TRANSCRIPT.html?pagewanted=print (accessed May 18, 2009).

39 www.dni.gov/press_releases/20070717_release.pdf (accessed May 18, 2009).

40 Transcript, "Democratic Debate in Philadelphia," *New York Times*, April 16, 2008. Available from: www.nytimes.com/2008/04/16/us/politics/16text-debate.html?pagewanted=print (accessed February 14, 2009).

41 Transcript, "Democratic Debate in Los Angeles," *New York Times*, January 31, 2008.

42 Transcript, Second McCain, Obama Debate, *CNN*, October 7, 2008.

43 Richard Rose, *The Post Modern Presidency. 2nd Edition.* Washington, DC: CQ Press, 1991.

44 These figures are taken from, "The Great Divide: How Westerners and Muslims View Each Other," Pew Global Attitudes Survey June 22, 2006, p. 4. Available from: www.pewglobal.org/reports/display.php?ReportID=253 (accessed March 16, 2009).

45 Pew Research Center for the People and the Press, "Muslims Americans: Middle Class and Mostly Mainstream," May 22, 2007, pp. 2, 5. Available from: www.pewresearch.org/assets/pdf/muslim-americans.pdf (accessed March 16, 2009).

46 Yaroslav Trofimov, Scott Neuman, and Daniel Pearl, "Import of bin Laden Video is in the Eye of the Beholder," *Wall Street Journal*, December 14, 2001; see also Howard Kurtz, "A Blood-Curdling Moment," *Washington Post*, December 14, 2001.

47 Glenn Kessler and Edward Cody, "U.S. Flexibility Credited in Nuclear Deal With N. Korea," *Washington Post*, February 14, 2007, A11.

48 Peter Baker, "U.S. to Ship Oil to North Korea Bush Cites Progress on Denuclearization," *Washington Post*, September 29, 2007, A13; see also Glenn Kessler, "Korea Nuclear Accord Reached Side Deal with U.S. Involves Terror List," *Washington Post*, October 3, 2007, A14.

49 Blaine Harden, "With Obama in White House, North Korea Steps Up Big Talk," *Washington Post*, February 4, 2009, A10.

50 Thomas Erdbrink, "Ahmadinejad Vows New Start As Clashes Flare," *Washington Post*, June 14, 2009.

51 Glenn Kessler, "Cautious Response Reflects Obama's Long-Term Approach," *Washington Post*, June 21, 2009.

52 At a White House briefing the following exchange took place:

Q: Robert, on Iran, is there an internal debate in the White House now between those who clearly support what the President is doing in terms of the hands-off approach and those who think the President needs to have some stronger language? Is that ongoing in the White House?

MR. GIBBS: *There's no debate in the White House.*

Q: Never?

Q: Is there division at all? Is everyone on the same page on this, or are there those who think that the President—internally, that the President is—

MR. GIBBS: *Everybody is on the same page. There's no difference of opinion.* I think the only thing I might take—the only thing I would take some exception to is the notion that the President has been hands-off. Again, the President—

See Press Briefing by Pres Secretary Robert Gibbs, June 18, 2009 (emphasis mine). Available at http://www.whitehouse.gov/the_press_office/Briefing-by-White-House-Press-Secretary-Robert-Gibbs-6-18-09/ (accessed June 29, 2009).

11 Obama's National Security Tasks: Worldview, Leadership and Judgment

1 Peter Baker, "As Democracy Push Falters, Bush Feels Like a Dissident," *Washington Post*, August 20, 2007, A01.
2 Ikenberry and Slaughter, "Forging a World of Liberty Under Law," p. 58.
3 Ikenberry and Slaughter, "Forging a World of Liberty Under Law," p. 59.
4 All data drawn from Karyln H. Bowman, "Public Opinion and the War in Iraq," AEI Studies in Public Opinion, updated as of March 16, 2007, pp. 74–76. Available from: www.aei.org/publicopinion2 (accessed February 10, 2007).
5 NBC/JSJ Poll, November 2007, Question 12. The poll is online at: www.msnbcmedia. msn.com/i/msnbc/sections/news/071107_NBC-WSJ_Full.pdf (accessed May 18, 2009).
6 Cf. NBC/Wall Street Journal Poll, December 2007, Question 17b. The poll is online at: www.online.wsj.com/public/resources/documents/wsjnbcpoll20071219.pdf (accessed May 18, 2009).
7 NBC/JSJ Poll, November 2007, Question 22. The poll is online at: www.msnbcmedia. msn.com/i/msnbc/sections/news/071107_NBC-WSJ_Full.pdf (accessed May 18, 2009).
8 Michael Kelly, "Hagel's Asian Trip, Time for Reflection," *World Herald*, 15, October 2006.
9 E.J. Dionne Jr., "Morning in America," *Washington Post*, March 20, 2007, A19.
10 Mark Mazzetti and Helene Cooper, "An Israeli Strike on Syria Kindles Debate," *New York Times*, October 10, 2007, A1.
11 Within Congress there are substantial party differences in strategic worldviews, and even within each party within Congress there is some variation. To some degree this is historically normal, but the level of acrimony, distrust, and assumptions of bad faith coupled with enormous and real strategic danger sets this historical period apart.
12 Barack Obama, *The Audacity of Hope*. New York: Three Rivers Press, 2006, p. 285.
13 Obama, *The Audacity of Hope*, p. 308.
14 Obama, *The Audacity of Hope*, pp. 308–9.
15 Obama, *The Audacity of Hope*, p. 309.
16 Quoted in Ben Smith, "'Invasion of Georgia' a '3 a.m. moment'," *Politico*, August 9, 2008.
17 Quoted in Ben Smith, "'Invasion of Georgia' a '3 a.m. moment'," *Politico*, August 9, 2008 (emphasis mine).
18 Peter Baker, "On Foreign Policy, Obama Shifts, but Only a Little," *New York Times*, April 17, 2009.
19 Clive Crook, "In Search of an Obama Doctrine," *Financial Times*, April 19, 2009.
20 Paul Koring, "Democracy Fades from Obama's Afghan Agenda," *Globe and Mail*, February 4, 2009.
21 Scott Wilson and Al Kamen, "'Global War on Terror' is Given New Name Bush's Phrase is Out, Pentagon Says," *Washington Post*, March 25, 2009.
22 "Remarks by Homeland Security Secretary Janet Napolitano to the International Association of Fire Fighters," Washington, DC, March 16, 2009. Available from: www.dhs.gov/ynews/speeches/sp_1237294788434.shtm (accessed April 20, 2009).
23 Editorial, "The doctrine of r-e-s-p-e-c-t," *USA Today*, April 20, 2009.
24 Scott Wilson, "Obama Closes Summit, Vows Broader Engagement with Latin America," *Washington Post*, April 20, 2009.
25 Ben Smith, "White House: No Bow to Saudi," *The Politico*, April 8, 2009.
26 Charles Krauthammer, "It's Your Country Too, Mr. President," *Washington Post*, April 10, 2009.
27 "Transcript: Obama's Summit of the Americas Press Conference," April 19, 2009. Available from: www.realclearpolitics.com/articles/2009/04/19/obama_summit_a-mericas_press_conference_96076.html (accessed April 20, 2009).
28 "Transcript: Obama's Summit of the Americas Press Conference," April 19, 2009 (emphasis mine).
29 "Transcript: President Obama News Conference," Strasbourg, France April 4, 2009. Available from: www.whitehouse.gov/the_press_office/News-Conference-By-President-Obama-4-04-2009/ (accessed April 20, 2009).

30 Richard Wolffe, *Renegade: The Making of a President*. New York: Crown, 2009, p. 323.
31 David Mendell, *Obama: From Promise to Power*. New York: HarperCollins, 2007, p. 201.
32 Mendell, *Obama*, p. 201 (emphasis mine).
33 Stanley A. Renshon, *Barack Obama and the Politics of Redemption*. New York: Routledge, 2011 (forthcoming).
34 Charles Krauthammer, "Its Your Country Too, Mr. President," *Washington Post*, April 10, 2009, A17.
35 Barack Obama, "Renewing American Leadership," *Foreign Affairs*, July/August 2007, p.11.
36 Obama, "Renewing American Leadership," p. 11.
37 Evan Ramstad, "North Korea threatens Military Strikes," *Wall Street Journal*, May 27, 2009.
38 Choe Sang-Hun, "North Korea Claims to Conduct 2nd Nuclear Test," *New York Times*, May 25, 2009.
39 Choe Sang-Hun, "North Korea is Said to Test-Fire 3 More Missiles," *New York Times*, May 27, 2009.
40 Remarks by President Obama at Strasbourg Town Hall, April 3, 2009 (emphasis added). Available from: www.whitehouse.gov/the_press_office/Remarks-by-President-Obama-at-Strasbourg-Town-Hall/ (accessed March 31, 2009).
41 Transcript – "President Obama's Remarks at a Student Roundtable in Turkey," *New York Times*, March 7, 2009 (emphasis mine). Available from: www.nytimes.com/2009/04/07/us/politics/07obama-turkey-transcript.html (accessed March 31, 2009).
42 Transcript – "President Obama's Remarks at a Student Roundtable in Turkey."
43 John Harwood, "Running on Risk, Then Sticking with it," *New York Times*, March 2, 2009.
44 Quoted in Harwood, "Running on Risk, Then Sticking with It."
45 Peter Nicholas, "Obama confronts doubts on stimulus, vows faster spending," *Los Angeles Times*, June 9, 2009
46 Justin Lahart and Erica Alini, "Americans Get Thriftier as Fears Persist," *Wall Street Journal*, June 2, 2009.
47 Transcript, "Democratic Debate in Philadelphia," *New York Times*, April 16, 2008.
48 Peter Baker, "Transition Holds Clues to How Obama Will Govern," *New York Times*, January 20, 2009.
49 Peter Wallsten, Julian Barnes, and Greg Miller, "Obama Administration to Release Bush-era Detainee Photos," *Los Angeles Times*, April 24, 2009.
50 Jeff Zeleny and Thom Shganker, "Obama Moves to Bar Release of Detainee Abuse Photos," *New York Times*, May 14, 2009.
51 Peter Finn, "Military Tribunals Will Resume, Obama Says," *Washington Post*, May 15, 2009.
52 All quotes drawn from Michael D. Shear and Peter Finn, "Obama to Revamp Military Tribunals," *Washington Post*, May 16, 2009.
53 Quoted in Mark Memmott and Jill Lawrence, "Obama Launches Tour to Highlight 'Judgment, Experience' on Iraq," *USATODAY*, October 1, 2007.
54 "Remarks of Illinois State Sen. Barack Obama Against Going to War with Iraq," 2 October 2002. Available from: www.barackobama.com/2002/10/02/remarks_of_illinois_state_sen.phps (accessed March 16, 2009).
55 Kenneth Pollack, *The Threatening Storm: The Case for Invading Iraq*. New York: Random House, 2002.
56 Remarks of Illinois State Senator …
57 Quoted in Andrew Malcolm, "Top of the Ticket," *Los Angeles Times*, July 16, 2008.
58 Mayhill Fower, "Obama: No Need for Foreign Policy Help from V.P.," *Huffington Post*, April 7, 2008 (emphasis in original).
59 Pamela Hess and Anne Gearan, "Officials: US Troops to Exit Iraq by August 2010," *Associated Press*, February 24, 2009.
60 Pamela Hess and Anne Gearan, "Officials: US Troops to Exit Iraq by August 2010," *Associated Press*, February 24, 2009.

61 Peter Baker and Elisabeth Bumiller, "Obama Favoring Mid-2010 Pullout in Iraq, Aides Say," *New York Times*, February 25, 2009.

62 Peter Baker and Elisabeth Bumiller, "Obama Favoring Mid-2010 Pullout in Iraq, Aides Say," *New York Times*, February 25, 2009.

63 Peter Baker and Elisabeth Bumiller, "Obama Favoring Mid-2010 Pullout in Iraq, Aides Say," *New York Times*, February 25, 2009.

64 "Transcript: Obama's Interview Aboard Air Force One," *New York Times*, March 8, 2009.

65 David S. Cloud, "Inside Obama's Iraq Decision," *Politico*, February 27, 2009.

66 David S. Cloud, "Inside Obama's Iraq Decision," *Politico*, February 27, 2009.

67 Elisabeth Bumiller, "Petraeus Warns About Militant's threat to Pakistan," *New York Times*, April 2, 2009.

68 David Stout, "Obama Sounds Cautious Note as He Sets Out Afghan Policy," *New York Times*, May 26, 2009.

69 Ann Scott Tyson, "Military Wants More Troops for Afghan War," *Washington Post*, April 2, 2009.

70 Robert Kagan, "Obama's Gutsy Decision on Afghanistan," *Washington Post*, March 27, 2009.

71 Transcript: President Obama, Part II, CBS News March 24, 2009. Available from: www. cbsnews.com/stories/2009/03/24/60minutes/main4890687.shtml (accessed April 15, 2009).

72 Helene Cooper and Eric Schmitt, "White House Debate Led to Plan to Widen Afghan Effort," *New York Times*, March 28, 2009 (emphasis mine).

73 Bill Gertz, "Inside the Ring: Afghanistan Debate," *Washington Times*, March 26, 2009.

74 Helene Cooper and Eric Schmitt, "White House Debate Led to Plan to Widen Afghan Effort," *New York Times*, March 28, 2009.

75 "Text: President Obama's Remarks on New Strategy for Afghanistan and Pakistan," *New York Times*, March 27, 2009. Available from: www.nytimes.com/2009/03/27/us/politics/27obama-text.html?ref=washington&pagewanted=print (accessed April 19, 2009).

76 Quoted in Jim Garamone, "Military Ready to Send More Troops to Afghanistan, Gates Says," *Armed Forces Press Service*, January 28, 2009. Available from: www.defenselink.mil/news/newsarticle.aspx?id=52832 (accessed April 15, 2009).

77 Quoted in Paul Koring, "Democracy Fades from Obama's Afghan Agenda," *Globe and Mail*, February 4, 2009.

78 The specific policy goals noted here and in the next paragraph are drawn from "Text: President Obama's Remarks on New Strategy for Afghanistan and Pakistan," *New York Times*, March 27, 2009.

79 Ann Scott Tyson, "Manhunter to Take on a Wider Mission," *Washington Post*, May 13, 2009.

80 Michael Powell, "Calm in the Swirl of History," *New York Times*, June 4, 2008.

81 Jess Bravin, "New Rift Opens Over Rights of Detainees," *Wall Street Journal*, June 30, 2009.

82 In a *60 Minutes* interview with Steve Kroft, he said, "Now, do these folks deserve miranda rights? Do they deserve to be treated like a shoplifter down the block? Of course not." See "Obama On AIG Rage, Recession, Challenges," *CBS/60 Minutes*, March 22, 2009.

83 Michael D. Shear and Peter Finn, "Obama to Revamp Military Tribunals Stance Is Reversal on Trials for Detainees," *Washington Post*, May 16, 2009; see also Review & Outlook, "Obama's Military Tribunals," *Wall Street Journal*, May 18, 2009.

84 Peter Finn, "Obama Endorses Indefinite Detention Without Trial for Some," *Washington Post*, May 22, 2009; see also Dafna Linzer and Peter Finn, "White House Weighs Order on Detention Officials: Move Would Reassert Power To Hold Terror Suspects Indefinitely," *Washington Post*, June 27, 2009.

85 Elisabeth Bumiller, "Iraq Can't Defend Its Skies by Pullout Date, U.S. Says," *New York Times*, July 29, 2009.

Bibliography

9/11 Public Discourse Project. *Report on the Status of 9/11 Commission Recommendations. Part III: Foreign Policy, Public Diplomacy, and Nonproliferation.* November 14, 2005.

ABC News. "Obama Order to Shut Gitmo, CIA Detention Centers." January 22, 2009.

Ackerman, Spencer. "The Obama Doctrine." *The American Prospect* 19, no. 4 (April 2008): 12–15.

Ajami, Fouad. "Maintaining Perspective." *U.S. News and World Report* 142, no. 8 (March 2007): 49.

Al Arabiya. "Transcript: Obama's Interview with Al Arabiya," January 27, 2009.

Albright, David. "North Korea's Alleged Large-Scale Enrichment Plant: Yet Another Questionable Extrapolation Based on Aluminum Tubes." Institute for Science and International Security, February 2007.

Albright, David, Jacqueline Shire and Paul Brannan. "Has Iran Achieved a Nuclear Weapons Breakout Capacity? Not Yet, But Soon." Washington, DC: Institute for Science and International Security, December 2, 2008.

Allen, Mike. "Democrats Want Gitmo Prisoners Sent to U.S." *Politico* (March 2007).

———. "Edwards Rejects the 'War on Terror,'" *Time* (May 2007).

American Forces Press Service, 13 March 2009.

Armitage, Richard L. and Joseph S. Nye, Jr. "A Smarter More Secure America: Report of the CSIS Commission on Smart Power." Washington, DC: CSIS, 2007.

Art, Robert. "A Defensible Defense: America's Grand Strategy After the Cold War." *International Security* 15, no. 4 (Spring 1991): 5–53.

———. "Geopolitics Updated: The Strategy of Selective Engagement." *International Security* 23, no. 3 (Winter 1998–99): 79–113.

———. *A Grand Strategy for America*. Ithaca: Cornell University Press, 2003.

Associated Press, November 13, 2006–February 20, 2009.

Australia. The Parliament of the Commonwealth of Australia. *Intelligence on Iraq's Weapons of Mass Destruction. (Parliamentary Joint Committee on ASIO, ASIS and DSD)*. Canberra. December 2003.

Bai, Matt. "Kerry's Undeclared War." *New York Times Magazine* (October 10, 2004).

Baker, Gerald. "Neo-conspiracy Theories." *The National Interest* no. 78 (Winter 2004–5): 130–35.

Baker, Peter. "Transition Holds Clues to How Obama Will Govern." *New York Times*, January 20, 2009.

———. "On Foreign Policy, Obama Shifts, but Only a Little," *New York Times*, April 17, 2009.

Baker, Peter and Elisabeth Bumiller. "Obama Favoring Mid-2010 Pullout in Iraq, Aides Say." *New York Times*, February 25, 2009.

Baker III, James A. and Lee H. Hamilton. *The Iraq Study Group Report*. Washington, DC: U.S. Institute of Peace, 2006.

Barnes, Fred. "The Return of Big Government." *Weekly Standard*, March 29, 2009.

Barry, Ellen. "Russia is Weighing 2 Latin Bases, General Says." *New York Times*, March 15, 2009.

Beehner, Lionel. "Iran's Involvement in Iraq." *Council of Foreign Relations*. February 12, 2007.

Beinart, Peter. "A Fighting Faith: An Argument for a New Liberalism." *The New Republic* 231, no. 24 (December 2004): 17–29.

——. *The Good Fight: Why Liberals—and Only Liberals—Can Win the War on Terror and Make America Great Again*. New York: Harper Collins, 2006.

Bender, Bryan. "US Weighs Tough Action on Pirates." *Boston Globe*, April 14, 2009.

Betts, Richard K. "Power, Prospects, and Priorities: Choices for Strategic Change." *Naval War College Review* 50, no. 1 (Winter 1997): 9–22.

——. "The Soft Underbelly of American Primacy: Tactical Advantages of Terror." *Political Science Quarterly* 117, no. 1 (Spring 2002): 19–36.

Biden, Joe. "Five Years After 9/11: Rethinking America's Future Security." Speech Delivered to the National Press Club". September 7, 2006.

Blair, Dennis C. Annual Threat Assessment of the Intelligence Community for the Senate Select Committee on Intelligence: Senate Select Committee on Intelligence, February 2009, Intelligence Community, Annual Threat Assessment, Unclassified Statement for the Record, February 12, 2009.

Blair, Tony. "Prime Minister Warns of Continuing Global Terror Threat." 10 Downing Street. March 5, 2004.

Bowman, Karyln H. "America and the War on Terrorism." American Enterprise Institute for Public Policy Research, 2007.

——. "Public Opinion and the War in Iraq. American Enterprise Institute for Public Policy Research," 2007.

Brands, H.W. "Presidential Doctrines: An Introduction." *Presidential Studies Quarterly* 36, no. 1 (March 2006): 1–4.

Brattan, Patrick C. "When is Coercion Successful?" *Naval War College Review* 58, no. 3 (Summer 2005): 99–120.

Bravin, Jess. "New Rift Opens Over Rights of Detainees," *Wall Street Journal*, June 30, 2009.

Bremmer, L. Paul and Malcolm McConnell. *My Year in Iraq: The Struggle to Build a Future of Hope*. New York: Simon & Schuster, 2006.

Broder, David S. "Obama in Command," *Washington Post*, May 21, 2009.

Brooks, William C. and William C. Wohlforth. "Hard Times for Soft Balancing." *International Security* 30, no. 1 (Summer 2005): 72–108.

——. *World Out of Balance: International Relations and the Challenge of American Primacy*. Princeton: Princeton University Press, 2008.

——. "Reshaping the World Order: How Washington Should Reform International Institutions." 88, no. 2 *Foreign Affairs* (March/April 2009): 49–63.

Bumiller, Elisabeth. "Petraeus Warns about Militants' Threat to Pakistan." *New York Times*, April 2, 2009.

——. "Iraq Can't Defend Its Skies by Pullout Date, U.S. Says," *New York Times*, July 29, 2009.

Bunn, M. Elaine. "Preemptive Action: When, How, and to What Effect?" *Strategic Forum*, no. 200 (July 2003): 1–8.

Bush, George W. "A Distinctly American Internationalism." Ronald Reagan Presidential Library, Simi Valley, CA. November 19, 1999.

——. "President Bush Delivers Graduation Speech at West Point." Washington, DC: The White House, June 1, 2002.

——. "President Delivers State of the Union Address." Washington, DC: The White House, January 29, 2002.

——. "President Delivers State of the Union." Washington, DC: White House, January 28, 2003.

Byman, Daniel. "Constructing a Democratic Iraq: Challenges and Opportunities." *International Security* 28, no. 1 (Summer 2003): 47–78.

Byman, Daniel and Kenneth M. Pollack. "Things Fall Apart: Containing the Spillover from an Iraqi Civil War." The Saban Center for Middle East Policy at the Brookings Institution (January 2007).

Campbell, Kurt M. and Michael E. O'Hanlon. *Hard Power: The New Politics of National Security.* New York: Basic Books, 2006.

Carter, Ashton B., John Deutch, and Philip Zelikow. "Catastrophic Terrorism: Tackling the New Danger." *Foreign Affairs* 77, no. 6 (November/December 1998): 80–94.

Cavanaugh, Jeffrey M. "From the 'Red Juggernaut' to Iraqi WMD: Threat Inflation and How it Succeeds in the United States." *Political Science Quarterly*, 122, no. 4 (Winter 2007–8): 555–84.

CBS Radio. "Donald Rumsfeld Interview" (November 14, 2002).

Chandrasekaran, Rajiv. *Imperial Life in the Emerald City: Inside Iraq's Green Zone.* New York: Knopf, 2006.

Chicago Tribune, December 1, 2008–January 31, 2009.

CIA. *Comprehensive Report of the Special Advisor to the DCI on Iraq's WMD*, September 30, 2004.

Cloud, David S. "Obama Team Looks for Opening in Iran." *Politico* (January 31, 2009).

——. "Secret Report Urges New Afghan Plan." *Politico* (February 3, 2009).

——. "Inside Obama's Iraq Decision." *Politico* (February 27, 2009).

CNN. "Russia Considers Terror Strikes" (September 17, 2004).

——. "Transcript, First Presidential Debate" (September 26, 2008).

——. "Transcript, Second McCain-Obama Debate" (October 7, 2008).

——. "Obama Takes Questions on the Economy" (February 9, 2009).

——. "State of the Union with John King: Interview with Admiral Mullen" (March 1, 2009).

CNN Live at Daybreak. "Disclosure: Bush Received General Warning Before 09/11 Prompting Criticism of Missed Signals" (May 17, 2002).

Coalition for a Realistic Foreign Policy. "The Perils of Empire: Statement of Principles by the Coalition for a Realistic Foreign Policy," 2004.

——. "The Perils of Occupation," 2004.

Codevilla, Angelo M. "No Victory, No Peace: What Rumsfeld's Memo Reveals … and Other Lessons from the War—So Far." *Claremont Review of Books* 4, no. 1 (Winter 2003).

Collier, Robert and Bill Wallace. "Iraq-Russia Spy Link Uncovered, SECRET FILES: Documents Reveal Iraqi Agents Trained in Moscow." *San Francisco Chronicle*, April 13, 2003.

Commission on the Intelligence Capabilities of the United States Regarding Weapons of Mass Destruction. *Report to the President of the United States.* Washington, DC, 2005.

Constitution of the United Nations Educational, Scientific and Cultural Organization. 1945.

Cooper, Helene. "Obama Weighs Adding Troops in Afghanistan." *New York Times*, February 12, 2009.

Cooper, Helene and Eric Schmitt. "White House Debate Led to Plan to Widen Afghan Effort." *New York Times*, March 28, 2009.

Cordesman Anthony H. *Weapons of Mass Destruction in the Middle East.* London: Brasseys, 1991.

Croft, Steve. Interview with President Barack Obama, *60 Minutes*, March 20, 2009.

Cronin, Audrey Kurth. "How Al-Qaida Ends: The Decline and Demise of Terrorist Groups." *International Security* 31, no. 1 (Summer 2006): 7–48.

Crook, Clive. "In Search of an Obama Doctrine." *Financial Times*, April 19, 2009.

Daalder, Ivo H. "Statement on the 2006 National Security Strategy." *The Brookings Institution*, (March 16, 2006).

Daalder, Ivo H. and James M. Lindsay. "Bush's Flawed Revolution." *The American Prospect* 14, no. 10 (November 2003): 43–45.

——. *America Unbound: The Bush Revolution in Foreign Policy.* Washington, DC: Brookings Institution Press, 2003.

Davis, Paul K. and Brian Jenkins. *Deterrence & Influence in Counterterrorism: A Component in the War on al Qaeda.* Santa Monica: Rand, 2002.

Del Quentin, Wilber and Peter Finn. "U.S. Retires 'Enemy Combatant,' Keeps Broad Right to Detain." *Washington Post,* March 14 (2009): A06.

Dershowitz, Alan. "Debunking the Newest—and Oldest—Jewish Conspiracy: A Reply to the Mearsheimer-Walt Working Paper." Working paper, Harvard University, John F. Kennedy School of Government, 2006.

DeYoung, Karen. "U.S. to Join Talks on Iran's Nuclear Program," *Washington Post,* April 9, 2009.

DeYoung, Karen and Joby Warrick. "Drone Attacks Inside Pakistan Will Continue, CIA Chief Says." *Washington Post*, February 26, 2009.

DiMascio, Jen. "Gates and Mullen Disagree on Iran." *Politico*, March 1, 2009.

Dinmore, Guy. "Bush Plans Overhaul of US Foreign Aid System." *Financial Times,* December 11, 2005.

Dombrowski, Peter and Roger A. Payne. "The Emerging Consensus for Preventive War." *Survival* 48, no. 2 (Summer 2006): 115–36.

Drexner, Daniel W. "The New New World Order." *Foreign Affairs* 86, no. 2 (March/April 2007): 34–46.

Dreyfuss, Robert. "Obama's Evolving Foreign Policy." *The Nation,* July 1, 2008.

Dueck, Colin. "New Perspectives on American Grand Strategy." *International Security* 28, no. 4 (Spring 2004): 197–216.

——. "Realism, Culture and Grand Strategy: Explaining America's Peculiar Path to World Power." *Security Studies* 14, no. 2 (Winter 2004–5): 195–231.

Edelman, Eric S. Comments by the Office of the Under Secretary of Defense on a Draft of a Proposed Report by the DOD Office of Inspector General Project NO. D2006DINTOl-0077.00. Review of pre-Iraqi War Activities of the Office of the Under Secretary of Defense for Policy (u). January 16, 2007.

Edwards, John. Senator John Edwards, Head, One America Committee; Candidate for the 2008 Democratic Presidential Nomination–via Satellite. The Seventh Annual Herzliya Conference. January 22, 2007.

El Baradei, Mohamed. Transcript, "Director General's Interview on Iran and DPRK (with Daniel Dombey)." *Financial Times,* February 19, 2007.

Elsea, Jennifer K. and Kenneth Thomas. Guantanamo Detainees: Habeas Corpus Challenges in Federal Court. Congressional Research Service Report for Congress. September 7, 2005.

Erdbrink, Thomas. "Ahmadinejad Vows New Start As Clashes Flare," *Washington Post,* June 14, 2009.

Feith, Douglass J. *War and Decision: Inside the Pentagon at the Dawn of the War on Terrorism.* New York: Harper, 2008.

Ferguson, Niall. "The Axis of Upheaval." *Foreign Policy* 171 (March/April 2009): 56–58.

Finn, Peter. "Obama Set to Revive Military Commissions Changes Would Boost Detainee Rights," *Washington Post,* May 9, 2009, A01.

——. "Military Tribunals Will Resume, Obama Says," *Washington Post,* May 15, 2009.

——. "Obama Endorses Indefinite Detention Without Trial for Some," *Washington Post,* May 22, 2009.

Fitzgerald, Michael and Richard Ned Lebow. "Iraq: The Mother of all Intelligence Failures." *Intelligence and National Security* 21, no. 5 (October 2006): 884–909.

Fletcher Forum on World Affairs. "Interview with Under Secretary of State John R. Bolton." *The Fletcher Forum on World Affairs* 29, no. 1 (Winter 2005): 5–8.

Fower, Mayhill. "Obama: No Need for Foreign Policy Help from V.P." *Huffington Post*, April 7, 2008.

Fox News. "Opinion Dynamics Poll." January 16, 2007.

"Fox News Interview with Secretary of State Clinton: North Korea and the Six-Party Talks." U.S. Department of State, February 20, 2009.

Fox News Sunday. "Interview with Nancy Pelosi." November 8, 2006.

——. "Interview with Jim Baker." December 10, 2006.

Freedman, Lawrence. *Deterrence*. Cambridge: Polity Press, 2004.

Freeland, Jonathan. "After a flurry of early activity, the Obama doctrine is taking shape," *Guardian*, March 11, 2009.

From, Al and Mark Penn. "A Chance to Rebuild Our Democratic Majority: If We Take it." Democratic Leadership Council. December 18, 2005.

Frum, David and Richard Perle. *An End to Evil: How to Win the War on Terrorism.* New York: Random House, 2003.

Fukuyama, Francis. *America at the Crossroads.* New Haven: Yale University Press, 2006.

G9 Summit. *Growth and Responsibility in the World Economy. Summit Declaration.* June 7, 2007.

Gaddis, John Lewis. *Strategies of Containment: A Critical Appraisal of American National Security Policy During the Cold War.* New York: Oxford University Press, 2005.

Gaddis, John Lewis and Paul H. Nitze. *The United States and the Origins of the Cold War, 1941–1947.* New York: Columbia University Press, 1972.

——. "NSC-68 and the Soviet Threat Reconsidered." *International Security* 4, no. 4 (Spring 1980): 164–76.

Garamone, Jim. "Military Ready to Send More Troops to Afghanistan, Gates Says." *Armed Forces Press Service* January 28, 2009.

Garthoff, Raymond L. *Detente and Confrontation American-Soviet Relations from Nixon to Reagan.* Washington: Brookings Institution Press, 1994.

Gat, Azar. "The Return of Authoritarian Great Powers." *Foreign Affairs* 86, no. 4 (July/August 2007): 59–69.

Gates, Robert M. "A Balanced Strategy: Reprogramming the Pentagon for a New Age." *Foreign Affairs* 88, no. 1 (January/February 2009): 28–40.

——. "Transcript: Secretary of Defense Robert Gates." *NBC Meet the Press*, March 1, 2009.

George, Alexander L. "The Operational Code: A Neglected Approach to the Study of Political Leaders and Decision Making." *International Studies Quarterly* 13, no. 1 (March 1969): 190–222.

——. "The Causal Nexus between Beliefs and Behavior." In *Psychological Models in International Politics*, ed. Lawrence S. Falkowski. Boulder: Westview, 1979.

——. *Presidential Decision Making in Foreign Policy: The Effective Use of Information and Advice.* Boulder: Westview, 1980.

——. *Forceful Persuasion: Coercive Diplomacy as an Alternative to War.* Washington, DC: U.S. Institute of Peace, 1991.

——. *Bridging the Gap: Theory and Policy in Foreign Affairs.* Washington, DC: U.S. Institute of Peace, 1993.

——. "The Role of Force in Diplomacy." In *Managing Global Chaos: Sources of and Responses to International Conflict*, ed. Chester A. Crocker, Fen Osler Hampson, and Pamela Aall. Washington, DC: U.S. Institute of Peace, 1996.

——. "From Groupthink to Conceptual Analysis of Policy-making Groups." In *Beyond Groupthink: Political Group Dynamics and Foreign Policy Making*, ed. Paul T. Hart, Eric K. Stern, and Bengt Sundelius. Ann Arbor: University of Michigan, 1997.

——. "The Need for Influence Theory and Actor-Specific Behavioral Models of Adversaries." In *Know Thy Enemy; Profiles of Adversary Leaders and Their Strategic*

Cultures, ed. Barry R. Schneider and Jerrold M. Post. Maxwell AFB: USAF Counter Proliferation Center, 2002.

——. *On Foreign Policy: Unfinished Business.* Boulder: Paradigm, 2006.

George, Alexander L. and Andrew Bennett. *Case Studies and Theory Development in the Social Sciences.* Cambridge: MIT Press, 2005.

George, Alexander L. and William E. Simmon. *The Limits of Coercive Diplomacy: Laos, Cuba, Vietnam.* Boulder: Westview, 1994.

George, Alexander L. and Richard Smoke. *Deterrence in American Foreign Policy: Theory and Practice.* New York: Columbia University Press, 1974.

Gephardt, Richard. "Transcript: Gephardt Holds Press Conference Regarding '9/11 Blame Game'," *CNN*, May 16, 2002.

Gerstein, Josh. "Why the Gitmo Policies May Not Change," *Politico*, January 23, 2009.

——. "Obama Defends Bush-era Secrets." *Politico*, February 21, 2009.

Gertz, Bill. "Inside the Ring: Afghanistan Debate." *Washington Times*, March 26, 2009.

Gholz, Eugene. "U.S. Interests in the Persian Gulf." *Partnership for a Secure America.* December 13, 2006.

Gholz, Eugene and Daryl G. Press. "Protecting the Prize: Oil and the National Interest." Paper presented at the annual meeting of the American Political Science Association, Chicago, Illinois, 2004.

Gholz, Eugene, Daryl G. Press, and Harvey M. Sapolsky. "Come Home America: The Strategy of Restraint in the Face of Temptation." *International Security* 21, no. 4 (Spring 1997): 1–43.

Gibbs, Robert. Press Briefing by Press Secretary Robert Gibbs, June 18, 2009.

Glaberson, William. "U.S. Won't Label Terror Suspects as 'Combatants.'" *New York Times*, March 14, 2009.

Glick, Caroline. "If Iran Gets the Bomb." *Jerusalem Post*, March 7, 2007.

Glover, Julian. "British Believe Bush is More Dangerous Than Kim Jong-il." *Guardian*, November 3, 2006.

Goldberg, Jeffrey. "The Unbranding." *New Yorker* 81, no. 5 (March 21, 2005): 32–37.

Goldgeiger, J.M. and P.E. Tetlock. "Psychology and International Relations Theory." *Annual Review of Political Science* 4, no. 1 (June 2001): 67–92.

Gordon, Michael R. and Bernard E. Trainor. *Cobra II: The Inside Story of the Invasion and Occupation of Iraq.* New York: Pantheon, 2006.

Grieco, Joseph. "Anarchy and the Limits of Cooperation: A Realist Critique of the Newest Liberal Institutionalism." *International Organization* 42, no. 2 (Spring 1988): 485–507.

Grieve, Tom. "What Hillary Won't Say about Iraq," *Salon*, February 14, 2007.

Grunwald, Michael. "Obama Power Will Be in the White House, Not Cabinet." *Time* (December 16, 2008).

Haass, Richard. *The Opportunity: America's Moment to Alter History's Course.* New York: Public Affairs, 2005.

——. "The Case for Integration." *The National Interest* no. 81 (Fall 2005): 22–29.

——. "The World That Awaits." *Newsweek* 152, no. 8 (November 3, 2008): 28–31.

Halper, Stefan and Jonathan Clarke. *America Alone: The Neoconservatives and the Global Order.* New York: Cambridge University Press, 2004.

Hann, Peter L. "Securing the Middle East: The Eisenhower Doctrine of 1957." *Presidential Studies Quarterly* 36, no. 1 (March 2006): 38–47.

Harbaugh, Erin E. "The Proliferation Security Initiative: Counterproliferation at the Crossroads." *Strategic Insights* 3, no. 7 (July 2004).

Harwood, John. "Running on Risk, Then Sticking with it." *New York Times*, March 2, 2009.

Harris, Stephen L. and Gloria Platzner. *Classical Mythology: Images and Insights.* Mountain View: Mayfield, 2001.

Harrison, Selig S. "Did North Korea Cheat?" *Foreign Affairs* 84, no. 1 (January/February 2005): 99–110.

Heath, Chip, Richard P. Larrick and George Wu. "Goals as Reference Points." *Cognitive Psychology* 38, no. 1 (February 1999): 79–109.

Heisbourg, Francois. "American Hegemony? Perceptions of the US Abroad." *Survival* 41, no. 4 (December 1999): 5–19.

Hennessy, Patrick and James Langton. "Why Kyoto Will Never Succeed, by Blair." *Telegraph*, September 24, 2005.

Herz, John H. "Idealist Internationalism and the Security Dilemma." *World Politics* 2, no. 2 (January 1950): 157–80.

Hess, Pamela and Anne Gearan. "Officials: US Troops to Exit Iraq by August 2010." *Associated Press*, February 24, 2009.

Hochman, Dafna. "Rehabilitating a Rogue: Libya's WMD Reversal and Lessons for US Policy." *Parameters* 36, no. 1 (Spring 2006): 63–78.

Holsti, Oli R. *Public Opinion and American Foreign Policy*. Ann Arbor: University of Michigan, 1996.

Huntington, Samuel P. "Why International Primacy Matters." *International Security* 17, no. 4 (Spring 1993): 68–83.

——. "Democracy for the Long Haul." *Journal of Democracy* 7, no. 2 (April 1996): 3–13.

——. "The Erosion of American National Interests," *Foreign Affairs*, September/October 1997.

Hurst, Steven. "Myths of Neocons." *International Politics* 42, no. 1 (March 2005): 75–96.

Hussain, Zahid and Matthew Rosenberg. "Pakistani Peace Deal Gives New Clout to Taliban Rebels." *Wall Street Journal*, April 14, 2009.

Hsu, Spencer S. "Obama Integrates Security Councils, Adds New Offices Computer, Pandemic Threats Addressed," *Washington Post*, May 27, 2009.

Ignatius, David. "Mr. Cool's Centrist Gamble." *Washington Post*, January 11, 2009.

Ikenberry, John and Anne-Marie Slaughter. "Forging a World of Liberty Under Law: U.S. National Security in the 21st Century." Final Report of the Princeton Project on National Security Forging a World of Liberty Under Law: U.S. National Security in the 21st Century, September 27, 2007.

Ishiba. "Japan to 'Counterattack' if N. Korea Prepares to Attack." *Yomiuri Shimbun/Daily Yomiuri* January 25, 2003.

Jentleson, Bruce W. and Christopher A. Whytock. "Who 'Won' Libya? The Force-Diplomacy Debate and its Implications for Theory and Policy." *International Security* 30, no. 3 (Winter 2005): 47–86.

Jervis, Robert. *Perception and Misperception in International Politics*. Princeton: Princeton University, 1976.

——. "Cooperation Under the Security Dilemma." *World Politics* 30, no. 1 (October 1977): 167–214.

—— "International Primacy: Is the Game Worth the Candle?" *International Security*, 17: 4 (Spring 1993).

——. "Realism in the Study of World Politics." *International Organization* 52, no. 4 (Summer 1998): 971–91.

——. "U.S. Grand Strategy: Mission Impossible." *Naval War College Review* 51, no. 3 (Summer 1998): 22–36.

——. "The Confrontation between Iraq and the US: Implications for the Theory and Practice of Deterrence." *European Journal of International Relations* 9, no. 2 (June 2003): 315–37.

——. *American Foreign Policy in a New Era*. New York: Routledge, 2005.

——. "Reports, Politics and Intelligence: The Case of Iraq." *The Journal of Strategic Studies* 29, no. 1 (February 2006): 3–52.

——. "The Remaking of the Unipolar World." *Washington Quarterly* 29, no. 3 (Summer 2006): 7–19.

Jones, Athena. "Obama: Change Comes from Me." *MSNBC* (November 26, 2008).

Judis, John B. "Purpose Driven." *The New Republic On-line* (December 8, 2004).

Kagan, Robert. "One Year After: A Grand Strategy for the West?" *Survival* 44, no. 4 (2002): 135–39.

——"End of Dreams, Return of History." *Policy Review* no. 144 (August/September 2007): 17–44.

——. "Obama's Gutsy Decision on Afghanistan." *Washington Post*, March 27, 2009.

Kagan, Robert and William Kristol. *Present Dangers: Crisis and Opportunity in American Foreign and Defense Policy.* San Francisco: Encounter Books, 2000.

Kahneman, Daniel and Amos Tversky. "Prospect Theory: An Analysis of Decision Under Risk." *Econometrica* 47, no. 2 (March 1979): 263–91.

——. "Choices, Values, and Frames." *American Psychologist* 39, no. 4 (April 1984), 341–50.

Kahneman, Daniel, Jack L. Knetsch and Richard H. Thaler. "The Endowment Effect, Loss Aversion, and Status Quo Bias." *The Journal of Economic Perspectives* 5, no. 1 (Winter 1991): 193–206.

Kaufmann, Chaim. "Threat Inflation and the Failure of the Marketplace of Ideas: The Selling of the Iraq War." *International Security* 29, no.1 (Summer 2004): 5–48.

Kelly, Michael. "Hagel's Asian Trip, Time for Reflection." *World Herald*, October 15, 2006.

Kennan, George F. [X, pseudo.]. "The Sources of Soviet Conduct." *Foreign Affairs* 25, no. 4 (July 1947): 566–82.

——. "Moscow Embassy Telegram #511: The Long Telegram." In *Containment: Documents on American Policy and Strategy, 1945–1950.* New York: Columbia University Press, 1978.

——. "The Sources of Soviet Conduct." In *Containment: Documents on American Policy and Strategy, 1945–1950.* New York: Columbia University Press, 1978.

——. "Containment 40 Years Later." *Foreign Affairs* 65, no. 4 (Spring 1987): 827–30.

——. "The Sources of Soviet Conduct." *Foreign Affairs* 65, no. 4 (Spring 1987): 852–68.

Kennedy, John F. President John F. Kennedy's University of Washington Speech. November 16, 1961.

Keohane, Robert O. "Theory of World Politics." In *Neorealism and its Critics.* New York: Columbia University, 1986.

Keohane, Robert O. and Lisa L. Martin. "The Promise of Institutional Theory." *International Security* 20, no. 1 (Summer 1995): 39–51.

Kessler, Glenn. "Cautious Response Reflects Obama's Long-Term Approach," *Washington Post*, June 21, 2009.

Kimbell, Jeffrey. "The Nixon Doctrine: A Saga of Misunderstanding." *Presidential Studies Quarterly* 36, no. 1 (March 2006): 59–74.

Kinsella, David. "No Rest for Democratic Peace." *American Political Science Review* 99, no. 3 (August 2005): 453–57.

Klein, Ezra. "Edwards on Iran." *The American Prospect*, February 2, 2007.

Klein, Joe. "National Security Team of Rivals." *Time*, June 18, 2008.

Kohut, Andrew. America's Image in the World: Findings from the Pew Global Attitudes Project. Remarks of the U.S. House Committee on Foreign Affairs; Subcommittee on International Organizations, Human Rights, and Oversight. March 14, 2007.

Koring, Paul. "Democracy Fades from Obama's Afghan Agenda." *Globe and Mail*, February 4, 2009.

Kozaryn, Linda D. "Cheney Says Grave Threats Require Pre-emptive Action." *American Forces Press Service* August 26, 2002.

Kralev, Nicholas. "Russia Vows Pre-emptive Terror Hits." *The Washington Times*, September 9, 2004.

Krasner, Stephen D. "Sharing Sovereignty: New Institutions for Collapsed and Failing States." *International Security* 29, no. 2 (Fall 2004): 85–120.

Krauthammer, Charles. "It's Your Country Too, Mr. President." *Washington Post*, April 10, 2009.

Krebs, Ronald R. and Chaim Kaufman. "Correspondence: Selling the Market Short? The Marketplace of Ideas and the Iraq War." *International Security* 29, no. 4 (Spring 2005): 196–207.

Kupchan, Charles A. "After Pax Americana: Benign Power, Regional Integration, and the Sources of Stable Multipolarity." *International Security* 23, no. 2 (Autumn 1998): 40–79.

——. *The End of the American Era: U.S. Foreign Policy and the Geopolitics of the Twenty-First Century*. New York: Alfred A. Knopf, 2002.

Kupchan, Charles A. and Clifford A. Kupchan. "The Promise of Collective Security." *International Security* 20, no. 1 (Summer 1995): 52–61.

Kurth, James. "American Strategy in the Global Era." *Naval War College Review* 53, no. 1 (Winter 2000): 7–25.

Kushner, Adam B. "A Return to Realism." *Newsweek*, January 26, 2009.

Lahart, Justin and Erica Alini. "Americans Get Thriftier as Fears Persist," *Wall Street Journal*, June 2, 2009.

Lake, Eli. "U.S. Spy Chief Retreats on Iran Estimate." *The Sun*, February 6, 2008.

——. "Small Change: Dick Cheney Has—Surprise!—A Paranoid View of Obama's War on Terrorism." *The New Republic*, March 4, 2008.

Lander, Mark and Elisabeth Bummiller. "Now, U.S. Sees Pakistan as a Cause Distinct From Afghanistan," *New York Times*, May 1, 2009.

Layne, Christopher. "From Preponderance to Offshore Balancing: America's Future Grand Strategy." *International Security* 22, no. 1 (Summer 1997): 86–124.

——. "Offshore Balancing Revisited." *Washington Quarterly* 25, no. 2 (Spring 2002): 233–48.

——. "The Unipolar Illusion Revisited: The Coming End of the United States' Unipolar Moment." *International Security* 31, no. 2 (Fall 2006): 7–41.

——. *The Peace of Illusions: American Grand Strategy from 1940 to the Present*. Ithaca: Cornell University, 2006.

Leffler, Melvyn P. *A Preponderance of Power: National Security, the Truman Administration, and the Cold War*. Stanford: Stanford University, 1992.

Leffler, Melvyn P. and Jeffrey W. Legro. "Introduction." In *To Lead the World: American Strategy After The Bush Doctrine*, eds. Melvyn P. Leffler and Jeffrey W. Legro. New York: Oxford University Press, 2008.

Leites, Nathan. *The Operational Code of the Politburo*. New York: McGraw-Hill, 1951.

Leopold, Evelyn and Irwin Arieff. "Russia Said to Still Object to UN Iran Statement." *Reuters*, March 20, 2006.

Lieber, Keir A. and Gerard Alexander. "Waiting for Balancing: Why the World is Not Pushing Back." *International Security* 30, no. 1 (Summer 2005): 109–39.

Lieber, Robert J. "Persistent Primacy and the Future of the American Era." *International Politics* 46, no. 2/3 (2009): 119–39.

Leibovich, Mark. "Speaking Freely, Biden Finds Influential Role." *New York Times*, March 29, 2009.

Lieven, Anatol and John Hulsman. *Ethical Realism: A Vision for America's Role in the World*. New York: Pantheon, 2006.

Linzer, Dafna and Peter Finn. "White House Weighs Order on Detention Officials: Move Would Reassert Power To Hold Terror Suspects Indefinitely," *Washington Post*, June 27, 2009.

Litwak, Robert S. "The New Calculus of Pre-emption." *Survival* 44, no. 4 (December 2003): 53–80.

Los Angeles Times, March 13, 2005–February 12, 2009.

Lustick, Ian S. *Trapped in the War on Terror*. Philadelphia: University of Pennsylvania, 2006.

Lynch, Timothy J. and Robert S. Singh. *After Bush: The Case for Continuity in American Foreign Policy*. New York: Cambridge, 2008.

Malcolm, Andrew. "Top of the Ticket." *Los Angeles Times* July 16, 2008.

Mann, James. *Rise of the Vulcans: The History of Bush's War Cabinet*. New York: Viking, 2004.

——. "Think Globally: Just How Many Elections Do Democrats Have to Lose before They Deal with Their Foreign-policy Problem?" *The American Prospect* 15, no. 12 (December 2004): 27–28.

Marshall, Joshua Micah. *Talking Points Memo* (December 9, 2004).

Marshall, Will, ed. *With All Our Might: A Progressive Strategy for Defeating Jihadism and Defending Liberalism*. Lanham, MD: Rowman & Littlefield, 2006.

Martin, Jonathan. "West Wing on Steroids in Obama W.H." *Politico*, January 25, 2009.

Mayer, J. "Behind the Executive Orders." *New Yorker*, January 25, 2009.

Maze, Rick. "No More GWOT, House Committee Decrees." *Army Times*, April 4, 2007.

McCain, John. "An Enduring Peace Built on Freedom." *Foreign Affairs* 86, no. 6 (November/December 2007): 19–34.

McCormack, Sean. "Department of State Daily Press Briefing." February 28, 2007.

McCurry, Justin. "Japan Warns it May Shoot Down North Korean Satellite Launcher." *Guardian*, March 13, 2009.

McDougall, Walter A. *Promised Land, Crusader State*. New York: Houghton Mifflin, 1997.

McGeough, Paul. "Warning That Pakistan is in Danger of Collapse within Months." *Sidney Morning Herald*, April 13, 2009.

Mead, Walter Russell. *Power, Terror, Peace, and War: America's Grand Strategy in a World at Risk*. New York: Knopf, 2004.

Mearsheimer, John J. "The False Promise of International Institutions." *International Security* 19, no. 3 (Winter 1994/1995): 5–49.

——. *The Tragedy of Great Power Politics*. New York: Norton, 2001.

Mearsheimer, John J. and Stephen Walt. "Can Saddam Be Contained? History Says Yes." Harvard University: Belfer Center for Science and International Affairs International Security Program Occasional Paper, November 2002.

——. "The Israeli Lobby and U.S. Foreign Policy. Faculty Working Paper No # RWP06–011." Harvard University, John F. Kennedy School of Government, March 13, 2006.

Meet the Press. "Robert Gates: Secretary of Defense" (March 1, 2009).

Memmott, Mark and Jill Lawrence. "Obama Launches Tour to Highlight 'Judgment, Experience' on Iraq." *USA TODAY*, October 1, 2007.

Mendell, David. *Obama: From Promise to Power*. New York: HarperCollins, 2007.

Merill, Dennis. "The Truman Doctrine: Containing Communism and Modernity." *Presidential Studies Quarterly* 36, no. 1 (March 2006): 27–37.

Monaghan, Elaine. "Clinton Planned Attack on Korean Nuclear Reactors." *The Times*, December 16, 2002.

Montgomery, Evan Braden. "Breaking Out of the Security Dilemma: Realism, Reassurance, and the Problem of Uncertainty." *International Security* 31, no. 2 (Fall 2006): 151–85.

Morgan, Patrick. *Deterrence: A Conceptual Analysis*. Beverly Hills: Sage, 1997.

Morgenthau, Hans J. *Politics Among Nations: The Struggle for Power and Peace*. New York: Knopf, 1967.

Mueller, John. "Is There Still a Terrorist Threat?" *Foreign Affairs* 85, no. 5 (September/October 2006): 2–8.

——. *Overblown: How Politicians and the Terrorism Industry Inflate National Security Threats, and Why We Believe Them*. New York: Free Press, 2006.

Mueller, Karl P., Jasen J. Castillo, Forrest E. Morgan, Negeen Pegahi, and Brian Rosen. *Striking First: Preemptive and Preventive Attack in U.S. National Security Policy*. Santa Monica: Rand, 2006.

Mullen, Admiral Michael. "Interview with Admiral Michael Mullen," *This Week*, May 24, 2009. (emphasis mine).

National Commission on Terrorist Attacks upon the United States. *The 9/11 Commission Report: Final Report of the National Commission on Terrorist Attacks upon the United States.* New York: Norton, 2004.

National Intelligence Council. National Intelligence Estimate: Prospects for Iraq's Stability: A Challenging Road Ahead. January 2007.

———. National Intelligence Estimate: The Terrorist Threat to the US Homeland. July 2007.

———. *Global Trends 2025: A Transformed World.* November 2008.

National Review Online. "Vanity Unfair: a Symposium" (November 2006).

National Security Archive. "New State Department Releases on the 'Future of Iraq' Project: New Documents Provide Details on Budgets, Interagency Coordination and Working Group Progress." *The National Security Archive* September 1, 2006.

National Security Council. *NSC 68: United States Objectives and Programs for National Security. A Report to the President Pursuant to the President's Directive of January 31, 1950.* Washington, DC, April 14, 1950.

Negroponte, John D. Annual Threat Assessment. Testimony Before the Senate Select Committee on Intelligence. Washington, DC, January 11, 2007.

Neustadt, Richard E. *Presidential Power and the Modern Presidents: The Politics of Leadership from Roosevelt to Reagan.* New York: Free Press, 1990.

Neustadt, Richard E. and Ernest R. May. *Thinking in Time: The Uses of History for Decision-makers.* New York: Free Press, 1988.

New York Times. "Text: President Obama's Remarks on New Strategy for Afghanistan and Pakistan." March 27, 2009.

———. "Obama to Appeal Detainee Ruling." April 11, 2009.

Nicholas, Peter. "Obama confronts doubts on stimulus, vows faster spending," *Los Angeles Times*, June 9, 2009.

Nincic, Miroslav and Monti Narayand Datta. "Of Paradise, Power and Pachyderms." *Political Science Quarterly* 122, no. 2 (Summer 2007): 239–56.

Nordlinger, Eric D. *Isolationism Reconfigured: American Foreign Policy for a New Century.* Princeton: Princeton University Press, 1995.

Nye, Joseph S. "Redefining the National Interest." *Foreign Affairs* 78, no. 4 (July/August 1999): 22–35.

———. "A 'Progressive Realist' Foreign Policy Begins with Modesty." *The Daily Star*, August 29, 2006.

Obama, Barack. "Remarks of Illinois State Sen. Barack Obama Against Going to War with Iraq." Barack Obama and Joe Biden: The Change We Need, October 2, 2002.

———. "Floor Statement of Senator Barack Obama on S.2271 – USA PATRIOT Act Reauthorization." February 16, 2006.

———. "Senator Barack Obama Floor Statement General Michael Hayden Nomination." May 25, 2006.

———. *The Audacity of Hope.* New York: Three Rivers Press, 2006.

———. "Speech to the Chicago Council of Global Affairs." April 23, 2007.

———. "Renewing American Leadership." *Foreign Affairs* 86, no. 4 (July/August 2007): 2–16.

———. "Responsibly Ending the War in Iraq." Prepared for Delivery at Camp Lejeune, North Carolina, February 27, 2009.

———. Transcript – "President Obama's Remarks at a Student Roundtable in Turkey," *New York Times*, March 7, 2009.

———. "Transcript: Obama's Interview Aboard Air Force One." *New York Times*, March 8, 2009.

———. "Transcript, President Obama, Part I, CBS News" March 24, 2009.

———. "Transcript, President Obama, Part II, CBS News" March 24, 2009.

——. Remarks by President Obama at Strasbourg Town Hall, April 3, 2009 (emphasis added)

——. "Transcript: President Obama News Conference." Strasbourg, France, April 4, 2009.

——. "Transcript: Obama's Summit of the Americas Press Conference." April 19, 2009.

Office of the Director of National Intelligence. *The National Intelligence Strategy of the United States of America: Transformation Through Integration and Innovation.* Washington, DC, 2005.

——. 2006. Declassified Key Judgments of the National Intelligence Estimate "Trends in Global Terrorism: Implications for the United States." April 2006.

Office of the Inspector General Department of Justice. *USDOJ/OIG Special Report. The FBI Laboratory: An Investigation into Laboratory Practices and Alleged Misconduct in Explosives-Related and Other Cases. Section D: The Bush Assassination Attempt.* Washington, DC, 1997.

Pach, Chester. "The Reagan Doctrine: Principle, Pragmatism, and Policy." *Presidential Studies Quarterly* 36, no. 1 (March 2006): 75–88.

Packer, George. "A Democratic World: Can Liberals Take Foreign Policy Back from the Republicans." *New Yorker* 80, no. 1 (February 2004): 101–8.

——. *The Assassins' Gate: America in Iraq.* New York: Farrar, Straus & Giroux, 2005.

Pape, Robert A. "Soft Balancing Against the United States." *International Security* 30, no. 1 (Summer 2005): 7–45.

——. "Empire Falls." *The National Interest* 99 (January/February 2009): 21–34.

Patten, Chris. "Democracy Doesn't Flow from the Barrel of a Gun." *Foreign Policy* 138 (September/October 2003): 40–44.

Paul, T. V. "Soft Balancing in the Age of U.S. Primacy." *International Security* 30, no. 1 (Summer 2005): 46–71.

Pena, Charles V. "Bush's National Security Strategy is a Misnomer." *The Cato Institute, Policy Analysis* 496 (October 2003): 1–26.

Perine, Keith. "Justice Department Again Defends Bush on State Secrets." *CQ Politics* (February 20, 2009).

Pew Global Attitudes Project. "The Great Divide: How Westerners and Muslims View Each Other." 2006.

——. "Global Unease with Major Powers." 2007.

Pew Research Center for the People and the Press. "Foreign Policy Attitudes Now Driven by 9/11." 2004.

——. "More Say Iraq Hurts Fight Against Terrorism." 2005.

——. "The Dean Activists: Their Profile and Prospects." 2005.

——. "Broad Opposition to Bush's Iraq Plan." 2007.

——. "Muslim Americans: Middle Class and Mostly Mainstream." 2007.

——. "Obama Faces Familiar Divisions Over Anti-Terror Policies." February 18, 2009.

Phillips, Kate, Shane Lauth, Erin Schenck, and W. Andrew Terrill, ed. "U.S. Military Combat Operations in Iraq; Planning, Combat and Operations." Carlisle, PA: Strategic Studies Institute of the U.S. War College, April 2006.

Pillar, Paul R. "Intelligence, Policy, and the War in Iraq." *Foreign Affairs* 85, no. 2 (March/April 2006): 15–27.

——. "Iran May Not Be Behind Coalition Attacks." *Council of Foreign Relations* (February 6, 2007).

Pollack, Kenneth M. *The Threatening Storm: The Case for Invading Iraq.* New York: Random House, 2002.

——. "Securing the Gulf." *Foreign Affairs* 82, no. 4 (July/August 2003): 2–16.

Posen, Barry R. *The Sources of Military Doctrine.* Ithaca: Cornell University Press, 1984.

——. "The Struggle Against Terrorism: Grand Strategy, Strategy and Tactics." *International Security* 26, no. 3 (Winter 2001–2): 39–55.

Posen, Barry R. and Andrew L. Ross. "Competing Visions for U.S. Grand Strategy." *International Security* 21, no. 3 (Winter 1996–97): 5–53.

Posner, Richard. *Law, Pragmatism, and Democracy*. Cambridge, MA: Harvard University Press, 2005.

Post, Jerrold M. "Saddam Hussein of Iraq." In *The Psychological Assessment of Political Leaders: With Profiles of Saddam Hussein and Bill Clinton*, ed. Jerrold M. Post. Ann Arbor: University of Michigan Press, 2003.

Powell, Michael. "Calm in the Swirl of History." *New York Times*, June 4, 2008.

Press, Daryl G. *Calculating Credibility: How Leaders Assess Military Threats*. Ithaca: Cornell University Press, 2005.

Press, Daryl G. and Benjamin Valentino. "A Balanced Foreign Policy." In *How to Make America Safe: New Policies for National Security*, ed. Steven van Evera. Cambridge: The Tobin Project: 2002.

Project for the New American Century. "Statement of Principles," June 3, 1997.

———. "Letter to President Clinton on Iraq," January 26, 1998.

Rabe, Stephan G. "The Johnson Doctrine." *Presidential Studies Quarterly* 36, no. 1 (March 2006): 48–58.

Ramstad, Evan. "North Korea threatens Military Strikes," *Wall Street Journal*, May 27, 2009.

Rasmussen Reports. "National Security Agency," December 28, 2005.

Ravenal, Earl. "The Case for Adjustment." *Foreign Policy*, no. 81 (Winter 1990–91): 3–19.

Renshon, Jonathan. *Why Leaders Choose War: The Psychology of Prevention*. Greenport: Praeger, 2006.

———. "Assessing Threat and Vulnerability: The Role of Overconfidence and Overestimation." Unpublished paper, Harvard University, 2007.

———. "Making Frames and Taking Chances: The Utility of Prospect Theory in International Relations." Unpublished paper, Harvard University, 2007.

———. "Mirroring Risk: Empathetic Failure and the Cuban Missile Crisis." *Intelligence and National Security* 24, no. 3 (June 2009): 315–338.

Renshon, Jonathan and Stanley A. Renshon. "The Theory and Practice of Foreign Policy Decision Making." *Political Psychology* 29, no. 4 (2008): 509–36.

Renshon, Stanley A. "The World According to George W. Bush: Good Judgment or Cowboy Politics." In *Good Judgment in Foreign Policy: Theory and Application*, ed. Stanley A. Renshon and Deborah Welch Larson. Lantham: Rowman & Littlefield, 2003.

———. *In His Father's Shadow: The Transformations of George W. Bush*. New York: Palgrave/St. Martin's, 2005.

———. "Psychological Reflections on Barack Obama and John McCain: Assessing the Contours of a New Presidential Administration." *Political Science Quarterly* 123, no. 3 (Winter 2008): 391–433.

———. *Barack Obama and the Politics of Redemption*. New York: Routledge, 2011.

Renshon, Stanley A. and Peter Suedfeld, eds. *Understanding the Bush Doctrine: Psychology and Strategy in an Age of Terrorism*. New York: Routledge, 2007.

Review & Outlook. "Sayonara Kyoto," *Wall Street Journal*, July 29, 2005.

———. "Ticking Tehran Bomb," *Wall Street Journal*, December 7, 2005.

———. "Kim Jong-Il's Bankers," *Wall Street Journal*, November 24, 2006.

———. "Uranium Do Over," *Wall Street Journal*, March 1, 2007.

———. "Mahmoud's 'Gift'," *Wall Street Journal*, April 5, 2007.

———. "Obama's Military Tribunals," *Wall Street Journal*, May 18, 2009.

Rice, Condoleezza. "A Balance of Power That Favors Freedom." Manhattan Institute for Policy Research. Wriston Lecture, October 1, 2002.

———. "America Has the Muscle, But it Has Benevolent Values, Too." *Telegraph-UK*, October 17, 2002.

——. "Interview with Andrea Mitchell of NBC News." *NBC News*, January 17, 2007.

Richter, Paul. "Biden Warns Israel Off Any Attack on Iran." *Los Angeles Times*, April 8, 2009.

Ricks, Thomas E. *Fiasco: The American Military Adventure in Iraq.* New York: Penguin, 2006.

Rose, Gideon. "Neoclassical Realism and Theories of Foreign Policy." *World Politics* 51, no. 1 (October 1998): 144–72.

Rose, Richard. *The Post Modern Presidency.* Washington, DC: CQ Press, 1991.

Rosen, Gary. "Bush and the Realists." *Commentary* 120, no. 2 (September 2005): 31–37.

——. ed. *The Right War; The Conservative Debate on Iraq.* New York: Cambridge University Press, 2005.

Rosenberg, Matthew and Zahid Hussain. "Pakistan's Leader Stirs Fresh Turmoil." *Wall Street Journal*, February 26, 2009.

Rosenthal, Justine A. "A Sit-down with Brent Scowcroft." *The National Interest* 99, (January/February 2009): 4–9.

Rumsfeld, Donald. Secretary Rumsfeld Speaks on "21st Century Transformation" of U. S. Armed Forces (Transcript of Remarks and Question and Answer Period). Remarks as Delivered by Secretary of Defense Donald Rumsfeld, National Defense University, Fort McNair. Washington, DC: US Department of Defense, January 31, 2002.

Russell, Richard L. "Iran in Iraq's Shadow: Dealing with Tehran's Nuclear Weapons Bid." *Parameters* 34, no. 3 (Autumn 2004): 31–45.

Samii, Abbas William. "The Iranian Nuclear Issue and Informal Networks." *Naval War College Review* 59, no. 1 (Winter 2006): 63–89.

Sanger, David E. "Hints of Obama's Strategy in a Telling 8 Days." *New York Times*, April 8, 2009.

Sang-Hun, Choe. "North Korea claims to Conduct 2nd Nuclear Test," *New York Times*, May 25, 2009.

Schlesinger, Arthur M., Jr. "An American Empire? Not So Fast." *World Policy Journal* 22, no. 1 (Spring 2005): 43–46.

Schelling, Thomas C. *Arms and Influence.* New Haven, CT: Yale University Press.

Schweller, Randall L. "Bandwagoning for Fun and Profit: Bringing the Revisionist State Back In." *International Security* 19, no. 1 (Summer 1994): 72–107.

Seib, Gerald F. "Obama will be a Hands-on Chief," *Wall Street Journal*, January 13, 2009.

Shane, Scott. "Interrogations' Effectiveness May Prove Elusive." *New York Times*, April 23, 2009.

Shapiro, Ian *Containment: Rebuilding a Global Strategy against Global Terror.* Princeton: Princeton University Press, 2007.

Shear, Michael D. and Peter Finn. "Obama to Revamp Military Tribunals Stance Is Reversal on Trials for Detainees," *Washington Post*, May 16, 2009.

Slackman, Michael. "Amid Crackdown, Iran Admits Voting Errors," *New York Times*, June 23, 2009.

Slaughter, Anne-Marie. "To Pursue Primacy for its Own Sake Seems an Odd Way to Reassure Other Nations." *Boston Review* (February/March 2005).

Smith, Ben. "'Invasion of Georgia' a '3 a.m. moment'." *Politico*, August 9, 2008.

——. "White House: No Bow to Saudi." *Politico*, April 8, 2009.

Smith, Ben and Jonathan Martin. "Can Obama's Team of Egos Co-exist?" *Politico*, November 20, 2008.

Smith, Tony. *A Pact with the Devil: Washington's Bid for World Supremacy and the Betrayal of the American Promise.* New York: Routledge, 2007.

Snyder, Jack L. *The Ideology of the Offensive: Military Decision Making and the Disasters of 1914.* Ithaca: Cornell University Press, 1989.

Squassoni, Sharon. "Proliferation Security Initiative (PSI)." *CRS Report to Congress*, September 14, 2006.

Starks, Tim. "Intelligence Policy: New Perspectives of Familiar Approach." *Congressional Quarterly* February 16, 2009.

Starobin, Paul. "The Realists." *National Journal* 38, no. 37 (September 2006): 24–31.

Stein, Janice Gross. "Anti-Americanism: Seeing Ourselves in the Mirror of the United States." In *Understanding the Bush Doctrine: Psychology and Strategy in an Age of Terrorism*, ed. Stanley A. Renshon and Peter Suedfeld. New York: Routledge, 2007.

Stout, David. "Obama Sounds Cautious Note as He Sets Out Afghan Policy." *New York Times*, May 26, 2009.

Sung-Ki, Jung. " South to Boost Surgical Strike Capability Against the North," *Reuters*, June 26, 2009.

Suskind, Ron. *The One Percent Doctrine*. New York: Simon & Schuster, 2006.

Tagliabue, John. "No Evidence Suspect Met Iraqi in Prague." *New York Times*, October 20, 2001.

Takeyh, Ray. "Time for Détente with Iran." *Foreign Affairs* 86, no. 2 (March/April 2007): 17–32.

Tavernsise, Sabrina, Richard A. Oppel, Jr., and Eric Schmitt. "Militants Unite in Pakistan's Populous Heart." *New York Times*, April 14, 2009.

Taylor, Terence. "The End of Imminence?" *Washington Quarterly*, 27, no. 4 (Autumn 2004): 57–72.

Tenet, George. *At the Center of the Storm: My Years at the CIA*. New York: Harper Collins, 2007.

Tetlock, Phillip E. *Expert Political Judgment: How Good is it? How Do We Know?* Princeton: Princeton University Press, 2005.

Thaler, Richard H., Amos Tversky, Daniel Kahneman, and Alan Schwartz. "The Effect of Myopia and Loss Aversion on Risk Taking: An Experimental Test." *Quarterly Journal of Economics* 112, no. 2 (May 1997): 647–61.

Thomma, Steven. "Obama Sends a Message: the United States Will Not Torture." *McClatchy Newspapers*, January 22, 2009.

Thrall, A. Trevor and Jane K. Cramer, eds. *American Foreign Policy and the Politics of Fear: Threat Inflation Since 9/11*. New York: Routledge, 2009.

Tobin, Gary and Aryeth K. Weinverg. *A Profile of American College Faculty. Vol. I: Political Beliefs and Behavior*. Institute for Jewish and Community Research, 2006.

Tucker, Robert W. "Containment and the Search for Alternatives: A Critique." In *Beyond Containment: Alternative American Policies Toward the Soviet Union*, ed. Aaron Wildavsky. San Francisco: Institute of Contemporary Studies, 1983.

Tyson, Ann Scott. "Military Wants More Troops for Afghan War." *Washington Post*, April 2, 2009.

——. "Manhunter to Take On a Wider Mission," *Washington Post*, May 13, 2009.

United Kingdom, Parliament. *Review of Intelligence on Weapons of Mass Destruction Report of a Committee of Privy Counsellors Chairman: The Rt Hon The Lord Butler of Brockwell KG GCB CVO*. London: The Stationery Office, 2004.

United Nations General Assembly. Fifty-ninth Session. *A More Secure World: Our Shared Responsibility: Report of the High-level Panel on Threats, Challenges and Change*. Prepared by Anand Panyarachun in pursuance of UN General Assembly Resolution A/59/565. 2004.

U.S. Department of Defense. *Quadrennial Defense Review Report*. Washington, DC, February 6, 2006.

U.S. Department of Homeland Security. "Remarks by Homeland Security Secretary Janet Napolitano to the International Association of Fire Fighters." Washington, DC, March 16, 2009.

U.S. Department of State. *U.S. Objectives with Respect to the USSR to Counter Soviet Threats to U.S. Security, Foreign Relations of the United States*, Vol. 1. Washington, DC: GPO, 1948.

——. *State Sponsors of Terrorism*. Washington, DC, 2007.

——. "Global Initiative Current Partner Nations."

U.S. House of Representatives. Investigative Status Report of the House Judiciary Committee Democratic Staff. The Constitution in Crisis: The Downing Street Minutes and Deception, Manipulation, Torture, Retribution, and Cover-ups in the Iraqi War. Washington, DC, December 20, 2005.

——. Making Emergency Supplemental Appropriations for the Year Ending September 30, 2007, and for Other Purposes. 110th Congress, 1st Session, H.R. 1591, Report No. 110–60. March 20, 2007.

U.S. Senate. Senate Select Committee, Report on the US Intelligence Community's Prewar Intelligence Assessments on Iraq. July 7, 2004.

——. Hearing of the Senate Select Committee on Intelligence Annual Threat Assessment. January 11, 2007.

USA Today. Editorial. "The doctrine of r-e-s-p-e-c-t." April 20, 2009.

Van Evera, Stephen. *The Causes of War: Power and the Roots of War*. Ithaca: Cornell, 1999.

——. *The War on Terror: Forgotten Lessons from World War II*. Cambridge: MIT Center for International Studies, 2006.

——. "Farewell to Geopolitics." In *To Lead the World: American Strategy After The Bush Doctrine*, eds. Melvyn P. Leffler and Jeffrey W. Legro. New York: Oxford University Press, 2008.

Von Drehle, David and R. Jeffrey Smith. "U.S. Strikes Iraq for Plot to Kill Bush." *Washington Post*, June 27, 1993: A01.

Wall Street Journal, 14 December 2001–6 March 2009.

Wallsten, Peter, Julian Barnes and Greg Miller. "Obama Administration to release Bush-era detainee photos," *Los Angeles Times*, April 24, 2009.

Walt, Stephen M. *The Origins of Alliances*. Ithaca: Cornell, 1987.

——. *Taming American Power: The Global Response to U.S. Primacy*. New York: Norton, 2005.

——. "In the National Interest: A New Grand Strategy for American Foreign Policy." *Boston Review* (February/March 2005).

Waltz, Kenneth N. *Man, The State, and War: A Theoretical Analysis*. New York: Columbia University Press, 1965.

——. *Theory of International Politics*. Reading: Addison-Wesley, 1979.

Washington Post. Editorial, "A Solution for Somalia: What it Will Take to Stop the Threats of Piracy and Terrorism." April 14, 2009.

Weisberg, Jacob. "The Brilliant Brain Trust." *Newsweek* 152, no. 21 (November 24, 2008): 34.

Wells, Jr., Samuel F. "Sounding the Tocsin: NSC 68 and the Soviet Threat." *International Security* 4, no. 2 (Autumn 1979): 116–58.

White House. *A National Strategy of Enlargement and Engagement*. Washington, DC, 1996.

——. "President Welcomes President Chirac to White House." Washington, DC, November 6, 2001.

——. "President Outlines Priorities." Washington, DC, November 7, 2002.

——. *National Strategy for Homeland Security*. Washington, DC, 2002.

——. *National Strategy to Combat Weapons of Mass Destruction*. Washington, DC, 2002.

——. *The National Security Strategy of the United States of America*. Washington, DC, 2002.

——. *National Strategy for Combating Terrorism*. Washington, DC, 2003.

——. *The National Strategy to Secure Cyberspace*. Washington, DC, 2003.

——. "President Addresses American Legion, Discusses Global War on Terror." Washington, DC, February 24, 2006.

——. "President Bush and Prime Minister Ehud Olmert of Israel Participate in Joint Press Availability." Washington, DC, May 23, 2006.

——. "President Bush and Prime Minister Tony Blair of the United Kingdom Participate in Joint Press Availability." Washington, DC, May 26, 2006.

——. "Joint Statement Announcing the Global Initiative to Combat Nuclear Terrorism." Washington, DC, July 15, 2006.

——. "Press Conference of the President." Washington, DC: White House, September 15, 2006.

——. "President Bush Meets with British Prime Minister Tony Blair." Washington, DC, December 7, 2006.

——. *The National Security Strategy of the United States of America.* Washington, DC, 2006.

——. *National Strategy for Homeland Security.* Washington, DC, 2007.

——. "Executive Order: Ensuring Lawful Interrogations." January 22, 2009.

——. "Executive Order: Review and Disposition of Individuals Detained at the Guantánamo Bay Naval Base and Closure of Detention Facilities." January 22, 2009.

——. "Executive Order: Review of Detention Policy Options." January 22, 2009.

——. "Presidential Policy Directive-1." Washington, DC, February 13, 2009.

——. "Presidential Study Directive." Washington, DC, February 23, 2009.

——. "Remarks by President Barack Obama," Washington, DC, Prague, Czech Republic, April 5, 2009.

Whiteneck, Daniel. "Deterring Terrorists: Thoughts on a Framework." *Washington Quarterly* 28, no. 3 (Summer 2005): 187–200.

Wilson, John K. *Barack Obama: This Improbable Quest.* Boulder: Paradigm, 2007.

Wilson, Scott. "Obama Closes Summit, Vows Broader Engagement with Latin America." *Washington Post*, April 20, 2009.

Wilson, Scott and Al Kamen. "'Global War on Terror' is Given New Name, Bush's Phrase is Out, Pentagon Says." *Washington Post*, March 25, 2009.

WOAI San Antonio News. "Dean: U.S. Won't Win in Iraq." December 4, 2005.

Woods, Kevin, James Lacey, and Williamson Murray. "Saddam's Delusions: The View from the Inside." *Foreign Affairs* 85, no. 3 (May/June 2006): 2–26.

Woods, Kevin, Michael R. Pease, Mark Stout, Williamson Murray, and James G. Lacey. *Iraqi Perspective Project: A View of Operation Iraqi Freedom from Saddam's Senior Leadership.* Norfolk, VA: The U.S. Joint Forces Command, 2006.

Woodward, Bob. *Bush at War.* New York: Simon & Schuster, 2002.

Wolffe, Richard. *Renegade: The Making of a President.* New York: Crown, 2009.

Yglesias, Matthew. "Big-Time Trouble." *The American Prospect: Online Edition.* December 20, 2005.

Zagorin, Adam. "Charges Sought Against Rumsfeld Over Prison Abuse." *Time,* November 10, 2006.

Zakaria, Fareed. *From Wealth to Power: The Unusual Origins of America's World Role.* Princeton: Princeton University Press, 1998.

——. "The Future of American Power: How America Can Survive the Rise of the Rest." *Foreign Affairs* 87, no. 3 (May/June 2008): 18–43.

Zeleny, Jeff and Thom Shganker. "Obama moves to Bar Release of Detainee Abuse Photos," *New York Times,* May 14, 2009.

Index